THE ECONOMIC MIND IN AMERICA: ESSAYS IN THE HISTORY OF AMERICAN ECONOMICS

In the history of economic thought, American economics is an area which has received insufficient attention. This volume demonstrates the variety and creativity of American economics and places American economic thought in its particular, non-European, context. The book consists of selected papers from the 1996 History of Economics Society Conference.

The opening part examines the concept of "American" economic thought from a variety of perspectives. The following parts provide a critical reassessment of pioneering American policy analysts such as Irving Fisher, Wesley Mitchell, Harold Moulton, and Leo Paslovsky, as well as some of the theoretical contributions of Herbert Davenport, Irving Fisher, and Frank Knight. The fourth part contains a detailed account of Thorstein Veblen's institutional economics, including an exploration of its links with Canadian and European economic thought, and an examination of the treatment of the individual in both Veblen's and J. R. Commons' writings. The unusual and original contributions of C. S. Peirce, Alvin Johnson, and science fiction author Robert A. Heinlein are also analyzed. The final part details American economists' interests in international issues from 1886 to 1995.

With contributions by an international array of leading economists, this volume is an important contribution to the literature on the history of American economics.

Malcolm Rutherford is Professor of Economics at the University of Victoria, B.C., Canada. He has written extensively on the history of institutional economics, and is the author of *Institutions in Economics: The Old and the New Institutionalism* (C.U.P.) and the co-editor of *John R. Commons: Selected Essays* (Routledge).

THE ECONOMIC MIND IN AMERICA: ESSAYS IN THE HISTORY OF AMERICAN ECONOMICS

Perspectives on the history of economic thought

Selected papers from the History of Economics Society Conference, 1996

Edited by Malcolm Rutherford

London and New York

First published 1998
by Routledge
11 New Fetter Lane, London EC4P 4EE

Simultaneously published in the USA and Canada
by Routledge
29 West 35th Street, New York, NY 10001

Typeset in Garamond by RefineCatch Limited, Bungay, Suffolk
Printed and bound in Great Britain by
Biddles Ltd, Guildford and King's Lynn

British Library Cataloguing in Publication Data
A catalogue record for this book is available from the British Library

Library of Congress Cataloguing in Publication Data
A catalogue record for this book has been requested

ISBN 0–415–13355–6

CONTENTS

LIST OF CONTRIBUTORS

William J. Barber is the Andrews Professor of Economics Emeritus at Wesleyan University. Recent books include *Breaking the Academic Mould: Economists and American Higher Learning in the Nineteenth Century* (ed.) and *Designs within Disorder: Franklin D. Roosevelt, the Economists, and the Shaping of American Economic Policy, 1933–1945*. He is also the General Editor of the 14-volume edition of *Works of Irving Fisher*.

Jeff Biddle is a Professor of Economics at Michigan State University. His research in the fields of labor economics and the history of economic thought has appeared in such journals as *The American Economic Review*, *The Journal of Political Economy*, *The Journal of Labor Economics*, and *History of Political Economy*. His current research concerns the development of the economics profession in the United States during the twentieth century.

Philippe Broda is a member of the Centre d'Histoire de la Pensée Economique (CHPE), Paris, and of the Institut Commercial de Nancy. His current area of research is institutionalism, old and new. His publications include "Commons and Veblen: Contrasting Ideas about Evolution," in L. Moss (ed.), *Perspectives on the History of Economic Thought: Joseph A. Schumpeter, Historian of Economics*, and "Veblen and the Vanishing of the 'Leisure Class,'" forthcoming in the collection edited by Professor Samuels on the occasion of the centenary of Veblen's *TLC* and Commons' *SVS*.

A. W. (Bob) Coats, Emeritus Professor of Economic and Social History, University of Nottingham. He has published articles on history, sociology, and professionalization of economics in, *inter alia*, *American Economic Review*, *Journal of Economic Literature*, *Economic Journal*, *Economica*, *Journal of Political Economy*, *H.O.P.E.*, and *Economic History Review*. He is the Editor of *British and American Economic Essays*, vol. 1, *On the History of Economic Thought*, 1992, and vol. 2, *The Sociology and Professionalization of Economics*, 1993; and also of *The Post-1945 Internationalization of Economics*, 1997.

Avi J. Cohen is Associate Professor of Economics at York University, Toronto, Canada. His research interests include history of economic thought, capital theory, and economic education. His work has been published in *H.O.P.E.*, *Journal of Economic Education*, *Journal of Economic History*, and *Journal of Post-Keynesian Economics*. Currently, he is working on a book for Cambridge University Press entitled *Capital Controversy from Böhm-Bawerk to Bliss: History versus Equilibrium*.

Robert W. Dimand, Professor of Economics at Brock University, St. Catharines, Ontario, is author of *The Origins of the Keynesian Revolution* (1988), *A History of Games Theory*, vol. 1 (with Mary Ann Dimand, 1996), and he has published articles in *The American Economic Review* (Papers and Proceedings), *The Economic Journal*, and *History of Political Economy*. He also edited (with Mary Ann Dimand and Evelyn Forget) *Women of Value: Feminist Essays on the History of Women in Economics* (1995).

Ross B. Emmett, Associate Professor, Augustana College. The focus of his research has been the work of Frank H. Knight and the Chicago economics department as an example of the changing nature of modernist social science during the twentieth century. He has published articles in *History of Political Economy*, *Research in the History of Economic Thought and Methodology*, *Against the Grain: Dissent in Economics*, and *The American National Biography*.

Craufurd D. Goodwin is James B. Duke Professor of Economics at Duke University, and is Editor of the journal, *History of Political Economy*, and of the book series, *Historical Perspectives on Modern Economics*, published by the Cambridge University Press. He has been working recently on the history of American economic thought and on the Bloomsbury Group. His book on the economic ideas of the art critic Roger Fry will be published late in 1997 by the University of Michigan Press.

J. Patrick Gunning is Professor of Economics in the Institute of Public Finance at National Chung Hsing University in Taiwan. He has published two books and several papers on Ludwig von Mises, including *The New Subjectivist Revolution* (1990) and a companion paper "Ludwig von Mises' Transformation of the Austrian Theory of Value and Cost" (1997). He has also published several papers on entrepreneurship and Austrian economics. He recently completed a manuscript in *Public Choice* called "Understanding Democracy."

Anne Mayhew is Professor of Economics and History at the University of Tennessee, Knoxville, and serves as Editor of the *Journal of Economic Issues*. Her major areas of research are institutional economic theory, U.S. economic history, and the history of American thought 1870–1940. Her published work has appeared in several journals, including the *History of Political Economy*, *Journal of Economic History*, and *Journal of Economic Issues*.

Stephen Meardon is an economics Ph.D. candidate at Duke University.

Earlier research (with Andreas Ortmann) on Adam Smith's ideas regarding the evolution of moral standards and the acquisition of self-command has been published in the 1993 Perspectives volume and in *Rationality and Society*. Current research includes his Ph.D. thesis on the influence of trade liberalization on the geographical location of industries in North America, and archiving the professional papers of Don Patinkin.

Robin Neill, Adjunct Professor, Carleton University, and Sessional Lecturer, University of Prince Edward Island, is the author of two books: *A New Theory of Value: The Canadian Economics of H.A. Innis*; and *A History of Canadian Economic Thought*. He is currently researching the information environment of economics in the 1950s, and the history of Island roads.

Neil B. Niman is an Associate Professor of Economics in the Department of Economics at the University of New Hampshire. His areas of interest include the history of economic thought, organizational economics, and electronic commerce. His publications have appeared in: *Journal of the History of Economic Thought*, *Scottish Journal of Political Economy*, *Contemporary Economic Policy*, *Journal of Post-Keynesian Economics*, and *Management Science*.

Jerry L. Petr is Professor of Economics at the University of Nebraska, Lincoln. His areas of scholarly interest include comparative economic systems, history of economics, and economic heterodoxy. His work has appeared in the *Journal of Economic Issues* and *Comparative Economic Studies*, and as chapters in *Market Power and the Economy* and *The Principles of Economics Course: A Handbook for Instructors*.

Robert P. Rogers is Associate Professor of Economics at Ashland University of Ohio. His research interests are industrial organization, econometrics, and the history of economic thought. He has published articles in the RAND *Journal of Economics*, *Southern Economic Journal*, *Contemporary Economic Policy*, and *Journal of Business and Economic Statistics*.

James R. Wible has been a member of the economics faculty at the University of New Hampshire in Durham for more than a decade. His research interests are the economics of science, the economics and philosophy of Charles Sanders Peirce, and macroeconomics and monetary theory. His monograph, *The Economics of Science: Methodology and Epistemology as if Economics Really Mattered*, contains a chapter on Peirce and will soon be published by Routledge.

ACKNOWLEDGEMENTS

The following people served in the capacity of an editorial board for this collection: Roger Backhouse, Ross Emmett, Steve Medema, and Warren Samuels. Their willingness to share in the task of refereeing manuscripts and providing suggestions to authors is gratefully acknowledged.

INTRODUCTION

Malcolm Rutherford

This volume contains seventeen papers presented at the 1996 History of Economics Society meetings in Vancouver. All the papers included deal in whole or in part with the history of American economic thought. That so many papers dealing with American subjects were presented at the conference was not an accident. At the History of Economics Society meetings in 1994 Mary Morgan and I started an informal network of historians of economics interested in the history of American economics. We felt this was an area of the history of economics that had received insufficient attention, and which, as a result, contained numerous opportunities for new and interesting research. Moreover, the standard presentation of American economics as derivative and of poor quality was, we thought, misleading. We were concerned that the variety and creativity of American economics, and the links between American economic thought and its particular, non-European, context, should become better appreciated. One of our objectives was to encourage papers on American themes to be given at the Vancouver conference. This volume is the result. The title, *The Economic Mind in America*, is an acknowledgement of the pioneering work of Joseph Dorfman in this area.

Part I contains a roundtable discussion concerning the "American-ness" of American economics. A.W. Coats was the lead speaker, with William Barber, Ross Emmett, and Anne Mayhew as commentators. Coats begins with a criticism of the excesses of Dorothy Ross's use of the notion of "American exceptionalism," but goes on to outline a number of hypotheses that have been advanced to account for the "distinctive qualities and features of American intellectual history." Some of these hypotheses conflict with each other, but others overlap or are complementary. Concern with practical matters, an eagerness to modify or scrap existing ideas in response to new conditions, and the high degree of specialization and compartmentalization in American academic life are all factors mentioned in a variety of ways in Coats's outline.

In response, Barber provides a defense of a limited version of the exceptionalist thesis, noting the efforts of Daniel Raymond and others to build an economics related to American circumstances, and suggesting that the peculiarities of American conditions have continued to play a role in affecting both the types of questions that have been raised and the "manner in which answers to them" have been sought. Emmett begins by adding a Canadian perspective to the discussion, but continues by focusing on the "discursive and institutional contexts in which economics is practiced." This he claims will enable the historian to discover the unique features of American economics without falling into the traps of the exceptionalist thesis. Finally, Mayhew points to the manner in which "specifically American economic *problems* shaped American economics," with particular emphasis on the issue of monopolies, trusts, and market power, and the policy environment that shaped the American reception of Keynes.

Part II contains three papers that were all presented at the same conference session on "Pioneers of American Policy Analysis." The first of these papers by William Barber details Irving Fisher's remarkable career as a policy advocate. As Barber points out, Fisher "was an inveterate crusader for causes," a point amply demonstrated by his tireless efforts to promote his schemes for monetary reform to promote price stability. Fisher's views on the appropriate role of the economist as policy advocate contrast sharply with those of Wesley Mitchell, the subject of the next chapter by Jeff Biddle. It is ironic that we see the relatively orthodox Fisher sometimes letting his advocacy get the better of his scholarship, while we observe the institutionalist Mitchell striving to keep the scientific enterprise free from political overtones or contamination. This is not because Mitchell thought reform was not necessary, or because he thought scientific investigation could not offer useful information to the policymaker, but because he wanted to keep a separation between social scientific investigation and political discourse in order to protect the former. This he did by creating and maintaining a detached stance. Scientific findings may affect political values, but the scientist as scientist is an investigator and not a policy advocate.

A different view held sway at Brookings. Here scientific objectivity did not mean detachment but the attempt to promote policy in the broad public interest—as opposed to narrow sectional interests. Craufurd Goodwin's chapter discusses the fascinating and ultimately successful efforts of Harold Moulton and Leo Pasvolsky to promote their "vision" of a new world order designed to ensure both peace and prosperity—a global vision unusual in American economists of the time.

Part III deals with some American contributions to economic theory and measurement. The first chapter in this part deals with Herbert J. Davenport. Patrick Gunning's chapter reveals the significant contributions made by Davenport to the Austrian theory of subjective value and cost and to the concept of the entrepreneur. It is perhaps not generally known that there was a considerable amount of interest in Austrian school ideas in America between the 1890s and the First World War. This was a part of the great ferment of economic ideas that existed in America at that time. Davenport was, however, an unusual Austrian as he was also influenced by Veblen's discussion of financial manipulation and predation. This aspect of Davenport's work was heavily criticized by Frank Fetter, something that may have contributed to his underappreciation by other Austrians.

Robert Dimand's chapter discusses another of Irving Fisher's crusades, this time his quest for an ideal index number. The debates over Fisher's ideas involved many economists on both sides of the Atlantic, including Allyn Young, Udney Yule, A.L. Bowley, and R.G. Hawtrey. As Dimand argues, the debate deepened the understanding of index numbers and of the statistical criteria by which they might be assessed.

The last chapter in this part is Avi Cohen's examination of Knight's work on capital theory that formed the center of the 1930s debate between Knight, Hayek, and Kaldor. The chapter deals with the influences of J.B. Clark and Irving Fisher on Knight, and comprehensively reviews Knight's various capital models. The various tensions and unresolved problems in Knight's work are brought out. The chapter exposes the wide variety of views to be found in the early neoclassical work on capital theory, but also points to the similarities between Knight's theoretical and methodological positions and those later expressed by Joan Robinson.

Part IV focuses on American institutionalism, but with some interesting angles on European and Canadian connections. Robin Neill deals with John Rae, Thorstein Veblen, and Harold Innis. Rae's thinking is seen as European and based on a Baconian view of science and Scottish Common Sense Philosophy. Neill argues that Veblen knew of Rae's work but was not closely familiar with it. The similarities between the two men on issues such as capital theory and the nature of human agency are explained by Neill in terms of the elements of Scottish Common Sense Philosophy that were passed through into American pragmatism. Innis, who was—via J.M. Clark—influenced both by Veblenian ideas and his Canadian economic environment, represents a more purely North American phenomenon.

Neil Niman's chapter deals with the evolutionary component in the work of Veblen and Alfred Marshall. Veblen, of course, was engaged quite explicitly in the attempt to develop an evolutionary economics along "Darwinian" lines. The place of evolutionism and biological analogy in Marshall's work has been much disputed. Niman argues that an evolutionary approach can be found in Marshall's work, and one that has some interesting commonalities with Veblen's.

The third chapter in this part is Philippe Broda's examination of the methodological divergences between Veblen and J.R. Commons. Broda argues that Veblen's Darwinian methodology led him to eliminate the teleological dimension of human action from his theory, while Commons made exactly that dimension the starting point for his research. Broda's chapter contains a particularly interesting section dealing with the role of "great men" in the treatments of Veblen and Commons. This is a point that is highly revealing of the differences between them.

Part V contains three chapters that each deal with writers who have combined different ideas or approaches in particularly interesting and original ways. The first of these chapters concerns the work on economics of the American philosopher Charles S. Peirce. Peirce is, of course, best known as the founder of American pragmatism. He was deeply influenced by evolutionary ideas, and his notions of science and his discussions of the active mind and of habit formation were, in turn, formative influences on American institutionalists such as Veblen and Commons. Because of this it is surprising to find that Peirce's explicitly economic writings are mathematical and make use of utility theory. He also used economic criteria in his appraisals of research, and it is an aspect of this part of Peirce's work that is the subject of James Wible's paper. For Peirce, because of the expense of experimentation, scientific examination of a hypothesis should be carried out in the most economically efficient manner possible, and the hypothesis itself should be stated in terms that facilitate testing. In the work discussed by Wible, Peirce applies these ideas to the drawing of hypotheses from ancient documents, specifically the works of Aristotle.

The second chapter in this part, by Jerry Petr, concerns the reform and advocacy efforts of Alvin Johnson. Johnson was a skilled exponent of the neoclassical economics of J.B. Clark, but became increasingly aware of its limitations in dealing with a dynamic economy and of the growing division between academic economics and the intelligent layman. Johnson turned his career in new directions, becoming editor of *The New Republic* and working editor for the first *Encyclopedia of the Social Sciences*, promoting adult education, directing the New School for Social Research, launching the "University in Exile" at the New School's graduate faculty to provide an American haven for European scholars fleeing Nazi persecution, and combatting racial discrimination at home. For Johnson, the values of human rights, nondiscrimination, and liberal democracy called for active involvement and dedication.

The last chapter in this part represents a shift away from academic economics to the economics of a popular science fiction writer, Robert A. Heinlein. As noted by Barber in his response to Coats, economic writing by amateurs has been something of a feature of the American landscape. Even within the area of science fiction there is the precedent of Edward Bellamy. Robert Rogers outlines Heinlein's economics as revealed in his various novels. Heinlein is strongly pro-market in his economic views, sometimes verging on libertarian views in his critique of government. Despite this, Heinlein often proposes a form of economic planning or coordination to be undertaken by a super computer. Heinlein thus appears unfamiliar with the full scope of the Austrian critique of planning, in that he does not take account of the necessarily subjective and dispersed nature of the information that would be required for effective planning.

The final part, Part VI, consists of a single chapter by Craufurd Goodwin and Stephen Meardon. This chapter charts the degree and type of interest in international matters displayed by American economists between 1886 and 1995. The technique used is a statistical examination of the contents of articles published in the three leading American economics journals. The findings indicate a "strikingly high" level of interest in international issues at the opening of the century. After 1907 there was something of a decline, with revivals as a result of the two world wars. A further decline began in 1960 with only a modest recovery in the years since 1980.

This collection can, of course, make no claims to achieving balance or completeness in its coverage. The chapters have a heavy emphasis on the American economics produced between 1900 and 1945, and most discuss individuals. Nevertheless, many features of the American scene are visible: the very close involvement of many economists in policy debate and policy formation, the conflicting views concerning the issue of advocacy vesus scientific objectivity (which are not always what one might expect), the important place of particular institutions of research and training such as Brookings, the NBER, and the New School, and—most of all—the wonderful variety and creativity that is to be found everywhere in the history of American economics.

Part I

ROUNDTABLE ON AMERICAN ECONOMICS

1

WHAT IS AMERICAN ABOUT AMERICAN ECONOMICS?

A.W. (Bob) Coats

INTRODUCTION

The organizer of this symposium deliberately posed a sweeping, over ambitious open-ended question to which there is obviously no single answer. As the first contributor I am privileged, for I am not constrained by the fear of duplicating what my fellow symposiasts are going to say. The duplication, in any case, is unlikely to be great given my somewhat idiosyncratic approach, which focuses on the general intellectual and social context of economic thought, rather than on the development of economic analysis. There is, of course, ample scope for both, and indeed other, interpretative standpoints.

ARE AMERICANS AND THEIR EXPERIENCES EXCEPTIONAL?

One obvious answer to the question "What is American about American economics?" is that it is a species of economics produced by Americans. Or, to adapt Jacob Viner's oft-quoted quip: "American economics is what American economists do (or have done)." This response is evasive; and it may seem trivial. Yet it raises a prior question: "What is an American?"—a question that has often formed the starting point of American Studies courses, and provoked endless debate. Much of this debate arises directly or indirectly from efforts to assess the impact and role in American history of the immense, irregular flow of immigrants over several centuries. In his late eighteenth-century *Letter from an American Farmer* St. John Crevecourt confidently asserted that "The American is a new man who acts on new principles" (Crevecourt [1782] 1981). If this is true, and applied to economics, it means the subject is culture-bound and not a universal science, as many economists want to believe.

Far greater thinkers than Crevecourt—such as Alexis de Tocqueville,

James Bryce, and Frederick Jackson Turner—have tackled Crevecourt's question "What then is this new man?" This is not the place to review the endless litany of attempts to define "*the* American character," or to provide a comprehensive and definite list of distinctive American "traits." But before abandoning these very abstract and general issues, let me warn you against one familiar and superficially attractive idea—the notion of American "exceptionalism." Like "the American character," and "American traits," this concept can be formulated in a variety of ways designed to pinpoint America's uniqueness. But it can be a snare and a delusion. A recent extreme example of this is Dorothy Ross's *The Origins of American Social Science* (Ross 1991), in many other respects an admirably scholarly volume, in which "exceptionalism" runs riot. Ross refers to it roughly a hundred times in just over 500 pages, and in a mind-boggling variety of definitions and characterizations which I shall not try to enumerate here.[1] One is tempted to adapt George Orwell, by saying that all countries are exceptional, but some are more exceptional than others! The pursuit of exceptionalism will not help us here.

The question "Who is an American?" is relevant to the history of American economic thought as soon as we differentiate between those economic writers who were born, bred, and trained (if at all) and lived in the colonies or the United States, and those who were born and educated (though not necessarily trained) abroad before arriving in this country—usually, but not invariably, from across the Atlantic. According to Joseph Dorfman's encyclopedic five-volume survey, *The Economic Mind in American Civilization* (Dorfman 1947–59), there were more noteworthy foreign-born economic writers in the pre-Civil War era than in the 1895–1918 period covered in his third volume. This is surprising, given the vast increase in the flood of immigrants into the United States around the turn of the century (although the pre-Civil War period was, of course, much longer). In the twentieth century, especially during and after the 1930s, a considerable number of so-called illustrious immigrants came to the United States from Europe. Several became president of the American Economic Association (AEA), and the list of American economist Nobel prizewinners includes a number who cannot be classified as pure Americans—for example, Coase, Debreu, Harsanyi, Koopmans, Leontief, Lewis, Modigliani, and perhaps Hayek. Some, but not all, did their prizewinning work before they were permanently domiciled in the United States. And an earlier example is Schumpeter, who was a well-established professor in Europe before he migrated to America in the early 1930s, becoming president of the AEA in 1947.

Even in a large and rapidly growing professional community of economists this small band of outstanding immigrants (together with others—for example, Kenneth Boulding, J.K. Galbraith), located in strategic institutions, doubtless made a disproportionate impact on research, and probably also on teaching. But it would take a historian of Bob Fogel's boldness and ingenuity to demonstrate counterfactually what the state of American economics would now be were it not for the immigrants' contributions.

SOME HYPOTHESES

A number of competing, conflicting, complementary, or overlapping hypotheses have been advanced to account for the distinctive qualities and features of American intellectual history, some of which apply to American economic thought. The following examples are not necessarily listed in order of importance, nor should the amount of space devoted to each be taken as an index of its significance.

1 Among the general characteristics of American ideas and intellectual life identified by American historians are: distaste for "pure" theory and speculative ideas; preference for "practical" or "applied" ideas; lack of interest in and ability at construction of elaborate intellectual or doctrinal systems; lack of originality, especially with respect to fundamentals; prevalent broad socio-political consensus.
2 The United States made no progress in the development of the theory of political economy prior to 1876 mainly because Americans were too preoccupied with the urgent needs of a new society to devote themselves to original thought (Dunbar 1886).
3 However, it has been argued that a new environment stimulates novel ideas appropriate to the circumstance, and there is abundant evidence of this in the early economic literature (Fetter 1943; Conkin 1980). Indeed, there was probably an excess of originality, flexibility, and ingenuity, especially on policy issues. American economic writers were eager to break free from inherited European economic ideas, or to adapt them to indigenous needs and interests.
4 Overreadiness to modify or scrap existing ideas in response to some new intellectual impulses or the pressure of current concerns helps to explain the inability or reluctance to undertake sustained analysis. In the crucial formative phase of professionalization in the social sciences during the late nineteenth and early twentieth centuries, there was excessive product differentiation among American economics textbook writers that reflected the intensity of personal and institutional competition. Numerous commentators have noted the prevalence of hypercriticism or "superindividualism" in economics (Laughlin 1906; Clark 1927; Norton 1969).
5 "*Plus ça change, plus c'est la même chose.*" In a recent symposium on the question "Is there a European Economics?" (Frey and Frey 1995), a number of distinguished economists argue that American economists are more susceptible to intellectual fashions; more introverted, more academically oriented, more narrowly specialized (see below, item 6), and less

tolerant intellectually than their European counterparts. (This is not based on a systematic opinion poll, but it has some echoes of earlier characteristics.)

6 The weakness and delayed development of theory is by no means peculiar to American economic thought. The American distaste for abstract and speculative inquiry, whether in philosophy, politics, or natural science, is a historiographical commonplace. (Religion, especially in the colonial period, may be an exception.) According to Daniel Boorstin: "this kind of knowledge which life in America made possible, precisely because it was factual and miscellaneous, required no preliminary training. . . . All knowledge seemed to come in small miscellaneous parcels" (Boorstin 1958: 162, 168). Curiously enough, when the late nineteenth-century revolution in American higher education occurred, the rapid expansion of university departments facilitated a high degree of specialization and compartmentalization of academic labor. This was not, of course, a uniquely American movement, but it seems to have started earlier, and proceeded more rapidly and with greater enthusiasm than elsewhere. The combined impact of secularization, late industrialism (by comparison with Europe), urbanization, and modernization accorded with the desire to make knowledge serviceable (knowledge as technology, that is, ideas that "work").

7 The conspicuous early American intellectual achievements in empirical studies were directly dependent on keen observation and assiduous data collection. In producing works of travel or natural history, or in undertaking investigations in geology rather than, say, physics, American authors were less constrained by the European heritage, which was a source of strength in elementary work, but inhibiting to advanced thinking or research in more theoretical fields. This bias against so-called pure theory persisted long after the late nineteenth- and early twentieth-century expansion of the academic profession. Caustic critics have argued that when a sophisticated indigenous intellectual system eventually emerged—that is, pragmatist philosophy—it was little more than an elaborate rationalization of deep-rooted and widely held beliefs and values. Pragmatism, it has been said, has rested glacier-like "on miles of submerged conviction . . . the American deals with concrete cases because he never doubts his general principles" (Hartz 1955: 59).

8 In the 1950s American historians emphasized the continuities and consensus features of their past. According to Hartz, the great majority of Americans have been liberals of one species or another. America never had a feudal aristocracy, and therefore did not need to develop a radical or socialist counterweight. The conflicts between American reformers and conservatives have lacked depth, "forever dissolving into common agreements," while Hartz's student, the brilliant British political scientist Bernard Crick, argued that this explained why American political

scientists had consistently failed to engage in fundamental thinking about the nature of politics (Crick 1959). (Needless to say, this thesis was not welcomed by American political scientists!) Have American economists, likewise, failed to examine the fundamental nature of an economic system, relying instead on European authors (e.g., Smith, Walras, Hayek)? Does the liberal predominance help to explain the weakness of radical and Marxist economics in the United States? (Ward 1979). Hartz has said of pragmatism, "it is only when you take your ethics [or politics, or economics?] for granted that all problems appear as problems of technique" (Hartz 1955: 10). Does this shed any light on the unusual strength of formalism and technical skill in contemporary academic economics? (Some symposiasts in Frey and Frey (1995) argued that European economists were concerned with deeper issues!) (N.B. the term "formalism" is used quite differently in Morton White's (1976) stimulating, pragmatist-flavored account of American turn-of-the-century intellectual development.)

9 Daniel Boorstin claimed that in the colonial period, "American life quickly proved uncongenial to any special class of knowers" (Boorstin 1958), while Richard Hofstadter maintained that anti-intellectualism has been both powerful and endemic throughout the nation's history (Hofstadter 1964). Deference and respect for intellectual, social, and political authority have been limited; and in a democratic and egalitarian society, "anti-establishment" sentiments have generally commanded widespread support.

In his influential education tract, *The School and Society* (Dewey 1900), John Dewey contrasted the impulse to create and produce with mere intellectual virtues. Separation of "theory" from "practice" threatened to perpetuate the division between "cultured" persons and ordinary workers. (This may underlie the distaste for "grand theory" which gives its originators undue influence and a sense of superiority to its followers.) In his *Reconstruction in Philosophy* (Dewey 1920), he made a comprehensive attack on "traditional" philosophy. The parallel with Richard Rorty's (1980) influential *Philosophy and the Mirror of Nature* is intriguing. (But this is no place to embark on a comparison between early and late twentieth-century American pragmatism, or its relationship to the philosophy and methodology of economics.)

10 Antiestablishment sentiments have long been sustained by geographical diversity and the persistence of regional rivalries (the Civil War being the most extreme example). In intellectual and cultural affairs there has been lasting suspicion, even hostility, between "east" and "west" (both geographically shifting concepts). The older eastern universities and prestigious liberal arts colleges have been seen as institutional representations of an elitist "genteel" tradition. By contrast, it has been said that in the newer state universities the main standards were quantitative, their main

concerns were materialistic, their education bias utilitarian, and their outlook optimistic (Foerster 1937). Is it a coincidence that the founding triumvirate of the principal antiestablishment movement in economics—Veblen, Commons, and Mitchell—were all born in the middle west?[2] On the other hand, the growing size and representativeness of the AEA has operated as a unifying force—and also as a forum wherein intra-professional and doctrinal divisions can be aired.

11 It has been argued that the decentralization and competitiveness of American academic life has been a positive stimulus to the growth of scientific knowledge (David 1991). On the other hand, the number, geographical dispersion, and heterogeneity of American academic institutions has facilitated the formation and survival of minority and/or heterodox intellectual interests and schools of thought. In his *History of Economic Analysis*, Schumpeter (1954) remarked that the rapid growth of American higher education between 1870 and 1920 meant that employment opportunities in academia outstripped the growth of "fully competent personnel." Many of the new entrants were "practically untrained"; sharply divergent educational backgrounds and levels coexisted; and "for a considerable period of time there were no professional standards, and competent teaching was not always guaranteed" (Schumpeter 1954: 864). However, in the past half-century, circumstances have changed markedly. The recent report of the AEA's Commission on Graduate Education in Economics (Krueger et al. 1991) reveals the remarkable homogeneity and uniformity of graduate training in the discipline. This has been facilitated by the expansion and increased efficiency of communication. The AEA has contributed to this general process.

12 Throughout American history (with the possible exception of the past two decades or so) the American intellectual and academic communities have been comparatively weak by European standards. This is in large part a by-product of the "practical" bias in American life, and the lack of respect for thinking rather than doing. Prior to the Civil War, and for a limited period thereafter, attacks on professors were usually based on charges of religious heresy. However, during the early phase of rapid university expansion (1870–1920), the social scientists, and especially the economists, were the primary targets of serious and well-publicized efforts to curtail academic freedom (Hofstadter and Metzger 1955). This generated what Mary Furner (1975) has called, in her classic study, the crisis of advocacy versus objectivity. Economists and other social scientists, in varying degrees, felt the need to be useful to society, while simultaneously seeking recognition as impartial scholars and/or objective scientists. For economists this often meant studying pressing contemporary problems and making constructive policy recommendations, which thrust them into the arena of public controversy. The extra-mural threats

to freedom of expression and job security led to the development of a consensus about the limits of acceptable academic behavior. This necessarily involved the discouragement or repression of radical views, and, according to some observers, a surrender to the growing power of the corporate business interests. Comparisons between expanding universities and expanding business organizations have become commonplace (Veblen [1918] 1954; Barrow 1990).

13 This, however, was an unstable accommodation, which provided little protection for intellectual freedom during the two World Wars and after 1945 (Gruber 1975; Schrecker 1986). To a European, it seems curious, to say the least, that in a country where professors and intellectuals have so often been viewed as weak and ineffectual, they should also be seen at times as a powerful subversive force, against which brutal and organized suppression was justified. Extended pressures on the academic community in the post-1945 period led to widespread self-imposed restraints on freedom of expression, and may well have contributed, in economics as elsewhere, to the shift toward politically safer quantitative and technical work (Schrecker 1986; Lazarsfeld and Thielens 1958).[3]

AFTERTHOUGHTS

In the preceding section I have deliberately concentrated on very general issues, in the hope of provoking discussion. The list of items is not, of course, exhaustive, and I have made no specific references to the history of American economic thought as such—in particular the hoary old question whether institutionalism is a uniquely American phenomenon. Other panellists may wish to take up this and related issues. (However, I cannot resist the comment that despite numerous earlier reports of its demise, institutional economics, both in its old and new forms, is nowadays enjoying a vigorous new lease of life—with exciting future prospects. Perhaps this is, after all, an example of American exceptionalism?)

Given the nature of this inquiry the foregoing account is necessarily somewhat sweeping and simplistic. Many qualifications are required, for example the distinction between academics and intellectuals. The organization of large-scale twentieth-century universities has, in many respects, been inimical to intellectual activity.

NOTES

1 See my review of Ross (Coats 1992). The most recent contribution to this literature is Seymour Martin Lipset's *American Exceptionalism: A Double-Edged Sword* (Lipset 1996).

2 The idiosyncratic Texas-trained, Colorado-based institutionalist, J. Fagg Foster, viewed institutional economics as a direct by-product of the American frontier experience (Miller 1994: 257).

3 It is tempting to suggest that European academics have, generally speaking, enjoyed greater intellectual, political, and social freedom and security than their American counterparts. However, I know of no systematic comparative study of these matters, and Nazi- and Communist-dominated eras obviously constitute major exceptions to any such generalization.

REFERENCES

Barrow, C. (1990). *Universities and the Capitalist State: Corporate Liberalism and the Reconstruction of American Higher Education, 1894–1928*, Madison: University of Wisconsin Press.

Boorstin, D. (1958). *The Americans: The Colonial Experience*, New York: Random House.

Clark, J.M. (1927). "Recent Developments in Economics," in Edward C. Hayes (ed.), *Recent Developments in the Social Sciences*, Philadelphia: Lippincott.

Coats, A.W. (1992). "Review of *The Origins of American Social Science* by Dorothy Ross," *Academe* 78 (January–February): 43–44.

Conkin, P. (1980). *Prophets of American Prosperity: America's First Political Economists*, Bloomington, Ind.: Indiana University Press.

Crevecourt, St. J. ([1782] 1981). *Letters from an American Farmer*, Harmondsworth: Penguin.

Crick, B. (1959). *The American Science of Politics*, London: Routledge & Kegan Paul.

David, J.B. (1991). *Scientific Growth: Essays on the Social Organization and Ethos of Science*, Berkeley: University of California Press.

Dewey, J. (1900). *The School and Society*, New York: McClure, Phillips.

——— (1920). *Reconstruction in Philosophy*, New York: Holt.

Dorfman, J. (1947–59). *The Economic Mind in American Civilization*, 5 vols, New York: Viking.

Dunbar, C. (1886). "Economic Science in America, 1776–1886," *North American Review* 122 (January): 124–154.

Fetter, F. (1943). "The Early History of Political Economy in the United States," *Proceedings of the American Philosophical Society* 87 (July): 51–60.

Foerster, N. (1937). *The American State University: Its Relation to Democracy*, Chapel Hill, NC: University of North Carolina Press.

Frey, R.L. and B. Frey (eds) (1995). "Is there a European Economics?," *Kyklos* 48 (2): 185–311.

Furner, M.O. (1975). *Advocacy versus Objectivity: A Crisis in the Professionalization of American Social Science 1865–1905*, Lexington, Ky.: University of Kentucky Press.

Gruber, C.S. (1975). *Mars and Minerva: World War I and the Uses of Higher Learning in America*, Baton Rouge, La.: Louisiana State University Press.

Hartz, L. (1955). *The Liberal Tradition in America*, New York: Harcourt Brace.

Hofstadter, R. (1964). *Anti-Intellectualism in American Life*, New York: Oxford University Press.

Hofstadter, R. and W.P. Metzger (1955). *The Development of Academic Freedom in the United States*, New York: Columbia University Press.

Krueger, A.O. et al. (1991). "Report of the Commission on Graduate Education in Economics," *Journal of Economic Literature* 29 (September): 1035–1053.

Laughlin, J.L. (1906). *Industrial America*, New York: Scribners.

Lazarsfeld, P. and W. Thielens, Jr. (1958). *The Academic Mind*, Glencoe, Ill.: The Free Press.

Lipset, S.M. (1996). *American Exceptionalism: A Double-Edged Sword*, New York: Norton.

Miller, E.S. (1994). "J. Fagg Foster," in Geoffrey Hodgson, Warren Samuels, and Marc Tool (eds), *The Elgar Companion to Institutional and Evolutionary Economics*, vol. 1, Cheltenham: Edward Elgar.

Norton, H.S. (1969). *The Role of the Economist in Government: A Study of Economic Advice Since 1920*, Berkeley: McCutchan.

Rorty, R. (1980). *Philosophy and the Mirror of Nature*, Oxford: Blackwell.

Ross, D. (1991). *The Origins of American Social Science*, Cambridge: Cambridge University Press.

Schrecker, E.W. (1986). *No Ivory Tower: McCarthyism and the Universities*, New York: Oxford University Press.

Schumpeter, J.A. (1954). *A History of Economic Analysis*, New York: Oxford University Press.

Veblen, T. ([1918] 1954). *The Higher Learning in America: A Memorandum on the Conduct of Universities by Businessmen*, Stanford, Calif.: Stanford University Press.

Ward, B. (1979). *The Ideal Worlds of Economics: Liberal, Radical and Conservative World Views*, London: Macmillan.

White, M.D. (1976). *Social Thought in America: The Revolt Against Formalism*, New York: Oxford University Press.

2

REMARKS ON "AMERICAN-NESS" IN AMERICAN ECONOMIC THOUGHT

William J. Barber

In the summer of 1995, the Whitney Museum in New York staged what was billed as a "blockbuster" exhibition of the works of Edward Hopper. Those responsible for preparing the exhibition notes and videos proclaimed Hopper to be the quintessential American artist. His canvases, they maintained, were distinctively American by virtue of their stark depiction of space—a phenomenon which allegedly reflected the openness and land abundance of the American experience. Similarly—the commentaries asserted—his representations of lonely people in his interior scenes should be understood as an expression of American "rugged individualism." To an amateur like myself, what the professional art critics had to say about all this had at least a surface plausibility. I thus found the review of this show that appeared in *The Economist* of London to be particularly arresting. *The Economist*'s art critic totally rejected the interpretation provided by the management of the Whitney Museum. There was no denying Hopper's central preoccupation with space—but, it was argued, there was nothing peculiarly American about that. The problem of the treatment of space was one that all artists were obliged to confront, whatever their geographical situation or national origin. In short, space was a universal category and not one to which any distinctive national characteristics could be assigned. I recount this episode as a reminder of pitfalls awaiting anyone who rushes into ascribing special national attributes to artistic and/or intellectual productions. The search for "exceptionalism"—as Bob Coats has observed—can be a snare and a delusion.

I too reviewed Dorothy Ross's book on *The Origins of American Social Science* and found it necessary to criticize her attempt to locate "exceptionalism" without exception. At the same time, it seems to me that it would be a mistake to suppress this category altogether. At various times in American history, the flow of economic discourse has been heavily conditioned by attempts to construct a political economy for the "New World" which would be sharply differentiated from that of the "Old World." Whether or not those attempts were successful, the motivating force inspiring them needs to be recognized. Clearly, Daniel Raymond in the 1820s believed it to be imperative that the new nation should have a political economy that it could call its own. And he also insisted that it needed to address head-on one of the special properties of the national reality: the institution of slavery. In a similar vein, Henry C. Carey proposed an American political economy from which all vestiges of European classicism should be banished. Indeed, his writings stood the central Ricardian and Malthusian propositions on their heads. Examples of this type of exercise abound. There are, for instance, more than trace elements of a claim to "exceptionalism" in the literature of the 1920s extolling the unlimited possibilities of the American economy of a "new era."

Note should be taken as well of another body of literature—one which does not reject imported ideas altogether, but instead adapts them as deemed appropriate to fit the American environment. This process of selective filtration has been in evidence throughout the nation's history. The most widely read American textbook before the Civil War—the Revd Francis Wayland's *Elements of Political Economy*—is a case in point. Wayland, writing in 1837, used classical categories as a point of departure, but he arrived at decidedly different conclusions. In America, the Ricardian analyses of land scarcity and the threat of a stationary state had no meaning. Nor were the findings of later British classicism concerning the divergent interests of various social classes acceptable: social harmony, not class conflict, was held to be the fundamental American reality. Adaptation of imported doctrines of a different type occurred in the last two decades of the nineteenth century. The "Young Turks" who studied in Germany in the 1880s and 1890 came home fired up to apply the teachings of the German Historical School in the United States. They soon came to realize that the role played by the state in the German economy could not be readily replicated on native soil in the absence of a competent and nonpartisan professional civil service. Selective accommodation of imported ideas has also occurred in the twentieth century. A Keynesian style of thinking which had come into official favor by the late 1930s was a domesticated version of the original, expressed with American accents by Alvin Hansen and Lauchlin Currie. What came through was not pure Keynes, but "Curried Keynes."

I should like to suggest that there is yet another way to address the issue of the existence (or non-existence) of a distinctive national dimension in economic discourse in the United States. Potentially, at least, it would seem to be fruitful to ask whether or not peculiarities of American circumstances leave a mark on the types of economic questions that are raised and the manner in which answers to them are sought. Let us consider a few of the properties of the local environment that have shaped the structure of argument at various times. By way of illustration, I itemize a few of them (and I am well aware that this listing can be considerably extended), as follows:

- Before the Civil War, the sectionalism that divided the country between slave states and free states certainly gave an extraordinary twist to economic debate over a wide variety of issues—and not least to controversies over free trade versus protection.
- The Morrill Act of 1863 and the land-grant college systems that stemmed from it provided a springboard for the specialism of agricultural economics (a field which the United States pioneered). These arrangements themselves were made possible by America's abundant endowment of land resources and by the policies developed by the Federal government for land disposal.
- The manner in which another subspecialism—labor economics—evolved was crucially influenced by the nation's experience with mass immigration. John R. Commons's findings (which documented the dominance of "group consciousness" over "class consciousness" among American workers) charted a course for this field that was quite different from the one typically taken in Europe.
- The system of American federalism—and its impact on capacities of various echelons of government to formulate and execute policies affecting money, banking, and public finance—has certainly left its mark on the character of American contributions to monetary and fiscal analysis.

Let me close by mentioning one additional characteristic of American life which may not be altogether singular, but which has certainly helped to shape the flow of economic discourse. I refer here to the unusual receptivity of the populace to arguments generated by economic amateurs and to the popular suspicion of experts based in the academy. Indeed, there are a fair number of moments in American history when the amateurs have had a lot to do with setting the agenda. Henry George (the single taxer), "Coin" Harvey (the bimetallist), and William Trufant Foster and Waddill Cathings (the underconsumptionists of the 1920s) were regarded by establishment economists of their day as untutored heretics. They nonetheless excited the public. In some measure, the behavior of the professionals was conditioned by that fact.

3

WHAT IS "AMERICAN" ABOUT U.S. ECONOMICS?

Ross B. Emmett

The title of my remarks is "What is 'American' about U.S. economics?" This differs somewhat from the title provided for the panel and therefore I begin with an explanation of my alternative title.

My growing familiarity with the literature of Canadian economics convinces me that many of the same issues that emerge in an examination of the unique features of U.S. economics (ranging from the early requirement of dealing with the needs of a "new" society to the twentieth-century problem of the role of the academic community in reshaping liberal democracy) also appear in an examination of the unique features of Canadian economics. That is not to say that the Canadian and U.S. responses to these issues are identical—the mixture of two founding nations, long peaceful relationships with Britain and with native peoples (for the most part), the presence of strong nationalist and social democratic traditions, and close proximity to a dominant power is enough to distinguish Canadian responses from those in the United States. Rather, a study of Canadian economic thought reveals simply that there is significant commonality in the issues faced by both U.S. and Canadian economists.

A few examples may help make this point. Robin Neill has argued that early Canadian economic thought was often either an "economics in the context of action" (Neill 1991: 57) or a branch of moral philosophy—an argument echoed in the literature about early U.S. economic thought (see Bob Coats's contribution to this same panel). Queen's University's refusal to appoint John Rae in the 1840s exemplifies the disdain moral philosophy had for practical political economy—Rae's ([1832] 1965) work was the outstanding North American contribution to economics prior to the late 1800s. Barry Ferguson's (1993) study of the political economy department of Queen's University at the turn of the twentieth century suggests that Canadian economists were engaged in the same kind of "re-making of liberalism" that economists and other social scientists in the United States were engaged in, although the final products in the two countries are different. And Harold

Innis's staple theory of the economic development of Canada shares much in common with U.S. histories based upon exceptionalist principles (see the conclusion to Innis 1930).

Hence, if we can speak of an "American" economics (and I believe we can), then recognition can also be given to its applicability in both the Canadian and U.S. contexts. It may be too much to expect a commonality of issues for economics in all of the Americas, but economists in the United States and Canada have enough common bonds to make us realize that what distinguishes "American" economics is not restricted to the U.S. portion of the American continents. That said, my own work has focused on U.S. economics in the twentieth century, and forms the basis for the remainder of my remarks.

Until recently, it has been a commonplace that location in time and place does not matter in the development of scientific ideas. Historians of economic thought have often accepted this modernist dogma, tutored in the "absolutist" approach by Blaug (1985) and others.

U.S. (and Canadian, it might be argued) intellectual history, meanwhile, has often accepted another commonplace: American exceptionalism—the notion that the unique historical circumstance, political structures, and geographic situation of North America provide a context which marks its ideas apart, especially from those developed in Europe (see Ross 1991).

Needless to say, the contrast in these two historiographic starting points has seldom brought the historian of economics and the intellectual historian together. Even when the latter rejects the exceptionalist position, as in the current vogue of "American studies," the historian of economics remains apart (although, in the case of cultural studies, the separation has as much to do with the economist's suspicions about social and cultural anthropology—from which the cultural studies movement emerged—as it does with the absolutism of the historian of economic thought).

However, the slow demise of "absolutism" among historians of economic thought, the fact that "exceptionalism" has fallen out of favor in American studies, the attraction of contemporary movements in science studies, for historians of economics, and the burgeoning volume of literature successfully linking the work of economists located in the United States (or elsewhere, for that matter) with their social and intellectual context suggests that it may now be appropriate to speak of "American" economics without implying that it is somehow exceptional within the economics profession.

What, then, might be American about U.S. economics? First, let us return to exceptionalism. Put positively, the argument that Dorothy Ross (1991) and others have made about U.S. social science during the post-Civil War, pre-Second World War period places central emphasis on the tensions created by the declining significance of the traditional sources of authority in U.S. thought (Protestantism, individualism, and so forth) and the perceived failure of other sources to provide the certainty that the traditional sources were assumed to have provided (e.g., science provided a language of social control, but what to do about uncertainty—the subjectivity of knowledge and prospect of individual opportunistic behavior?). While the U.S. response to these tensions is similar to the European response in some regards, there are sufficient differences to warrant separate treatment (see Kloppenberg 1986 for one comparison). Given the differences between European and U.S. responses in other disciplines, it would not be surprising to find U.S. economics facing these tensions in ways unfamiliar to Europeans. The conflux of competing traditions in U.S. economics prior to the interwar period is one such difference—while marginalism places an important role, neoclassicism does not reach its hegemonic position in the United States until the Second World War (see Goodwin 1973).

Secondly, we need to mention the academization of public intellectual discourse. A topic of some dissension among intellectual historians is the changing institutional context of professionalization. Thomas Bender (1993) puts the strong case: In the nineteenth century intellectual discourse found its place in urban culture (think of New York, London, Paris, Berlin, Vienna, etc.). The process of professionalization created a tension between the intellectual and the citizen which was resolved by the creation of a new institutional context—the American university. The same tension occurred in Europe, but the resolution was somewhat different—intellectual and public discourse remained more closely linked (for example, through the role of academics in government service) in Europe than it did in the United States, where intellectual and public discourse were separated and the former sought legitimation through the authority of science within the university. Bender's argument is probably overstated—one thinks of the relationship between Chicago social scientists and their urban culture—but recent interest in the difference between European economists and U.S. economists suggests there might be something to it (see references in Bob Coats's contribution to this text).

An interesting aspect of this academization of intellectual discourse in the United States is the fact that the U.S. academic community was more international in scope than the larger U.S. public during the early decades of the twentieth century. Freer to travel than most U.S. citizens, academics remained in contact with their South American and European colleagues even during periods of U.S. isolationism. From the late 1920s to the 1940s, this contact was reversed in a sense—instead of U.S. citizens going to Europe, the European intellectuals came to America, as émigrés. American universities, then, became entrepôts of foreign ideas and scholars. The reception granted émigré scholars and the transformation of the ideas of European and other economists in the American context continues to provide fodder for historians of economics. However, greater contact with historians of intellectual life and academic communities could provide a better understanding of the institutional context in which that reception and transformation occurred.

Finally, another aspect of American economics that requires attention is the relationship of social science and technology in the post-Second World War era—what Phil Mirowski (forthcoming) calls cyborg science. American economics in the postwar period was shaped by America's economic, financial, and technological position at the end of the Second World War, the society's acceptance of science being the means by which American superiority would be maintained, and the emergence of government and foundation spending on an unprecedented scale. The implications of this combination are only beginning to be studied.

These three aspects of U.S. economics are not intended to provide a comprehensive list of those attributes which might mark it as "American." My intention has been to focus attention on the discursive and institutional contexts in which economics is practiced, and to suggest that historians of U.S. economics will benefit from a closer examination of those contexts. The same can be said of the study of the history of Canadian economics. Only by engaging in such "thick" descriptions will we discover what is unique about U.S. economics, without feeling compelled to label it exceptional.

REFERENCES

Bender, T. (1993). *Intellect and Public Life: Essays on the Social History of Academic Intellectuals in the United States*, Baltimore: Johns Hopkins University Press.

Blaug, M. (1985). *Economic Theory in Retrospect*, 4th edn, Cambridge: Cambridge University Press.

Ferguson, B. (1993). *Re-Making Liberalism: The Intellectual Legacy of Adam Shortt, O.D. Skelton, W.C. Clark, and W.A. Mackintosh, 1890–1925*, Montreal and Kingston: McGill–Queen's University Press.

Goodwin, C.D. (1973). "Marginalism Moves to the New World," in R.D. Collison Black, A.W. Coats, and C.D. Goodwin (eds), *The Marginal Revolution in Economics*, Durham, NC: Duke University Press.

Innis, H.A. (1930). *The Fur Trade in Canada*, New Haven: Yale University Press.

Kloppenberg, J.T. (1986). *Uncertain Victory: Social Democracy and Progressivism in European and American Thought, 1870–1920*, New York: Oxford University Press.

Mirowski, P. (forthcoming). "Machine Dreams: Economic Agent as Cyborg," *History of Political Economy* 28 (suppl.).

Neill, R. (1991). *A History of Canadian Economic Thought*, London: Routledge.

Rae, J. ([1832] 1965). *Statement of Some New Principles on the Subject of Political Economy*, in R.W. James (ed.), *John Rae, Political Economy*, vol. 2, Toronto: University of Toronto Press.

Ross, D. (1991). *The Origins of American Social Science*, Cambridge: Cambridge University Press.

4

COMMENT ON "WHAT IS AMERICAN ABOUT AMERICAN ECONOMICS?"

Anne Mayhew

Bob Coats has provided an excellent survey of reasons that intellectual historians have given, or might give, for the Americanness of American economics. What seems to me—an institutional economist and economic historian—to be missing is sufficient attention to the ways in which specifically American economic problems shaped American economics. The influence of economic issues that have been especially American has tended to be obscured by the understandable tendency for historians of economic thought to focus on consistencies/inconsistencies of American thought with European (primarily English) thought. Even more important in obscuring the role that public issues in the United States have had on American economic thought has been the dominance of U.S. economic thought in the industrial world in this century, and particularly in the last half of the century. Let me illustrate with three examples of the way in which three specifically American episodes affected our texts, texts that came from America but have shaped thought elsewhere.

American economics, as an organized and separate discipline, came into being after the Civil War and in the midst of a spirited public debate over the role of new, large, and powerful firms in a democratic nation. The simultaneous commercialization of agriculture, and the beginning of a relative decline of that sector as a source of employment and income, sharpened the debate and allowed the farmers, who were still the majority of income earners, to articulate the issues of the debate. They saw the issue as one of powerful monopolists versus the farmers (and by intellectual extension, if not political practicality, "the people" more generally). The result was the Sherman Antitrust Act, a bill that was opposed, or at least not supported, by economists at the time. However, over the following decades, and via a process that still requires investigation, this Act came to be seen as an important linchpin of modern capitalism.

The key political issue was how to reconcile the fairly obvious effectiveness of large concerns with public concern over their power, and a series of Administrations and courts struggled with the problem. Out of a parallel intellectual struggle came the field of industrial organization (Phillips and Stevenson 1974). That field—with its paradigm of structure–conduct–performance, and its emphasis on degree of market power—was, I submit, especially American. It grew out of an American political and social battle. That elements of the intellectual resolution offered by economists can be traced to English thought (as Phillips and Stevenson do) makes it no less an American development. Nor is it any less an American development because, following the Second World War, Americans pressured the defeated nations to adopt something like the Sherman Antitrust Act and the economics that had grown around it.

Another illustration of how an American problem gave rise to an American economics, and yet again to Americanism that has in this age of U.S. hegemony become part of an international economics: In their recent and important book David Colander and Harry Landreth (1996) describe, by way of interviews, how "Keynesian economics" came to America. It is a most enlightening book, especially if you have ever read Samuelson's *Economics* of 1948 just after reading *The General Theory*, or read Hansen's *A Guide To Keynes* just after reading what Keynes actually wrote. It is obvious that some things happened to Keynes in the crossing of the Atlantic. Colander and Landreth's book makes it clear that one thing that happened was that a fairly anecdotal retelling of what Keynes may have been saying in Cambridge was transported into a world in which economists had become government bureaucrats, organizing an economy during a massive war and worrying all the while about the Depression that might yet return. Is it any wonder that "Keynesian economics" came to be about fiscal policy?

The other thing that happened was that Keynes did not make explicit the understanding that he had of the workings of the "City of London." Those who read and used Keynes on this side of the Atlantic did not have comparable familiarity with the inner workings of the financial sector. Money and the supply of credit was up to the Federal Reserve Bank and could be put aside for quite separate treatment and quite separate chapters in the textbooks. I think it not too farfetched to argue that the shape of the Friedman-led counterrevolution was part and parcel of this separation of fiscal policy and business investment from money and banking, a separation more extreme than that required by the English inheritance of a veil of money from the classicals. The American experience and the American uses of Keynes gave shape to modern macrotheory in the texts of the United States and in the rest of the world as well. That shape was one that, as Hyman Minsky has argued, involved a crucial missing step, "the explicit consideration of capitalist finance within a cyclical and speculative context" (Minsky 1975: 130).

Finally, I will mention in passing that modern development economics has been profoundly affected by the American structure of agriculture. Issues about the willingness of peasant farmers to be innovative, to take risks in adopting new technology and techniques, and their attitudes toward thrift and spending have been framed to a large extent by assumptions that the extension-trained farmers of the American Midwest represented both the real and the best nature of farmers worldwide. Though "development" as it came to be understood in the 1950s and 1960s when the field of economic development was new was not about an issue in the United States, it was very much about American frustration with a failure of those in the Third World to respond as they assumed U.S. farmers would. From that experience there has grown a literature that, even though it is about elsewhere, reflects a strongly American bias. So, my answer to the question "What is American about American Economics?" is to suggest that we might profitably look to the American political and social context for answers, and then look to the texts to see how it is that many of us have been led to assume that the rest of the world is really like America.

REFERENCES

Colander, D.C. and H. Landreth (eds) (1996). *The Coming of Keynes to America: Conversations with the Founders of American Keynesian Economics*, Brookfield, Vt.: Ashgate Publishing Co.

Minsky, H.P. (1975). *John Maynard Keynes*, New York: Columbia University Press.

Phillips, A. and R.E. Stevenson (1974). "The Historical Development of Industrial Organization," *History of Political Economy* 6 (fall): 324–342.

Part II

PIONEERS OF AMERICAN POLICY ANALYSIS

5

IRVING FISHER AS A POLICY ADVOCATE

William J. Barber

Irving Fisher was an inveterate crusader for causes. While the concern of this chapter is with his approach to monetary innovation, it is worthwhile to recall the multifaceted character of his interventions to set the world to rights. In 1925—at a moment when he could relish some extraordinary (though transitory) affluence—he wrote to his son that the financial resources generated by the sale of one of his inventions would enable him to further the "four chief causes . . . [he] had at heart." He ranked them in the following order: "the abolition of war, disease, degeneracy, and instability of money."[1] Whatever the crusade—world peace, health and life extension, eugenics, or stable money—Fisher approached it with missionary zeal.

Fisher's conception of the policies required for monetary stability underwent considerable modification over the course of his lengthy professional career. The first phase of his policy advocacy on this subject emerged as a by-product of his work when preparing *The Purchasing Power of Money* (which appeared in 1911). This study had been conceived as an analytic statement of the quantity theory of money, with supporting documentation intended to demonstrate its empirical validity. And he might well have left it at that, namely, as a scholarly treatise on the conditions under which changes in the quantity of money generated proportionate variations in the general price level. But Fisher was not content to offer only an analytic explanation for fluctuations in the purchasing power of money. Convinced as he was that monetary instability produced distributive injustices through distortions in the relative positions of creditors and debtors, he felt obliged to suggest a corrective. When the book was approaching completion, he wrote to Princeton's monetary expert, Edwin W. Kemmerer, that he had "restrained himself from putting in [his] remedy until the last moment" and that he would have "felt so dissatisfied having written a book on the problem" if he had failed to provide a solution.[2]

This aspect of Fisher's view of the relationship between analysis and policy had been heavily conditioned by unpleasant personal experience. In his first years as a professional economist, his correspondence indicates his negative attitude toward those who rushed to judgment with appeals to "do something" to fix problems. What was needed instead, he then argued, was quiet, detached analysis to strengthen the theoretical foundations upon which informed policies could be built. Premature action would lead to nothing but mischief. But he shed this attitude following his recovery from a potentially fatal bout with tuberculosis. The post-TB Fisher became the impatient reformer who insisted on "action now" to uplift the human condition. Thus, with respect to a cure for monetary instability, he had inserted into a scholarly study a recommendation for a "compensated dollar"—i.e., one with constant purchasing power but with varying gold content. This proposal was an acknowledged afterthought as the book was being put to bed. But there was a difficulty here: his policy recommendation did not mesh with the analytic argument of *The Purchasing Power of Money*. The "compensated dollar" scheme rested essentially on a "commodity theory of money"; within that framework, the real value of money was determined by the value of its gold equivalent. That conclusion did not follow from the "equation of exchange" that Fisher had presented as his "quantity theory of money." J.A. Schumpeter (1948) and Don Patinkin (1993) have drawn attention to this oddity, suggesting that it can be explained because Fisher, the reformer, got the better of Fisher, the scholar.

For his part, Fisher entertained no doubts about the theoretical soundness or about the practical feasibility of monetary stabilization through the mechanism of a compensated dollar. He corresponded prolifically with professional colleagues, seeking to mobilize support for this scheme. He was also the prime mover in an effort to launch an International Commission on the Cost of Living that he hoped could be used in promoting his vision of what needed to be done. There was some payoff from these efforts. An impressive array of world leaders endorsed, in principle, the plan to create an International Commission to study these matters and, in 1912, he managed to persuade President William Howard Taft to recommend that an international conference for this purpose be convened. This proposal, though approved by the U.S. Senate, failed in the House of Representatives. Events intervened to put Fisher's "compensated dollar" project on hold. By 1913, American policymakers were preoccupied with a monetary reform of a quite different sort, namely, the creation of the Federal Reserve System. In the following year, the outbreak of war in Europe meant that any attempt at international collaboration on monetary stabilization would be a nonstarter.

Fisher kept the idea alive and mounted a major push for its adoption at the end of the First World War. In his view, the inflationary derangements bred by war made monetary stabilization all the more imperative. Moreover, President Wilson's initiative in calling for the formation of a League of Nations—an instrumentality that Fisher supported wholeheartedly—seemed to brighten the prospect for cooperation between nations. His hopes were bruised when the U.S. Senate blocked American membership in the League, but he persevered nonetheless in his advocacy. Much good could still come, he maintained, if the United States, unilaterally, adopted the "compensated dollar" plan. The United States could lead by example, and the merits of the scheme when demonstrated would convince the rest of the world to follow suit. He recognized that this would not happen without backing from an aroused public. Accordingly, he played the leading role in the formation of the "Stable Money League" in early 1921 to popularize this program.

Throughout the 1920s, a number of bills that would proclaim price level stabilization to be the overriding objective of American economic policy were presented to the Congress. Fisher was regularly the star witness in hearings before the appropriate Congressional Committees. The particulars of how this objective could best be reached, however, changed over time. In the early 1920s, he placed the main weight on varying the gold content of the dollar, as called for in the "compensated dollar" scheme. By the middle 1920s, on the other hand, he emphasized the importance of the Federal Reserve's conduct of open-market operations. This technique for monetary control had not been foreseen when the Federal Reserve Act was drafted: indeed, the manner in which the central bank's purchases and/or sales of government securities could affect the reserves of member banks was discovered, virtually by accident, in 1922. Fisher was quick to appreciate the significance of this finding.

In the version of a price stabilization bill that Fisher supported in 1926, the Federal Reserve's ability to alter the lending capacity of commercial banks through its open-market operations was identified as the primary instrument of monetary control. When endorsing this view, he noted that "today it is the volume of credit that determines the purchasing power of the dollar—the price level—more than the volume of gold." Even so, he argued: "You have got to have your gold control as well as your credit control, if you are going to prevent the terrible evils of inflation and deflation in the future" (Fisher 1926a). He held that the Federal Reserve's stabilizing role might be compromised unless discretionary authority to alter the gold content of the dollar were available. At one extreme, the system's capacity to fight deflation could be immobilized because of its legal obligation to maintain at least a 40 percent gold backing for the Federal Reserve note issue. It was at least conceivable that expansionary policies would be blocked because the entire gold stock was committed to satisfying that requirement. (In the United States in the spring of 1932, this was not just a hypothetical situation—it was real.) Nor, at the other extreme, could success of a counterinflationary policy be assured when gold reserves were abundant. The Federal Reserve's ability to make the open market sales called for in that situation presupposed that it had a portfolio to trade with: if it were obliged to sell all its securities, its "ammunition" would be exhausted. (In 1926, Fisher believed that this state of affairs might be in prospect.)

Fisher's advocacy notwithstanding, legislation mandating price level stabilization via monetary manipulations went nowhere in the 1920s. He was, however, all the more persuaded of its necessity. The analyses he produced in the mid-1920s indicated that changes in the general price level typically preceded changes in the volume of trade by seven months or so. This insight had a clear implication for policy: i.e., that the way to stabilize economic activity was to stabilize the price level. Monetary policy, properly conducted, could thus eliminate the phenomenon of the business cycle. The evils associated with an unstable dollar were no longer primarily those of distributive injustices. He was now to stress the unfortunate consequences of changing price levels for the volume of production and employment. But, as he argued with some passion, serious disturbances in the economy's performance did not have to be tolerated (see Fisher 1923, 1925, 1926b).

The events of the early years of the Depression posed formidable challenges to Fisher as an economic theorist and as an economic policy advocate. He had been totally unprepared for this crisis. The lesson of the theories he had worked out in the 1920s seemed to be that significant changes in economic activity were triggered by changes in the price level. But that model could not explain what had happened to the American economy following the stock market crash in the autumn of 1929. For the preceding half decade or so, the general price level had been remarkably stable—a condition that would appear to have augured well for continued macroeconomic stability. The realities of the early 1930s, it should be noted, presented Fisher with more than analytic perplexities. There was a decided urgency as well about his own financial circumstances. He had believed that "new era" prosperity in the 1920s was solidly based and that it was prudent to accumulate common stocks on margin. Following the collapse on Wall Street, he was spared the embarrassment of declaring personal bankruptcy only because he was able to borrow heavily from a wealthy sister-in-law.

In late 1932—in his Presidential Address to the American Statistical Association—Fisher offered an account of why his prognostications in the late 1920s had been so drastically wrong:

> I did not then know certain scientific laws and I did not know, as well as I should, the historical background of conditions. For instance, I had counted on the continuance of the open market policy of Benjamin Strong of the Federal Reserve Bank of New York, not knowing that these had largely died with Governor Strong the year before. As to the laws governing depressions, I did not then know, what since I have learned and embodied in my book *Booms and Depressions*, the important role of over-indebtedness and its tendency to break down the price level through distress selling, contraction of deposit currency, and slackening of its velocity.
>
> (Fisher 1933a: 9–10)

When he made these remarks, Fisher was convinced that his newly conceived "debt-deflation theory of Great Depressions" explained the catastrophe that had struck the American economy. And there was a moral to that tale as well: the perspective of this new model indicated that deflationary shocks had no inherent self-correcting properties.

In Fisher's judgment, the most arresting finding of the analytic insight he had come to in 1932 was that deflation simply generated more deflation. Bankruptcies and shrinking profits led to reductions in output and employment. These circumstances bred pessimism, hoarding, and further slowdown in the velocity of monetary circulation. The remedy, however, was implicit in the diagnosis: "reflating the price level up to the average level at which outstanding debts were contracted by existing debtors and assumed by existing creditors, and then maintaining that level unchanged" (Fisher 1933b: 346). Debt burdens would thereby be relieved. Debtors would then have more discretionary income available for spending on goods and services, and the resulting resurgence in purchasing power would reinvigorate production and employment.

Fisher's position in 1932 differed in details from analyses he had worked out in the preceding decade, but still maintained a continuity in theme. The call for stabilization in the 1920s had now become a call for "reflation." The latter term, he insisted, should not be confused with "inflation." The objective was simply to restore an earlier price level—say, that of 1926. Once that had been accomplished, price stabilization would again be the order of the day. At this time, Fisher poured virtually all of his extraordinary energies into getting this message out. It was not just a matter of spreading the word in the usual manner—through books, articles, newspaper columns and interviews, testimony before Congressional committees. Though he had never been reticent about urging his views on high public officials, the crisis atmosphere of 1932 enhanced the priority he assigned to this dimension of his lobbying work.

Some of the techniques of monetary manipulations he recommended to engineer "reflation" built on foundations he had laid earlier. He was certainly in character when urging the Federal Reserve to launch an aggressive program of open-market purchases, with the objective of expanding the quantity of "check book" money. A residue from his early thinking about the "compensated dollar" was apparent as well when he identified himself with ideas presented by Professor George F. Warren, an agricultural economist from Cornell. Warren maintained that the commodity price level was governed by the price of gold and offered elaborate correlations to demonstrate such a connection. The clear implication here was that raising the price of gold was the route to "reflation"—a conclusion resting at base on a "commodity theory" of money. (When Warren came prominently into the public eye, Fisher—even though he had moved beyond the thinking that had gone into his "compensated dollar" scheme—spoke approvingly of Warren's argument, describing it "as *exactly* my doctrine.")[3] But the package of Depression remedies that Fisher was then pushing contained an added ingredient. The idea of "stamped money" dated back to 1890 when Silvio Gesell had first advanced it. Fisher learned about it in 1932 and he quickly assimilated it into his program. In his view, a healthy stimulant to the velocity of monetary circulation would be forthcoming if government issued a special series of dollar bills that would depreciate in value by 2 cents each week unless a 2 cent stamp were affixed to them. This would amount to a direct attack on the hoarding of currency: the holders of "stamp-scrip" had an obvious incentive to move it before its value shrank. Fisher peddled this proposition to officials at all echelons of government. He leaned hard on the Mayor of New Haven, Connecticut, for example—though without success—to meet the municipal payroll in "stamp-scrip."

Prospects that the "reflation" message might get a sympathetic hearing at the highest levels of government brightened with Franklin D. Roosevelt's electoral success in the presidential campaign of 1932. Official receptivity to heterodox monetary experimentation was further heightened in 1933 by the paralysis that afflicted the American banking system which impelled Roosevelt to declare a national "Bank Holiday." Fisher perceived these events to be moments of opportunity. He worked feverishly to sell his economic program to the new president and bombarded the White House with memoranda. Though his advice was unsolicited, Fisher liked to think of himself as an unofficial member of Roosevelt's "Brains Trust." Roosevelt met with him on a number of occasions—and there was a monumental flow of Fisher to Roosevelt correspondence. Though Fisher was inclined to exaggerate his own importance in presidential decision-making,[4] Roosevelt did act on one of the points on Fisher's policy agenda when embarking on the program that raised the dollar price of gold by nearly 70 percent between October 1933 and January 1934. Fisher drew satisfaction from the implementation of this "reflationary" recommendation. (The decisive advice that moved this policy forward, however, came from Warren and Fisher's Yale colleague, James Harvey Rogers.) For his part, Fisher believed that the exercise in manipulating the gold price would have been much more effective had an additional item of his counsel been heeded. He had proposed that the nominal "gold profit"—the increment in the official value of the Treasury's gold stock—be monetized. The supply of the circulating medium could be substantially enlarged, he argued, if the "gold profit" were used to back a new currency issue to be known as "yellowbacks" (so styled to distinguish them from "greenbacks"). If holders of maturing government debt, for example, were paid out in "yellowbacks," the money supply would instantly be increased, with an impact on the "reflationary" program that could only be positive.[5] This recommendation fell on deaf ears.

During the years of the First New Deal (1933–35), two additional features of Fisher's style of policy advocacy were on display. In the first instance, it was clear that he believed that the challenge of winning converts to his positions was not solely a matter of persuading officialdom of the inherent merits of his recommendations. He was convinced that valuable points could be carried as well when he introduced arguments to demolish other approaches to policy then competing for official favor. In his view, prospects for the economy's recovery hinged almost exclusively on "reflation" achieved through monetary measures. He was well aware of an alternative approach to macroeconomic stimulation, namely, a "massive" (in the vernacular of the time) program of spending on public works. This strategy, in Fisher's judgment, was totally misguided. As an employment-creating device, it would fail dismally. Given the magnitudes involved, the task of creating worthwhile public-sector jobs to absorb the unemployed was not feasible. Attempts to address joblessness in this way would generate unacceptable economic inefficiencies. But, even if a public works program could pass a test of feasibility, it would still be a mistake. Fisher insisted that it would be far better for government to assist in supporting re-employment in the private sector. Toward that end, he recommended that the Federal government (through the offices of the Reconstruction Finance Corporation) extend interest-free loans to those private employers who agreed to enlarge their payrolls. Ideally, the government should finance this lending through the creation of new money. This in itself would be a plus for the "reflationary" program which was needed to make the job-creation effort successful. His policy recommendation, Fisher insisted, would avoid what he labelled as the "double-wrench": "wrench one" was the strain involved in getting workers into public sector jobs, which were artificial in any case; "wrench two" was the strain that would ultimately have to be addressed in transferring those engaged in public works back to private sector jobs where they belonged all along. But he also held that government should be generous in providing relief for the jobless. Commitments of public resources to their support were essential. They could best be honored, he argued, if the Federal government moved into the "stamped-scrip" business. After all, a 2 cent-per-week tax per dollar of scrip would yield receipts of $1.04 over the course of the year. This would permit retirement of the scrip—with something left over. This program was twice-blessed: it would accelerate the velocity of monetary circulation, and generate revenues to fund relief for the residually unemployed.[6]

Fisher left no one in any doubt about what he opposed as well as what he supported. He was realist enough to recognize that policies he was not pleased with might still carry the day. When that happened, there was an opportunistic component in his advocacy. National policy was not moving in the way he preferred in May 1933 when Congress was about to approve an appropriation for public works—unprecedented in its peacetime magnitude—as part of the National Industrial Recovery Act. Fisher still hoped to have some of his own thinking embodied in this legislation. He urged the Ways and Means Committee of the House of Representatives to specify that the debt service charges arising from this appropriation should be paid in "stamped scrip." When this effort failed, he called upon the Senate Finance Committee to authorize state governments to issue "stamped scrip" to fund the latter's contribution to public works spending (in which the sharing was expected to be 70 percent Federal and 30 percent state) (see Fisher 1933b, 1933c). This appeal also went nowhere.

Fisher's distaste for public works spending—even when financed by deficits—was further in evidence in his reactions to Keynes's presentation favoring this policy which he heard at a meeting of economists in New York in June 1934. Keynes then had set out his case for "loan expenditure" on public works, supplementing it with an explication of the concept of the "multiplier." When reporting this event to his wife, Fisher wrote: "His paper was interesting but to me—and I think to everyone else—rather obscure and unconvincing. He was very skilful in answering questions but seemed to get nowhere."[7] Aware that Keynes had already put his argument before Roosevelt, Fisher took it upon himself to instruct the president on what he should absorb from Keynes's message:

> I had a long talk with J. Maynard Keynes and find myself in substantial agreement with him, but it should be noted that:
>
> (1) "loan expenditure" is really a *monetary* measure involving added (government) deposits and their use as purchasing power;
> (2) the quickest, cheapest and most beneficial loan expenditure is, it seems to me, . . . to lend to all those going concerns a year or more old, who want it a dollar and a half per day per employee added to payroll for one hundred consecutive days;
> (3) public works make the slowest, dearest, and usually least beneficial form. It will require something of a wrench later to get millions of workers out of jobs under government into their normal jobs in industry. Under the plan I propose, most would be re-employed in their normal jobs to start with.[8]

With respect to policy choices that ought not to be made, Fisher made no bones about his sharp dissent from the structuralist thinking underlying the First New Deal's direct intervention in the agricultural and industrial sectors. He registered his distress with the supply management approach of the Agricultural Adjustment Administration in a letter to his son:

> It's all a strange mixture. I am against the restriction of acreage but much in favor of inflation. Apparently FDR thinks of them as similar—merely two ways of raising prices! But one changes the monetary unit to restore it to normal while the other spells scarce food and clothing when many are starving or half-naked.[9]

He rejoiced—and so informed the president—when the Supreme Court struck down the National Recovery Administration (NRA) and its authority to grant antitrust immunity to trade associations with approved "codes of fair competition." Two years of that experiment seemed to demonstrate that this procedure amounted to legalized collusion. As Fisher saw the matter, NRA should properly be described as the "National Retardation Association."

Fisher was consistent when sticking to his guns about the primacy of monetary measures to promote recovery. But there was still room for maneuver with regard to the type of monetary reform he backed. His policy advocacy took yet another turn in mid-1934 when he embraced the doctrine of "100 percent money."

He first learned of this idea from contacts with a group of economists at the University of Chicago, headed by Henry C. Simons. As worked out by Simons and his colleagues, this proposal for banking reform—which would require commercial banks to hold 100 percent reserves behind demand deposits—would differ from the fractional reserve system of banking in fundamental ways. In the first instance, the linkage between extending (or calling) loans and the creation (or destruction) of money would be broken. Henceforth the supply of money would be the exclusive jurisdiction of a governmental body—Simons proposed that it be called a National Monetary Authority.

For Fisher, this scheme had a compellingly attractive feature: if implemented, it would eliminate the destabilizing properties of the existing system in which the volume of "check-book money" was essentially a by-product of the activities of private lenders in their pursuit of profits. In a well-ordered system, control of the money supply should unambiguously be a public function. But he insisted that a National Monetary Authority should be given precise directives about how it should behave. There was nothing surprising in his recommendation that a new governmental body be charged to restore the 1926 price level and thereafter to stabilize. He also proposed a novel technique for keeping the members of a National Monetary Authority on course. If the price level deviated from the targeted norm by as much as 10 percent for three consecutive months, its officers would automatically forfeit their jobs.

Though a latecomer to the doctrine of "100 percent money," Fisher embraced it with characteristic enthusiasm and became its most ardent public champion. He poured his energies into mobilizing support through his writing, speaking, and lobbying. At a White House meeting with Roosevelt in January 1935 he sought, unsuccessfully, to persuade the president that this reform should be the centerpiece of his legislative program for that year. Though again frustrated, Fisher continued to campaign relentlessly. By early 1937, he spoke with qualified optimism about the prospects. As he then wrote to Simons:

> There seems to be no doubt that the 100% Money idea has taken root in many minds in Washington, in the executive departments, the House and the Senate. It seems too good to prove true that it will win out, but it is worth fighting for.[10]

The sharp downturn in economic activity that set in in August 1937 sent alarm bells ringing throughout official Washington. In Fisher's view, this unexpected turn of events should be treated as a wake-up call. He volunteered advice to Roosevelt on how to deal with this crisis:

> One result of the present stock market crash is stagnation of money. This deflationary effect is aggravated by the actual destruction of money ("check-book money") now coming about through the selling of Government bonds by banks. This reverses the process by which, largely, you have been creating more purchasing power by selling bonds to banks for new check-book money. In other words, we are now threatened by the same sort of deflation as followed 1929 after which eight billions of deposits were destroyed. The chief difference is that Government bonds now play the role then played by private debts. *Under our present laws there is nothing dependable to prevent this new deflation from proceeding far beyond the old deflation. The only dependable way is through new legislation.*[11]

To supplement this memorandum, Fisher attached an "Outline of Proposed New Monetary Legislation" which summarized the now familiar principles of 100 percent reserves and the steps necessary to activate this reform.

Fisher was again disappointed by his failure to bend economic policymakers in his direction. Meanwhile there were signs of strain in the relationship between Fisher and the Chicago economists who had first set him on this particular course. Simons, for example, distanced himself from Fisher's style of advocacy. Indeed there were indications that Simons had come to regard some of Fisher's ambitious claims for the 100 percent money program to be something of an embarrassment. Fisher, in Simons's judgment, had gone too far in the direction of premature popularization. What was needed instead was further technical analysis to fine-tune the proposed reform, and it should be subjected to expert criticism. From that point of view, it appeared again that the spirit of the crusader had dominated that of the scholar.[12]

Fisher remained undeterred. "100 percent money" stayed at or near the top of his policy agenda for the rest of his days. In company with five collaborators, he developed a more systematic statement of "A Program for Monetary Reform" which circulated in 1939 and again in 1941 (in a slightly modified version). Its substantive recommendations incorporated the essentials of Fisher's monetary thinking—most notably, the enactment of 100 percent reserves and the creation of a monetary authority charged to maintain a dollar of "constant purchasing power" through its control over the supply of money. After Pearl Harbor, serious lobbying for this proposition was suspended for the duration. Though the suggestion was brushed aside, he did urge John Maynard Keynes—in mid-1944—to supplement the Bretton Woods plan for reform in the international monetary system with a recommendation that national governments adopt the 100 percent plan.[13] After V-J Day, Fisher resumed his effort to persuade the members of the American Economic Association that they should unite behind his banner. He continued to believe that a massive demonstration of support by the professionals would be decisive in moving political actors to adopt the policies he deemed to be essential. He was not acutely sensitive to—nor was he well informed about—the momentum behind a new fiscal orientation toward policy-making that was coming into official as well as professional favor.

Despite his brilliance as an economic theorist and his ingenuity as a formulator of "solutions," there was little to show in his lifetime for the abundant energies he poured into crusading for specific economic-policy recommendations. Nor did he leave behind a "school" of disciples—there was no "New Haven Circus" to match Keynes's "Cambridge Circus." Fisher was far too busy with his many causes to take the steps needed to make that happen. One should look elsewhere for evidence of the longer-term impact of his message. Through his activities as an advocate and popularizer, Fisher —perhaps as much, if not more, than any other individual economist— contributed to raising public consciousness about the hazards associated with monetary instability.

NOTES

1 Fisher to Irving Norton Fisher, June 17, 1925, Fisher Papers, Yale University Archives.
2 Fisher to Kemmerer, January 11, 1911, Kemmerer Papers, Princeton University Archives.
3 Fisher used these words when writing to his wife on Warren's testimony to the Senate Committee on Banking; see Fisher to Margaret Hazard Fisher, May 12, 1932, Yale University Archives.
4 It is worth noting that Fisher did not endear himself to the more partisan members of Roosevelt's inner circle because it was no secret that he had supported Hoover in the campaign of 1932.
5 Fisher to Roosevelt, September 6, 1934, Yale University Archives.
6 Fisher put these views before Roosevelt in numerous memoranda dispatched in 1933 and 1934.
7 Fisher to Margaret Hazard Fisher, June 7, 1934, Yale University Archives.
8 Fisher to Roosevelt, June 11, 1934, Yale University Archives.
9 Fisher to Irving Norton Fisher, August 15, 1933, Yale University Archives.
10 Fisher to Simons, January 29, 1937, Simons Papers, University of Chicago Archives.
11 Fisher to Roosevelt, October 24, 1937, Yale University Archives.

12 Simons explained his difficulties with Fisher's preferred course of action as follows: "I'm afraid you'll find me either useless or a liability in connection with any drive for definitive legislation for carrying out the 100% scheme. . . . I have little faith in any simple legislative prescription. To me, the scheme (whatever its potentialities during the banking crisis) is significant only for its definition of an ideal objective of gradual reform; and in such a gradual unfolding, changes outside formal banking seem even more important and indispensable than the things which we stressed in the beginning" (Simons to Fisher, February 3, 1937, University of Chicago Archives).

13 Fisher to Keynes, July 4, 1944, Yale University Archives. Fisher maintained that Keynes thus "might follow success internationally by success nationally. In this way one of the greatest, if not the greatest, economic problem might be solved 'in our time' with you in the leading role again."

REFERENCES

Fisher, I. (1911). *The Purchasing Power of Money*, New York: Macmillan.

——— (1923). "The Business Cycle Largely a 'Dance of the Dollar'," *Journal of the American Statistical Association* 18 (December): 1024–1028.

——— (1925). "Our Unstable Dollar and the So-Called Business Cycle," *Journal of the American Statistical Association* 20 (June): 179–202.

——— (1926a). Testimony before the Committee on Banking and Currency, House of Representatives, 69:1, March 26, 1926.

——— (1926b). "A Statistical Relationship between Unemployment and Price Changes," *International Labour Review* 13 (June): 785–792.

——— (1933a). "Statistics in the Service of Economics," *Journal of the American Statistical Association* 28 (March): 1–13.

——— (1933b). Testimony before the Committee on Ways and Means, House of Representatives, 73:1, May 19, 1933.

——— (1933c). Testimony before the Committee on Finance, U.S. Senate, 73:1, May 31, 1933.

Patinkin, D. (1993). "Irving Fisher and His Compensated Dollar Plan," *Federal Reserve Bank of Richmond Economic Quarterly* 79 (summer): 1–33.

Schumpeter, J.A. (1948). "Irving Fisher's Econometrics," *Econometrica* 16 (July): 219–231.

6

SOCIAL SCIENCE AND THE MAKING OF SOCIAL POLICY

Wesley Mitchell's vision

Jeff Biddle[1]

Wesley Mitchell believed that social science research could provide the knowledge that would allow mankind to control social forces. Just as the application of natural science knowledge to the technologies of production had led to unprecedented growth in material prosperity, the wise application of social science knowledge to the making of policy could lead to an era of rapid social progress.

As a number of recent books on the history of the social sciences make clear, Mitchell was not alone in this belief. His optimistic opinion of what could be achieved through the application of social science knowledge was shared, at least in its general outlines, by numerous other social scientists and intellectuals, as well as by prominent business and political figures.[2] Ross (1991, 1994) has identified this attitude toward social science as a variant of cognitive modernism, a response to the loss of the nineteenth-century faith that science could reveal the hidden order in the world and provide answers to the problems of human existence. The cognitive modernists accepted that the subjectivity of perception made the notion of objective, empirically based scientific knowledge problematic, and they had largely abandoned, in the face of the disturbing events of the early twentieth century, nineteenth-century notions of an orderly plan underlying history. But if they frankly recognized that science did not have all the answers, they continued to see science as mankind's best hope for understanding a confusing world and coping with an uncertain future. A disciplined application of the scientific method to the study of natural and social processes remained the best procedure for minimizing the problems created by the subjectivity of the individual observer. Moreover, if humanity indeed had to build its own future, the knowledge of social processes provided through an application of the scientific method would prove the most reliable foundation upon which to do it.

Several of Ross's cognitive modernist social scientists, including Mitchell, are also profiled by Smith (1994). He sees behind their fundamental agreement on the importance and practical utility of a scientific study of social processes a crucial disagreement over the proper role of social science and the social scientist in the policy process. Smith classes Mitchell with the "service intellectuals," who believed that the purpose of social science was to produce objective knowledge of society, ideally to be used in the design of social policy, but who saw no place for social science in the processes that determined the ends that social policy would serve. Opposing them were the purposivists, who believed that social scientists, by virtue of their knowledge of social processes, deserved and should take a more active role in determining the values that would guide both social research and social policy.

Both Ross and Smith provide informative accounts of Mitchell's career and his general views on the relationship between social science and social policy, while accurately identifying the parallels between his views and those of other important figures in American social science. There will necessarily be some overlap between this chapter and those accounts. However, while many shared Mitchell's general views on the role of social science in the policy process, each had a more or less specific vision of how their ideals might be realized: how exactly the institutions of government and the institutions of social science should be reformed both to produce the most useful knowledge and to insure its optimal use in making public policy. I will focus on Mitchell's particular vision and the steps he took to realize it, steps that left a permanent imprint on the development of American social science.

I will also focus on Mitchell's experience as he tried to put his ideals into action. The world of policy-making is a particularly harsh one into which to carry the ideal visions of objectivity and rationality shared by Mitchell and like-minded social scientists, and one would expect disappointment and disillusionment to be the rule among those who made the attempt. Mitchell's career as an economic researcher was punctuated by several assignments that gave him at least potential influence over policy decisions; not all could be considered successful. But Mitchell remained optimistic about the prospects for improving social policy through the application of social science knowledge, and confident that his own efforts toward that end had not been wasted. As I shall explain more fully below, Mitchell's vision of social progress through more rational social policy involved reforms in three areas: pure social science research, applied social science research, and the application of social science knowledge in the making of policy. He believed the first area, however, to be by far the most important, and the bulk of his effort in the service of his vision involved contributing to and promoting institutional innovations in the area of pure social science research. These efforts were successful to a degree that, when faced with potential or actual frustrations in posts closer to the actual making of policy, Mitchell could step back into the world of pure research, consolidate and expand his successes there, and never feel that he had compromised on his commitment to improving society through the application of science.

MITCHELL'S VISION: AN OVERVIEW

Though the notion that social scientists could contribute to solving social problems seemed to be "in the air" during Mitchell's formative years, Mitchell's particular conception of how this could take place reflects the thinking of the two men he identified as mentors, Thorstein Veblen and John Dewey.[3] Following Veblen, Mitchell viewed culture or society as a complex system of interrelated institutions, patterns of behavior influenced and being influenced by conventional habits of thought. The system evolved in a cumulative process, and social problems arose due to uneven institutional evolution, as changes in behavior patterns in one area of society caused other more settled and previously benign patterns of behavior to generate new and unwanted consequences (Mitchell 1933: lxx).

To his Veblenian view of the social system and its tendency to generate problems Mitchell hitched a Deweyian notion of "planning" as a strategy for dealing with those problems. Planning, in Mitchell's lexicon, meant choosing responses to new and problematic situations after forecasting the consequences of various possible courses of action, with the forecasts being based on experiential knowledge. Such planning was a part of the ordinary life of individuals, and it characterized the policy choices of businesses, communities, and nations. The key to successful planning was reliable knowledge, and Mitchell believed the social sciences could provide knowledge that would improve the quality of both individual and business planning. One theme in Mitchell's writing on business cycles was that economic research could make businessmen aware that certain of their actions could exacerbate economic fluctuations. If businessmen were then provided with information regarding economic circumstances (in the form of statistical data, for example), they would formulate their plans in ways that would stabilize the economy.[4]

But Mitchell was also interested in the contributions that social science could make to the planning activity of governments. The uncoordinated activities of individuals and businesses, no matter how well planned, could generate problematic social consequences. The planning of governments involved responding to those consequences.[5] With solid knowledge of the social system and how it evolved, provided by the social sciences, governments could anticipate the emergence of social problems and rationally evaluate proposed solutions.

Mitchell tried to destigmatize the notion of "national planning" by pointing out that the Federal government had long engaged in planning, choosing discrete policy responses to perceived national problems: war efforts, canal building programs, prohibition, and so on (Mitchell 1937: 100). Unfortunately, in the past this planning had not been done in anything like a scientific manner. Problems were usually addressed only after they had become emergencies; and emergencies prompted hurried, emotional, politically motivated reactions rather than careful analytical thought. Planning was piecemeal, tending to focus on problems one at a time without regard to how they might be related to each other or to broader social conditions. Little thought was given to how policy action in one area of the social system might affect other areas of the social system, and different policy initiatives often ended up working at cross purposes (Mitchell 1937: 100).

Mitchell offered "scientific" national planning as an alternative to this ad hoc process. National planning would become a full-time responsibility of government, handled by a professional workforce trained in conducting and interpreting natural and social scientific research. Social trends would be studied, measured, and monitored to spot or anticipate emerging problems. Political decision makers would be given information about alternative policy responses to these problems and their likely consequences. Suggestions would be made for coordinating the programs of the various agencies and levels of government in light of existing knowledge of the interrelationships between social phenomena. Planners would have the power to make recommendations, but final decisions would remain the province of elected officials.

The social sciences, Mitchell believed, were not currently producing the quantity or type of knowledge required for scientific social planning, and the government was not organized to make use of such knowledge if it existed. In keeping with his view of society generally, however, he thought that the institutions through which social science knowledge was generated and through which social policy was made were malleable and subject to intelligent human control (Mitchell 1939c: 604). Mitchell formulated a vision of the social sciences reorganized, expanded, and redirected to produce more serviceable knowledge, and of governmental institutions that both supported social science research and saw that it was brought to bear on policy decisions as a matter of routine.

There was a particular role in the vision for which Mitchell felt himself most suited: that of a social science researcher, adding to the fundamental knowledge of the social system that was a prerequisite to intelligent social planning. Joseph Schumpeter called Mitchell's founding and direction of the National Bureau of Economic Research (NBER) —probably his most significant professional activity—"an act of self realization" (Burns 1952: 336). Schumpeter was right. Through the NBER Mitchell created a space and secured resources for doing the sort of work he loved: the analysis of quantitative economic data. One sees in many of Mitchell's other institutional involvements some of the same motives: the desire to secure resources for, to promote and to otherwise facilitate the sort of research he enjoyed and believed in. These acts of self-realization, however, were by Mitchell's way of thinking also acts of public service. In what he admitted might be an act of rationalization, he had convinced himself early on that in doing the work he found most satisfying lay his greatest chance to make a contribution to the public welfare, and that institutional reforms making it easier for others to do the same sort of work were the first and most important step in putting the making of public policy on a scientific footing.

REMAKING SOCIAL SCIENCE IN THE IMAGE OF NATURAL SCIENCE

In 1911 Mitchell wrote an "autobiographical letter" to his future wife, Lucy Sprague, in which he sketched out his vision of how the social sciences could contribute to the solution of social problems:

> In the latest fraction of human history we have made rapid industrial progress. . . . But in all matters of social organization we remain backward; we don't know how to recast our inherited ways of treating each other with anything like the success we have had in recasting our inherited ways of treating materials. It is not lack of will that impedes progress, but lack of knowledge. We putter with philanthropy and coquette with reform when we would fain find a definite method of realizing the demand for social justice which is so strong an element in human nature. . . . What we need . . . is sure knowledge of the causal interconnections between social phenomena.
>
> Such knowledge we have little chance of getting while we are immersed in our daily tasks, whether these be the tasks of philanthropy, politics or business. The "reformer," indeed, strikes me as being in about the same predicament as the practicing physicians of two generations ago. These men were doing the work which someone had to attempt, with a professional air of confidence which they had to assume for the benefit of their patients, and with an ambition to learn from experience. But the progress of medical science has not come from them. Instead it has come from the laboratories, where the issues of life and of death in individual cases are replaced as the immediate object of attention by little problems of chemical reactions and bacteriological detail for which the busy practitioner had neither time nor patience. So must it be in other subjects. If we are ever to have an economics of use in guiding our efforts at social reconstruction, it must come from men who find some way of resolving the vital social problems into simpler elements. And these won't

be the men who are doing their manful best to bear the burden and heat of the passing day.

(L.S. Mitchell 1953: 187–188)

Mitchell never stopped believing what he wrote in 1911, and as he rose to professional and public prominence in subsequent years, he had the opportunity to present and elaborate upon his vision in essays and addresses prepared for a variety of audiences. He continued to maintain the premise, which he apparently felt little need to defend, that the natural sciences had succeeded in increasing our understanding and control of natural forces, and that to become useful as a guide to policy the social sciences needed to become more like the natural sciences.[6] Such a transformation was possible because science was defined not by its subject matter, but by the spirit that motivated inquiry: a devotion to careful observation and systematic analysis, a willingness to submit one's results to the scrutiny of fellow researchers, a knowledge of one's own potential for biased thinking coupled with a desire to overcome it. And there were signs that progress was being made. "Realistic" research involving analysis and observation of actual social phenomena was growing up beside the older speculative, deductive approaches to theorizing. Monographs and technical papers containing objective, disinterested analyses were supplanting treatises that offered new theoretical systems or promoted normative agendas. Doctrinal and methodological controversy was on the decline.[7]

Mitchell admitted to his audiences that the social sciences lagged behind their natural counterparts; they had been established later and had progressed more slowly. There were good reasons for this, however. Simply put, social science was harder to do properly than natural science. As members of society, social scientists had normative feelings about the behaviors and institutions they studied unlike any a natural scientist might have about the behavior of a gas or a geological structure. In the natural sciences, the methods of observation and controlled experimentation allowed scientists to check their own and each other's speculative theorizing against the facts, a process that rooted out error and bias. But in the social sciences, where the problem of bias was greater and the phenomena to be studied more complex and variable, controlled experiments were seldom possible. Even systematic observations of social phenomena in the form of social statistics had only recently begun to be subjected to analysis. In the face of such difficulties, there was no guarantee that the study of social phenomena would ever become truly scientific.[8] The benefits to be achieved, however, from a large body of tested knowledge of the social system were so great that any promising efforts toward building such knowledge deserved society's support.[9]

Mature social science, like natural science, would have well-developed basic and applied branches. Mitchell compared the proper relationship between basic and applied social scientists to that between physicists and engineers, or, as in his letter of 1911, biological scientists and physicians. Basic social science research would look into how the social system functioned and evolved. Applied social science would attack specific social problems, using the discoveries of basic researchers to design possible solutions or forecast the likely consequences of solutions proposed by others. Basic social scientists would choose research questions with at least one eye toward producing knowledge that would be of use to those in the applied fields, and in the course of their work applied researchers would develop new research techniques that would aid basic researchers, just as engineers and technicians designed the laboratory instruments that helped advance basic research in the natural sciences.[10]

The application of social science knowledge to the making of social policy could not be expected to proceed as rapidly as had the application of natural science knowledge to the development of new technology, for the latter process had been powered by the profit motive. A technological innovation could earn a trial if one entrepreneur were persuaded of its potential for increasing profits, and if successful, it would spread rapidly as other businessmen copied it. Past instances of the lucrative application of science to the production process created a demand for technicians and engineers, an openness to their methods, and a respect for the scientific research upon which their work was based. Proposed social policy innovations faced a tougher road, for many, perhaps millions, had to be convinced of their reasonableness before they could be implemented. No one stood to make an individual fortune from the successful application of social science to social policy, limiting the labor market demand for would-be applied social scientists. Because of this, the task of designing and promoting plans for ameliorating social problems had in the past fallen largely to "inspirational reformers," people gifted in persuasion, motivated by and appealing more to emotion than reason. Their plans were based on feelings and hunches rather than sound knowledge of the social system, and as a result their efforts were often ineffectual if not counterproductive. Still, Mitchell could point to hopeful signs. He saw potential branches of applied social science emerging in the fields of social work, education, and personnel management, as well as in the work of trained economists employed by business and government.[11]

In his discussions of social science and the making of social policy, Mitchell maintained a distinction between the ends and means, that is, between the social values to be promoted by social policy and the specific actions most likely to promote those values. Social science was concerned only with means: "It is not the business of the social sciences to say what is good and bad, all they can do is trace functional relationships among social processes, and so elucidate the most effective means of attaining whatever ends we set ourselves." The applied social scientists, using basic social science knowledge, would provide policymakers a list of possible courses of action, and forecasts of the possible social consequences of each. But their scientific work ended there—the question of which bundle of consequences was the most desirable was a problem of ends. On the troublesome matter of choosing the ends of social policy, Mitchell usually made brief remarks about democratic processes or the will of the majority.[12] He granted that social scientists should participate, on an equal footing with other citizens, in discussions of the appropriate ends of social policies and in movements to influence those ends. But such activities were outside the realm of science. All social scientists needed was to be on guard against "offending the scientific spirit" by subconsciously allowing their personal scale of social values to color their scientific findings.[13] It is hard to imagine that a close follower of Dewey would not be aware of the subtle relationship between means and ends, and the problematic nature of drawing a hard line between them. But Mitchell drew the line frequently, perhaps in the service of driving home his message about the importance of scientific objectivity in the study of social processes.[14]

THE ROLE OF GOVERNMENT

Mitchell's addresses and essays devoted far more attention to the question of how the social sciences should be transformed than to the question of how the institutions of government should be altered to facilitate the application of social science knowledge to the policy process. In the 1910s and 1920s his discussion of the latter question concentrated mainly on government's role as a collector and disseminator of statistics. "More and better" was the general theme. In the absence of data generated by controlled experiments, the scientific study of society depended on reliable statistical records of human behavior in society as its empirical base. Statistics would also aid the planning of businessmen and would guide policymakers. Businesses were collecting more statistics on their own as they came to recognize their value, but the government was needed to collect those statistics that, despite their potential usefulness to both government and business planning, it was in no individual businessman's interest to collect.[15]

A brief job with the Census Bureau in 1899–1900 left Mitchell with serious doubts about the competency of those employed by the government for statistical work, but he believed that higher salaries would clear up a number of problems by attracting more able and qualified workers. In the mid-1910s he began to encourage the creation of a single bureau to oversee and coordinate all federal data collection efforts. Additional experience as a government economist during the First World War reinforced these views: the extent of the government's statistical effort before the war had been woefully inadequate even for peacetime needs; government statistical workers were inadequately paid and underqualified; there was wasteful duplication in the data collection that did take place. During the war Mitchell and his supervisor Edwin Gay had successfully pushed for the creation of a central statistical bureau for the war effort, even managing to get appropriations to extend its life beyond the Armistice, but their hopes that it would be transformed into a permanent central statistical bureau were dashed in 1919.[16]

In the 1930s Mitchell began to offer more concrete proposals for governmental planning agencies, including descriptions of a national planning board. The essence of his blueprint for a national planning board is found in this passage from a 1936 address:

> First, the organization should be a continuing one, . . . for social problems are ever assuming new forms and the task of dealing with them is never finished. Second, to be effective the organization should center in a small board, responsible not for making technical studies and formulating plans . . . but for seeing that studies are made and plans are formulated. It would be the board's task to make sure that in this work available knowledge is utilized to the full—not merely such contributions as social scientists could make, but also the contributions of experienced men of affairs . . . and natural scientists, which are fundamental to many social problems. The board should endeavor to take up problems before they reach the emergency stage, while there is still time for full consideration before reaching a decision. . . . [T]he board should have a technical staff including men of many qualifications, means for obtaining professional assistance from anyone whose counsel is needed, and close contacts with government agencies. . . . It should foster the planning attitude toward public problems, cooperating with state, regional, and municipal planning organizations. . . . Finally, it should give all the interests affected by the issues under consideration an opportunity to present their views before it formulates proposals.
>
> (Mitchell 1937: 132–133)

The board would be purely an advisory body; only then would it fit into the American scheme of institutions.[17] The establishment of a planning board with a particular organizational structure was less important to Mitchell, however, than the general acceptance of the idea that social planning, done on an ongoing basis by full-time professional personnel, was a proper responsibility of government.

BUILDING A WORKSHOP FOR HIS LABOR OF LOVE: INSTITUTIONAL INNOVATIONS IN THE AREA OF PURE SOCIAL SCIENCE RESEARCH

When Mitchell wrote to his future wife in 1911 of his vision of scientifically guided social reform, he called it a "reasoned conviction" in support of his "temperamental craving" for self-directed research; a justification for his conduct, he joked, that he had "manufactured after the offense was committed." Basic social science research was both the foundation of Mitchell's vision (social progress, like progress in medicine, would come from the laboratories, from people working on research projects seemingly far removed from the pressing problems of the day) and the professional activity to which Mitchell was always most strongly drawn.[18] His dissertation involved the sort of quantitative research for which he later became famous, but he was eager to follow this up with a more significant project—a theory of the evolution and functioning of the complex of modern economic institutions he called "the money economy." After several years of work on this project, however, he was unsatisfied. Believing his theorizing to be too speculative, he narrowed his focus to a quantitative study of recent business cycles. In justifying this decision, he wrote:

> Has it not really been one of the great sources of weakness in economics that people have been content with plausible speculations, attractively presented . . . ? Is it not really better to establish firmly a few simple propositions than to elaborate many in a speculative manner? Do not the real sciences proceed in the more humble manner? The more I read of the recent theorizing on crises the more I am convinced that statistical measurement of the various factors involved is the thing needed to substitute certainty for plausibility.
> (Burns 1952: 91)

Although he promised at the time that he would return to his "money economy" project, he never did. Quantitative research on business cycles became his central research task for the rest of his life, and he persisted in his belief that the sort of work most needed in the basic social sciences was "realistic" research, based on the study of actual human behavior as reflected in statistics.

Mitchell's initial attraction to basic research was only strengthened as he tried other roles early in his career. His job with the Census Bureau proved most unsatisfying. "I learned I could never be happy except as my own master," Mitchell later wrote, "finding my own problems and nursing my own interests." He left for an academic job. A supervisory job with the U.S. Immigration Commission a few years later held his interest, and he discovered a talent for managing the work of others. But this type of activity did not seem as "worth while" as his research, and he returned again to academe. Teaching came easy to him, but he resented the time it took away from research. A stint at Harvard as a visiting professor 1908–9 left a particularly strong impression on him. The emphasis on teaching he found there created a "danger of yielding to the temptation to put too much time on class work." "I am becoming infected," he wrote to a friend. "I find myself more concerned with what my classes do than with the progress of my MSS—a frame of mind of which I do not seriously approve." He rejected two permanent job offers from Harvard over the next three years, citing Harvard's overemphasis on teaching as a reason, and he never lost the sense that demands of the classroom contributed greatly to making academe a less than ideal environment for basic social science research (L.S. Mitchell 1953: 170, 174–175, 183–187).

The publication of *Business Cycles* in 1913 established a reputation for Mitchell beyond the economics profession and brought new opportunities for him to advance both his personal research agenda and his vision of scientifically based social progress. Such opportunities multiplied further in subsequent years as Mitchell's performance in the tasks he chose for himself further enhanced his reputation. Not long after *Business Cycles* appeared, Mitchell was asked by the Department of Labor to advise them on the revision of their wholesale price index numbers. This task was consistent with Mitchell's view that while the government could and should handle routine data collection tasks, the problems of defining what should be measured and how, and of reducing the measurement process to routine, were better left to trained specialists. Mitchell's work during the war led to contacts with influential business and political figures, and left a strong impression on him, as it did on so many of the scholars and businessmen who came to Washington for the war effort. His faith that the government could, in theory, plan effectively in the face of national problems was unshaken if not strengthened, but his sense of the deficiency of the existing knowledge and data base of the social sciences was considerably enhanced.

The National Bureau of Economic Research (NBER) was not founded until after the war, but its story begins in the years before.[19] Edwin Gay, at that time the director of Harvard's Bureau of Business Research, asked Mitchell in 1914 to head a project estimating the national income, but the start of the war in Europe meant that the idea was put to one side. Gay was approached with the same idea by Malcolm Rorty of AT&T in 1916. Again Gay asked Mitchell to take charge, but the entry of the United States into the war put an end to this initiative. After the war Rorty revived the idea, obtained financial support, and by 1920 the National Bureau was up and running under Wesley Mitchell's direction.

The discussions that went on between the people involved with these initiatives were very much in tune with Mitchell's thinking about the contributions social science could make to social policy.[20] One common theme was that a number of disagreements over policy arose from disagreements over questions of fact, such as the size and distribution of the national income, which could be resolved if the facts were ascertained in a scientific manner. A second theme was that either the team of investigators involved with the project or a committee overseeing their work should be comprised of representatives of competing schools of thought or opposing interest groups. This would serve as a check on the biases inherent in social science research, and perhaps more importantly, reassure the public that the results of the investigation were not slanted to support any particular ideological or policy position. When approached by Rorty in 1916 Mitchell had proposed, as a condition of his participation in the project, a board of directors representing a wide range of opinions and interests. Rorty's first proposal after the war relied on funding from a committee of businessmen that had recently formed to promote "education in opposition to Bolshevism," but this potential infringement on the appearance of scientific objectivity was quickly shot down by others involved. The idea that was finally accepted by the Commonwealth Fund, the first major backer of the Bureau, was for an independent agency with a board of directors along the lines Mitchell had proposed.

With financial support assured for at least two years, the proposed committee to estimate the national income organized itself as the National Bureau of Economic Research, an ongoing institution dedicated to "investigation, research and discovery, and the application of knowledge to the well-being of mankind" (L.S. Mitchell 1953: 351). It was an institution that pledged, as a mark of its dedication to disinterested scientific research, to refrain from making policy recommendations. Mitchell was chosen as director of research. Estimation of the national income became the "first" Bureau project, because knowledge of the size and distribution of the national income was a prerequisite to intelligent discussion of such a wide range of social problems. Other equally important research initiatives would presumably follow.

From the beginning Mitchell referred to the innovative constitutional design of the Bureau, with its board of directors representing diverse interests and its pledge of policy neutrality, as a "bold experiment" toward giving the results of social science research their proper place in discussions of policy. It was an attempt to "raise the discussion of public questions to a higher level," to make "a contribution to the working methods of intelligent democracy." The NBER experiment had missionary potential: "The practical demonstration that we have given that men of otherwise divergent views can unite in scientific investigation of controverted social facts will give a powerful stimulus to all movements like ours."[21] In later years Mitchell would explain the appearance of university-supported social science research bureaus as a response to the success of the NBER and similarly constituted independent institutes (Mitchell 1937: 66–67).

But if the external structure of the Bureau was an experiment designed to increase public acceptance of social science research, the Bureau's internal organization became for Mitchell an experiment designed to increase the quality of social science research. "Organization," Mitchell once said, "is often a critically important factor in determining the efficiency of group action" (Mitchell 1937: 131), and Mitchell wanted to establish at the Bureau an effective social science counterpart to the team-oriented laboratory research he believed to be an important feature of modern natural sciences.[22] At the Bureau's first staff meeting he talked of experimenting with procedures to achieve the "best combination of system and spontaneity," and gradually there developed a settled way of doing things at the Bureau with certain noteworthy features. Members of the research staff (usually around half a dozen senior economists in Mitchell's time, most of whom also had university appointments) would work on projects assigned or approved by Mitchell. An acceptable project would have to be seen as complementary to other ongoing Bureau projects, related in some way to an overall Bureau program of research, and, by tacit understanding, would involve the analysis of statistical data. There were standing meetings in which staff members discussed work in progress, inviting the suggestions of others and hopefully revealing instances in which the findings of one staff member might contribute to the research of another. When a staff member completed a draft research report, it was assigned to a panel of other staff members who were to read and criticize it, a duty that was taken very seriously.[23]

The approach to research established by Mitchell at the Bureau, according to his wife, was "the approach he was most interested to follow himself . . . the National Bureau was organized for research in the special kinds of economic problems, through the special kinds of techniques, around which he wished to focus his own work" (L.S. Mitchell 1953: 333). Certainly the Bureau answered many of Mitchell's research needs. Prior to 1910 he had complained of intellectual loneliness, and yearned for colleagues with similar research interests. Within a few years of the publication of *Business Cycles* he worried that the book was becoming obsolete, and began to consider revising his theoretical discussion of the cycle on the basis of a much wider range of statistical data processed with more up-to-date statistical techniques. This would involve huge amounts of the tedious routine calculations that accompanied statistical research in those days, and, because Mitchell did not feel sufficiently trained in statistics to keep up with the field, the aid of statistical experts. Mitchell had earlier turned down an opportunity to head a "statistical laboratory" at Harvard for reasons discussed earlier, but by the late 1910s he was looking with admiration and perhaps envy at the sophisticated statistical research on business cycles being led by Warren Persons at that laboratory.[24] The National Bureau became Mitchell's statistical laboratory. He hand-picked a research staff of quantitative economists that included statistical experts Frederick Macauley and Frederick Mills. There was also room in the budget for a support staff, including statistical calculators. Not surprisingly, it was decided fairly early on that the NBER's second major research area after national income would be business cycles.[25]

Mitchell was involved in two other "experimental" movements in the 1920s that dovetailed in one way or another with both his plans for promoting social progress and his personal research agenda. In 1918, before the NBER was off the drawing board, he was approached about joining in the initiative that led to the founding of the New School for Social Research. Mitchell shared the concerns with academic freedom that motivated the other founders, believing that the lack of such freedom was one more reason that universities were not the ideal environment for social science research. But he saw other advantages to the project as well. During preliminary discussions he pushed for the school to be devoted to basic social science research. He wrote to his wife that the group was developing "two currents of policy": Herbert Croley wanted to "make the school primarily a concern for 'social engineering,'" but Mitchell backed the plan to "make it primarily a scientific body, though one alert to developments of a social sort." His confidence that the position he supported would win out was sufficient to allow him to resign from Columbia to join the New School faculty in 1919 (L.S. Mitchell 1953: 344–345).

In letters and talks promoting the New School in its early years Mitchell sounded some familiar themes: the New School would contribute to the movement to apply the scientific method to the study of complex social phenomena, and to replace policy-making on the basis of untested hunches with policy-making on the basis of the scientifically proven facts. He also seemed to envision the New School as a training ground for future applied social scientists, and its nontraditional students as potential assistants to the faculty in ongoing research projects. Learning at the New School, he wrote in 1920, would "lead up to research work which is the New School's chief function." Students would join with faculty in the fieldwork and data collection efforts required by the modern social sciences. A traditional university graduate student, Mitchell complained, might be able to solve a technical problem in statistics, or gather data for a historical study, but "did not have sufficient practical acquaintance with affairs to equip him for any serious investigation" (L.S. Mitchell 1953: 337–42).

Mitchell's plans to use New School students as research assistants while training them for research careers did not work. Although he remained peripherally involved with the New School for most of his life, Mitchell resigned from the faculty in 1922 and returned to Columbia because he had come to realize that "the graduate students there who expected to become professional economists would have more influence than the students at the New School on the development of economic science." The School's growing emphasis on adult education rather than research probably contributed to Mitchell's decision as well, as did the fact that in 1922 Mitchell could be more sure than in 1919 of his statistical laboratory at the NBER surviving as a going concern.[26]

It was also in 1922 that Mitchell joined with a group of other social scientists, led by Charles Merriam, to establish the Social Science Research Council (SSRC). Merriam and Mitchell had very similar ideas about the potential for social science knowledge to facilitate scientific social control, and about the sorts of changes needed in the social sciences if this potential were to be realized. In particular, they agreed—and this was a central point of SSRC rhetoric—that social science research would benefit from a more interdisciplinary approach. Mitchell's version of the argument was that all the social sciences were studying human behavior, but many of the traditional social science disciplines had abstracted out one or another aspect or motive of human behavior and constructed deductive theories around it. Dealing effectively with social problems, however, would require the realistic study of actual social phenomena, phenomena that typically involved the interplay of all these aspects and motives. By the 1920s, Mitchell did not believe that the answer lay in the creation of a single discipline, or in the borrowing of theories and concepts developed in one discipline by members of another. Specialized training in the existing disciplines should continue, but "cross-fertilization" of the disciplines, and effective problem-solving research, would occur when specialists of several social science disciplines worked together on the same concrete research problem.[27]

The SSRC soon developed into a grant-making agency, funding research proposals deemed worthy by appropriate council committees. The SSRC in turn was funded by foundations, particularly the Laura Spelman Rockefeller Memorial, whose director Beardsley Ruml entertained hopes for the social sciences remarkably like those articulated by Merriam and Mitchell.[28] An early policy of the council, pleasing to Mitchell, was that priority would be given to proposals for "merged research" involving joint work by "scientists trained in different techniques" (Social Science Research Council 1929: 3). In 1928 Mitchell, in his report as chairman of the SSRC, described the sort of research he hoped the council would promote:

> The research interests of the Social Science Research Council . . . comprehend both "pure" researches and more "practical" or "applied" activities. . . . [T]he first question the Council prefers to ask when confronted with . . . "social problems" is, "What is Happening?" Only after that question has been answered can intelligent consideration be given to the question: "What are the possibilities of more effective control in this particular area of human behavior?" . . . It is interested in encouraging greater fertility and diversity of scientific attack. . . . It believes that such fertility is encouraged when specialists from more than one discipline . . . are enabled to formulate a common problem and join in planning and executing a common program of research.
>
> (Social Science Research Council 1928: 16)

As first chairman of the SSRC's committee on research fellowships, Mitchell took an opportunity to direct council resources toward correcting what he saw as a serious flaw in the existing institutional structures of the social sciences. The research fellowship program was an "experiment," Mitchell reported, and the committee had decided that its goal would be to "promote the development of research workers, rather than . . . aid in the execution of research projects." Fellowships would be granted mainly to applicants in their late twenties and early thirties, because:

> Generous as American Universities have been in helping graduate students to obtain doctor's degrees, they have not been generous or wise in treating their young instructors. A newly-fledged doctor . . . is usually assigned a heavy teaching schedule, when he neither knows thoroughly the subjects he has to cover, nor knows how to teach. During the years when he would be most likely to make discoveries, he is kept exceedingly busy mastering new subjects, marking papers, acquiring classroom skills. . . . That is a most effective system for discouraging research. Only the most vigorous or the most fortunate men keep their creative faculties intact for the years when promotion enables them to command a scanty leisure by becoming exploiters of a new generation of youthful scholars. We say little about this scandal of which we are all conscious, but which we have not thought we could mend. . . . If our few research fellowships can give the ablest . . . men who aspire to do scientific work in the social field opportunity to develop their powers while they are still in their flexible years, we may hope for large results, ultimately if not immediately.
>
> (Mitchell 1926: 606–607)

Mitchell's concern with the corrosive influence of teaching duties on the nations' potential social scientific manpower, dating back no doubt at least to his youthful stint at Harvard, was sufficiently strong that he later established a similar fellowship program at the NBER (Mitchell 1940: 70).

In addition to being a means through which Mitchell could help promote in a general way the transformation of the social sciences, participation in the SSRC became a means of securing additional resources for the NBER. For example, in the mid-1920s the NBER conducted studies of various economic aspects of immigration using funds granted by the SSRC, or more precisely, the Laura Spelman Rockefeller Memorial acting through the SSRC. Mitchell worked with Ruml putting together a proposal for this research, with the understanding that the SSRC would use funds provided by the Memorial to underwrite the project (Fisher 1993: 40–41).

FORAYS INTO THE POLICY PROCESS: MITCHELL, HOOVER, AND THE NBER

While Mitchell was "experimenting" during the 1920s with new institutions and programs with the potential to further both basic social science research in general and his own research agenda in particular, he and the NBER became involved with Herbert Hoover's new model for economic policy-making. Mitchell and Hoover first met while both were in Washington for the war effort, and each was impressed by the other. In 1921 Hoover became Secretary of Commerce, a position from which he hoped to have a prominent voice in shaping national economic policy. Hoover, like Mitchell, supported the timely dissemination of economic statistics to businessmen as a means of improving business planning and thus contributing to macroeconomic stabilization; he also supported the consolidation of the government's statistical services in a single agency. In part to provide a show of expert support for these initiatives which he hoped to advance at the Commerce Department, Hoover early on appointed an Advisory Committee on Statistics that included Mitchell along with several other prominent economists (Barber 1985: 5–8). A few months later Hoover asked Mitchell to serve as his economic adviser, to help in making the Department of Commerce "the economic interpreter to the American people." Mitchell, involved at this time with the NBER's first project and his second year of teaching at the New School, declined, citing "obligations both of a personal and professional sort which bind me to New York."[29]

A few months later, however, Mitchell said yes to a different form of involvement with Hoover's program at Commerce, one more in keeping with his vision of the place of social science in the policy process. In response to the economic slump of 1921, Hoover had convinced President Harding to put him in charge of a "President's Conference on Unemployment." Hoover then appointed an advisory committee to the Conference which included Mitchell as a member. As Hoover explained it, the Conference would not only consider policies for the relief of unemployment, but also evaluate longer-term plans for stabilizing employment and controlling the business cycle. This important aspect of the Conference's work would be handled by a Committee on Unemployment and Business Cycles, which would commission a "careful technical investigation" to uncover factual information about the problem of unemployment that would raise the level of policy discussions in the area. If properly done, the investigation would also lend credibility to the recommendations of the committee (Alchon 1985: 79–80).

Hoover saw the independent NBER, with its nonpartisan board of directors, as an ideal agency for handling the technical investigation and lending the desired air of scientific objectivity to the Committee's work. Mitchell quickly agreed to Hoover's plan. It would fit in, after all, with the Bureau's planned project on business cycles. It would provide an influx of funds that would subsidize other ongoing Bureau projects at a time when the Bureau's financial future was not entirely secure. In accepting Hoover's proposal, Mitchell stressed that he would need funds not only to hire investigators but to cover such overheads as research assistants, office space, secretaries, and statistical clerks (Alchon 1985: 79–80).

In addition, this model of involvement in policy was more in tune with Mitchell's thinking than that of serving as an economic adviser to the Commerce Department. Hoover was proposing a disinterested investigation by social scientists in order to ascertain "facts"; this would be followed by a review of the results by a committee of business, labor, and government representatives who would then propose plans for economic reform to policymakers. As Mitchell understood it, the role of the Bureau investigation was to "present not recommendations concerning what ought to be done, but facts which ought to be considered by those who have the responsibility of formulating policies." Mitchell drew up a plan of research calling for the Bureau to commission studies of various aspects of the related problems of unemployment and business cycles. Drafts of the studies were to be ready for the committee's consideration in six months, a time period that Mitchell apologetically admitted on more than one occasion was too short to allow the appropriate level of scientific thoroughness.[30]

Not all involved in the undertaking saw the role of the committee and of the Bureau's investigation in the same way that Mitchell did. In the view of E.E. Hunt, the Hoover lieutenant overseeing the investigation, the committee's main job was public education, building an understanding of and enthusiasm for stabilization policies that had already been worked out. The technical reports would demonstrate support for these policies among social scientific experts. Hunt considered the plan for research submitted by Mitchell to be fine "from the point of view of pure research," but it lacked "the sort of pointing up which is necessary to spur action." Upon seeing the pile of drafts generated by the technical investigation, committee chairman Owen Young of General Electric expressed the opinion that they would be of little use in drafting recommendations. He preferred to formulate the committee's recommendations after consultation with business and labor leaders. Some members of the committee were unhappy with the fact that public unemployment insurance was discussed in a noncondemnatory fashion in the technical reports; their unease was increased by Mitchell's expression to the committee of his personal opinion that they should endorse both public and private plans for unemployment relief (Alchon 1985: 86–87, 91–96).

Mitchell does not appear to have been too discouraged by these developments, and he would later express the opinion that when conflict arose between the committee view and the scientific view, Hoover's man Hunt would support the scientific view. As the investigations progressed, and later while the committee was deliberating, Mitchell emphasized the significant additions being made to basic knowledge of unemployment and business cycles. He was no doubt pleased by the fact that when published in early spring of 1923, the technical reports were in general favorably received by academic reviewers. The recommendations of the Committee on Unemployment and Business Cycles were published in the same volume as the technical reports, and, in part as a result of the disagreements over public unemployment insurance, included a statement that the committee was in no way responsible for the content of the Bureau's reports, and the Bureau in no way endorsed the committee's recommendations.[31]

The Hoover camp was also satisfied with the outcome of the committee's work, to the extent that they proposed in 1927 a second project organized along the same lines. The project would again take place under the auspices of the President's Conference on Unemployment, and would study the prosperity of the previous four years. It was proposed that the National Bureau would once again conduct or commission studies of a number of aspects of recent economic performance. A Committee on Recent Economic Changes would then consider the studies and offer a set of policy recommendations aimed at consolidating and sustaining the prosperity.[32]

The Bureau's acceptance of this proposal came jointly from Mitchell and Edwin Gay, who was now co-director of research at the NBER. They expressed interest in doing the work as a scientific proposition: studies of the sort proposed would help determine the extent to which the recent prosperity was due to fortuitous events, and the extent to which it might be due to specific policy actions and other factors that could be controlled through "wise planning." The studies would also provide the impetus for collection and analysis of data on a wide range of economic activities. Hoover's involvement would allow the Bureau to do this fundamental research at a low cost, for with his backing the cooperation of government agencies and other research organizations could be obtained on better terms. There was some concern about the possible politicization of the project, for an election year was approaching and Hoover seemed certain to be a candidate. The NBER did not want to be involved in something that appeared to be propaganda for the achievements of Hoover and the Republicans. Hunt offered reassurances that since the committee's report would not be written and released until after the election, it would not appear tainted by political considerations (Alchon 1985: 135–140).

Mitchell and Gay put together a team of investigators to conduct studies of various sectors of the economy, and of prices, population, and business cycles. The studies were done between February and October of 1928, and the committee prepared a first draft of its report in January of 1929. The technical studies and the committee report were published in May. The tone of the committee report was upbeat, as one might expect given the period with which it dealt. A central theme was that the recent prosperity was a result of a "balance" that had been achieved between the various sectors of the economy; making it important to study the period and develop a technique, or set of policies, for maintaining the balance (Committee on Recent Economic Changes 1929: ix–xxx).

Mitchell wrote an essay summarizing the technical studies, and cited as a chief factor behind the prosperity the increased application of intelligence to the daily activities of life. The findings of science were continuously being used to modify production processes, resulting in increases in labor productivity. Employers were experimenting with innovative management techniques and showing an increased willingness to plan using economic statistics. "Wise" government policy measures such as the establishment of the Federal Reserve System contributed as well. Mitchell did not neglect to mention certain negative aspects of the period, including technological unemployment and poor performance in certain sectors such as mining and agriculture. He also noted that, although the crash of 1921 had inspired an admirable caution on the part of businessmen for several years thereafter, there were disquieting signs of a return to unduly speculative behavior. Economic balance was a delicate thing, Mitchell warned, and continued intelligent action was required to preserve it (Committee on Recent Economic Changes 1929: 841–910).

The *Recent Economic Changes* technical report was well received by the scholarly community. Although the economic events of 1929 and 1930 would detract somewhat from the relevance of the studies, all of which covered only up to 1928, they would be frequently cited by economists for many years after. The investigation was seen, as Mitchell hoped it would be, as a solid contribution to social scientific knowledge.

As Barber (1985: 65) has noted, however, Hoover and his aides saw a different purpose in the work of the Committee on Recent Economic Changes: it was a means of promoting Hoover's ideas for scientifically based economic reform, already formulated and initiated during his time as Secretary of Commerce, now to be completed during his presidency. In the fall of 1929, Hoover enlisted Mitchell in a similar effort designed to promote a scientific approach to social reform in general, an effort that became the President's Research Committee on Social Trends. Mitchell was to chair the committee, with his SSRC colleague Charles Merriam serving as vice-chair. The committee restricted its role to "fact-finding," holding that the making of policy recommendations was the prerogative of the president. A proposal was put together for a research project exceeding in size and scope the report on Recent Economic Changes. It would cover topics as diverse as trends in religion, uses of leisure time, communication media, and the arts, but an underlying theme would be the unity of the social system. All investigators, regardless of disciplinary background, would be attentive to the interrelationships existing between all social phenomena. The committee assured Hoover that such a study would take a large step toward "bringing the scientific method to bear on the solution of social problems," although Mitchell personally believed that a thorough and scientific study of social trends would not be possible within the three-year time span proposed for the investigations. Hoover's aides moved to obtain funding for the committee's investigation from the Rockefeller Foundation, promoting it as a way "to produce a well rounded and explicit picture of the whole American social scene, with such a wealth of facts and statistics and conclusions as to form a new and unique basis of thought and action for social scientists, social workers, and . . . officers of government," language that must have resonated with Mitchell in spite of its hyperbolic nature (Karl 1974: 210–214).

Although the social trends study was patterned on the technical investigation/committee report model of the Unemployment and Recent Economic Changes projects, Mitchell's role in and experience with the study was different. Mitchell was this time chair of the committee, but had no direct involvement with the research end of the project. The studies were being administered by the SSRC, and the NBER was involved only peripherally. And although Mitchell had learned by now that the technical investigation/committee report model did not really fully insulate social science researchers from political concerns, in the case of the Social Trends study the model's weakness in this respect became more apparent than ever.

The work of the investigators began in early 1930 and continued through 1932 as the nation sank deeper into the Depression. Hoover had from the beginning wanted to be personally involved with the committee, viewing its work as a contribution to building a program for his second term. In 1931 Merriam protested against White House requests to view preliminary material from the investigations, arguing that it might create the appearance of a presidential attempt to influence the content of the investigators' studies. In early 1932 Hunt and other presidential aides began suggesting the possibility of using some of the committee's preliminary findings as campaign material, but the committee objected. They believed themselves to be overseeing a monumental and fundamentally important social science research project, and did not want the public to get the impression that their work was in reality political propaganda. As the presidential campaign became increasingly strident, committee members became concerned and even argumentative about the tone of the reports. Were the reports sufficiently grounded in fact? Were they too optimistic? Were they written on a scientific level, or did they pander to a popular audience (Karl 1974: 214–219)?

The committee's report, entitled *Recent Social Trends in the United States*, was issued after the election in January of 1933. It consisted of two volumes containing over two dozen essays. The social science community was once again impressed, but there were also criticisms of the committee's approach, and, by implication, of Mitchell's view of the role of social scientists in the policy process, which Mitchell would hear again, namely, that in a time of crisis, a compilation of the facts is not enough—social science should say something about what is to be done in light of the facts, of what values the nation should pursue and how. A.A. Berle commented that "one may regret that the academic community has fallen out of the habit of interpreting its data; feel . . . that the desire for objectivity has been carried too far."[33]

WITHDRAWING THE NBER INTO THE REALM OF PURE RESEARCH

Though not directly involved in the Social Trends project, the NBER continued to receive funds from the Committee on Recent Economic Changes into the 1930s for the purposes of generating a statistical profile of the economic downswing. Still, the depression had created a financial crisis at the Bureau—the budget fell by two-thirds, staff size and salaries were cut, and projects were suspended (Gay and Mitchell 1933: 13, 22–23). Interestingly, the Bureau's crisis almost became fatal in 1932 as a result of the Bureau's cooperation with Hoover's committees during the 1920s.

By the late 1920s, the Carnegie Corporation had become an important benefactor of the National Bureau. One of Carnegie's directors, however, Russell Leffingwell, had spoken against the foundation's involvement with the Recent Economic Changes project, and by the 1930s he felt that events had vindicated his opposition: "[T]he National Bureau disgraced itself and the Carnegie Corporation by its work on Recent Economic Changes." "Presumably under political pressure," he wrote to Carnegie president Frederick Keppel in 1932, it "completely disregarded the prospect of disaster which had actually occurred after its publication."[34] Leffingwell had in 1930 blocked Carnegie's participation in the extension of the Recent Economic Changes research, and he became an obstacle to any attempt by the Bureau to get Carnegie Funds.

In 1932 Oswald Knauth, former Bureau research staff member and now chairman of the NBER board, approached Leffingwell with a deal. Knauth had confided with another Bureau board member that he had lost confidence in the organization, that although it had done important work in its early years, the "driving impulse of discovering facts" had now left it. Knauth told Leffingwell that if Leffingwell would assent to a pending Bureau request for Carnegie funds, the Bureau would use the money to complete ongoing projects, and then close itself down. The Carnegie Board voted the Bureau a one-year emergency appropriation (Alchon 1985: 162–163).

Alchon (1985), in reporting this series of events, expresses uncertainty as to whether Mitchell or co-director Gay knew anything of the arrangement between Knauth and Leffingwell. Mitchell was in England at the time, as a visiting professor at Oxford. In any case, the Bureau did not close down. Early in 1933, both the Carnegie Corporation and the Rockefeller Foundation made large long-term financial commitments to the Bureau. The Bureau's case in seeking these funds was strengthened by promises to reduce outside commitments (such as the projects done for Hoover's committees) in favor of the basic programs of the Bureau (national income and business cycles), and to give Mitchell more control over Bureau operations. Gay resigned as co-director of research at about the same time, but there is no indication that he was pushed out (Alchon 1985: 163–165).

The NBER had originally fitted into Mitchell's vision as an organization dedicated to pure social science research (and a place for him to do such research). Whatever Mitchell might have hoped, however, the Bureau's high-profile activities for Hoover in the 1920s created an impression of a different sort of research organization, one moving closer to the applied pole of social science research, working on problems identified by policymakers, and, in the eyes of some, subject to political pressures. The annual reports written by Mitchell in the years after the 1932–33 crisis express a strong commitment to the original mission of the Bureau as an institute for basic social science research. In his 1934 report, Mitchell noted that the Bureau had frequently been "called upon by governmental or private agencies to take part in the deliberate study of some specific problem and to suggest practical policies for dealing with it." The Bureau did not regret having aided such proceedings, he added, but in the future would devote most of its energy to studying "the general features of economic life" and "relationships among inter-connected processes." Such studies might not show how to solve problems of the day: "But the knowledge slowly and painfully acquired . . . is valuable . . . as a part of the foundation upon which an economic science that treats dynamic problems in a realistic fashion will be built." In 1939, Mitchell defended the Bureau's refusal to state opinions on policy, and reiterated its commitment to basic research: "[I]n trying to establish a few economic fundamentals firmly . . . we are contributing more toward the improvement of economic organization than we could by tackling what are commonly called 'practical problems.'" He also spoke of the practical social science experts outside the Bureau who "will apply to the betterment of economic organization whatever the National Bureau and its co-workers discover." In 1945, he contrasted what he called ad hoc or piecemeal investigations into particular problems, initiated at the request of "public officials and private philanthropists," with systematic, integrated research into the functioning of the economic system as a whole. Dealing with the former was "exciting; it attracts public attention . . . the men so engaged feel they have a share in determining policy." The Bureau was honored to have done such work in the past, but now devoted its resources exclusively to systematic research. "Dealing energetically with one question for a year does not necessarily make an investigator better qualified to deal next year with a different question," Mitchell observed, while "anything learned about the basic features of economic organization applies to a host of practical problems."[35]

Why this change in course for the Bureau in the 1930s? A reason offered by Mitchell was that the multiplication of research institutes eager to work on "practical problems" relieved the Bureau of what it had regarded in the 1920s as a burdensome civic duty. One might also speculate, on the basis of Alchon's account of the Bureau's near-death experience, that in re-emphasizing the Bureau's basic research function Mitchell was doing what he had to do to save the Bureau, whether or not his preferences ran in that direction. Dorothy Ross (1991) has suggested a change in Mitchell's attitude in the 1930s, with the Depression impressing upon him firmly how much was still unknown about the workings of the economic system, and how much more basic research was necessary before social scientists could offer effective policy advice. Information reported by Edwin Gay's biographer, however, indicates that even in the 1920s Mitchell had lost enthusiasm for the Bureau's work on outside commitments. He felt the unemployment study had distracted him from his own business cycle research, and did not want the Bureau to be thought of as a general service research institute to be called upon by state and federal agencies. Gay, who was given the public relations/fundraising role when he became co-director of research, emphasized the public service aspect of the special studies, as well as the money they brought in. Gay's departure allowed Mitchell to do what he wanted with the Bureau, and the foundations happened to see things Mitchell's way.[36]

The Bureau did continue to work on cooperative projects with the government after 1930, but the cooperation was of a sort that had always been part of Mitchell's vision for the Bureau, and on a level far removed from the realms in which policies were made. During the mid-1930s, Bureau personnel worked with staffers at the Department of Commerce to facilitate the transfer of the task of making annual estimates of the national income from the Bureau to the government. The Bureau had unsuccessfully pressed the Commerce Department to take over the preparation of the annual estimates as early as 1921, with then-secretary Hoover refusing on the grounds that the independent NBER was better suited to the task than the government (Barber 1985: 199–200). The government takeover of national income accounting in the 1930s would begin a series of transfers to the government of projects begun at the Bureau, including the preparation of estimates of consumer installment credit and the construction of an index of economic indicators, all consistent with the Mitchellian goal of expanding the government's role as the provider of fundamental statistics needed for business and governmental planning.

MITCHELL'S LAST MAJOR INVOLVEMENT IN THE POLICY PROCESS: THE NATIONAL PLANNING BOARD

While Mitchell was steering the Bureau back toward its program of basic research in 1933, he personally accepted a post closer than ever to the political aspects of the policy process. The closing section of Mitchell's summary report of the Committee on Social Trends had been an argument for his (and Merriam's) version of scientific social planning, and had raised the possibility of a National Advisory Council, "able to contribute to the consideration of the basic social problems of the nation" (Mitchell 1933). In July of 1933, Harold Ickes, secretary of the interior, created the National Planning Board (NPB) to advise him on the distribution to local communities of funding for public works projects. Mitchell was appointed to the Board along with Charles Merriam and Frederic Delano. Mitchell and Merriam saw the Board as a move in the direction of the sort of national planning agency they envisioned, and the official description of the Board's duties—preparation, maintenance, and development of comprehensive and coordinated regional plans; research into trends in natural resources, population, social and economic habits; and the coordination and sequencing of proposed projects to prevent duplication and overlap—could only have reinforced this view.[37]

Mitchell noted in the Board's first meeting an important difference between the work of the Social Trends committee and the work of the new National Planning Board: Hoover had wanted fact-finding, while Roosevelt wanted plans of action. During its year of operation, the NPB encouraged and funded the formation of local government planning agencies, commissioned various studies designed to aid local planning efforts, developed criteria for the disbursement of public works funds, and worked to coordinate Public Works Administration projects with projects supported by other government agencies. It closed its first year with a report promoting the Mitchell/Merriam view of national planning and recommending the creation of a permanent National Planning Board, "directly responsible to the country's chief executive." The report explained that this board and its technical staff would coordinate and supplement the work of other planning agencies, and conduct or finance research to identify emerging trends and problems. The Board would be useful only "in proportion as it was detached from immediate political power and responsibility, as a general staff gathering and analyzing facts, . . . constantly preparing and presenting to the authorities its impressions, findings, conclusions and recommendations for such disposition as those entrusted with governmental responsibility may deem appropriate" (National Planning Board 1934: 35–38).

Roosevelt responded positively to the idea of a planning board reporting directly to him, but Ickes did not. He saw the Board as his board, and was angered by the proposal that it be removed from cabinet control. In a compromise, the National Planning Board was reorganized as the National Resources Board (Roosevelt wished to avoid the word "planning"), with Ickes and two other cabinet secretaries joining Mitchell, Merriam, and Delano as members. Mitchell, however, resigned about a year later in 1935.[38]

Mitchell explained in his letter of resignation that proper performance of the duties of a national planning organization required a full-time commitment that he was unwilling to make; he wished to return to his research. Four years later he elaborated on this in a talk to economics students at Columbia:

> For several years I was a member of the National Planning Board and of its successor the National Resources Board. The problems on which we were allowed to advise were of a relatively simple nature. . . . But when I got solidly "up against" any of these problems and had to make a responsible decision, I found I needed a great deal of knowledge that I lacked and could acquire only by painstaking inquiries by myself or by members of a staff. I believe strongly that a community needs to have such planning done. But after taking an active share in the work for some time I resigned, because I realized that I could not do the job properly without devoting my whole energy to it.
>
> (L.S. Mitchell 1953: 546)

It is not hard to accept Mitchell's reason given his "temperamental craving" for basic research and the fact that he was falling behind on his personal project of revising his 1913 study of business cycles.[39] Mitchell was also possibly put off by the frequent intrusion of politics into the work of the board. The disagreement over the proper position of the Board vis-à-vis the president and the cabinet has been mentioned, and the Board was frequently running into turf battles with other agencies that did not want to submit their own plans and projects to be "coordinated." Mitchell must have been particularly discouraged by an early dispute with the War Department, which, in defending the priority of the Army Corps of Engineers in certain projects dealing with waterways, questioned a central premise of Mitchell's thinking on social planning: the need for coordinated planning in dealing with a complex system. Secretary of War Henry Dern argued that flood control, improvement of navigation, pollution abatement, reforestation, and irrigation were distinct problems, each "to be handled by a special group of experts if satisfactory results are to be obtained. . . . [T]oo much coordination, or the coordination of unrelated activities, might prove harmful instead of beneficial." Mitchell was also disappointed that the Board's duties were in practice limited to projects related to land and water use, and that it was not developing into the broader agency for general social and economic planning for which he hoped (Karl 1974: 241–242, 324).

The National Resources Board was Mitchell's last major involvement in the political side of policy-making. Over the last decade of his life he devoted his time increasingly to the revision of his business cycle theory, ultimately giving up even the management of the NBER in his unsuccessful attempt to complete the project he had started some twenty-five years before. He continued to speak and write about the desirability, indeed the urgency, of adopting a scientific approach to social policy, but as always gave a place of priority to the need to support, reorganize, and expand basic social science research. Even as the nation mobilized for the Second World War, Mitchell worked to preserve the flow of resources to basic research activities. When

Mitchell's friend Joseph Willets, head of the Division of Social Sciences of the Rockefeller Foundation, asked about how social science could best contribute to the war effort, Mitchell argued that "it seems to me the part of wisdom to devote at least a small fraction of what intelligence we possess to economic research, and to the training of young investigators" unless "our fortunes sink to so low a pass that no energy can be spared for any other end than mere survival." He questioned the wartime use of so many trained economists in administrative work or routine analysis, lamenting that "few, if any, economists are used by the government to carry on researches of a more fundamental sort."[40]

Shortly after the war, Mitchell got the opportunity to present his case before Congress. A Senate subcommittee was considering a proposal to create an agency for channeling federal funds to support scientific research, and the question of whether and how the social sciences would fit in. Mitchell was testifying as a representative of the SSRC. The official statement of the SSRC predictably emphasized the great need for and potential benefits from social science research. It mentioned the concern that federal funding of social science research could lead to political influence on that research, but argued that past experience showed there to be practicable institutional arrangements for channeling federal funds to social science research without endangering objectivity. During subsequent questioning, a sympathetic Senator Fulbright noted that as a political matter it was important to be able to point to short-term results from investments of government money, and that while most citizens were aware of positive results flowing from natural science research, the benefits of long-term social science research were less clear. Mitchell offered as an example the difference between the economic mobilizations for the two World Wars. The second effort was a great improvement over the first, according to Mitchell, largely because the people involved in the more recent mobilization "had at their disposal a great deal of careful inquiry, and inquiry of a more thoroughgoing and realistic kind than used to be carried out in the social sciences." Apparently, Mitchell believed that social science was beginning to make its way into the policy process.[41]

MITCHELL AND HIS (FRIENDLY) CRITICS

Not surprisingly, Mitchell's bold talk of "social engineering" and "social planning" was criticized by the conservatives of his day. Mitchell's wife recalled his felt need to combat the widespread belief that planning was "un-American." While Mitchell was working on the National Planning Board, his old ally Herbert Hoover wrote to him that his proposed national planning organization, if appointed by Roosevelt, would attempt "to create of a Socialist State—or at least a Regimented one" (L.S. Mitchell 1953: 368, 371). Even Mitchell's protégé, Arthur Burns, raised conservative concerns in his comments on Mitchell's essay on "Intelligence and the Guidance of Economic Evolution." The results of applying intelligence to social policy, Burns argued, would depend on the values of those doing the guiding, and Burns felt that Mitchell had said too little about how those values would be determined:

> I suppose that at bottom, I am inclined to quarrel because I do not quite share the liberal faith you profess. Intelligence is a fuzzy word. It has given to mankind both religion and atheism; democracy and fascism, free trade and autarchy; it has produced wars and prevented them; it has soaked the rich and oppressed the poor; and so on, and on. You seem to start (and end) with a preference for an economic system built upon (mainly, though progressively less so) private enterprise. You therefore want intelligence to improve the working of *this* system. Norman Thomas starts with a collectivist bias. Writing on your subject, he would argue that intelligence will begin guiding economic evolution when we set about scrapping private enterprise.[42]

It is also possible, however, to identify conservative elements in Mitchell's vision and in the approach to research he cultivated at the Bureau, and some of Mitchell's contemporaries did so. Mitchell's position that wise policy design required a knowledge of the working of the social system, and his frank admissions of the current inadequacy of such knowledge, could be used by those opposing changes in the status quo to argue that plans for reform must be delayed until more accurate forecasts of their effects could be made. Mitchell spoke against this interpretation of his position, on one occasion telling an audience: "We must do what we can in our own generation to improve both our economic knowledge and our economic practice. That we cannot do a perfect job until we have perfect knowledge is no excuse for not doing the best job our imperfect knowledge permits."[43] He also felt compelled to answer unnamed critics, both "impatient" and "thoughtful," who saw the Bureau, with its refusal to take positions on policy matters and its pursuit of "basic research" seemingly unrelated to pressing social problems, as giving little aid to, if not draining resources from, the cause of social reform (Mitchell 1940: 9–13).

One of Mitchell's "thoughtful" critics from the left can be readily identified. In 1939 Robert Lynd, Mitchell's friend and colleague both at Columbia and on the SSRC, published *Knowledge for What?*, a "critique of the current focus and methods of social science research." Lynd was troubled by the direction social science had taken in the attempt to be objective, and by certain consequences of the drive to make the social sciences more thoroughly empirical. He singled out the work of the NBER to illustrate some of his misgivings. Lynd argued that the NBER's pursuit of objectivity through descriptive empiricism could actually result in a loss of true objectivity, which included a willingness to question existing cultural arrangements and the values they served and reinforced, along with a willingness to consider the possibilities for human fulfillment held out by very different sets of cultural arrangements and values. A neutral program of gathering facts about one's own culture tended to involve a tacit acceptance of that culture's values and goals. The choice of what facts to gather was based on the culture's own definition of its problems. The refusal to interpret the facts gathered meant leaving their interpretation, and the conclusions to be drawn from them concerning the cultural situation, to powerful interest groups. The Bureau hoped to contribute to social reform by providing knowledge of the functioning of the social system, but Lynd argued that research into the functioning of the existing economic system, while perhaps allowing the design and evaluation of incremental reforms to that system, could not "carry us far along the road to understanding the potentialities of a culture not dominated by the price system operating under the quest for private profit" (Lynd 1939: ix, 121–123, 186, 221–222).[44]

Lynd was troubled by a social science that professed to have nothing to say about values, and he argued that social scientists should research the question of values, attempting to identify what was truly valuable from the point of view of the fundamental cravings and desires of the human species, as opposed to those things deemed valuable by the prevailing culture. Armed with hypotheses concerning fundamental human values, and knowledge gained from the testing of these hypotheses, the social sciences could go beyond the question of how to make the existing social system better able to meet the goals it defined for its members, and begin to explore the problem of what institutional system best satisfies basic human cravings and desires (Lynd 1939: 185–202, 205–206).

Mitchell was invited by a Columbia student organization to speak on Lynd's book shortly after it appeared; Lynd attended at Mitchell's invitation. Mitchell informed the group that he agreed with Lynd that the present culture was flawed, and that the social sciences should contribute to developing social institutions "better suited to the requirements of human personalities." He differed with Lynd, however, on how the social sciences could best accomplish this goal. As he had many times before, he argued that "what we need to improve our social institutions is what we need to improve our medical practice and our industrial technology—knowledge on which we can rely and that we can apply." He spoke of having learned while young the importance of cultural institutions in shaping economic behavior, and of his early criticisms of economists' assumptions about human behavior; but "accomplishing something constructive" required determining how men actually behaved, and how institutions actually affected human behavior. His desire for concrete knowledge resting on evidence had led him into detailed quantitative research. He suggested that when Lynd decided to "advance" from criticism to attempting to solve the problems he had identified in *Knowledge for What?*, he would find himself going back to research involving careful observation of the existing system, of the sort he did for his book *Middletown* (Lynd and Lynd 1929). Mitchell noted, for example, that Lynd had proposed a tentative list of fundamental human cravings. Would he really, Mitchell wondered, be willing to reconstruct American society in accordance with those fundamental cravings before careful research had shown his list of cravings to be accurate (L.S. Mitchell 1953: 561–564)?

Mitchell then took issue with Lynd's argument that social scientists should concentrate "less on the workings of the present culture and more upon the changes that ought to be made in culture." Any attempt to appraise proposals for changing a culture, large or small, would require predictions of the effects of those changes, Mitchell argued. Moreover, any proposed cultural change would have to be introduced into the existing culture, so that the effects of the change would depend upon the reactions of the people whose culture was being changed. The way to obtain knowledge required to predict these reactions was to study the existing culture (L.S. Mitchell 1953: 565).

Both Lynd and Burns were troubled by Mitchell's position on the relationship between values, social science, and social reform. Burns, like Mitchell, believed that social scientists should pursue the ideal of objective knowledge, but worried about where the application of that knowledge to social reform might lead if left in the hands of leaders with unspecified values. Lynd believed that Mitchell's style of "objective" research would embody the dysfunctional values of the existing culture, and argued for research that would offer an alternative to those values and that culture. Neither man moved Mitchell very far.

Mitchell was, as he claimed, close to Lynd on many points regarding the shortcomings of both social science and capitalist society.[45] He had often called for research into values: how they were formed, the extent to which they were culturally determined rather than intrinsic. He was aware of the tendency for social science to become apologetics for the existing order.[46] In spite of the errors of the past, however, Mitchell was not willing to abandon the ideal of objective knowledge. He was also aware of the power of the concept of objectivity in the public mind. If social scientists wished to contribute to social reform, Mitchell pointed out in his response to Lynd, their findings must be accepted by many people. Mitchell undoubtedly believed that, in the society in which he lived, the public would more readily accept the findings of researchers who enforced upon themselves a discipline of objectivity than the findings of those who, following Lynd, boldly stated as their guiding hypothesis that the capitalist system had failed and could not be repaired—even if the findings of both researchers pointed to the same program for reform.[47]

In response to Burns, Mitchell offered the hope that greater knowledge could clarify—that is, improve—the values of those responsible for making policy. Against this, one might argue (although Burns did not) that all the knowledge in the world would not diminish, say, the cravings for power and order that led to fascism. But Mitchell seemed to believe that at bottom the values of the American electorate were sound, and the democratic process ultimately effective in giving people what they thought they wanted.[48] Many disagreements over policy were disagreements over the effects of particular policies, not over the ends to be served by policy. Mitchell believed that ignorance, rather than the evil or selfish motives of people or politicians, was the chief obstacle to social progress, and the chief danger to democracy and freedom—the ignorance of policymakers, who failed to prevent or even exacerbated social and economic problems, and the ignorance of voters, who turned for relief to attractive-sounding schemes, not understanding how damaging the schemes might be to their pocketbooks or the values they cherished.[49]

CONCLUSION

Mitchell died in 1948. His remarks in his final years continued to emphasize work yet to be done, but also revealed, as did his testimony before Congress, a belief that progress had been made. "The years near at hand," he told an audience in 1945, "may see the beginnings of an economics worthy to be called a science." Smith (1994: 80) writes of Mitchell feeling "the tension between his humanitarian sentiments and his firm belief in empirical, inductive science," especially during the late 1930s, as he withdrew entirely from the realm of policy-making and devoted both his own efforts and those of the National Bureau to pure research. I tend to doubt that Mitchell felt such tensions, however, or accepted the opposition between humanitarianism and his empirical research posed by Smith. Although Mitchell spoke of the need for reforms in public policy and the institutions through which it was made, and participated in the policy process in hopes of contributing to such reforms, it was his position from the beginning that pure research was the most important prerequisite to the social progress for which he hoped. Early on, he decided that through pursuing an activity he found personally satisfying he could also pursue his ethical ideals. Subsequently, he had more successes and ran up against fewer frustrations working on his research than when he accepted posts with the potential for more immediate impact on policy. Mitchell's actions in the 1930s should be viewed in this light. Though he could have made more aggressive attempts to mold the National Resources Board into a true national planning agency, or accepted other government posts, or publicly aired his opinions about the problems of a capitalist society, Mitchell made the determination that he could better serve his humanitarian goals by devoting his remaining time and effort to increasing knowledge of the workings of the social system.

In believing that the knowledge obtained through (social) scientific research offered the best hope for social progress, Mitchell was, as noted in the introduction, part of a larger movement in the social sciences. The decades following his death saw the establishment and the extension of the sorts of programs, policies, and institutions for which he and like-minded cognitive modernists had pushed. The National Bureau of Economic Research, with its board of directors and its pledge of policy neutrality, survives today, as do a number of other independent social science research institutes. Funding flows to social science researchers from foundations and from various levels of government. At the state and federal government one finds agencies and departments, staffed by trained economists, charged with the mission of providing the objective economic analysis that policymakers need to make informed decisions.

Social science research, however, has not been able to disentangle itself from debates over "what ought to be." Alongside the putatively independent social science research institutes are those organized to generate and publicize social science research supporting a particular policy or ideological agenda, their partisan activities supported by funds from private and foundation sources. And government agencies established to provide objective economic information, from the Council of Economic Advisors and the Congressional Budget Office on down, are routinely accused of shaping their analyses to support the positions of those who appointed them. The sorts of disagreements that arise when agencies with different patrons analyze the same question often support such accusations.

This problem, I think, stems partly from the failure of an assumption that is ultimately crucial to Mitchell's vision: that the main problem in public policy is ignorance over the workings of the social system, rather than conflicts over the values that should guide policy. Mitchell occasionally opined that most arguments over public policy were arguments over facts that could be resolved through the scientific method; a few years after Mitchell's death the same assertion appeared in the influential essay "The Methodology of Positive Economics" by his student Milton Friedman (1953). But this idea, and the implied assumption that fundamentally people share the same values, was questioned by Mitchell's contemporary critics, and however enthusiastically it may have been embraced by mainstream economists following Friedman's essay, each new controversy in the realm of economic policy seems to cast more doubt upon it. And without the assumption of shared set of values, Mitchell's vision and prescriptions for social science and public policy are at best incomplete.

NOTES

1 The author would like to acknowledge the helpful comments of Warren Samuels and Perry Mehrling.

2 A long list of these could be compiled including Herbert Hoover (Barber 1985), Walter Lippmann (Goodwin 1995), Charles Merriam (Karl 1974), Beardsley Ruml and other key figures at the Ford and Carnegie Foundations (Alchon 1985: 118–124); along with John Dewey and a number of the social scientists profiled in chapters 10 and 11 of Ross (1991).

3 Burns (1952: 97). Mitchell once wrote to Dewey: "There is no one to whom I feel under heavier intellectual obligation than yourself" (Letter of December 7, 1934, Dewey folder, correspondence section, Mitchell papers).

4 Mitchell (1937: 18); Mitchell (1913: 588–596). Mitchell's view on economic research and business planning was shared by Herbert Hoover both as Secretary of Commerce and as President. For more on Mitchell and Hoover's view of how the education of and dissemination of information to businessmen could moderate business cycles, see Barber (1985: 8–13, 41).

5 Mitchell (1927: 167–173); Mitchell (1937: 88–93, 117).

6 Late statements of this view are found in L.S. Mitchell (1953: 553, 561–562, 567) and Mitchell (1941: 13–16).

7 Mitchell (1939b: 1); Mitchell (1937: 403–410).

8 Mitchell (1937: 51); Mitchell (1939b: 9); Mitchell (1939c: 605); Mitchell (1940: 10–13).

9 Mitchell (1939b: 31); Mitchell (1941: 16–17).

10 Mitchell (1939b: 10); Mitchell (1940: 20–21); Mitchell (1941: 14); Mitchell (1945: 13).

11 Mitchell (1931: 107); Mitchell (1940: 10–11, 20–21); Mitchell (1941: 13, 16–17).

12 For example, "Science properly considered does not undertake to say what ought to be done. That is the responsibility in this country of the representatives of the people who have been chosen by the democratic process" (U.S. Congress 1945: 739).

13 Mitchell (1939a: 3). See also Mitchell (1937: 127); Mitchell (1934a: 26–27); Mitchell (1931: 107); Mitchell (1939c: 605); L.S. Mitchell (1953: 374–375, 567–568).

14 Mitchell once wrote to J.M. Clark (Letter of January 19, 1944, J.M. Clark folder, correspondence section, Mitchell papers): "If one wishes to make anything clear by talking, it is . . . best to concentrate on what the people before you need to hear and not confuse them by mentioning all the points pertinent to your theme or by putting in all the qualifications, even of your main proposition, that you would think requisite in a full presentation," and almost all Mitchell's writings on social science and social policy were originally public addresses. Rutherford (1994: 138) writes that Mitchell "made no sharp distinction between means and ends," which probably reflects what Mitchell thought, but not what he repeatedly stressed to a variety of audiences. A few times Mitchell did point out that social science research could help contribute to the formation of social values by making clear the consequences of pursuing particular values and the possible conflicts between simultaneously held social values (Mitchell 1937: 135; Mitchell 1939c: 603; L.S. Mitchell 1953: 374–376). The argument appears most prominently in Mitchell's address "Intelligence and the Guidance of Economic Evolution" (Mitchell 1937: 103–136, delivered in 1936), but was placed there only at the prompting of his colleague Arthur Burns. Mitchell asked Burns for comments on

a draft of the address, and Burns wrote in the summer of 1936: "I should like your essay better . . . if you devoted a page or two to the 'ends' which 'science' must serve, to the union between ethics ('ends'), pure science ('relations') and applied science ('means'). It seems to me that in so doing you will also show more concretely how the social disciplines can make a unified attack on the problem before you." Mitchell responded in August that he had inserted a paragraph on ends into the address (Burns folder, correspondence section, Wesley Mitchell papers). That social science was about means and not ends was, I think, a main proposition for Mitchell; that it could clarify thinking about ends was a qualification.

15 Mitchell (1922); Mitchell (1937: 20–57).

16 L.S. Mitchell (1953: 184); Mitchell (1937: 46–47, 55); Alchon (1985: 35–37).

17 Mitchell (1937: 101, 134). See also Mitchell (1934b: 613).

18 In the 1911 letter quoted earlier (L.S. Mitchell 1953: 183) he wrote that while still a doctoral student, "I knew definitely that I had found my work in research." That Mitchell truly loved his research work comes through clearly at many points in his wife's account of their lives (see e.g., L.S. Mitchell 1953: 180).

19 The next three paragraphs are based on Alchon (1985); L.S. Mitchell (1953: 350–356); and Stone (1945: 5–10).

20 There are conflicting accounts of who originated certain aspects of the program that eventually became the National Bureau, but it is certainly conceivable that key figures arrived at certain ideas independently.

21 Mitchell's report to the Bureau Board of Directors upon completion of the first National Income estimates, quoted in L.S. Mitchell (1953: 355–356).

22 L.S. Mitchell (1953: 332) notes Mitchell's opinion that "social and economic problems are best attacked through group work" (see also p. 348).

23 The quote is from L.S. Mitchell (1953: 352). The account of internal Bureau organization is drawn from the author's interviews with Geoffrey Moore and Moses Abramovitz, June 1993. See also Mitchell (1945: 34–35).

24 L.S. Mitchell (1953: 171); Burns (1952: 37–8); Mitchell (1919).

25 On Mitchell's choice of Macauley and other original staff members see Alchon (1985: 59). Mills was Mitchell's colleague at Columbia and author in the mid-1920s of the leading textbook on statistical methods for economists. On business cycles as the second NBER research project see Alchon (1985: 74).

26 The quote is from L.S. Mitchell (1953: 343); Mitchell to R. Meeker October 13, 1922, correspondence section, Mitchell papers; Ross (1991: 404).

27 On Mitchell's ideas on cooperation between the disciplines see Mitchell (1937: 361–362, 369–372), and L.S. Mitchell (1953: 345–347).

28 On the founding of the SSRC and Ruml's role see Fisher (1993: chapter 2); on Ruml's views see Fisher (1933: 33) or Alchon (1985: 118–124).

29 Hoover to Mitchell July 29, 1921; Mitchell to Hoover August 3, 1921; both in L.S. Mitchell (1953: 364–365).

30 Mitchell et al. (1923: 2); Alchon (1985: 85–86, 102).

31 Alchon (1985: 89, 100–102, 107–108, 137); Mitchell et al. (1923: xxxiii).

32 Barber (1985: 65–66); Alchon (1985: 140).

33 Berle (1933); see also Beard (1933).

34 Mitchell to Keppel, quoted in Alchon (1985: 156).

35 Mitchell (1934a: 27–28); Mitchell (1940: 9–15); Mitchell (1945: 14–15).

36 Mitchell (1945: 15); Ross (1991: 419); Heaton (1952: 198–203).

37 Karl (1974: 235–236); Clawson (1981: 43).

38 Clawson (1981: 45–46); Karl (1974: 245–249).

39 Mitchell's failure to stay on his research schedule during this period is shown

by reading Mitchell (1933: 17), Mitchell (1934a: 14–16), and Mitchell (1935: 23).

40 Mitchell to Willets December 29, 1941 and May 22, 1942, Willets folder, correspondence section, Mitchell papers.

41 When Fulbright remarked that he thought the job of the social sciences was to prevent wars, not to help fight them, Mitchell noted that the nation's current approach to postwar international affairs was also an improvement over that which had prevailed after the First World War (U.S. Congress 1945: 739–744, 779–782).

42 Burns to Mitchell, summer 1936, Burns folder, correspondence section, Mitchell papers.

43 Mitchell (1931: 107). Elsewhere, speaking for the NBER, he wrote (Mitchell 1940: 10) that "Emphatically we do not hold that all attempts to improve economic organization should be postponed until economic science has been perfected. On the contrary, our annual reports have recognized the necessity of attacking issues as they arise with whatever insight men possess."

44 Lynd's arguments are representative of a more widespread "purposivist" position in American social science, as described by Smith (1994).

45 Not surprisingly for such a strong advocate of scientific objectivity, Mitchell said little in his public addresses that would reveal his political views. In my opinion Alchon (1985) and Ross (1991), who label Mitchell a social democrat and a liberal respectively, are closer to the mark than Fisher (1993: 32), who characterizes him as a "sophisticated conservative who wished to preserve the underlying structure of society."

46 Mitchell (1937: 27, 369–370, 381–383); Mitchell (1939c: 3).

47 L.S. Mitchell (1953: 566); Lynd (1939: 220).

48 Though he was well aware of problems in the process, such as the ability of self-serving interest groups to hinder attempts to improve the general welfare.

49 See Mitchell (1934b: 611–613) or Mitchell (1933: lxxiv).

REFERENCES

Alchon, G. (1985). *The Invisible Hand of Planning: Capitalism, Social Science, and the State in the 1920s*, Princeton: Princeton University Press.

Barber, W.J. (1985). *From New Era to New Deal: Herbert Hoover, the Economists and American Economic Policy, 1921–1933*, Cambridge: Cambridge University Press.

Beard, C. (1933). "Recent Social Trends," *Yale Review* 22 (March): 596.

Berle, A.A. (1933). "Review of *Recent Social Trends*," *Saturday Review of Literature* 9: 533–535.

Burns, A.F. (ed.) (1952). *Wesley Clair Mitchell: The Economic Scientist*, New York: NBER.

Clawson, M. (1981). *New Deal Planning: The National Resources Planning Board*, Baltimore: Johns Hopkins University Press.

Committee on Recent Economic Changes (1929). *Recent Economic Changes in the United States*, 2 vols, New York: McGraw-Hill.

Fisher, D. (1993). *Fundamental Development of the Social Sciences: Rockefeller Philanthropy and the United States Social Science Research Council*, Ann Arbor: University of Michigan Press.

Friedman, M. (1953). *Essays in Positive Economics*, Chicago: University of Chicago Press.

Gay, E. and W. Mitchell (1933). *Thirteenth Annual Report of the Directors of Research*, New York: NBER.

Goodwin, C.D. (1995). "The Promise of Expertise: Walter Lippmann and the Policy Sciences," *Policy Sciences* 28: 317–345.

Heaton, H. (1952). *A Scholar in Action: Edwin F. Gay*, Cambridge, Mass.: Harvard University Press.

Karl, B. (1974). *Charles E. Merriam and the Study of Politics*, Chicago: University of Chicago Press.

Lynd, R.S. (1939). *Knowledge for What? The Place of Social Science in American Culture*, Princeton: Princeton University Press.

Lynd, R.S. and H. Lynd (1929). *Middletown*, New York: Harcourt Brace.

Mitchell, L.S. (1953). *Two Lives: The Story of Wesley Clair Mitchell and Myself*, New York: Simon & Schuster.

Mitchell, W. (1913). *Business Cycles*, Berkeley: University of California Press.

——— (1919). "Review of *The Review of Economic Statistics*," *American Economic Review* 9 (December): 872–876.

——— (1922). "The Crisis of 1920 and the Problem of Controlling Business Cycles," *American Economic Review* 12 (March): 20–32.

——— (ed.) (1923). *Business Cycles and Unemployment*, New York: McGraw-Hill.

——— (1926). "The Research Fellowships of the Social Science Research Council," *Political Science Quarterly* 41 (December): 604–607.

——— (1927). *Business Cycles: The Problem and its Setting*, New York: NBER.

——— (1931). "Engineering, Economics, and the Problem of Social Well-being: The Economist's View," *Mechanical Engineering* 53 (February): 105–110.

——— (1933). "Review of Findings," in President's Research Committee on Social Trends, *Recent Social Trends in the United States*, 2 vols, New York: McGraw-Hill.

——— (1934a). *Fourteenth Annual Report of the Director of Research*, New York: NBER.

——— (1934b). "Mr. Hoover's Challenge to Liberty," *Political Science Quarterly* 49 (December): 599–614.

——— (1935). *Fifteenth Annual Report of the Director of Research,* New York: NBER.

——— (1937). *The Backward Art of Spending Money*, New York: McGraw-Hill.

——— (1939a). "Science and the State of Mind," *Science* 89 (January 6): 1–4.

——— (1939b). *The National Bureau Enters its Twentieth Year: Report of the Director of Research*, New York: NBER.

——— (1939c). "The Public Relations of Science," *Science* 90 (December 29): 599–607.

——— (1940). *The National Bureau's Social Function: Twentieth Annual Report of the Director of Research*, New York: NBER.

——— (1941). "Economic Resources and their Employment," in *Studies in Economics and Industrial Relations*, Philadelphia: University of Pennsylvania Press, 1–23.

——— (1945). *The National Bureau's First Quarter Century: Twenty-Fifth Annual Report of the Director of Research*, New York: NBER.

National Planning Board (1934). *Final Report, 1933–34*, Washington, DC: USGPO.

Ross, D. (1991). *The Origins of American Social Science*, Cambridge: Cambridge University Press.

——— (1994). *Modernist Impulses in the Social Sciences*, Baltimore: The Johns Hopkins University Press.

Rutherford, M. (1994). *Institutions in Economics: The Old and the New Institutionalism*, Cambridge: Cambridge University Press.

Smith, M. (1994). *Social Science in the Crucible*, Durham, NC: Duke University Press.

Social Science Research Council (1928). *Fourth Annual Report, 1927–28*, New York: SSRC.

——— (1929). *Fifth Annual Report, 1928–29*, New York: SSRC.

Stone, N.I. (1945). "The Beginnings of the National Bureau of Economic Research," in W. Mitchell, *The National Bureau's First Quarter Century*, New York: NBER, 5–10.

United States Congress (1945). *Hearings on Science Legislation*, Senate, Committee on Military Affairs, Hearings, 79th Congress, 1st Session, parts 1–6, Washington, DC: USGPO.

7

VISION ACCOMPLISHED

Harold Moulton and Leo Pasvolsky of the Brookings Institution as champions of a new world order

Craufurd D. Goodwin

INTRODUCTION

Economic policy advisers come in various sizes, shapes, and flavors. It may be useful to construct a simple taxonomy. One distinction suggested by Alvin Gouldner is between intellectuals in the vanguard of a popular movement and technical intelligentsia who simply serve those in power (Gouldner 1979). A more fine-grained categorization is possible within these two types. Within the technical intelligentsia there are economists who are prepared to hold a mirror for princes, or to serve presidents, so long as they may remain true to their principles in so doing. Martin Feldstein fits in this category, resigning from the Reagan administration when it acted on principles with which he had no sympathy. Also within the technical intelligentsia are economists like Arthur Okun who, as chair of Lyndon Johnson's CEA, disagreed with the administration but remained to confront it in private. The most reprehensible variant of the technical intelligentsia, presumably, is the economist who is prepared to advise princes, no matter how distasteful their objectives or methods.

All of the pioneers of economic policy advice examined in this part seem to fall under the category of "vanguard intellectual" rather than technical intelligentsia. They bring their own ideas more than just their technical expertise to the policy table. The ideas are of three kinds, again reflective of distinctive types of adviser. The first, Irving Fisher, comes to macroeconomic policy problems with a single solution, more or less, which is to maintain stable prices. Others in this genre include Henry George with the single tax and more recently, Hall and Robushka, with the flat tax. The second example, Wesley Mitchell, comes to policy with an eye on systems. In particular, he looks for better economic policy to emerge from better systems of governance that deliver wise policy where it really counts. Outside of government he calls for excellent policy-relevant economic research to be conducted in universities and such bodies as the National Bureau of Economic Research and the Social Science Research Council.

The two persons whose careers are examined in this chapter fall in a third category of vanguard intellectual—those with a vision. Such persons have a picture in their minds of something approaching a policy utopia, and their task is to persuade others of this vision and to figure out how to get there. In our own day, the most prominent visionary policy intellectuals are those who see an unrestricted free market delivering efficiency, justice, and human liberty. Milton Friedman expresses this vision well and sees the path to it paved with monetary growth rules, automatic stabilizers, and deregulation in all directions.

The bright picture seen by these two visionaries, Harold Moulton and Leo Pasvolsky, was not of a nation on a hill, but of the entire planet on a hill. Over a quarter century as president and program director, respectively, at the powerful Brookings Institution, they set forth a conception of an integrated world economy coordinated by cooperative nation states that at a minimum would eliminate Depression and prevent war. What is most unusual about this case is that, unlike almost all other economic visionaries before and since, they concluded by the ends of their careers in the years after the Second World War, that they had achieved their objective.

ROOTS OF THE GLOBAL VISION

The Brookings Institution was established in 1927 primarily to bring "economy and efficiency" into the *domestic* affairs of government. This was the intention of the founder Robert Brookings and of the original staff. Quickly, however, foreign affairs began to intrude. Indeed, a remarkable and striking feature of Brookings in its early days was the rapid internationalization of its agenda. Between the First World War and the Second World War, international relations presented to the United States and to Brookings three challenges: how to prevent a recurrence of the First World War into which the United States might again be drawn; how to facilitate American membership in a rapidly changing global economic system and thereby assure high employment and growth; and how to formulate policy toward close neighbors in whom the United States had an inevitable special interest, particularly countries in the hemisphere. In response to these three challenges the senior staff at Brookings formulated a vision of how the world worked and of how it might be reformed in better days. In a remarkably short time the compelling power of this vision caused international affairs to dominate purely domestic issues and to remain a central focus of the Institution up to the present time.

During the early years Brookings' major successes on the domestic scene were to improve governmental performance through the introduction of a Federal budget, and to provide critiques of such revolutionary new public policies as the National Industrial Recovery Act. These were achieved well outside government, almost as if Brookings were a public conscience. Indeed, some New Dealers thought of Brookings as their most annoying opponent, always ready to expose your faults in a more or less friendly way. In foreign affairs, however, a characteristically different Brookings stance emerged, that of sympathetic partner with those in government who were committed to working together for common aims, even though the two parts of the Brookings public policy agenda, domestic and international, were, as it turned out, perfectly consistent. On the domestic scene Brookings was a leading critic of most New Deal policies that required fundamental interference with the free-market system. The enemies of the domestic economy, the Brookings staff thought, were a mix of misguided intellectuals and selfish special interests who threatened through their devices to damage or destroy the delicate free-market mechanism. In foreign affairs, Brookings found itself closely allied with leaders of the Department of State, and against those inside and outside of government who believed that America must remain a relatively closed economy. Brookings' "internationalist" policy posture, just as its domestic one, was that misguided meddling in either domain, either by reformists and interventionists at home, or by protectionists and isolationists abroad, could injure the delicate structure upon which peace and prosperity depended.

The Brookings staff performed two tasks in particular during the early years of their attention to American international relations: they struggled to understand seeming policy enigmas presented by changing conditions overseas, and they prepared public opinion for support of broad internationalist approaches and particular policies that they became convinced should be implemented. The early writings of Brookings' economists were addressed either to structural features of the world economy, like trade flows and exchange rates, or to the behavior of individual constituent nations like the United Kingdom, Japan, Bulgaria, and Poland. Both kinds of study recognized the interdependence of the parts of the global system and the relevance to the United States even of a remote Balkan nation. Some pioneering comparative economic studies were conducted at the request of foreign governments. Others, such as "confidential analyses with reference to the British financial situation for use by the Treasury Department," were commissioned by the U.S. government (H.G. Moulton to F.P. Keppel, October 31, 1933, Carnegie Corporation Archives). There is little attention in these works to the need for complex modelling of conditions, to the possibility that several equally reasonable but alternative policy paths might exist, or to the chance that "the people" might never be made to appreciate and endorse the policy that was "best" for them in some objective sense.

Despite its professed dependence on "fact," rather simple market theory more than empiricism lay at the core of Brookings' international policy position. The Brookings economists were captivated less by an ideology that associated political and social liberty necessarily with economic freedom, than they were by the potential of the international market mechanism, if cherished, to yield high incomes for all, and if neglected or mistreated, to bring economic collapse and a frustrated resort to totalitarian alternatives to democracy.

THE GLOBAL VISION OF HAROLD MOULTON

Harold Moulton, the first head of the Institute of Economics, a predecessor body to the later Brookings, became the first president of the new consolidated Brookings Institution in 1928. The Institute retained a separate identity within the Institution until 1942, and this was where Moulton's heart remained. It was Moulton and his close associate Leo Pasvolsky who drew attention repeatedly to the importance of the health of the world economy for American peace and prosperity. In the years after the First World War, the Institute carried out eighteen studies of various aspects of the economic dislocations caused by the war that had now to be resolved: crushing war debts for some of the victors and reparations burdens for the vanquished; the rise of new economic powers like Japan; and crises in various world markets both for raw materials and finished products. The most important of these studies were conducted by Moulton and Pasvolsky themselves. They include: *America and the Balance Sheet of Europe*, 1921; *Germany's Capacity to Pay*, 1923; *Russian Debts and Russian Reconstruction*, 1924; *The French Debt Problem*, 1925; *War Debts and World Prosperity*, 1932; and *Japan: An Economic and Financial Appraisal*, 1931.[1]

Moulton saw the roots of the interwar economic difficulties of the United States to lie in the nation's substantial and growing involvement in the world economy. Moulton had received his training and early employment at the University of Chicago in a strong market-oriented tradition. Indeed, his treatment of America's economic fate sounded very much like that of several prominent members of the contemporary Chicago faculty. Their central message was that growth in efficiency and output depended inevitably upon the extent of the market, and this meant buying and selling overseas—for the United States as for any other nation. Yet this route to economic growth contained hazards, which the interwar years were revealing with painful clarity.

The explanation for the interwar economic troubles, provided by Moulton on numerous occasions in the 1920s and 1930s, was roughly as follows. During the First World War the physical destruction reduced the capacity of European nations to produce and at the same time stimulated expansion of production in competitors, especially the United States. At the end of the war the Europeans sought to regain their productivity and their former markets, while the Americans tried hard to retain their new, more favored, position. These "maladjustments" had somehow to be resolved in a cooperative spirit. But the wrong road was chosen to do so. A series of ultimately self-destructive public policies were adopted in almost all the major trading nations of the world, and these combined to produce collective disaster. Both the weak and the strong resorted increasingly to protective devices to achieve their desired trade balances. Together restrictive measures threatened the growth of world trade, the only means by which the otherwise irreconcilable objectives could be achieved. Moulton explained to a Chicago audience in 1933: "The effect of these progressive and accumulating restrictions, intended to preserve stability for each particular nation, has been to demoralize international trade in general and with it the production of wealth. Instead of enabling men and women in all countries to produce and trade with the people of other countries, these policies have everywhere resulted in unemployment and impoverishment" (Moulton, "International Economic Recovery," March 25, 1933, p. 3, Moulton Papers).

To compound the problem of a crumbling global economic system the victors in the war insisted on severe reparations from the vanquished. However, in order for a substantial capital transfer to take place from losers to winners it was necessary, in particular, for Germany to achieve a substantial trade surplus, and for the United States to run a trade deficit. In Germany's weakened condition a continuing trade surplus of great magnitude was simply impossible; in the United States, on the other hand, a sustained trade deficit was unacceptable because like other nations its principal objective was to provide "maximum employment and economic activity within its borders" (Moulton, "International Economic Rehabilitation," p. 7). The result for the Allies of insisting upon a wholly unworkable policy of international economic relations, Moulton said, was to generate panic all around. "Confidence," upon which the world economy depended, simply melted. The effect of panic, and the runs which ensued on commercial and central banks, was to cripple the reconstructed gold standard that had just been put in place. With foreign exchange uncertainties added to growing trade protection, the global economic system unravelled and with it the prosperity of the constituent nations. The Dawes Plan of economic assistance to Germany (1924–30) temporarily limited the decline, but when it ended, collapse ensued. It was an unassailable fact, Moulton said, that "American trade and industry" depended upon "a revival of European trade and the restoration of stable conditions abroad." Some American citizens were lulled into a false sense of safety by the knowledge that their own markets were predominantly domestic. He listed a wide range of industries that were, in fact, heavily dependent on foreign sales (e.g., cotton, tobacco, lard, typewriters, sewing machines) (Moulton, "International Economic Rehabilitation," pp. 8–9), and he observed that weakness in these markets passed quickly through the entire economy.

The attempt of nations to achieve economic autarky, Moulton claimed, was based not on evidence and real calculations of the opportunity cost but on dangerous myth. "*What is needed above all else in this distressed world*," he said, "*is economic stability and an expanding purchasing power in Europe*" (italics in original) (Moulton, "International Economic Rehabilitation," p. 12). Moulton explained how an international free-market system could become the engine of American progress, absorbing large proportions of the output of farm and factory. When this world trading system was damaged or crippled in any way the transmission belt of trouble to the domestic economy was the banking and financial system, which was inherently fragile. The root of the problem must not be thought of as monetary or financial, however. The cause lay offshore in global market crises, and that was where the solution too must lie.

Moulton was convinced that policies of domestic market intervention and restriction, such as those proposed under the National Recovery Act, would simply worsen the Depression, and he was never attracted to Keynesian schemes for stimulation of aggregate domestic effective demand. The only hope for salvation, he insisted, lay in creating and sustaining a strong and effective global trading system. He explained: "There are three primary lines along which business recovery may be promoted by international cooperation: (1) by the revision of commercial policies; (2) by the restoration of the gold standard in all the leading countries; and (3) by the settlement of the reparation and war debt problems" (Moulton, "International Economic Rehabilitation," p. 2). Accordingly, one of the principal components of a Brookings "Program for the Future," set forth in 1938, was "fundamental studies in the reconstruction of international economic relations" ("Memorandum sent to Will Hays by Leverett S. Lyon, February 17, 1938," p. 8, Moulton Papers). At this date Moulton identified public policy errors as the main causes of economic distress, but he did not propose political research on how these policies came to be or how the policy-making process could be improved. His approach was, instead, to root out as many of the errors as possible by exposing them to the truth. Then he hoped nations would construct an international economic system that would be resistant to future tinkering.

Even though charges of superficiality in its diagnosis and lack of scientific rigor remained among the most serious obstacles faced by Brookings to gaining full acceptance among policymakers and professional economists, Moulton and his colleagues did not lose confidence. On the contrary, they became pioneers in the unabashed marketing of their policy advice. For example, in 1933 Brookings presented a series of radio broadcasts on domestic economic topics, and Moulton sought funds to extend the radio coverage on an even grander scale to problems of the world economy. He argued that the ordinary journalist was ill-equipped to interpret complex questions of international economic policy and needed the assistance of professional interpreters like himself. He wrote as follows to the Rockefeller adviser Raymond Fosdick, soliciting a personal contribution from John D. Rockefeller, Jr. for the media program: "it is highly essential that broadcasts undertaken to interpret the complex economic issues which will be before the World Economic Conference [in 1933] should be genuinely authoritative in character and presented in popular style." Moulton proposed to send a team of three broadcaster-analysts to London for the duration of this conference: Felix Morley, Leo Pasvolsky, and Lewis Lorwin. Despite some interest from the Rockefeller Foundation staff who were consulted by Fosdick, the request was denied (H.G. Moulton to Raymond B. Fosdick, April 14, 1933, Rockefeller Family Papers, Record Group 2, Box 154, Cultural Interests File, Rockefeller Archive Center).

In the mid-1930s Moulton made repeated attempts to reorganize the Institution's structure so as to emphasize the priority he placed on the health of world systems. In 1935 he proposed to the Rockefeller Foundation that he organize and they pay for "An Institute of International Affairs" with an intensified focus on comparative international studies so as "to make the experience of foreign countries, which have attempted to meet problems with which we are currently grappling, available to American legislators and administrators" (Docket, Meeting of Rockefeller Foundation Board of Trustees, April 10, 1935, p. 70, Record Group 1.1, Series 200, Box 310, Folder 3697, Rockefeller Foundation Archives). In 1937 Moulton and Pasvolsky asked Rockefeller also for support of a major three-year project "to formulate a long range commercial policy for the United States with regard to the relation of this policy to the policies of other countries." They contended that "a Brookings study appearing during a period of intense public discussion," prior to expiration in 1940 of the president's authority to enter into foreign trade agreements, "might play a decisive role in the formation of public opinion and public policy" (Memo, J.V.S. [John Van Sickle], April 30, 1937, "Brookings Institution—Study of International Commercial Policy: Interview H. Moulton and L. Pasvolsky," Record Group 1.1, Series 200 S, Box 313, Folder 3752, Rockefeller Foundation Archives).

Moulton's argument in defense of this latter request was straightforward: The depression had clogged the "channels of international trade" with "restrictions" and had induced "exchange demoralization." International cooperation leading to "a series of international commercial agreements" was essential for the "re-establishment of world prosperity." To help accomplish this goal Brookings would provide for public policymakers "a broad comprehensive analysis of the problems and issues involved in the formulation of new constructive policies." It would also help to create an "informed public opinion" supportive of such moves. The specific studies proposed were on the nature of tariffs and what are now called "non-tariff barriers," treaty negotiation, and alternative foreign-exchange regimes ("Memorandum on a Research Project Entitled International Commercial Relations and Policies Prepared by the Brookings Institution," Record Group 1.1, Series 200S, Box 313, Folder 3752, Rockefeller Foundation Archives).

Moulton and Pasvolsky believed that arid college teaching on international economics contributed to unsatisfactory public understanding of policy problems, and they proposed also "to produce a modern up-to-date textbook on the theory and practice of international trade." They called for collaborative international research on international economic policy and suggested that Pasvolsky travel through Europe to explore the possibility of joint endeavors (Memo, J.V.S., April 30, 1937, loc. cit.). A travel grant was provided by the Rockefeller Foundation for Pasvolsky to explore the possibility of systematic international collaboration. Raymond Fosdick, the Foundation's president, explained to Pasvolsky that he felt "this an opportunity to take leadership in attack on one of the most vexing international situations of world today." Pasvolsky traveled widely in 1937, found a positive response to his overtures, and received offers of cooperation from, among others, Henry Clay, Josiah Stamp, and Hubert Henderson in the United Kingdom, Charles Rist in France, William Rappard in Switzerland, and Dupriez in Belgium. But, in the end, his efforts came to naught. Rockefeller continued its longstanding general support to Brookings but declined to fund the collaborative commercial policy study. The high cost may have been a factor, but a conversation between Rockefeller staff member John Van Sickle and Herbert Feis, economic adviser to the State Department, may have been determinative. Van Sickle reported that Feis "gave project one in ten chance of being really useful. Thinks critical analyses in Germany and Italy quite impossible, better chance for factual studies, but even here not complete freedom. Very desirable that Germany participate in discussion of the international synthesis. Work would not bring out any really creative new ideas unless the noneconomic imponderables received adequate consideration and the Germans would certainly thrust these into the discussion" (Chronology, Brookings Institution Study of International Commercial Policy, Record Group 1.1, Series 200, Box 314, Folder 3733, Rockefeller Foundation Archives). Another reason why this imaginative multilateral project never progressed was because, as Feis hinted, war was just over the horizon. The time for brave discussion of systemic regeneration had passed—at least for a while.

THE PROSPECT OF WAR CONCENTRATES THE MIND

The outbreak of the Second World War seemed virtual confirmation to Moulton and his colleagues of the correctness of their diagnosis of critical problems in international relations. During the interwar years, they explained, a "profound disruption of foreign trade and virtual dissolution of the international monetary and credit system" had led to "the complete collapse of the League of Nations and of other instrumentalities designed to eliminate war and to promote constructive co-operation among nations." Thus economic disaster was followed by "a reversal of the great democratic movement of the nineteenth century and the emergence and adoption of conceptions which are in fundamental conflict with the principles—political, economic, racial, and religious—upon which the so-called American system has been based" ("Reorientation of America's Foreign Policy," 1/28/41, Moulton Papers). Moulton's message was slightly different from that of Friedrich Hayek who a few years later pictured the "road to serfdom" through creeping socialism, and Joseph Schumpeter who foretold the demise of capitalism from destruction of the entrepreneurs. Moulton believed more simply that all humans insisted upon employment and an opportunity for self-improvement. If one set of political arrangements would not yield these results, people would try another. The conditions required for economic growth and prosperity—a free, well-functioning world economy—could be sustained by a democracy, but there was no guarantee that it would do so. If the world economy were damaged, as it had been in the 1920s and 1930s, the people of the injured nations could be expected to reject the political system which permitted this to happen. This the peoples of the fascist nations had done. Authoritarian rule and international conflict followed necessarily.

So as to be ready at the end of the war with policy proposals that would prevent such an economic and political breakdown from occurring again, with the assistance of consultants led by John B. Condliffe of the University of California, Moulton "formulated a rather comprehensive program of research, which builds upon previous studies in the international field and integrates these and other inquiries in relation to the great problem of world economic reconstruction." Moulton's conviction in March of 1940 was that at the end of the Second World War the Allies would have one more chance to do right what had been done so badly at the end of the First World War. This time they must recognize clearly that economic issues had primacy over all others and that a healthy world economy must be their overriding goal: "the neglect of economic considerations after the World War was a major cause of the economic and political insecurity which has characterized the ensuing twenty years . . . the fundamental economic disequilibrium then existing has been aggravated. . . . It is only too clear from past experience that the fundamental bases of enduring peace are economic in character." Moulton requested a grant of $110,000 from the Rockefeller Foundation to conduct a comprehensive investigation "of the world's experience in the field of international economic relations during the twenty-year period from 1919 to 1939" so as to increase the "knowledge and understanding on the part of the public of the significance of the economic factors" as a basis for a postwar "constructive program" ("Application to the Rockefeller Foundation for Support of a Research Project Entitled 'Economic Bases of Enduring Peace'," Moulton Papers). Moulton was outraged when Joseph Willits of the Rockefeller Foundation replied that some parts of the program proposed were already underway at the Council on Foreign Relations and elsewhere, while for other parts the project "would scarcely permit any adequate new work" (Joseph A. Willits to Harold Moulton, April 12, 1940, Moulton Papers).

This exchange with the Rockefeller Foundation epitomized the tone of the Brookings Institution program on international affairs during most of its first two decades. Moulton was confident that he had found the secret of the worldwide economic depression: collapse had been brought on in an extremely fragile international economic system stressed by war, buffeted by foolish protectionist and reparations policies, and brought to its knees finally by the failure of nations to cooperate in improving the system and making it work. He was absolutely certain that he had arrived at the correct diagnosis and that given adequate support he could discover the right remedy, and yet sponsors seemed unwilling to listen or even to try to understand. He exclaimed in disgust to Willits: "You say you don't think that the proposal bags a particular target; we think you haven't yet seen the target" (Harold Moulton to Joseph H. Willits, April 17, 1940, Moulton Papers). It was in this mood of the frustrated prophet, unappreciated by those with the power to help, that Brookings entered the war years.

THE MISSIONARY COMMITMENT OF LEO PASVOLSKY

Moulton's closest colleague and research collaborator from the early 1920s onward was Leo Pasvolsky, an economist trained at City College (A.B., 1916), Columbia University, the University of Geneva, and Brookings' own Graduate School (Ph.D., 1936). Although their policy positions were virtually identical, Moulton and Pasvolsky came from very different backgrounds and traditions. The latter came with his parents to the United States from Russia as a child in 1905 and as a young man became an expert on the Soviet Union and Eastern Europe. During the First World War he edited a newspaper and a magazine in the Russian language and was editor of the English-language *Russian Review*. After joining the Institute of Economics in 1922 he became one of the pioneer "think-tank in-and-outers" serving on leave from Brookings for periods in the Department of Commerce (1934–35) and in the Department of State (1935–46). Pasvolsky was a student of European affairs and of authoritarian regimes, and he brought the perspective of the Russian émigré to his investigations of global political and economic issues. If Moulton carried the vision to academia and to "the people," Pasvolsky brought it within government.[2]

During the 1930s and in the war Moulton and Pasvolsky polished their vision of a postwar world in which an open and stable world economy would be preserved within some structure of political cooperation among nations. In order for the vision to become reality, however, a major challenge in political architecture lay before them. Although Pasvolsky spent most of the prewar years in the State Department his presence was still evident at Brookings, and his hand can be seen in a proposal in January 1941 to the Carnegie Corporation to carry out a study of how to achieve "reorientation of American foreign policy" so as "to meet the impact of changed conditions and to promote eventual economic and political reconstruction." Pasvolsky believed that it was essential before war's end to identify the best strategy for America (not yet a combatant) under three possible outcomes: (1) a German victory, (2) a British victory, and (3) a "stalemate." In the case of the third outcome, which before Pearl Harbor seemed quite possible:

> Three alternatives would present themselves to the United States: (1) to maintain a policy of political, if not economic, isolation from Europe, meanwhile developing the most powerful defenses possible; (2) to conclude a political and economic alliance with the British Empire for the purposes of mutual defense and constructive cooperation; or (3) to attempt to work out with both the British Empire and the totalitarian regimes some new conception of world organization which might ensure peace for the future and promote economic reconstruction.
>
> ("Reorientation of American Foreign Policy," January 28, 1941, Moulton Papers)

There is a good deal of high-flown speculation in Pasvolsky's proposals about how best to reach "enduring peace and prosperity." What were required, he contended, were "military, economic, and moral disarmament." How to achieve this blessed state was the question. Free trade was a primary starting point, followed by global political reorganization. An "alliance of the democracies" alone was probably not desirable because it would not be enduring and over its life might be weak and defensive in objective. Moreover, an alliance of democracies might lead to "an alliance of dictatorships" thus negating any strategic benefits it might yield. With so much ill-feeling in Europe Pasvolsky doubted that a more restricted "European federation" could be achieved for at least a decade after the war. He concluded that a successor to the League of Nations was called for, with international police power accompanied by widespread disarmament among member nations ("International Post-war Problems," undated, 22 pp., Moulton Papers). These early notions are especially interesting in light of Pasvolsky's later role in the birth of the United Nations.

A theme that emerges clearly in the 1941 Pasvolsky proposal and that he repeated throughout the war, and thereafter, is that because of an unalterable and growing dependence of the American economy on raw materials beyond its borders, the United States would be bound ever more tightly into the world economy as the years went on. Whereas Brookings studies in the 1920s and 1930s stressed the importance of foreign markets for their demand stimulus to American output and employment, the emphasis shifted now to sustained access to those inputs essential to production and supply. With considerable prescience, and OPEC still two decades away, the Brookings blueprint in the 1940s called for "suppression of all the *preferential* measures benefiting the inhabitants of the countries which possess these materials" and "measures to be taken to avoid or repress the abuse of the international private monopoly of raw materials, should these monopolies adopt a restrictive policy of curtailment of the products in order to maintain high prices" (ibid., p. 19).

The distinctive characteristic of the 1941 Pasvolsky plan was a creative political dimension to complement the familiar economic doctrine; this feature did not, however, appeal to the potential sponsors. Moulton and Pasvolsky after years of criticizing the foreign policies of the United States and other nations believed that now was the time to spell out alternative and optimum policies in detail. Their vision of a strong, well-constructed, global free-market system had always guided their recommendations. Now, they suggested, the time had come to figure out how to make this vision a practical reality. Yet this creative task of institutional and policy innovation was unfamiliar to sponsors and the need unpersuasive to them. Elihu Root, Jr., a Carnegie Corporation trustee, noted that the proposed Brookings research on "political policies" was "probably outside their bailiwick, although I do think that somebody ought to import some realism into that discussion." Others at Carnegie shared this view (Elihu Root, Jr. to Frederick P. Keppel, January 31, 1941; and Edward Mead Earle to Frederick P. Keppel, February 3, 1941, Carnegie Corporation Archives).

The Carnegie Corporation joined the Rockefeller Foundation in rejecting even the economic component of Pasvolsky's blueprint for a new foreign policy, and Moulton was again deeply distressed at the declination. (Vannevar Bush, on the boards of both the Carnegie Corporation and Brookings, reported Moulton's anguish to the Carnegie staff (Vannevar Bush to Walter A. Jessup, May 16, 1941, Carnegie Corporation Archives).) America's entry into the war ended further searches for support of the Brookings "reorientation" study. However, the conception did not die and Pasvolsky pressed many of the same ideas within government as special assistant to Secretary of State Cordell Hull. In anticipation of Pasvolsky's ultimate return and as part of a reorganization of Brookings, a proposal was discussed for a new "Division of International Studies" to be concerned with postwar reconstruction, international commercial, monetary, and cooperative problems, and "comparative studies of significant problems common to various countries."

Under this plan an "international center" would also be created within the proposed new division to bring together for extended conferences "mature scholars [connected both with academic and government agencies] from various countries . . . on international economic and political problems" ("Division of International Studies," no date, Moulton Papers). Brookings seemed determined to extend its global thrust and seek converts to its visions. But again the war cut off discussion of the proposal for the duration of hostilities.

Government was the paramount target constituency for Brookings' output in the eyes of its founder, trustees, and early staff. Therefore, it seemed quite natural for Pasvolsky to carry the Brookings message within government walls, where it was at least as liable to be heard and have impact as without. Moreover, the work style of pursuing a single visionary program followed by Moulton and Pasvolsky made the message to be carried nicely unambiguous. Pasvolsky found among the senior officials of the State Department, and especially in his patron Cordell Hull, a sympathetic audience for the Brookings position. Nevertheless, he kept up a steady repetition of his recommendations for action to "re-open the channels of international trade." As he made the case in 1937 to Undersecretary Sumner Welles these included "a gradual relaxation and eventual abandonment of such extraordinary barriers to trade as quotas . . . downward adjustment of unreasonably high tariff rates . . . firm re-establishment of the most-favored nation principle . . . stable foreign exchange . . . adjustment of existing international debt obligations . . . resumption of international lending . . . and safeguards against dumping." Pasvolsky recommended pursuing both bilateral and multilateral routes to achieve these goals. He favored also creation of an ad hoc committee with representatives of six nations to explore "ideas and proposals that might arise" including one for an "International Fund" to relieve the foreign exchange problem (Confidential memorandum, Leo Pasvolsky to Sumner Welles, November 10, 1937, Box 1, Subject file: International Economic Relations 1937, Pasvolsky Papers). To support his internationalist agenda Pasvolsky fed to the senior State Department officials reports on the views of others who shared his own judgment, for example those of Paul Van Zeeland, the Dutch economist, whose inquiries were supported by the Carnegie Endowment for International Peace ("Paul Van Zeeland's Ideas on Post-war Economic Reconstruction," March 12, 1940, Box 1, Subject file: International Economic Relations 1940–41, Pasvolsky Papers).

Even before America entered the war Pasvolsky was thinking about the postwar world. Here was an opportunity, he saw, in effect to plan for Utopia, and he urged that it be grasped ("Suggestions for the Secretary's Conversation with the Secretaries of the Treasury, Commerce and Agriculture Regarding our Consultations with Neutrals," Box 1, Subject file: International Economic Relations 1940–41, Pasvolsky Papers). By September of 1941 he had developed an outline for an extended study of "The United States and the Post-War World" through which after the "destruction of the totalitarian systems" the United States, although not a combatant, would take the lead in "the establishment and maintenance of enduring peace and the promotion of economic development" ("The United States and the Post-War World (Outline of a Study)," September 16, 1941, Subject file: Postwar Planning 1941, Pasvolsky Papers). In his discussions within government of the need for a reorientation of American foreign policy in the months before America's entry into the war, Pasvolsky seemed almost to treat Brookings and "other research agencies" as analytical arms of government ("Reorientation of American Foreign Policy," Subject file: Postwar Planning 1941, Pasvolsky Papers).

Pasvolsky was assigned by Hull after war began "specifically to work on long-range problems bearing on the postwar future," and in this task he must have felt that he and Moulton would be vindicated at last. Hull remembered afterwards that Pasvolsky's "capacities were splendid, his service exceedingly valuable" (Hull 1948: 1626). Pasvolsky became, in effect, the first director of policy planning at State when in February 1941 he was made chief of a Division of Special Research to analyze and appraise "developments and conditions arising out of present disturbed international relations." This division was replaced in January 1943 by separate divisions of "economic studies" and "political studies" still under the general supervision of Pasvolsky ("Work in the Field of International Organization in the Department of State Prior to October 1943," October 4, 1944, Subject file: International Organizations State Department, Pasvolsky Papers). In 1942 Pasvolsky became director of research for an Advisory Committee on Post-war Foreign Policy (with Alger Hiss as a member of his staff). It was in connection with the work of this committee and its several subcommittees that Pasvolsky made use of the Council on Foreign Relations, and the Carnegie Endowment for International Peace, as well as their leaders such as James T. Shotwell, Isaiah Bowman, and Hamilton Fish Armstrong, the last two being made subcommittee chairmen. Clearly, the State Department felt itself faced for the first time with the need for large-scale social science research. Pasvolsky turned naturally for help to the communities he knew best, academe and the nongovernmental research institutions. In 1943 Pasvolsky was placed in charge of International Organization and Security Affairs in the State Department with responsibility for drafting the United Nations Charter; he was present at Bretton Woods, Dumbarton Oaks, and San Francisco; and he became chairman of the Coordination Committee of the United Nations Conference on International Organization at San Francisco. Secretary Hull depended heavily on Pasvolsky to explain the plans and proposals for the UN to President Roosevelt (Hull 1948: 732, 1628–1635, 1687). It is striking how close a resemblance Pasvolsky's statement of objectives for the new international organization bears to the positions he had taken with Moulton throughout the previous decade.[3] If Pasvolsky was one of the parents of international organization in the postwar world, then Brookings had been the day-care center.

Pasvolsky was by no means universally loved and admired in State. For some, the Brookings prescription for all the ills of the world economy seemed too simple, and even tiresome. Dean Acheson referred disparagingly to the "Hull–Pasvolsky establishment" and wrote that "Leo Pasvolsky was Mr. Hull's principal speech writer. Or, one might say, he wrote Mr. Hull's principal speech: for, whatever the occasion or title, the speech was apt to turn into a dissertation on the benefits of unhampered international trade and the true road to it through agreements reducing tariffs" (Acheson 1969: 55, 64). Acheson denigrated Pasvolsky's postwar planning:

> The whole effort, except for two results, seems to have been a singularly sterile one, uninspired by gifts either of insight or prophecy. One of these results was the foundation work for the United Nations Charter, the other, which laid an even broader foundation, the education of Senator Arthur Vandenburg to understand that beyond the borders of the United States existed a "vast external realm" which could and would affect profoundly our interests and our destiny!
>
> (Acheson 1969: 64)

POLICY ADVICE AT PEACE

The conditions to which Pasvolsky returned at Brookings and in the country at the end of the war were markedly different from those he left more than a decade before. In those earlier times Brookings perceived itself as a policy critic with a consistent explanation for both depression and conflict rooted in the breakdown of the international economic order. This explanation had found some sympathetic ears in the State Department, but outside most policymakers still sought diagnosis and remedy mainly at home. Now, after five years of war, not only had Pasvolsky moved to the center of power and been involved in key postwar planning, but also the Truman administration was set to follow closely precepts very similar to those policy prescriptions laid down by Moulton and Pasvolsky during the 1930s and repeated by Pasvolsky during the war. No reparations or unreasonable capital transfers were exacted from the Axis powers. Indeed, quite the opposite occurred: strenuous efforts were made to rehabilitate the losers as well as the winners in Europe and Asia through a host of programs, including a generous occupation, the Marshall Plan, and Point Four. The overall goal of American policy was to overcome the dislocations of war rather than add to them. Peace, it was agreed virtually all around, required a smoothly functioning world economy, and it should be the American objective to see that one was created. This had been the Brookings line for a quarter of a century.

The United States was now committed unequivocally to a policy of free trade, in recognition of both the growing importance of export markets and the mounting dependence on imported raw materials. The point made repeatedly by Moulton during the 1930s was now accepted unquestioningly, namely, that when a system of free trade began to crumble it acted as an international transmission belt for the creation of macroeconomic difficulties worldwide. The abortive International Trade Organization and its replacement, the General Agreement on Tariffs and Trade, were cornerstones of a policy to constrain this possibility.

Finally, with the objective of strengthening the international monetary and financial system the meeting at Bretton Woods had yielded an attractive alternative to the fragile gold standard. The new scheme preserved some of the gold standard's presumed merits, such as short-run stability of exchange rates, and saw the creation of the International Monetary Fund and World Bank to handle individual country needs and avoid the panics and periodic losses of confidence which had cursed the 1920s and 1930s.

Perhaps of greatest importance for Pasvolsky, Moulton, and Brookings, the postwar programs were carried out with a clear consciousness of inevitable international interconnections, the impossibility of autarky for any nation in the modern world, and the potential economic and political gains from cooperative action under such a structure as the new United Nations. The message of Moulton and Pasvolsky about the international origins of domestic problems and their solutions seems to have been heard loud and clear. These visionaries had the rare experience of seeing their vision realized in their own lifetimes, at least in part as the result of their own efforts.

NOTES

1 "The Enforcement of Peace," Moulton Papers, Brookings Institution Archives. A complete list of "Brookings Studies in the International Field" up to 1940 is contained in "Application to the Rockefeller Foundation for Support of a Research Project Entitled 'Economic Bases of Enduring Peace,'" Moulton Papers.

2 A "biographical note" on Pasvolsky is contained with his personal papers in the Manuscript Division, Library of Congress.

3 See, for example, two State Department planning documents: "International Activities in which the United States Must Participate to Re-establish and Maintain Peace and to Promote General Welfare," August 9, 1943, and "Bases of our Program for International Economic Cooperation," October 6, 1943, both in subject file: International Economic Relations, Pasvolsky Papers.

REFERENCES

Acheson, D. (1969). *Present at the Creation*, New York: Norton.
Carnegie Corporation Archives, New York.

Gouldner, A.W. (1979). *The Future of Intellectuals and the Rise of the New Class*, New York: Oxford University Press.
Hull, C. (1948). *Memoirs*, New York: Macmillan.
Moulton Papers, Brookings Institution Archives, Washington, DC.
Pasvolsky Papers, Library of Congress, Washington, DC.
Rockefeller Family Papers, Record Group 2, Box 154, Rockefeller Foundation Archives, Rockefeller Archive Center, Pocantico, New York.

Part III

CONTRIBUTIONS TO THEORY AND MEASUREMENT

8

HERBERT J. DAVENPORT'S TRANSFORMATION OF THE AUSTRIAN THEORY OF VALUE AND COST

J. Patrick Gunning

This chapter is about Herbert J. Davenport's contribution to the Austrian theory of value and cost.[1] The term "theory of value," in today's words, means "theory of price."[2] "Price" includes the prices of consumer goods and the prices of the factors of production. An all-inclusive theory of price would aim to discover every cause of prices in the market economy. No Austrian economist has tried to achieve this aim. The Austrians have excluded theft and deceit. Also, while being careful to recognize that money is not neutral, Austrians have presented the theory of price independently of the theory of money. By doing so, they have disregarded the demand for and supply of cash balances. Besides these, Austrian authors have typically excluded time preference as a cause in order to achieve simplicity. Finally, in this field, the Austrian theory has not tried to account for credit and the money based on credit.

My point is only that when we speak of the Austrian theory of value, we are not talking about an all-inclusive theory but a special theory designed to show the relationship between the prices of goods and factors in isolation of the above-mentioned influences. Following this lead, this chapter also assumes fully defined property rights, no fraud, neutral money, absence of time preference, and no credit.

The word "cost" is included in the title of this chapter to indicate that the theory of relative prices should also describe or explain cost as we understand it in everyday life. Cost in this sense means opportunity cost, which may be different from the prices that a producer must pay for the factors of production.

When modern Austrian economists use the term "cost," they invariably refer to cost as subjective, meaning that it is a cost as perceived by some subject. When they use the term to refer to the cost of production in the market economy, they refer to cost as it is perceived by some entrepreneur.[3] They may not realize that this mode of expression is distinctly modern. In the early Austrian theory of value and cost, as espoused by Carl Menger, Friedrich von Wieser, and Eugen Böhm-Bawerk, there were references to the entrepreneur. However, it was only with the publication of Mises's *Human Action* that the entrepreneur as a role became central to the Austrian theory.[4] Mises did not see his contribution in this respect as original. In saying that "Entrepreneur means acting man in regard to the changes occurring in the data of the market," he referred to J.B. Clark (Mises 1966: 254). Moreover, he had favorable comments for Frank Knight's 1921 book on the entrepreneur, particularly as regards Knight's distinction between risk and (intersubjective) uncertainty (Mises 1966: 292). But Mises went far beyond these writers by embodying in the entrepreneur role all distinctly human action. It is precisely this fact that distinguishes the later Austrian theory of value and cost from the earlier theory.[5] However, Mises was anticipated on this issue. I will establish in this chapter that an American economist, Herbert J. Davenport (1861–1931), presented a modern Austrian view of value and cost as early as 1908 and that he did so in the context of assessing the theories of Böhm-Bawerk and Wieser.

A common belief among modern American Austrian economists is that following the first generation (or first two) of Austrians—Carl Menger, Friedrich von Wieser, and Eugen Böhm-Bawerk—there was a thirty-year hiatus in the spread of Austrian economics by true Austrians to monolingual, English-speaking economists. During that time the only economics of the Austrian masters available in English was that of Wieser and Böhm-Bawerk. Their books had been translated into English even before 1900 and they had written a few papers for British and American journals. These books and papers, however, were not the best that Austrian economics had to offer. Wieser had been attracted to socialism and thus did not maintain his focus on the theory of price. Böhm-Bawerk, on the other hand, had made a serious error in his materialistic view of capital and in the period of production. Menger's seminal work was not available in English. Thus the English-speaking world was deprived of an opportunity to learn what was best in Austrian economics.[6]

Austrian historians of thought acknowledge that some Americans either absorbed early Austrian ideas or arrived at them independently. Mises was aware of and complimented Frank Fetter, an early twentieth-century American, for having anticipated his own unique view of time preference and interest.[7] Moreover, he complimented Frank Knight's handling of the competition and uncertainty concepts.[8] But so far as I know, the only Austrian economist to have shown at least some awareness of the work on value and cost in American economics was Richard Ebeling (1977).[9] But Ebeling was mainly concerned with writers who sought to present the early Austrian theory to an English-speaking audience. He cites no references to American writers after 1891 until Mises's American students began to write on the subject.

If my interpretation is correct, it should surprise the American Austrians to find that Davenport, an American contemporary of Böhm-Bawerk, fully articulated the ideas contained in the nineteenth-century Austrian theory of value and cost, criticized them, and proceeded to advance the theory to a point that is similar to Mises'.[10] Indeed, in my view, Davenport's exposition was superior to that of Mises, although it lacked Mises's grounding in epistemology.[11]

The first part of this chapter reviews the Austrian theory as presented by Böhm-Bawerk and as later modified by Mises. The second part presents a lengthy review of Davenport's contribution. The third part presents some hypotheses on why Davenport's work has been disregarded. A major factor appears to have been Fetter's highly negative review of Davenport's 1914 book. The final part presents a conclusion.

BRIEF REVIEW OF THE AUSTRIAN THEORY OF VALUE AND COST

The early Austrian theory of value can be traced to Menger's *Principles* (1871). But Menger had little to say about cost.[12] Around 1890, the *Principles*, Wieser's *Natural Value* (1888), and Böhm-Bawerk's *The Positive Theory of Capital* (1889) were all available in German. James Bonar was apparently the first to present the Austrian ideas in English to an American audience in an 1889 *Quarterly Journal of Economics* paper.[13] In 1891, William Smart published a book in England on the Austrian school. Also, in 1891, Wieser wrote a paper in English for the British *Economic Journal* explaining the Austrian theory.[14] In the United States, there followed a criticism by S. Macvane in the *Quarterly Journal of Economics* in 1890, to which both Böhm-Bawerk and Wieser responded.[15] Macvane replied with two papers, one in the *QJE* (1893a) and the other in the *Annals of the American Academy of Political and Social Science* (1893b). Meanwhile, Böhm-Bawerk ([1891] 1962) wrote a paper introducing the Austrian school for the 1891 *Annals*. Also in 1893, Simon Patten published a paper relating to the Austrian theory and David Green wrote two papers. All this stir led to no less than three defenses of the Austrian theory in 1894 in the *QJE*, *Annals*, and the brand new *Journal of Political Economy*. The first, by David Green, was a refutation of Macvane's 1893 *QJE* paper. The second, by Böhm-Bawerk (1894a), included a long and scholarly survey of the literature, which discussed the Macvane and Patten papers as well as papers and books by German, Italian, and British writers. The primary target of his paper, however, was Marshall's doctrine of real costs. I discuss this paper below as representative of the early Austrian theory. The third was Davenport's first paper. It differed from the rest in that, although it contains a clear statement of the doctrine of subjective value, it did not mention the Austrian school. Davenport went on to publish three major academic books over the next twenty-two years, each representing a higher stage in his subjectivism. I will describe these stages below.

The early Austrian theory

The Austrian theory of value argued that the ultimate cause was the choices of individuals. By definition, the goal of each choice is utility and every choice entails forgone utility. In the market economy, such choices lead to a tendency, argued the Austrians, to make prices equal to marginal opportunity costs. Since opportunity costs are nothing but forgone utility, the ultimate cause of all prices is marginal utility.[16]

The main opponents of this view at the time argued that labor and waiting are the sources of value. They defined these things in terms of either (1) quantity, (2) price, or (3) pain or disutility. In his 1894a paper, Böhm-Bawerk disposed of the first by saying that it is impossible to form a clear idea of the quantity of labor. Because of specialization, labor differs in nature and quantity as among individuals. As a result, we cannot use the quantity of labor to help us explain the prices of goods (1894a: 327).[17] He accepted the second and went on to argue that the equilibrium market price of labor is merely forgone utility. In equilibrium, the price of labor equals, for the most part, the marginal utility of the alternative goods that could be produced with the labor, in terms of money. The main question that Böhm-Bawerk addressed was the extent to which labor disutility (the third source) was also a contributing factor to the cost of production. He answered basically that although Crusoe might produce goods up to the point where the marginal utility of the goods equals the marginal disutility of the labor expended, the production of goods in the market economy requires different kinds of complementary labor and other factors that are limited in supply. As a result, most people who perform work are not given the opportunity to work for as many minutes as they would like at the wage offered by the employer. Thus, for most types of labor, the subjective marginal utility of the goods that can be bought with a dollar earned is higher than the combined marginal disutility of labor required to produce them. It follows that while marginal disutility of labor is a source of cost, it is substantially less significant in determining wage rates than the marginal utilities of the alternative goods that could be produced with the labor (1894a: 327–343).

It should be noted that Böhm-Bawerk's theory of value and cost, based on marginal utility, is not contradicted by the idea that cost is partly determined by the marginal disutility of labor. After all, marginal disutility is just as important as marginal utility. The idea of positive and negative utility implies a standard for defining zero, which is not an essential part of the subjective theory of value. Böhm-Bawerk did not stress this point, although it came through clearly in Davenport's argument that it is better to regard the foundation of economics as *sacrifice* than as the utility entailed in a choice (1902: 383; 1908: 330). Menger also used this term, as quoted above in his brief discussion of cost.

I would like to describe a methodological element in Böhm-Bawerk's analysis, since it provides the starting point for the Austrian theory as it developed later. As implied above, Böhm-Bawerk began his argument about whether cost could be associated with the marginal disutility of labor with a discussion of the meaning of cost in a Crusoe situation. Then he proceeded to consider what he called the "synchronously reckoned money cost of the entrepreneur" (1894a: 325, 363). This is the cost that competing entrepreneurs would cause to emerge in the market. It is a kind of equilibrium cost. In order to understand this cost, one must put oneself in the shoes of the entrepreneurs. Many errors, Böhm-Bawerk implied, had resulted from the failure to distinguish correctly between the "synchronously reckoned" cost and "historical cost": "It would . . . be a very serious sin of omission, on the part of economic science, to attempt an explanation [of prices] without any reference to the characteristic circumstance that these prices represent the present cost to the entrepreneur"(1894a: 366).

Finally, I would like to point out a continuity between (1) Menger's initial point that for an item to be a good, someone must have knowledge of the causal connections between the item and the want it can be used to satisfy (Menger 1981: 52), and (2) Böhm-Bawerk's reference to the entrepreneur. Böhm-Bawerk did not discuss the possibility that the concept of the entrepreneur might be used to represent, in part at least, what Menger had meant by knowledge of the causal connections. For Mises, however, appraisement of the factors of production and dealing with uncertainty were the central characteristics of the entrepreneur function.[18]

The Misesian theory

In a companion paper (Gunning 1997b) I describe how Mises's image of entrepreneurship in the market transformed the Austrian theory of value and cost. I shall not describe it again here. However, some amount of repetition is necessary in order to show the reader the difference between the early and later theories. I repeat the section that shows how Mises might have traced cost from the standpoint of a particular entrepreneur in a particular market for a first-order good to the markets for higher-order goods. This will enable us to see clearly the difference between the idea that prices and costs equal marginal utilities and the idea that prices and costs are phenomena of subjective evaluation and appraisement. We begin by noting that the cost of producing a marketable consumer (first-order) good, as perceived by the entrepreneur who produces it, consists for the most part of the prices of the marketable factors of production needed to produce the good. Let us call this entrepreneur the first entrepreneur. The prices of the factors that he faces are determined in factor markets through entrepreneur bidding. Since the first entrepreneur must bid higher than the next highest bidding entrepreneur, we can say that the cost of a given marketable factor is equal to the highest price bid by a second, *marginal* entrepreneur—marginal in the sense that he is the entrepreneur who would have bid the highest price for the factor if the first entrepreneur did not. Following the trail to this second entrepreneur, we proceed to ask what led him to attach such a high appraisal to the factor. The answer is that he anticipated that if he combined this factor with other complementary factors, he could earn a profit. Thus the cost to the first entrepreneur depends on the profit that the second entrepreneur believed he could earn with the factor.

Now we might stop here and conclude that the second entrepreneur's anticipated profit from using the factor is, in some sense, a measure of the marginal utility that would result from using the factor in that employment. We could go on to reason that costs are the same as marginal utility by assuming an equilibrium in which all profit is zero. But this surely is insufficient, if not contradictory. The cost of a factor is not equal to its marginal utility in other uses for five important reasons. The first is that the presence of entrepreneurship is incompatible with the assumption of equilibrium. We can construct an image of entrepreneurs in which some entrepreneurs' anticipated profits from using a factor enter as costs of production in the calculations of other entrepreneurs. Or we can construct an image in which there is no entrepreneurship and therefore no cost calculation. The two images cannot legitimately be mixed.

The second reason, which was recognized by Böhm-Bawerk, is the disutility of labor. The complementarity of factors prevents most workers from being employed up to the point where the marginal disutility of labor equals the wage. Thus the entrepreneur's cost of the last minute of an employee's labor does not equal the worker's disutility of working for that minute.

Third, we have the problem of "utility margins." How many additional units of the second consumer good could be produced if the second entrepreneur gained control of the factor that is now being used by the first entrepreneur to produce one more unit of his good? The inability to answer this question in a definite way for the general case is why we should conceive of cost not as based on marginal utility—as Böhm-Bawerk and Wieser were prone to do on occasion—but on the less quantitative and less continuous idea of sacrifice, or subjective value. To be sure, some consumer gain is lost because the second entrepreneur cannot use the factor for which the first entrepreneur bids higher. But we should not pretend that the concept of *marginal* utility in any way helps us comprehend that loss.

The fourth reason is the complementarity of factors. Although entrepreneurs attach definite appraisals to factors—in other words, although they compute a contribution of each factor to the business revenue—we cannot directly relate this computation to forgone utility because of the "insolubility of the problem of physical imputation" (Mises 1966: 494).

The fifth reason—and this is the most important one in the transformation of the Austrian theory of value—is that the alternative cost clearly depends not only on the entrepreneur's estimate of consumer utility but also on the assumption that there is an entrepreneur in the first place! Suppose that we take away the second entrepreneur and put the third highest bidder for the factor in his place. Then the cost to the first entrepreneur would be lower.[19] This is not simply a displacement problem of complementary factors of production. What is displaced is not a physical factor but one of the unique human agents, who "represents a different aspect of the consumers' wants."[20] The agent is someone who we assume is a maker of prices and costs.

This example illustrates a source of prices and costs that was entirely missing from the early Austrian analysis, namely, the limited supply of unique appraising and price-setting entrepreneurs.[21] Thus it is that Mises transformed the old Austrian theory of value and cost, based on marginal utility, to a theory based on the appraisals and decision-making of entrepreneurship, although I am not aware of his actually making a claim that he had done so.

DAVENPORT

Davenport (1861–1931) was born in Vermont in 1861. Joseph Dorfman (1949: 375–376) writes that he was descended from two Puritan statesmen. It appears that he was mostly self-educated. In 1882, at the age of 21, he entered Harvard Law School and attended for two-and-a-half years as a special student. He studied at an accelerated pace and passed the final examination. Because he was a special student, however, the school did not grant him a degree. Then he went into business in South Dakota. He spent 1890–1 in Europe attending first the University of Leipzig and then L'Ecole des Libre des Sciences Politiques in Paris, after which he returned to business in South Dakota.[22] In 1894, when he published the above-mentioned article on relative price, he had at best the equivalent of a modern master's degree at universities where (I believe it can safely be assumed) no distinguished contributors to the Austrian theory of value and cost were located. Perhaps he had read the Austrian theory of value while in Europe or while studying for his degree in South Dakota.[23]

Although this chapter is not about Davenport's life, a few more words are worth writing in order to further indicate his apparent independence and self-reliance. Following his 1894 paper, he obtained a formal undergraduate degree from the University of South Dakota around 1895, having taken "all the examinations for the four-year course," although he "apparently attended no classes" (Dorfman 1949: 376). He proceeded to publish two books, one on general economic theory (1896) and the other ostensibly designed as a high-school economics text (1898). In 1897, he entered the University of Chicago, where he completed his Ph.D. in one year. He moved off to Nebraska to be a high-school principal, and then returned in 1900 to join the faculty of the University of Chicago. While there, he formed a close friendship with Thorstein Veblen, which was to last for the rest of Veblen's life.

The *Outlines* and relative marginal utility

Davenport made the subjective value theory the foundation of his first book, *Outlines of Economic Theory* (1896)—although he did not credit the Austrians with the theory! He quoted Böhm-Bawerk's *Capital and Interest* in several places, but he did not mention Menger or Wieser, and he quoted Marshall and Sidgwick more often.[24] Moreover, he criticized Böhm-Bawerk's theory of interest.[25] Thus there is no obvious reason to believe that he learned the subjective value theory from the Austrians.

Generally speaking, *Outlines* represents an early stage in Davenport's thinking. However, one feature of this book that takes on special relevance when we look at his later work is his conception of the entrepreneur as an *agent* for both consumers and the owners of the factors of production.[26] This idea later surfaced in Knight[27] and is related to Mises's role of the entrepreneur in consumer sovereignty and competition (see below).[28]

Davenport's book was well received[29] and undoubtedly was the reason why J. Laurence Laughlin was able to arrange a fellowship for him at the University of Chicago (Dorfman 1949: 380). The book also contained a subjectivist-based theory of credit, capital, and interest, which will not be discussed here.[30]

By 1902, Davenport had become sufficiently familiar with the Austrian theory to venture a paper entitled "Proposed Modifications in Austrian Theory and Terminology." The following quotation from the introduction gives a good idea of what he accomplished:

> As against the cost of production theory, it will be urged that the price point of adjustment is not fixed *by* marginal cost of production, but merely, tendency-wise, *at* the marginal cost of production. As against the marginal demand theory it will be urged: (1) that the marginal demand also gives merely the point of fixation, not the cause of the fixation—that in this case likewise the preposition should be *at*, and not *by*; (2) that it is only by a sleight of hand in terms that marginal utility is made identical with marginal demand; and (3) that marginal utility strictly and accurately used, has nothing directly to do with the value [price] problem.
>
> (Davenport 1902: 358–359)

Davenport explicitly addressed the writings by Austrian economists. He cited Wieser but mainly aimed his discussion at Böhm-Bawerk. He gave no indication of having read Menger, although he referred to Jevons, Gossen, and Walras (1902: 362). Aside from what was said above, Davenport argues that Böhm-Bawerk and Wieser often wrote as though the market price of a good (marginal cost of a factor) equates the marginal utilities (cost) of all buyers and that this implies a comparison of utilities at the margin. He pointed out that the market price of a good (and the market price of a factor) equals marginal utility only for the marginal buyer and seller.

What Davenport was really worried about was the assumption of complete divisibility. Examples of marginal utility in demand assume divisibility of each good and divisibility of each buyer's evaluation of each good. In addition, they assume that a person's comparisons of different goods are divisible so that each buyer can compare, with perfect continuity, any given quantity of each good with any given quantity of some other good.

On the sellers' side, the problem is worse. When the idea of marginal utility is extended to the theory of imputation in order to explain the relative prices of factors, it assumes that there is divisibility of producer appraisals as among different units of the same factor, different factors, and even by different producers. That factors are not divisible is evident. More importantly, there is clearly no continuum among human agents.

Thus Davenport proposed substituting the term "marginal relative utility" for "marginal utility."[31] However, the logic of his argument should have led him away from the terms "marginal" and "utility." That it did not is probably due to the fact that these terms were so widely used. A close reading of his detailed criticism of Böhm-Bawerk and Wieser in his 1908 book shows that he would have preferred to replace these terms with the term "sacrifice," as expressed in his original 1894 paper.[32]

In the paper, Davenport also objected to terms like "objective exchange value" and "subjective exchange value." The paper said nothing about entrepreneurship, which was to become the hallmark of his later work.

According to Frank Knight (1921), who was a student at Cornell during Davenport's tenure beginning in 1916, Davenport never mastered mathematics. If this is true, he would probably not have ventured a criticism of Walras but would rather have focused on the imprecise and clumsy language of the Austrian expositors. On the other hand, as Davenport himself recognized, it is surely not in the *spirit* of the Austrian school to claim that they assumed the equivalent of complete divisibility.[33] For this reason, the most accurate view of the 1902 paper seems to be that it was an early statement of a later point that is now well accepted by the Austrian economists, namely, that the significance of the "marginal utility" revolution was not marginalism but subjective utility.[34] And if we go on to look at what Mises says about utility, it is not utility that is important, but the "causal relevance for the removal of felt uneasiness."[35] This seems identical to what Davenport meant by the "formula of sacrifice" in his 1894 paper.

Value and Distribution

By 1908, Davenport had made entrepreneurship the central idea in his theory of price. The preface of his 1908 book *Value and Distribution* says that the book's emphasis is "upon the entrepreneur point of view in the computation of costs and in the analysis of the process by which distributive shares are assigned" (1908: vii). "The entrepreneur point of view" refers to a point of view that focuses on the entrepreneur's opportunity cost. It is distinguished from a collectivist, or social, point of view, which assumes that costs are calculated by the minister of a collectivist society. Davenport goes on to give credit to the person he believes to be the discoverer of the correct notion of opportunity cost—David Green! He does not mention the Austrians, apparently because he associated the Austrian analysis with marginalism.[36]

Another feature of the preface is modesty. He claimed that he did not regard his book as presenting a new doctrine. Its contribution was to select, delimit, and articulate the old. Reading between the lines, however, it is clear that he believed (1) that he had clarified the relationship between cost and entrepreneurship; (2) that he had furthered the development of the idea of "marginal relative utility," particularly on the supply side of the Marshallian scissors; (3) that he had used the idea of competitive entrepreneurship to derive what he called the loan-fund doctrine of capital; and (4) that he had made an advance on Fetter's interest theory through his loan fund doctrine. Moreover, the book was largely a critique of other economic writings, although it was a constructive one.[37]

In this book, he points out the difference between Menger, who was concerned with subjective value, and Jevons and Walras (1908: 334). However, although he has three chapters (out of twenty-seven) on the Austrian theory of value and cost, he focuses entirely on Wieser and Böhm-Bawerk, since their works "stand today as the most authoritative expression of what is characteristic and dominant in the unfolding of Austrian theory" (1908: 338). His first chapter on the Austrians was mainly a repeat of his 1902 paper pointing out the imprecise and clumsy language that he regarded as typical of Böhm-Bawerk and Wieser.

Austrian theory disregards the human agent-entrepreneur

He spends his second chapter dealing almost exclusively with a disagreement between Böhm-Bawerk and Heinrich Dietzel over the meaning of value and cost.[38] In describing this debate, Davenport correctly identifies this as the heart of the early Austrian view of cost. He points out that the classical school did not explain costs. The Austrian school must be credited with facing this issue fully. However, on the question of whether the Austrians succeeded in explaining costs, Davenport says that Böhm-Bawerk's discussion in the paper only makes "a passable showing" (1908: 346)

In explaining costs, Böhm-Bawerk invoked the standard Austrian theory described above, namely, that in calculating costs, the entrepreneur takes account of the prices of the factors, which are ultimately derived from the marginal prices that consumers are willing to pay for the products that they aid in producing. This is insufficient, says Davenport, because it fails to adequately account for the human agent, as evidenced by *entrepreneur reckoning* in the competitive system (1908: 347). What he means by this is that Böhm-Bawerk fails to consider all of the distinctly different human agents whose appraisals go into determining the price of a factor of production.[39] I discuss this issue further below.[40]

Critique of the Positive Theory *and* Natural Value

Davenport addresses the third chapter on the Austrian theory to Böhm-Bawerk's *The Positive Theory of Capital* and Wieser's *Natural Value*. He makes two points. The first and less substantive is that Böhm-Bawerk and Wieser used such slippery language that it is difficult to tell whether they understood the more essential points of the cost doctrines they aimed to promote.[41] The second and more substantive point is an extension of the critique of Böhm-Bawerk on his failure to recognize the full importance of entrepreneurship. The marginal entrepreneur—that is, the entrepreneur who actually gains control over a factor and determines its use—is not in any reasonable quantitative sense infinitesimally different from his closest competitor, either in the product market or the factor market. He is different in a *human* sense; and his reduction to infinitesimals is a fundamental error. A good example is his discussion of Wieser. The following quotation is illustrative:

> There is, therefore, for any particular production good, no such thing possible as one specific marginal use or marginal service or marginal utility or marginal productivity, as attributable to it in its own right and independently, or even as dependent solely on the relation of the [factor] in question to some other production good or goods, but only as also related to the situation and aptitudes and needs of a specific entrepreneur. There must, then, be as many specific marginal productivenesses as there are different entrepreneurs to come into relation with the good in question.
>
> (Davenport 1908: 364)

That Davenport recognized his contribution to the modern Austrian theory of value and cost, as defined here, is clear from his remarks on Wieser's deficiency.

> [M]y appeal to the entrepreneur computation and the entrepreneur bid supplies the missing link in the argument of Wieser with reference to the different equations; somehow, he says, the market out of all the different equations, arrives at a marginal-utility imputation for each productive good. If it really does so, it is done by the bidding of entrepreneurs.
>
> (1908: 366)

Davenport goes on to correct a statement in Wieser about imputation by inserting a reference to the entrepreneur's calculation at every stage where Wieser speaks of a marginal utility or a marginal product.[42]

Finally, anticipating Mises in the socialist calculation debate, Davenport says: "It is, indeed, only as working out through entrepreneur computations and entrepreneur competitions, that production goods of any sort acquire value or rental, or rank as costs, and come thereby to have their little or much bearing on the relative volumes of goods seeking exchange against one another" (1908: 368). However, so far I have not seen any evidence that Davenport recognized the importance of this to the debate over socialism. Of course, that debate did not occur until much later.

The Economics of Enterprise

In *The Economics of Enterprise* (1914)—the book that so much raised the ire of Fetter (see below)—Davenport refined his theory of value and cost. The book covers much the same ground as *Value and Distribution*. However, in the earlier book, Davenport presented his views within the context of a review of the economic doctrines of other economists, meticulously relating each view to historical and contemporary writers. In this book, he seems to go out of his way to avoid referring to other economists. Instead, he systematically develops his economic theory in treatise fashion.

Subjectivism, economics, and knowledge

His introduction to the theory of price contains the clearest introduction to subjectivism of which I am aware. He begins by taking the perspective of the outsider who is observing price adjustments, for example on the stock exchange. The outsider sees sellers' offers and buyers' bids. But he has no knowledge of other offers or bids that remain to be disclosed. Then Davenport shifts to the perspective of "any actual trader." "The bids of the prospective purchaser are intended to give the scantiest possible information as to how high he will go. . . . Each of the traders is shrewd to mislead the other as to his own limit" (1914: 43). Finally, he shifts to the economist's perspective:

> [W]e, as economists, have . . . to concern ourselves with the psychology of bargaining and with the influences that the different traders' limits have on the method by which the market equilibrium is reached or is disturbed. . . . We have to adopt the point of view of each of the different agents in the process rather than that of the mere observer. . . . As economists, we assume only the very facts that the traders are doing their best to guess at—a range of actual conditions, which, as actual, the traders are conjecturing as best they can.
> (1914: 44, 45)

Economics had to wait twenty-nine years for a comparable statement on subjectivism.[43]

He goes on in this chapter to draw demand and supply curves (emphasizing that supply curves are really reservation price curves). He attributes the marginal concepts implicit in the curves to the "Austrian school of economic doctrine" (ibid.: 53). He repeats his criticism of marginalism, however, only this time it takes a more modern form that anticipates Hayek's (1937) argument. Instead of referring to supply and demand, he refers to equilibrium analysis. He says, in effect, that "[a]ll these questions [about equilibrium based on marginal prices and marginal traders] really resolve themselves into the one great question: What are the causal forces in the market adjustment?" (1914: 54). These causal factors, as we shall see, can all be classified by one label—entrepreneurs. In a later chapter he consummates this line of thinking by anticipating the Mises–Hayek–Kirzner notion that "[i]n the study of the market process, the economist is interested in those forces at work tending to establish an equilibrium of price *under given conditions*" (1914: 76).

Supply and cost

Davenport's book then proceeds by discussing supply and demand in three chapters, to which the discussion here will mostly be confined. The subject of the first is "Supply and Cost." In this relatively long chapter, he introduces the concept of opportunity cost in the modern sense of a producer's foregone profit from alternative uses. There are two points worth noting. First, he sharply distinguishes between cost in the market (what he calls "competitive costs") and costs in a collectivist society. The latter are computed "parallel to the Crusoe computation." The manager of the collectivist society would presumably calculate cost in terms of displacement, according to the value he attaches to the displaced items.

Second, his example of a typical cost account, as faced by the entrepreneur, seems broader than modern Austrians would ordinarily make it. Like the modern notion (and the Austrian notion of Davenport's contemporaries), it includes the "value of entrepreneur's own time and supervision," possibly calculated by referring to the utility of a nonmarket alternative. "A cost calculation that is adequate and exhaustive must reduce to the price denominator all of the different resistances which bear on the case" (1914: 70). These include pain costs, disrepute costs, and danger costs.

> [I]t is evident . . . not only that all outlays are elements of cost, but also that personal preferences, repugnancies, considerations of climate, neighborhood, home ties, national prejudice, wholesomeness, cleanliness, good repute, are all elements in cost to the extent that they impose expense to overcome them—to the extent, that is, that they restrict supply and so increase the price of the remaining supply.
>
> (1914: 82)

He emphasizes that the cost account is forward looking and intended to enable the producer to make a profit estimate. So far so good. But he also includes taxes. This is appropriate if one's aim is to describe cost in the hampered market economy. However, Davenport makes no distinction between the hampered and unhampered economies. Moreover, in discussing the individuals in the market economy who act in the role of entrepreneurs and thus make cost accounts, he includes the example of the safe-cracker (1914: 70)! This is a prelude to his later argument that because cost is subjective, economists should not restrict the study of the "market process" to producers' actions that are assumed to benefit consumers. Whether the outcome of the "market process" is desirable or undesirable ought to be considered separately from the method of study and the logic of the deductions.

The main argument against this point of view is that if the economist's ultimate goal is to evaluate arguments relating to market intervention, it would be more convenient to start by imagining an economy in which no intervention is warranted. On the other hand, the danger is that having constructed such an image, we shall mistake it for the only kinds of systems that are practically feasible, namely, systems with incompletely defined property rights, enforcement costs, and goods (perhaps essential ones like national defense) that have the characteristic of jointness in demand.[44]

The critique of marginal utility

I now turn to Davenport's chapter on utility. His discussion of demand is standard textbook fare up to a point. He presents the theory of marginal utility and demand in the usual fashion. But then he follows it with a devastating critique:

> [O]ver and over again it is asserted—by economists who ought to

> know better—that the marginal utility to the bidder determines his bid; or that his bid expresses his marginal utility; or that the marginal bid expresses the marginal utility; or that the marginal utility determines, or is commensurate with, the market price. In truth, no one of these formulations is defensible. . . . All talk, then, of the fixation of price by either or both of the margins (buyer or seller) is nonsense. . . . At the most, the market price is simply commensurate with the marginal offer or with the marginal selling price.
>
> (1914: 92, 94–95)

Two other notable aspects of the chapter are as follows. First, he deals with Böhm-Bawerk's horse trade (without mentioning Böhm-Bawerk), pointing out that among the many horse traders in a market, there is no reason to suppose that any pair will be "at or near the margin of indifference" (1914: 97). Second, in his summary of the chapter he says that an individual's money demand for a good only shows that the marginal utilities from competing goods are *approximately* equal:

> Nor does the fact that two individuals are marginal at the same purchase price imply that the marginal utilities respectively involved are equal, but only that the ratios are the same between the utility in question and the utility forgone. And finally: utility being purely a relation to an individual, and men being different—their desires different and incommensurable, and their money resources different—there is no possibility of finding, either in the demand price of any individual or in the market, any expression or measure of utility or of marginal utility.
>
> (1914: 104–105)

Entrepreneur cost

Now I discuss Davenport's chapter on "The Significance of Cost of Production," which contains the methodological foundation of his theory of value and cost. He begins by pointing out that (right thinking) economists, in their search for the causes of cost in the competitive system, have always used the concept of *entrepreneur cost*. They have always asked: What constitutes cost to the entrepreneur? Entrepreneur cost is not the ultimate cost. It is superficial but nevertheless necessary "as an intermediate step in the great value problem." "The whole process is captained by" the entrepreneurs. "Thus, the point of view from which to attack this problem of causes is the entrepreneur point of view." In a competitive society, the "ultimate causes are forced to obtain expression" [through the entrepreneur process] (1914: 109). "[W]e must study an entrepreneur economics in terms of the entrepreneur process" (1914: 110).

He proceeds to make a point that is disregarded in explanations of value based on utility alone. He says that "[m]an as consumer is the end of the economic process. . . . But he is not merely the end; as producer he is also the means" (1914: 111).

He gives the following description of the causal nexus *on the supply side* of value as between products and factors:

> [Given the demand for a product], [t]he causal sequence on the supply side of the problem runs from the relative scarcity of the factor to the relative scarcity of its product, thence to the relatively high price of the product, thence to the relatively high remuneration of the factor. . . . But the hire of any factor as cost gets its immediate explanation not directly from the scarcity of the product but, *as an entrepreneur computation*, from the price of the product which price is in turn due to scarcity.
>
> (1914: 111)

In short, the entrepreneur perceives the demand for the product and the complementary factors that can be used to produce it. He then makes a computation, the result of which is a recognition of the scarcity of the factor. Knowing the scarcity of the factor (i.e., anticipating the prices that others will bid for the factor), he decides to ask a high price for the product. Believing that he can obtain a sufficiently high price for his product, he proceeds to bid, in competition with others, a high price for the factor.

This viewpoint marks the difference between the old Austrian theory of value and cost and the new theory. Under the old theory, prices can be traced exclusively to utility. But Davenport maintains that prices cannot emerge except through entrepreneurship. While the entrepreneur must account for utility indirectly when he estimates the demands of consumers, he must also use his knowledge. Moreover, in considering the "entrepreneur process," we must consider all entrepreneurs simultaneously. There are many different entrepreneurs, each with different knowledge and each using his particular knowledge to make appraisals of factors. These factors are partly complementary, meaning that no entrepreneur has a useful way to calculate the marginal revenue product of a particular factor. Yet somehow each entrepreneur must attach a money value to the factor in order to decide how much to bid for it. In light of this (and other considerations), it is insufficient and misleading to say that market price can be traced only to the utility of the consumers:

> It thus appears that costs to the entrepreneur are merely the guise in which, in an entrepreneur economy, the underlying and controlling situation of human needs on the side of demand, and of productive ability, and productive equipment on the side of supply, present

> themselves to the entrepreneur and bear upon him in his process of placing a particular product upon the market. Costs are merely one point or aspect—but the central point or aspect—in the process of production and distribution in the competitive regime.
>
> (1914: 118)

This says that costs represent both the entrepreneur's estimate of demand and his specialized knowledge and expectations about the money outlays and other resistances to satisfying those demands that are implied by the concept of scarcity. The inclusion of "productive equipment" is not a slip from subjectivism, since he is referring to what the entrepreneur perceives.

The role of the entrepreneur

I have argued elsewhere that the main contribution of Mises to economics was that he, in effect, defined entrepreneurship as a distinctly human action.[45] Whether this interpretation is correct, it is surely true that with respect to the problem of tracing the source of value in the pure market economy, the only method we have is to try to isolate the distinctly human action and show how it would operate in relation to a model of an economy that contains producers, consumers, savers, and factor suppliers. Just as the source of value in a Crusoe situation is the humanness of Crusoe—his ends and means as he perceives them—so also is the source of value in a market economy the humanness of the people. And if we can capture the active part of that humanness in a single personage, we shall be able to describe the source of value by referring to that personage. Now what I call here the active part of humanness or "distinctly human action" would have to include what we know from intuition and experience about the nature of human wants. Surely, we know that these wants are continually changing. However, when we focus on the problem of cost, clear thinking requires that we hold those wants constant. If we assume that ends are given, then entrepreneurship must refer entirely to means. Thus we arrive at the definition of the entrepreneur as the representative, or embodiment, of a distinctly human element involved in causing given wants to be satisfied. Davenport, as I see now, was the first, to my current knowledge, to recognize this point:

> In the main, then, the process is captained by the entrepreneur, is guided and supervised by him, and worked out through him. It may, indeed, be said to be entirely so worked out and guided, if only the concept of entrepreneurship be given its proper extension. All employers of labor or of instrumental goods for hire are entrepreneurs, no matter whether the prospective product is to be offered for sale or not. If it have no sale price, it is because it has a reservation price; it is still a price product. The client of the lawyer or the patient

> of the doctor, the master in his hiring of his house servants or his valet, the employer of labor in the raising of garden products for the home table, are all bidders for factors of production and are entrepreneurs for this—and for every other—purpose of economic analysis.
>
> (1914: 139)

Related to this definition of entrepreneurship was Davenport's definition of profit. He considers three possibilities: (1) "exceptional, unclassified, irregular gains," (2) "compensation for the independently working factor of *in production*," or (3) "the still broader notion of compensation for the independent human factor in the *quest for gain*." Logically, he chooses the third. "*Profit* . . . points to gain *without the intervention of an employer*; it is, then, remuneration to the entrepreneur for entrepreneur activity as such" (1914: 404).

FETTER'S REVIEW

Frank Fetter attacked *The Economics of Enterprise* viciously in a fifteen-page review.[46] His criticism might not concern us were it not for the facts that: (1) Fetter was praised by Mises, (2) his papers and books have been referred to favorably by several other American Austrian economists, and (3) one of the papers referred to includes this attack. Lacking the time to read every relevant paper and book, the American Austrians naturally rely on the references of others whom they respect. In the case of Fetter, they have made a mistake.

Fetter's paper contains five criticisms of Davenport. They are: (1) lack of scholarly attitude; (2) the definition of economics as the theory of price; (3) the inclusion of predation and exploitation; (4) the loan fund theory of capital; and (5) the position of technical productivity in the theory of price and interest. In this chapter, I shall focus on the first two of these criticisms because these appear most relevant to the Austrian theory of value and cost.[47]

Lack of scholarly attitude

Fetter claimed that while Davenport's ideas had become quite familiar to most American students, marking Davenport as a progressive and member of the group who were in the process of revising fundamental theory, he presents his ideas as if they are almost entirely new (1914b: 550). "Such a standard of scholarship is to be condemned, for, without conscientious references, essays in the field of controverted doctrines can attain but little of their possible service" (1914b: 551). Fetter used the example of Davenport's treatment of "social capital." He claimed that Davenport had ignored the writings of Clark, Fisher, and himself. In Fetter's opinion, these writers had made it possible to end the error of confusing what he called business economy with political economy. Business economy uses the private concept of capital, meaning that capital is what business entrepreneurs perceive it to be. Political economy, which includes discussions about whether the goods produced in a society and the means of production are desirable, uses the "social wealth" concept. He chastised Davenport for failing to credit the abovementioned authors for developing the business economy–political economy distinction.

Three points should be made about this criticism. First, it is misleading. There is little doubt that Davenport was guilty of neglecting the doctrines of others since he seems to have intentionally avoided referring to other economists in the 1914 book. However, his earlier 1908 book methodically laid out each of his ideas in the context of the history of economic thought, giving credit to and often criticizing practically all of his important predecessors, including Fetter. Fetter indicated in his review that he was aware of the 1908 book. However, he neglected to note the vast difference between the two books on this score, suggesting to the uninitiated reader that "lack of scholarship," by Fetter's definition, was a characteristic of Davenport's writing in general.

Second, Fetter appears to have been wrong in his judgment that the distinction between private point of view and the social point of view had taken hold in professional economics. One piece of evidence stands out. It is the professional reaction to Davenport's 1910 *QJE* paper in which he criticized the "social point of view" and claimed primacy for the individual point of view.[48] A year later, the *QJE* published a lengthy paper, in two parts, by L.H. Haney (1911, 1912), which sought to defend the social point of view.[49]

Third, Davenport's concept of private capital was different from that which Fetter and the others were using. To the others, private capital referred to the market value of assets anticipated by "business entrepreneurs." To Davenport, it referred to the money value of assets perceived by all individuals, each acting in the role of the entrepreneur. This difference in concepts of private capital changed the nature of the business economy–political economy distinction. In retrospect, it seems reasonable for Davenport to have assumed that a reader like Fetter would have appreciated this fact. Unfortunately, Fetter did not. If he had, he might have constructively shown how it can be used to embellish the business economy–political economy distinction instead of criticizing Davenport for not giving Fetter and others credit.

A final point regarding the scholarship issue is that, all things considered, Fetter himself appears to be more guilty of the sin with respect to Davenport than Davenport is with respect to Fetter. Besides his 1908 book, Davenport had described his views on capital as early as 1904 in a paper entitled "Capital as a Competitive Concept," which made several references to Fetter's work. One of Davenport's papers (1905) had Fetter's name in the title. Then there was the 1910 paper referred to above.[50] I have reviewed practically all of Fetter's academic papers, including his 1914 paper on interest theories (Fetter 1914a). No reference to Davenport appears until Fetter's 1927 paper.

Economics as the theory of price

Davenport defines economics as the science that "treats phenomena from the standpoint of price." "Price, then, must attend and characterize all things that are economic; and all things so attended are so far economic in character" (Fetter 1914b: 554, quoting from Davenport). This definition, says Fetter, excludes self-production, barter, and psychic incomes. After making such a definition, Davenport nevertheless proceeds to include these things in his discussion of the cause of price. "This reversal of the plain sense of the definition [of economics] is done by the simple expedient of introducing the idea of reservation prices, or refusal prices, and then assuming a hypothetical price for everything" (1914b: 554–555).

It is not entirely clear what Fetter objects to here. One possibility is that he defines price and all related phenomena in an empirical sense. Under this interpretation, Davenport's definition of economics would indeed exclude the items Fetter mentions. However, Davenport's notion of the theory of price refers to calculations in terms of price. A thing is economic if someone uses price to evaluate it (or, more accurately, if someone *appraises* it). Thus self-production and barter are economic if an individual appraises them in terms of money. Psychic income is the same. In fact, there is no difference between Davenport's definition and that of Mises, who makes economic calculation (in terms of money) the defining character of economic phenomena. To say that economics treats all phenomena from the standpoint of price does not necessarily rule out monetary calculations based on the prospect of self-production and barter. The problem is that Fetter does not appreciate the reservation demand approach.

The reservation demand approach

When we take the reservation demand approach, we view each actor as both a demander and supplier. By considering both simultaneously, we avoid the error of conceiving of cost in any other sense than sacrifice (forgone opportunities). This leaves us free to explore the economic organization of supply (i.e., production with the use of factors) from a purely subjective viewpoint. Using this approach, every limitation on the nonhuman factors of production is regarded entirely in terms of how it is perceived and interpreted by a human demander–supplier.

To understand how the reservation demand approach is used, we begin with a single market. We assume that market participants own a fixed amount of an already-produced good. The pricing problem is that of finding a price at which each potential consumer is satisfied with the amount that he has in light of the offers to buy and sell of his fellow consumers. Thus we construct an image of an equilibrium price.

Using the single market as a metaphor, we try to envision a similar phenomenon at the market economy level. The difference is that to achieve the goal of considering each actor as both a demander and a supplier, we cannot assume a fixed supply of produced goods. We must assume that the goods are produced with factors of production. The metaphor suggests that we might assume that there is a fixed amount of various types of factors. However, this is not realistic. Production as we know it in everyday life requires human factors of production, both in the production process and in identifying and allocating the other factors. In other words, we try to construct an image in which each individual can be said to have a reservation demand for his factors, including his own effort. But this immediately leads us to consider the personal uses and the psychic income associated with the factors, along with the entrepreneurship entailed in appraising the factors and allocating them to various uses.

Seen in this way, the reservation demand approach is simply a means of incorporating the a priori assumption that the owners of factors perceive alternative uses associated with the alternative demands for factors. Moreover, the reservation demand approach pushes one in the direction of considering entrepreneurship in a broad sense. Every owner of a factor would appear as an entrepreneur when he is making a decision on how to use his factors. And, of course, it is Davenport's procedure of regarding every individual as an entrepreneur that establishes his intellectual kinship with Mises.

CONCLUSION

Davenport advanced the Austrian theory of value and cost in ways that have not been recognized by modern economists who associate themselves with the Austrian school. He anticipated Mises's criticism of the Austrian school's presentation of the subjective theory of value, albeit from a less sympathetic perspective. He presented the first clear statement of the subjectivist viewpoint in economics. He employed the reservation demand approach to factor markets as the proper complement to Menger's "orders of goods" approach. He anticipated Mises's theory of prices and markets by placing entrepreneurship at the center. And he defined entrepreneurship in virtually the same way as Mises.

Mises, of course, was the first to identify the praxeological foundations of economics. Davenport did not do this. Nor did Davenport attack positivism, mathematical economics, and econometrics; the reason for this is probably that these tendencies in professional economics were not so evident at the turn of the century. Another important point must be that although neither man achieved great success in the eyes of professional academics, Mises was able to gather around him in the 1920s a number of ardent followers. So far as I know, Davenport operated independently and tried to achieve success in the eyes of his peers through his writings. Perhaps in the academic struggle that was then taking place in American universities among competing worldviews and conceptions of the nature of economics, it was not possible for an independent writer to persuade the profession of the usefulness of his ideas. In any case, modern Austrians have made a serious mistake in relying on Fetter's discussion. They would be wise to look thoroughly at Davenport's works.

NOTES

1 The chapter was shortened in accord with the request of the editor. The original version (Gunning 1996) contains more extended quotations of Davenport's works and a discussion of some of his controversial ethical claims. The latter version is available as a working paper and can be accessed through my web site:

web.nchulc.edu.tw/~gunning/pat/subjecti/workpape/dav_valu; and
www.showtower.com.tw/~gunning/subjecti/workpape/dav_valu.htm

2 In the terms of the interpreters of the Austrian theory, it is a theory of one species of objective value, as opposed to subjective value (e.g., utility) or other species of objective value (the power of a commodity to produce certain effects) (Bonar 1888: 13; Endres 1996: 85–86).

3 See e.g., Pasour (1977) and Vaughn (1980).

4 See Lachmann (1951) for a confirmation of the idea that the central economic concept in *Human Action* was entrepreneurship.

5 One must regard Israel Kirzner's definition of entrepreneurship as subconscious, spontaneous alertness (Kirzner 1973, 1979) as a deviation from this path, however. In his notion of alertness, Kirzner seems to have isolated an important intuitive aspect of human behavior which is implicit in all informed writings about entrepreneurship. However, this idea of the entrepreneur is narrower than Clark's functional concept. For a discussion of the relationship between Mises's and Kirzner's concept of the entrepreneur, see Gunning (1997a).

6 That Menger should be regarded as the primary source for early Austrian ideas in economics is argued in Streissler (1972) and Streissler and Weber (1973).

7 Mises (1966) makes four positive references to Fetter. One might presume that Mises's references were the reason Rothbard resurrected some of Fetter's writings (Fetter 1977) and that Gerald O'Driscoll (1980) wrote a brief paper about similarities. Fetter is also cited by Kirzner (1975).

8 See the index of *Human Action* (Mises 1966).

9 Ebeling mainly presented a bibliography on the concept. He did not present the theory and did not describe the American commentary on it.

10 See e.g., Kirzner's discussion of "most economists in the early twentieth century" (1992: 101–102). Kirzner's discussion is only indirectly about cost.

11 Mises is well known for his encyclopedic knowledge of economics. Thus I was puzzled at not being able to locate any references to Davenport's work in Mises's writings. Aside from their familiarity with the writings of the early Austrians

and of Fetter, the only link I could find between the two economists was a common reference to the work of Dutch economist N.G. Pierson. Mises mentions him as a contributor to the socialist calculation debate (Mises 1978: 111). (Also see Pierson's paper in Hayek 1935.) Davenport has a long and critical footnote on Pierson's notion of cost. The footnote begins with the statement that the critique will shed "some light upon the later trend of cost doctrine with the Austrian school" (Davenport 1908: 268 ff.).

12 As usual, however, what he did say was highly revealing: "Freight costs, loading charges, tolls, excise taxes, premiums for marine and other insurance, costs of correspondence, commissions and other sales costs, brokerage charges, the entire cost of the commercial banking system, even the expenses of traders and all their employees, etc. are nothing but the various economic sacrifices which are required for the conduct of exchange operations and which absorb a portion of the economic gains resulting from the exploitation of existing exchange opportunities" (Menger 1981: 189).

13 See Ebeling (1977). Bonar (1889) also published a review of Böhm-Bawerk's *Positive Theory*. For a recent discussion of the difference between Wieser and Böhm-Bawerk, see Elzas (1988).

14 Edgeworth criticized Böhm-Bawerk in an 1892 issue of the *Economic Journal*. Also Marshall had sought to deal with the Austrian ideas in the second edition of his *Principles* (1890) and in a later book, *Elements of the Economics of Industry* (1892). Böhm-Bawerk wrote a paper for the *Economic Journal* (1894b). Much of this is discussed in Böhm-Bawerk (1894a). Because I am interested in the developments in America, I shall not pursue the British discussion.

15 See Böhm-Bawerk (1890) and Wieser (1892).

16 We should exempt Menger from this characterization on the grounds that he did not express the Austrian theory in marginal terms (Streissler 1972).

17 He did not directly discuss abstinence but the argument would presumably be similar. One person's abstinence cannot be compared with another's in terms of quantity.

18 Kirzner (1992: ch. 4) is nevertheless correct to point out that Menger's focus was on the relationship between consumer evaluation and the prices of factors and not on entrepreneurship. Menger simply did not develop the knowledge theme and neither did Böhm-Bawerk. As Kirzner points out (1992: 102), and so far as I know, the stimulus for further development by Austrians was the economic calculation debate. But that debate was less about the production and use of knowledge than about how money and prices are necessary for the transmission of valuations and appraisals. It was not until 1937 that Hayek shifted the focus toward knowledge and 1940 that Mises shifted it toward entrepreneurship.

19 I am, of course, speaking loosely here. The difference between the costs in a market economy with n entrepreneurs and those in the same economy but with $n-1$ entrepreneurs should be described in terms of a different configuration of all prices and costs. In terms of our example, instead of saying that the cost of using this factor would be "less," I should say that the cost of using many, or possibly all, factors would be different. But it is not necessary to go into such detail in order to make the essential point.

20 Mises (1966: 338).

21 Menger (1981: 172) clearly recognized that entrepreneurial activity was limited. However, as stated previously, he did not focus on appraisement.

22 Philip Newman (1952: 246) says that he spent two years in Europe, one year at the University of Leipzig and the second at the University of Paris. He goes on to say that he lost all his money in the panic of 1893 and had to become a

high-school principal. After 4 years of boredom, he sought a job as a professor, but lacked a B.A. But Newman appears to have his timing mixed up because he has Davenport writing his textbooks five years after the 1893 panic.

23 His 1908 book had a chapter on Say in which he makes a qualified argument that Say was more advanced in his thinking about utility and the entrepreneur point of view than all the modern writers on the subject (1908: 115). In that chapter, he quotes correspondence between Say and Ricardo on the cause of market prices (1908: 110). Thus it is possible that he learned about the theory of value and cost by reading Say. In any case, his 1894 paper contains only two references, one to Courcelle-Seneuil and the other to Jevons.

24 One might surmise that in preparing his book, he read several treatises but remained largely ignorant of the Austrian school as a whole as well as other schools.

25 Davenport (1896: 134–136). His criticism was against the view that interest is the market premium of present over future goods. Although he pointed out that this view was an improvement over earlier formulations, it neglected to distinguish between loans made to consumers and those made to producers. Modern Austrians may not appreciate this point, since they have attributed the same theory that Davenport criticized to Mises. However, although Davenport did not fully articulate his view until later, his point was that in an economy with production, the market premium of present over future goods cannot be calculated unless one takes account of the appraisals of entrepreneurs who are contemplating financing the production of goods for future consumption. His argument was in no way based on the idea of physical productivity for which Mises criticized Böhm-Bawerk and Hayek. See Mises (1966: 527–528).

26 Davenport (1896: 151). In this book, he preferred to use the terms "imprenditor" and "employer."

27 See Gunning (1993). I wrote in that paper, following a hint by Yoram Barzel, that Knight was a precursor of the modern theory of agency. At that time, I was only vaguely aware of Davenport's work. It is clear to me now that while Knight dealt more thoroughly than anyone with the concept of entrepreneurial judgment, Davenport's formulation of the entrepreneur concept was in most respects superior to that of Knight. It is not surprising, then, to find that Davenport also conceived of the entrepreneur as an agent. This particular passage predates Knight's notion of the entrepreneur as an agent by twenty-five years.

28 In speaking of real employers, as opposed to those of economic theory, Davenport goes on to point out that the differential profits of employers often result "from superior ability and readiness in tricks of adulteration, in the lying of advertising, and in oppression of employees"(1896: 152). This statement is also a prelude to Davenport's later work and hints at the reason why Fetter found that work unacceptable. This issue, along with Fetter's criticism, is discussed in my longer, web version.

29 J.B. Clark (1897) wrote a brief praiseworthy review. W.G. Langworthy Taylor (1897) wrote a good long review in which he complimented Davenport for his treatment of money but, in the spirit of Simon Patten, complained that the book treated the issue of justice separately from the theory of price. Taylor was professor at the University of Nebraska and Davenport later (1899–1902) was appointed principal of the high school in Lincoln, where the university is located. I am uncertain whether they were related in any other way, however. Taylor is distinguished by a highly provocative and neglected book on the credit system as a stage in the evolution of human relations (1913).

30 The best sources for Davenport's theories of these subjects are his 1908 and 1914

books, partly because he had by that time become more acquainted with the professional literature.

31 See Davenport (1902). Davenport's criticism is similar to that made later by Mises, the difference being that Davenport did not use the term "subjectivism." Mises referred to "stylistic faults in the presentation of the subjective theory of value" (1981: 167).

32 See especially (1908: 329–330) and surrounding discussion.

33 That Menger's theory of price did not assume divisibility has been recently argued by Endres (1995).

34 Streissler points out that Menger "was the least marginalist of the Austrians. *The further his pupils escaped him, the more marginalist they became, precisely because they assimilated other traditions*" (italics in original) (1972: 429). Mises conceived of the nineteenth-century revolution not in terms of marginalism, but in terms of the subjective theory of value (Mises 1981: chs 5 and 7).

35 Mises (1966: 120).

36 Davenport (1908: 93 n.). In the same footnote, Davenport also points out that his own paper published later in 1894 covered "very much the same ground" and that he was entirely ignorant of Green's paper at the time. It is also interesting to note that one year before his 1894 paper, Green had published two papers related to the Austrian theory of value. So it is possible to hypothesize that Green's notion of value and cost was rooted in the Austrian theory. Davenport never indicated that he had seen the earlier papers.

37 Wesley Mitchell points this out in his review of Davenport's later book (Mitchell 1914).

38 This disagreement is demonstrated by a series of papers in the German-language journal *Jahrbücher*. For a list of references see Davenport (1908: 339).

39 Not only does he criticize Böhm-Bawerk for not making the human agent part of his explanation of value, he goes on to show that Böhm-Bawerk unconsciously slipped the human agent in as part of his explanation. I discuss this in greater detail in Gunning (1996).

40 Davenport also stresses the advantage to clear thinking of regarding supply as reservation demand or, in other words, of describing equilibrium price in terms of reservation prices (see below for a fuller discussion of this point). This procedure brings to the fore the implicit assumption of a "fixed supply" in all economic analysis. Wicksteed (1914) made the same point. And, apparently, the point was implicit in Wicksteed's ([1910] 1933) earlier book, according to Robbins (1934: n. 9). Robbins (1934: 27) also adopted Davenport's suggestion that we conceive of utility in its relative sense and not its marginal sense. Nevertheless, Robbins apparently overlooked Davenport's 1914 book, as well as Davenport's posthumously published critique of Marshall. Fixed supply, in this context, means entrepreneurship's belief that the means of satisfying consumer demands are not unlimited. They are scarce.

41 See Gunning (1996) for quotations.

42 This is perhaps an opportune time to point out a misreporting of Davenport by Israel Kirzner (1975: 102–103). Kirzner lumps Davenport with Vilfredo Pareto and others as being among a group that was concerned only with the consequences of human behavior—prices. He is unlike Frank Fetter and Jacob Viner, according to Kirzner, who "insisted on the need to dig below the surface phenomena of prices for their explanation." On the contrary, it might be said that Davenport dug deeper than any of his contemporaries, including the Austrians of the day.

43 See Schuetz (1943). The source of Davenport's subjectivism may have been

Henri Bergson, since there is a brief reference to Bergson's notion of time (1914: 174).

44 This issue, along with Fetter's criticism, is discussed in Gunning (1996).

45 See Gunning (1997a).

46 Fetter (1914b).

47 The third is discussed in Gunning (1996). The last two are discussed in Gunning (1997c).

48 This paper, by the way, also had few references. If Fetter had read it—and it seems likely that he had—he would presumably have had the same complaint against it.

49 The interested reader should also consult J.M. Clark's review of the 1914 book (J.M. Clark 1914).

50 This is discussed more fully in Gunning (1997c).

REFERENCES

Böhm-Bawerk, E. ([1889] 1959). *Capital and Interest*, vol. 2, *The Positive Theory of Capital*, transl. George D. Huncke and Hans F. Sennholz, South Holland, Ill.: Libertarian Press.

——— (1890). "Macvane's Political Economy," *Quarterly Journal of Economics* 4 (April): 331–339.

——— ([1891] 1962). "The Austrian Economists," in *Shorter Classics of Eugen von Böhm-Bawerk*, South Holland, Ill.: Libertarian Press.

——— ([1894a] 1962). "The Ultimate Standard of Value," in *Shorter Classics of Eugen von Böhm-Bawerk*, South Holland, Ill.: Libertarian Press.

——— (1894b). "One Word More on the Ultimate Standard of Value," *Economic Journal* 4 (December).

Bonar, J. (1888). "The Austrian Economists and Their View on Value," *Quarterly Journal of Economics* 2 (October): 1–31.

——— (1889). "The Positive Theory of Capital," *Quarterly Journal of Economics* 3 (April): 336–351.

Clark, J.B. (1897). "Book review of H.J. Davenport's *Outlines of Economic Theory*," *Journal of Political Economy* 5 (June): 384–385.

Clark, J.M. (1914). "Davenport's Economics," *Political Science Quarterly* 29 (June): 315–323.

Davenport, H. (1894). "The Formula of Sacrifice," *Journal of Political Economy* 2 (September): 561–573.

——— (1896). *Outlines of Economic Theory*, New York: Macmillan.

——— (1898). *Outlines of Elementary Economics*, New York: Macmillan.

——— (1902). "Proposed Modifications in Austrian Theory and Terminology," *Quarterly Journal of Economics* 16 (May): 355–384.

——— (1904). "Capital as a Competitive Concept," *Journal of Political Economy* 13 12 (December): 31–47.

——— (1905). "Doctrinal Tendencies: Fetter, Flux, Seager and Carver," *Yale Review* (November).

——— (1908). *Value and Distribution*, Chicago: University of Chicago Press.

——— (1910). "Social Productivity Versus Private Acquisitions," *Quarterly Journal of Economics* 25 (November): 96–118.

——— (1914). *The Economics of Enterprise*, New York: Macmillan.
——— (1916). "Fetter's 'Economic Principles'," *Journal of Political Economy* 24 (April): 313–362.
Dorfman, J. (1949). *The Economic Mind in American Civilization*, vol. 3, New York: Viking.
Ebeling, R. ([1977] 1990). "On the Theory of Costs," repr. in Stephen Littlechild (ed.), *Austrian Economics*, vol. 1, Brookfield, Vermont: Edward Elgar Publishing Company, 8–9.
Edgeworth, F. (1892). "Review of Eugen Böhm-Bawerk's *The Positive Theory of Capital*," *Economic Journal*, repr. in id., *Papers in Political Economy* ([1925] 1963), New York: Burt Franklin.
Elzas, B. (1988). "On the Austrian Notion of 'Cost' in 1889," *Journal of Economic Studies* 34: 36–54.
Endres, A. (1995). "Carl Menger's Theory of Price Formation Reconsidered," *History of Political Economy* 27: 261–287.
——— (1996). "Some Microfoundations of Austrian Economics: Böhm-Bawerk's Version," *The European Journal of the History of Economic Thought* 3 (spring): 84–106.
Fetter, F. (1914a). "Interest Theories, Old and New," *American Economic Review* 4 (March): 68–92.
——— (1914b). "Davenport's Competitive Economics," *Journal of Political Economy* 22 (June): 550–565.
——— (1927). "Clark's Reformulation of the Capital Concept," in J. Hollander (ed.), *Economic Essays Contributed in Honor of John Bates Clark*, New York: Macmillan.
——— (1977). *Capital, Interest, and Rent*, ed. Murray Rothbard, Kansas City, Kan.: Sheed Andrews & McMeel.
Green, D. (1893a). "Marginal Utility and Value," *Quarterly Journal of Economics* 7 (April).
——— (1893b). "The Austrian Theory of Value," *Annals of the American Academy of Political and Social Sciences* (November).
——— (1894). "Pain-Cost and Opportunity-Cost," *Quarterly Journal of Economics* 8: 218–229.
Gunning, J. (1993). "Entrepreneurists and Firmists: Knight vs. the Modern Theory of the Firm," *Journal of the History of Economic Thought* 15 (March): 31–53.
——— (1996). "Herbert J. Davenport's Transformation of the Austrian Theory of Value and Cost," working paper, Dept. of Economics, Taiwan: National Chung Hsing University.
——— (1997a). "The Theory of Entrepreneurship in Austrian Economics," in W. Keizer, B. Tieben, and R. Van Zijp (eds), *Austrians in Debate*, London: Routledge.
——— (1997b). "Ludwig von Mises's Transformation of the Austrian Theory of Value and Cost," *History of Economics Review* (forthcoming).
——— (1997c). "H.J. Davenport's Loan Fund Theory of Capital," manuscript.
Haney, L.H. (1911). "The Social Point of View in Economics: I," *Quarterly Journal of Economics* 27 (November): 115–139.
——— (1912). "The Social Point of View in Economics: II," *Quarterly Journal of Economics* 27 (February): 292–321.
Hayek, F.A. von (ed.) (1935). *Collectivist Economic Planning: Critical Studies on the Possibilities of Socialism*, London: Routledge.

Hayek. F.A. von ([1937] 1948). "Economics and Knowledge," repr. in id., *Individualism and Economic Order*, Chicago: University of Chicago Press.

Kirzner, I. (1973). *Competition and Entrepreneurship*, Chicago: University of Chicago Press.

——— (1975). *The Economic Point of View: An Essay in the History of Economic Thought*, Kansas City, Kan.: Sheed & Ward.

——— (1979). *Perception, Opportunity, and Profit*, Chicago: University of Chicago Press.

——— (1992). *The Meaning of the Market Process: Essays in the Development of Modern Austrian Economics*, London: Routledge.

Knight, F. (1921). *Risk, Uncertainty, and Profit*, New York: Houghton Mifflin.

——— (1927). "Comment on Fetter," *American Economic Review* 17 (March): 120–121.

Lachmann, L. ([1951] 1977). "The Science of Human Action," repr. in *Capital, Expectations, and the Market Process*, Kansas City, Kan.: Sheed Andrews & McMeel.

Macvane, S. (1890). "Böhm-Bawerk on Value and Wages," *Quarterly Journal of Economics* 4 (October): 24–43.

——— (1893a). "Marginal Utility and Value," *Quarterly Journal of Economics* 7 (April): 255–285.

——— (1893b). "The Austrian Theory of Value," *Annals of the American Academy of Political and Social Science* (November).

Marshall, A. (1890). *Principles of Economics*, London: Macmillan.

——— (1892). *Elements of the Economics of Industry*, London: Macmillan.

Menger, C. ([1871] 1981). *Principles of Economics*, tr. J. Dingwall and B. Hoselitz, New York: New York University Press.

Mises, L. von (1966). *Human Action: A Treatise on Economics*, Chicago: Henry Regnery Company.

——— (1978). *Notes and Recollections*, South Holland, Ill.: Libertarian Press.

——— (1981). *Epistemological Problems of Economics*, tr. G. Reisman, New York: New York University Press.

Mitchell, W. (1914). "Book review of H.J. Davenport's *The Economics of Enterprise*," *American Economic Review* 9 (September): 602–605.

Newman, P. (1952). *The Development of Economic Thought*, Englewood Cliffs, NJ: Prentice-Hall.

O'Driscoll, G. (1980). "Frank A. Fetter and 'Austrian' Business Cycle Theory," *History of Political Economy* 12 (winter): 542–556.

Pasour, E.C. (1977). "Cost and Choice—Austrian vs. Conventional Views," *Journal of Libertarian Studies* 2: 327–336.

Patten, S. (1893). "Cost and Expense," *Annals of the American Academy of Political and Social Science* (May).

Robbins, L. (1934). "Remarks Upon Certain Aspects of the Theory of Costs," *Economic Journal* (March): 1–19.

Streissler, E. (1972). "To What Extent Was the Austrian School Marginalist?" *History of Political Economy* (fall): 426–441.

Streissler, E. and W. Weber (1973). "The Menger Tradition," in J.R. Hicks and W. Weber (eds), *Carl Menger and the Austrian School of Economics*, Oxford: Clarendon Press.

Taylor, W.G.L. (1897). "A New Presentation of Economic Theory," *Journal of Political Economy* 5 (June): 518–528.

——— (1913). *The Credit System*, New York: Macmillan.

Vaughn, K. (1980). "Does It Matter That Costs are Subjective?" *Southern Economic Journal* 46: 702–715.

Wicksteed, P. ([1910] 1933). *The Common Sense of Political Economy*, London: Lund Humphries.

——— (1914). "The Scope and Method of Political Economy in the Light of the 'Marginal' Theory of Value and Distribution," *Economic Journal* 24 (March): 3–26.

Wieser, F. ([1888] 1956). *Natural Value*, tr. A. Malloch and ed. W. Smart, New York: Kelley & Millman.

——— (1891). "The Austrian School and the Theory of Value," *Economic Journal* 1: 108–121.

——— (1892). "The Theory of Value: A Reply to Professor Macvane," *Annals of the American Academy of Political and Social Science* (March).

9

THE QUEST FOR AN IDEAL INDEX

Irving Fisher and *The Making of Index Numbers*[1]

Robert W. Dimand

INTRODUCTION

Measuring movements in the general level of prices was crucial for Irving Fisher's monetary economics. His distinction between real and nominal interest rates depended on changes in the general price level. His statement in *The Purchasing Power of Money* (Fisher 1913) of the quantity theory of money, holding that, other things being equal, a change in the quantity of money leads in the long run to a change in the price level of the same proportion, also depends on the concept and measurement of an index of the average level of prices, as did his educational campaign to eradicate money illusion. His compensated dollar proposal called for stabilization of an index of commodity prices. The gold standard, the policy rule which Fisher's compensated dollar plan was intended to replace, created no comparable need for calculation of a price index. Fisher's schemes for neutralizing monetary shocks by indexation, such as the indexed bond that he persuaded Remington Rand to issue in the 1920s or the indexation of his secretary's weekly pay, also depended on a price index. Fisher drew on his great energy and determination in his effort to decide upon and calculate an ideal index number for prices, along with the corresponding index for quantities. Although Fisher had predecessors whom he generously acknowledged (notably Edgeworth and Walsh, who shared the dedication of *The Making of Index Numbers* (Fisher 1922)), Arthur Vogt (Vogt and Barta 1997) rightly states that one may call Fisher's *The Purchasing Power of Money* the old testament and *The Making of Index Numbers* the new testament of statistical index theory.

The test approach to the statistical theory of index numbers, to which Fisher (1913, 1922) and Walsh (1901, 1921) contributed, sought to find an index number formula that would satisfy a list of statistical criteria. Walsh introduced the proportionality test, which Fisher included in a more comprehensive set of criteria. Fisher claimed, on the basis of these criteria, to have found an "ideal index," a particular formula which was best for all purposes. The economic theory of index numbers, exemplified by Bennet (1920) and Konüs (1924), sought a "true index" of the cost of achieving a constant level of utility. Unlike this approach, the criteria for Fisher's ideal index did not require knowledge of the utility function. Konüs and Byushgens (1926) linked the two approaches by showing that certain index number formulae are equivalent to assuming particular functional forms, in particular that Fisher's ideal price and quantity indexes would be exact for a homogenous quadratic aggregator function. In the 1970s, W. Erwin Diewert (1993c) introduced the concept of superlative indexes, statistical indexes that are exact to flexible functional forms (functional forms providing a second-order approximation to an arbitrary twice-differentiable aggregator function).

The importance of index numbers for Fisher's monetary theory and policy set him apart from the Austrian approach exemplified by Ludwig von Mises's *Theory of Money and Credit*, first published in German in 1912, a year after *The Purchasing Power of Money*. Mises and later Hayek were skeptical of reasoning in terms of aggregates such as the price level and, while adamantly against inflation, opposed price level stabilization as a policy rule because they considered deflation a necessary part of adjustment.

TOWARD AN "IDEAL INDEX"

Chapter 10 of *The Purchasing Power of Money* (Fisher 1913) discussed "The Best Index Numbers of Purchasing Power" and had a 45-page appendix testing index number formulae for theoretically desirable properties (Fisher 1913: 198–233, 385–429). Some reviewers found Fisher's coverage too comprehensive: John Maynard Keynes objected that "In the long appendix on index numbers, in which marks for different kinds of merit are given to 44 different formulae, it seems a waste of time to have demonstrated the unsuitability of numerous expressions which have never previously been suggested, far less advocated, by anyone" (Keynes 1983, 11: 381). Undeterred by such protests, Fisher went on to a deductive and empirical investigation of the properties of 134 index number formulae in *The Making of Index Numbers*.

Fisher's concern in chapter 10 of *The Purchasing Power of Money* was with the appropriate index number for P, the price level in the equation of exchange $MV + M'V' = PT$, and with T, the corresponding index of trade. PT would be the value of transactions at actual prices, while T would measure what the value of transactions would have been had quantities been sold at base prices. P would then be a measure of general purchasing power suitable as a standard for deferred payments. The context of the equation of exchange shaped Fisher's choice of criteria for a useful index number, even though he was to make the controversial claim that his preferred index number was best for all purposes. While Fisher (1913: 200) accepted that "it seems theoretically impossible to devise an index number, P, which shall satisfy all of the tests we should like to impose," he held that it is "nevertheless, possible to construct index numbers which satisfy these tests so well for practical purposes that we may profitably devote serious attention to the study and construction of index numbers."

In a lengthy appendix, Fisher listed eight tests for a good index number, and then examined how well 44 index number formulae satisfied them. The first six tests were in pairs, for the price index and the corresponding trade index. The proportionality tests held that if all prices (or quantities) changed by the same proportion, so should their index. Determinateness tests held that the price index (or correlative trade index) should not become zero, infinite, or indeterminate if an individual price (or quantity) became zero. Tests of withdrawal or entry would be satisified if the index was unaltered by adding or removing a price or quantity ratio whose value was the same as the index. The ratios between price indexes (and the correlative trade indexes) should be unaffected by reversing or changing the base. Finally, the index should be independent of units of measurement, so that it would not matter whether a quantity was measured in tons or in pounds.

These eight tests sounded intuitively appealing and not terribly restrictive, yet they were inconsistent with some of the best-known and most widely used index number formulae. William Stanley Jevons's essays in the 1860s (collected posthumously in his *Investigations in Currency and Finance* in 1884) were saluted in Fisher's "Landmarks in the History of Index Numbers" (appendix IV of *The Making of Index Numbers*), for "Jevons seems to have been the first to have kindled in others an interest in the subject and may perhaps be considered the father of index numbers." Jevons's geometric average of price ratios fails Fisher's determinateness test, because the index would become zero if any of its components was zero. Perhaps the most common index was an arithmetic average of price ratios, simple or weighted, with the price indexes published by *The Economist* and *The Statist* (both of London) being simple arithmetic averages. Arithmetic averages are not invariant to the choice of base year. Indeed, Fisher found no formula satisfying all his tests, and Swamy (1965) and Eichhorn (1976) have shown that no such formula can exist. Out of a possible score of seven (counting the withdrawal or entry test only for the price index), the highest score found by Fisher was 5.5, with six other formulae satisfying five tests. Four formulae even failed the unit-shifting test (changing the physical units of one commodity), including the simplest, Bradstreet's ratio of sums of current and base prices per pound of 96 commodities.

Since he did not consider the tests to be of equal importance, Fisher's choice of index number was not simply determined by the raw score. He attached little importance to the determinateness tests (regarding zero prices or quantities as of little practical significance), and placed most stress on the proportionality test. With proportionality, a change in M (currency) and M′ (bank money) by the same proportion would, if velocities of circulation and quantities were unchanged, cause each individual price and the price index to change in the same proportion.

If each year's price index was to be expressed on a common base, Fisher's preferred index was the total value of quantities sold in a year divided by what the value would have been reckoned at base prices. When each year was expressed in terms of the preceding year as base (a chain index), Fisher considered price index formulae using the arithmetic or geometric average of the quantities in the two years as slightly superior in theory for year-to-year comparisons. Fisher (1913: 425) asserted that "Practically, however, there is little if any advantage" in these latter formulae as they are "practically far more laborious" to compute and "weighting is of little importance." Keynes (1983, 11: 379–380) complained in his 1911 *Economic Journal* review of *The Purchasing Power of Money* that "Professor Fisher's theory, that the weights employed in compiling an index number seldom affect the result, naturally leads him to think that an index number made for one purpose is equally suitable for another, and that the method of compilation can be safely determined by considerations of taste and convenience. . . . [W]hen Professor Fisher comes to the separate determination of P and T, he is content to publish what seem to the present reviewer to be unscientific guesses of the wildest character."

Fisher (1921) returned to the question of "The Best Form of Index Number" in talks to the American Statistical Association in Atlantic City in December 1920 and to the American Academy of Arts and Sciences in Boston in April 1921. As the paper had "not yet been completed in all the detail desirable for publication," the *Quarterly Publications* of the American Statistical Association for March 1921 published only a four-page abstract, followed by a very brief discussion by Wesley Clair Mitchell of Columbia, editor of the *History of Prices During the War*, a little less than two pages of discussion by Warren M. Persons of Harvard, seven pages of discussion by Correa Moylan Walsh, and a five-page rejoinder by Fisher. In the course of revision for publication, "The Best Form of Index Number" grew into *The Making of Index Numbers*.

In his short abstract and long book, Fisher put aside several of the tests for a good index number proposed in his earlier book, not as mistaken but as being of little quantitative importance (as well as dropping the so-called circular test as unsound in theory). While keeping a subordinate role for tests of determinateness, proportionality, and commensurability (independence of the units of measurement), he stressed two tests as most important, one from *The Purchasing Power of Money* and one new. The test from the earlier book was the time-reversal test: in comparing two years, an index calculated with one year as the base should be the reciprocal of the index calculated using the other year as the base. The new test was the factor-reversal test: the price index multiplied by the quantity index should give the correct figure for the index number of value. Few formulae conformed to both criteria. One that did satisfy both was proposed by Fisher as the ideal index number for all purposes. This was the square root of the product of an aggregative average weighted by base-year quantities (a Laspeyres index) and an aggregative average weighted by given-year quantities (a Paasch index), with the downward bias of the Laspeyres index offsetting the upward bias of the Paasch index. This formula, number 353 in *The Making of Index Numbers*, was formula 16 in *The Purchasing Power of Money*, but had not then been singled out by Fisher as the best formula. Fisher's ideal index does not, however, satisfy the circular test that a price index should be independent of the choice of a third time point (decomposing it into the product of two similar price indexes).

Fisher's principal discussant at the American Statistical Association was C. M. Walsh. This was highly appropriate: Fisher (1922) dedicated *The Making of Index Numbers* "To F.Y. Edgeworth and Correa Moylan Walsh Pioneers in the Exploration of Index Numbers." The dedication to Walsh recognized Walsh's *The Measurement of General Exchange-Value* (1901), which Fisher had reviewed in the *Yale Review* in May 1902. Fisher's appendix to *The Making of Index Numbers* on "Landmarks in the History of Index Numbers" hailed Walsh (1901) as "the largest and best work, and the only general treatise on the theory of the subject up to the present time" (1922: 459). The only work of comparable stature were the reports from 1887 to 1889 of a British Association committee on index numbers, of which Edgeworth was secretary (reprinted in Darnell 1991, 6: 1–126). While Mitchell and Persons demurred at Fisher's claim that a particular index number formula was best for all purposes, rather than being simply a good general purpose index, Walsh largely accepted Fisher's view of the ideal price index. While acknowledging Fisher's priority and suggesting that the index be known as Fisher's index number, Walsh drew attention to support for that index in his forthcoming short book, *The Problem of Estimation* (1921: 102–103). Walsh was one of five people thanked by Fisher in the preface of *The Making of Index Numbers* for reading and commenting on the whole manuscript. A letter from Fisher to Mitchell inviting Mitchell to New Haven for a weekend to discuss index numbers mentioned that Walsh was coming (Fisher to Mitchell, June 24, 1921, Mitchell Papers, Columbia University). Another letter from Fisher to Mitchell mentions a conference Fisher held with several members of the American Economic Association's Committee on Index Numbers, which Mitchell (who chaired the committee) was unable to attend (Fisher to Mitchell, August 20, 1921).

Well before *The Making of Index Numbers* was published, and even before the manuscript was finished, Fisher's ideal index number formula was the subject of several articles. Warren Persons discussed it in the *Review of*

Economic Statistics in May 1921, again holding it to be a good general purpose index rather than ideal for all purposes. Royal Meeker (1921) of the International Labour Office in Geneva, later a collaborator with Fisher in the Index Number Institute, also expressed doubt about the existence of a single ideal index in the *Quarterly Publications of the American Statistical Association*.

Fisher sent a rough draft of his manuscript to Wesley Mitchell on November 10, 1921, asking Mitchell to return it to Fisher's New Haven address as soon as he had finished it, so that parts of it could be forwarded for Fisher to perfect in Europe, for which he would sail on November 23 (Fisher to Mitchell, Mitchell Papers, Columbia University). On the evening of March 30, 1922, Irving Fisher made his first radio broadcast, about his European trip, just a few months after regular radio broadcasts began in the United States, then took the manuscript of *The Making of Index Numbers* to the Railway Express office: "I've been in a whirl with my book and so many other things. *But the book is now really off!* I took it down to the station and sent it myself, insured for $1,000! It seems too good to be true" (Fisher to Margaret Hazard Fisher, March 30, 1922, Fisher Papers, Yale University).

The Making of Index Numbers: A Study of Their Varieties, Tests, and Reliability, Fisher's fully worked-out version of his American Statistical Association paper, was finally three times as long as he had initially expected. With more than five hundred pages, 123 charts, and 33 pages of tables of numbers, and what was expected to be a limited scholarly audience, it did not appeal to ordinary commercial publishers. Houghton Mifflin's Riverside Press published the book for the Pollak Foundation for Economic Research, which made *The Making of Index Numbers* the Foundation's publication no. 1: "Some of the work must have been abandoned had not the Pollak Foundation for Economic Research come to the rescue," paying for calculations as well as publication, wrote Fisher in the preface. The Pollak Foundation—directed by William T. Foster, a teacher of rhetoric and former president of Reed College, and financed by Waddill Catchings of the investment bankers Goldman Sachs & Company—provided a forum for the underconsumptionist views of those monetary heretics. Their sponsorship of major scholarly works such as Fisher's *The Making of Index Numbers* and later a book on real wages by Paul Douglas (who had been an instructor at Reed College during Foster's presidency) provided Foster and Catchings with visibility and access to the economics profession rare for dissenting amateurs. So did their sponsorship of a $5,000 prize for the best criticism of their book, *Profits* (1925). Foster was among those credited in the preface to *The Making of Index Numbers* with helping Fisher with the book, and was thanked by Fisher (1928) in the acknowledgements for *The Money Illusion*. Foster and Catchings gave similar thanks to Fisher in the prefaces to their Pollak Foundation volumes on *Money* (1923) and *Profits* (1925). Another connection linking Fisher to Foster and Catchings was Hudson Bridge Hastings, Professor of Administrative Engineering at Yale and author of the third Pollak publication, *Costs and*

Profits (Hastings 1923). When Fisher thanked Hastings in the preface to *The Making of Index Numbers* as one of five people who had read the entire manuscript, he gave the Pollak Foundation rather than Yale as an affiliation for Hastings.

To Fisher's "pleasant surprise," a second edition was called for within five months of the December 1922 publication. Only a few corrections were made in the second edition, and a detailed table of contents of appendix I was added. The third edition of 1927 added only appendix IX, surveying recent literature on the subject. Franklin Ho, a former student of Fisher at Yale who went on to work for him before returning to China, translated *The Making of Index Numbers* into Chinese. The Central Statistical Office of the USSR published a Russian translation in 1928. Soviet interest in index numbers had been demonstrated by the Conjuncture Institute's publication of A.A. Konüs ([1924] 1939) which sought to find bounds on a "true" constant-utility index of the cost of living, as distinct from Fisher's "ideal" index satisfying certain statistical tests, and Konüs and Byushgens (1926), whose techniques of proof for exact index number formulae developed the concept of duality and were to influence the work of Erwin Diewert (see Diewert 1993a, b). S.S. Byushgens (1925) and Konüs and Byushgens (1926) showed that Fisher's ideal index is exact if demand is governed by a homogenous quadratic utility function (see Afriat 1987: 212–214). Soon thereafter, such an interest in Western economics or economic conditions became dangerous in the Soviet Union: N.D. Kondrat'ev's Conjuncture Institute was closed in 1928 and the Central Statistical Office was purged for "wrecking activities," with one of the allegations being that "Kondrat'ev with his staff of henchmen in the Conjuncture Institute was engaged in the study of the economy of foreign countries and described it in numerous bulletins and books" (Jasny 1972: 164). Kondrat'ev vanished in the purges, Slutsky became a meteorologist, but Konüs survived to resume writing about index numbers after Stalin's death and to become a Fellow of the Econometric Society in 1975.

RECEPTION, CRITICISM, AND RESPONSE

The Making of Index Numbers stimulated great debate in scholarly journals. Journal editors allocated space for substantial review articles by leading quantitatively inclined economists and to Irving Fisher's extensive and vigorous responses. In one journal, the *Journal of the American Statistical Association*, discussion of Fisher's tests for a good index number continued for some years, as Fisher's inability to find an index number that fully satisfied all his tests led to the conjecture that the tests were mutually inconsistent. Ragnar Frisch (1930, 1934, 1936) argued that Fisher's tests were mutually inconsistent, but S. Subramanian (1934) showed that a weakness in Frisch's attempted proof left the question of consistency of the tests open. Another proof of inconsistency of Fisher's tests, by Abraham Wald (1937), also turned out to be flawed (see Swamy 1965). Later Subramanian Swamy (1965) offered a proof that no index number could satisfy all of Fisher's proportionality, circular, commensurability, and factor-reversal tests, and argued that the factor-reversal test was suspect. Eichhorn (1976) extended Swamy's proof, dropping the requirement of partial differentiability of the price index, and developed a weaker but consistent set of five tests (cf. Eichhorn and Voeller 1976; Jazairi 1972a, b; Diewert 1992).

The Statist sprang to the defense of its price index, a simple arithmetic average that failed both the time-reversal and factor-reversal tests. *The Statist* compiled and published such a simple and theoretically unsound index even though the periodical's founder, Sir Robert Giffen, had served in the 1880s on Edgeworth's British Association for the Advancement of Science committee, which had recommended an aggregative average. *The Statist* defended its index editorially five times (January 27, February 3, February 10, April 14, and May 26, 1923) and published four letters to the editor from Fisher (March 31, April 7, May 26, and July 28, 1923, the second and fourth of which are quoted in appendix IX). Fisher got the last word in the argument and had the stronger case. Felix Klezl of the Austrian Statistical Office, writing in the *International Labour Review* (August 1924), was the only supporter of *The Statist*'s stand on the simple arithmetic index. Fisher was forced, however, to admit in his April 7 letter to a clerical error that overstated the bias in the Sauerbeck–Statist index number (an error noted by Bowley, Snyder, and Yule in reviews), and to make the corresponding correction in the text and in chart 55 in his second edition.

Apart from his controversy with the editors of *The Statist*, Fisher replied in print to reviews or review articles by the Harvard economist Allyn Young (1923) in the *Quarterly Journal of Economics*, the London School of Economics statistician and mathematical economist A.L. Bowley (1923) in the *Economic Journal*, Carl Snyder (1923) of the Federal Reserve Bank of New York in the *American Economic Review*, and the British statistician G. Udney Yule (1923) in the *Journal of the Royal Statistical Society*. Fisher's replies amounted to 33 journal pages. In appendix IX of the third edition of *The Making of Index Numbers*, Fisher noted major reviews of his book in Italy, Germany, and Switzerland, describing Ladislaus von Bortkiewicz (1924) of Berlin University as "my most constructive critic" for improving some of Fisher's formulae for the coefficient of correlation between price relatives and quantity relatives. The book captured international scholarly attention, all (except a few British critics) praising Fisher for an important and massive contribution to the field, even when reviewers dissented from his downgrading of the circular test or his claim that his ideal index number formula was best for all purposes.

The first and longest review article of *The Making of Index Numbers* was by Allyn Young. Twenty-three pages long, it appeared in print in February

1923, a mere two months after the book was published. Young had corresponded with Fisher before publication, calling Fisher's attention to the appearance of his "ideal formula" along with other formulae in an 1899 article by Bowley in *Palgrave's Dictionary of Political Economy*. Frederick Macaulay noticed the "ideal formula" recommended (with inadvertent omission of the square root sign) by A.C. Pigou in *Wealth and Welfare* (1912). Wesley Mitchell wrote to tell Fisher of its recommendation (with the square root sign) in Pigou's *Economics of Welfare* (1920), already spotted by Fisher (Fisher 1922: xv, 241; Mitchell to Fisher, February 16, 1922; Fisher to Mitchell, February 18, 1922).

Young praised *The Making of Index Numbers* as

> a notable scientific achievement. The book has the qualities of deft and finished workmanship one has come to expect in what Professor Fisher does. . . . The practical significance of this general winnowing of the whole field of index numbers can hardly be overestimated. . . . It is an important contribution to knowledge, and reflects honor on American scholarship.
>
> (Young 1923: 342, 345, 364)

He found the factor-reversal test "ingenious and important" and Fisher's discussion of bias "one of the most valuable, as well as the most original, parts of the work" (1923: 350–351). Young "agree[d] with Professor Fisher respecting the formulas which give the best year-with-year comparisons," but demurred at Fisher's abandonment of the circular test: "But I believe that in the practical construction of standard series of index numbers it is quite as important, on the whole, that the series should be self-consistent as that each number of the series should afford an impeccably accurate comparison with the base of the series" (1923: 347). Consequently, Young could not accept that Fisher's ideal index was best for all purposes.

Young's review article led to the longest of Fisher's replies to critics of *The Making of Index Numbers*, a 14-page rejoinder in the August 1923 issue, in which Fisher (1923b: 754–755) overoptimistically held that "it would seem that such discussions as Professor Young's, Professor Persons's, Professor Bowley's, the *Statist*'s, and the present article mark the approach of the end, to all intents and purposes, of the age-long controversy over index number formulae." Fisher (1923b: 754) drew attention to Young's (1923: 363) "acceptance of the 'ideal' index number as 'beyond much doubt, the most accurate single index number of the movement of prices between any two years.' He gives no support to the common false belief that one formula is best for one 'purpose' and another for another."

In another very early review, in the *Economic Journal* for March 1923, A.L. Bowley omitted any initial praise of Fisher's book in general terms, and went straight into questioning whether the time-reversal and factor-reversal tests were in fact tests of universal validity, suitable regardless of the purposes for which the index number might be computed: "A test to which so much importance is attached, one which is used to condemn well-known index-numbers, ought not to have been put forward on so slender a basis" (Bowley 1923: 94). Fisher (1923a: 251) responded in June:

> While thanking Professor Bowley personally both for his favourable expressions and for his criticisms, I confess to a regret that he seems to hesitate to throw his strong influence wholeheartedly in the direction of what might be called index-number reform, so much needed to-day in the interests of statistical science. This would seem especially appropriate, as the "ideal" index-number which has been associated with my name should, as shown in my book, be more properly associated with his.

Bowley was not mollified: "My point about the factor-reversal test was that it had no theoretical justification; for this it is irrelevant to say that in fact index-numbers held to be good on other grounds satisfy it."

G. Udney Yule (1923) objected to Fisher's claim that "The purpose to which an index-number is put does not affect the choice of formula" (Fisher 1922: 229):

> "Marry, that's a bountiful answer that fits all questions!" Professor Fisher's belief that he is able to give the correct answer to a question without knowing what the question is does not appear to me well founded. An unknown question cannot be answered at all. A vague and indefinite question cannot be answered definitely, and unless the purpose of an index-number—the question that it is intended to answer—is settled with complete precision, the correct formula to use cannot be stated. . . . The volume will serve as a useful encyclopaedia of formulae, and collection of arithmetical tests of such formulae. From the standpoint of principle it is wholly disappointing.
>
> (Yule 1923)

Fisher replied sharply in the January 1924 *Journal of the Royal Statistical Society*, at greater length than Yule's original review. Referring to his 1902 review of Walsh (1901), Fisher noted that he had once believed that the purpose of an index number must have something to do with its measurement:

> Having changed from Mr. Yule's position to (essentially) that of Walsh, I should be quite willing to change back if Mr. Yule had any real evidence to offer. But he offers none nor does he refute the evidence presented in my book. I am forced to the conclusion that he has here also missed the point. Mr. Yule is an able statistician and

> analyst, but, in his self-confidence, he seems hastily to have assumed that what was really a conclusion empirically reached is a "basis" absurd *a priori*. The other reviewer [Fisher himself in 1902] fell into just this error.
>
> (Fisher 1924: 91)

Fisher also remarked that "Mr. Yule, while evincing a lively sympathy for the *Statist*, and, apparently, even resentment against me for my criticism of the *Statist*'s index-number, does not venture to defend it; nor does he include in the above list of alleged different formulae for different purposes any case of the simple arithmetic" (1924: 94).

Carl Snyder's *American Economic Review* review article concluded that

> it seems as if, as a recent writer in the *Economist* expresses it, the United States is being driven by the force of ineluctable circumstance to some kind of an experiment with index number control, in the endeavor to regain that economic stability which it lost in the war, and in the topsy turvy conditions since prevailing. Nothing could offer a firmer base for this, nor, in the end, lend greater confidence to the use of index numbers than such a painstaking work as that which Professor Fisher has carried through. He has cleared away much debris, so that the solid structure built up in the last fifty or sixty years stands forth in clear and precise outline.
>
> (Snyder 1923: 421)

Fisher's brief reply (1923c) concentrated on his criticism of the simple arithmetic average as a price index.

R.G. Hawtrey objected that

> If a price index has to be constructed to verify Professor Irving Fisher's Equation of Exchange and for no other purpose, there is something to be said for including prices of securities. Professor Fisher includes in the totality of transactions all dealings in securities. But to my mind that is a defect in his formula, and it would be an improvement to exclude all dealings in stocks, shares and pecuniary rights and to restate the Equation of Exchange, as Professor Pigou has proposed, in terms of transactions in goods and services only.
>
> (Hawtrey 1930: 152–153)

Disregarding Fisher's argument for the geometric average of the Paasche and Laspeyres indexes as his ideal index, Hawtrey argued that

> much of that controversy [as to the ideal methods of averaging and weighting index numbers] is in reality irrelevant to the selection of

> an index-number for Professor Fisher's Equation of Exchange. The equation of exchange itself determines its own type of index-number. Since the equation of exchange proceeds from a comparison of two aggregates of wealth, it must employ the type of index-number which arises from such a comparison, that is to say, the weighted arithmetic mean. The ambiguities inherent in that index, owing to the differences in weighting appropriate to the different periods to be compared, are inherent in the equation of exchange itself.
>
> (1930: 131)

Thus the economist closest to Fisher's monetary theory of economic fluctuations was not only unpersuaded by Fisher's proposed ideal index, but failed to see any purpose in Fisher's *The Making of Index Numbers*.

Although Correa Moylan Walsh agreed with Fisher's choice of an ideal index number, both Walsh and Francis Ysidro Edgeworth continued to attach more importance to the circular test than did Fisher. In appendix IX, added in the 1927 third edition of *The Making of Index Numbers*, Fisher printed a letter from Edgeworth (Fisher 1927a: 523) and stated that part of the criticism in Edgeworth's letter and two 1925 articles by Edgeworth was well considered:

> In particular, I wish to admit that my book largely neglects the theory of selecting and revising the items to be included in an index number when, as is usually the case, those items are samples intended to represent a larger group. This neglect was partly intentional, as my book was primarily devoted to the discussion of formulae; but it was also partly due to my lack of appreciation of the importance of this subject of Sampling. . . . I hope before long to publish a paper [read at the 1926 meeting of the American Statistical Association] on the stock market index, in which this matter of improper Sampling, and other results, including the proposed remedy, will be fully treated.
>
> (1927a: 524–525)

In that paper, Fisher (1927b) took the construction of a price index for industrial common stocks listed on the New York Stock Exchange as his example, and proposed a "total value criterion" for sampling analogous to his factor reversal test for the index formula:

> our samples are to be so chosen that their *price index* multiplied by their *quantity index* shall give the *true value index* for the *whole field* represented by those samples. The necessity of such a criterion was forced on my own attention in a study of stock market indexes.

> Without it, a stock market index of prices, and even more, a stock market index of quantities is apt to wander surprisingly far afield.
>
> (1927b: 421)

> This *sampling* bias is a new concept in Index Numbers and is quite distinct from the *formula* bias (whether "type" bias or "weight" bias) discussed in *The Making of Index Numbers*. To indicate a reliable method of insuring, to a reasonable extent, against sampling bias is the chief objective toward which this article is aimed.
>
> (1927b: 432)

This article (with Fisher's characteristically optimistic view of what he had achieved) rounded out his theoretical work on index numbers.

CONCLUSION

Although the U.S. Bureau of Labor Statistics began to publish its index of wholesale prices in 1902 and its cost of living index (later renamed the Consumer Price Index) in 1919, Fisher worked in an era of limited compilation of statistics by government. Consequently, he took it upon himself to carry his index number prescriptions into practice. Fisher founded the Index Number Institute in January 1923, a month after *The Making of Index Numbers* appeared. Beginning in that month, the *New York Times* and other papers published the Institute's weekly index number of commodity prices (a wholesale price index) every Monday. By 1929 the index was published in newspapers with a combined circulation of seven million, and the Institute published other indexes, such as a weekly index of stock prices. Fisher wrote all the weekly articles accompanying the index until the end of 1930. Thereafter, some were written by Royal Meeker, a former Princeton economics professor and Commissioner of Labor Statistics in the Wilson administration, hired by Fisher as president of the Index Number Institute. Fisher continued to write many himself until he sold the Index Number Institute to the Institute of Applied Econometrics, writing, for example, 28 of the articles in 1932. This privately produced index was discontinued only in 1942, after which government statistics held the field (Allen 1993: 173, 244).

Like his annual article in the *American Economic Review* on the equation of exchange, the weekly newspaper article and price indexes of the Index Number Institute show Fisher harnessing his great energy and power of perseverance for the empirical follow-up to his monetary theories. Unlike defenders of the gold standard or Austrian critics of aggregate reasoning, Fisher needed a meaningful price index for statistical verification of his quantity of money theory of the price level and of his monetary theory of economic fluctuations, for his proposed compensated dollar monetary policy rule, and for his proposed indexation of bonds. Fisher not only attempted the statistical verification of his version of the quantity theory of money and his monetary theory of economic fluctuations (see Dimand 1993); he also composed a monumental work on the best method of calculating the statistical indexes to be used for this purpose. As with the compensated dollar or 100 percent reserve banking, Fisher presented his ideal index number as a simple, definitive solution to an apparently complex problem. He undertook the daunting task of compiling these index numbers, without financial support from government or philanthropic foundations. He was determined not merely to add to knowledge, but to stabilize the economy by vanquishing money illusion and by persuading monetary authorities to stabilize a commodity price index rather than just the price of a single commodity, gold. This required reliable index numbers of prices. If these were lacking, Fisher would remedy the lack himself. Responsibility for producing such index numbers has since shifted to the public sector. Even so, the trail now followed is the one blazed by Fisher: in 1995, the U.S. Department of Commerce adopted Fisher's "ideal index number" for calculation of the GNP deflator, and the associated quantity index.

What Fisher contributed to index number theory was the testing of a wide range of possible index number formulae for the degree to which each satisfied a list of desirable properties such as proportionality and independence of units of measurement, an approach continued by Eichhorn (1976) and Eichhorn and Voeller (1976). Inspired by the work of Correa Moylan Walsh, Fisher carried this test approach to index numbers much further than Walsh had. From this exhaustive testing, Fisher concluded in *The Making of Index Numbers* that a single formula, the geometric mean of the Paasche and Laspeyres indexes, was the ideal index number for all purposes. The reception of *The Making of Index Numbers* shows the deep-seated resistance to this idea of a single index number for all uses, typified in Bowley's review and in the title of Edgeworth's last article, "The Plurality of Index-Numbers." Over time, Fisher's notion of the same index number formula being suitable for different applications has become generally accepted in statistical index number theory, which deals with parameter-free statistical indexes, not dependent on the estimator or assumed functional form for the underlying utility, production, or cost function. Moreover, Fisher's ideal index is still the index number formula that best satisfies the tests of this approach, with the Divisia index second (Serletis 1997: 324; Divisia 1925). However, Diewert (1993c) has shown that all known superlative indexes (i.e., indexes that are exact to flexible functional forms) are second-order approximations to each other, so that the choice of which superlative index to use in an application does not matter much. The journal discussion of Fisher's test approach, extensive both in terms of journal pages and of years, deepened understanding of why even Fisher's ideal index fully satisfied only five of his seven tests, and partially satisfied a sixth. Fisher's tests turned out to be inconsistent, so that no index number formula could meet all his criteria. One of Fisher's tests must be dropped to produce a mutually consistent set of criteria, but it remains an open question which one should go. The concept of exactness of an index emerged from the journal discussion of Fisher's book, with the demonstration by Byushgens and Konüs that Fisher's ideal index is exact for a homogenous quadratic utility, production, or cost function. Three-quarters of a century after the first edition of *The Making of Index Numbers*, index number practice is catching up with Fisher's recommendations, and Fisher's claim that the index that best satisfied a set of statistical criteria is best for all purposes, so startling to many of his reviewers, no longer seems so controversial.

NOTE

1 I am grateful to William J. Barber and James Tobin for comments on a related manuscript, the editorial introduction and postscript to a new edition of *The Making of Index Numbers*, in *The Works of Irving Fisher* (14 vols, general editor William J. Barber, assistant editors Robert W. Dimand and Kevin Foster, consultant editor James Tobin, London: Pickering & Chatto, 1997).

REFERENCES

Afriat, S.N. (1987). *Logic of Choice and Economic Theory*, Oxford: Clarendon Press.

Allen, R.L. (1993). *Irving Fisher: A Biography*, Oxford: Blackwell.

Bennet, T.L. (1920). "The Theory of Measurement of Changes in Cost of Living," *Journal of the Royal Statistical Society* 83: 455–462.

Bortkiewicz, L. von (1924). "Review of Fisher's *The Making of Index Numbers*," *Archiv für Sozialwissenschaft und Sozialpolitik* 51: 848–853.

Bowley, A.L. (1923). "Review of Fisher, *The Making of Index Numbers*," *Economic Journal* 33: 90–94.

Byushgens, S.S. (1925). "Ob Odnom klasse giperpoverkhostey: po povodu 'idealnovo indeksa' Irving Fisher'a pokupatelnoi sili denig [On a class of hypersurfaces: Concerning the 'ideal index' of Irving Fisher]," *Mathematischeskii Sbornik* 32: 625–631.

Darnell, A. (1991). *Early Mathematical Economics*, 6 vols, London: Pickering & Chatto.

Diewert, W.E. (1992). "Fisher Ideal Output, Input, and Productivity Indexes Revisited," *Journal of Productivity Analysis* 3: 211–248, repr. in Diewert (1993c), 317–354.

——— (1993a). "Overview of Volume 1," in Diewert (1993c), 1–31.

——— (1993b). "The Early History of Price Index Research," in Diewert (1993c), 33–65.

——— (1993c). *Essays in Index Number Theory*, ed. W.E. Diewert and A.O. Nakamura (vol. 1 of Diewert's *Collected Papers*), Amsterdam: North-Holland.

Dimand, R.W. (1993). "The Dance of the Dollar: Irving Fisher's Monetary Theory of Economic Fluctuations," *History of Economics Review* 20: 161–172.

Divisia, F. (1925). "L'Indice monétaire et la théorie de la monnaie," *Revue d'Economie Politique* 29: 980–1008.

Edgeworth, F.Y. (1925a). "The Element of Probability in Index-Numbers," *Journal of the Royal Statistical Society* 88: 557–575.

——— (1925b). "The Plurality of Index-Numbers," *Economic Journal* 35: 379–388.

Eichhorn, W. (1976). "Fisher's Tests Revisited," *Econometrica* 44: 247–256.

Eichhorn, W. and J. Voeller (1976). *Theory of the Price Index: Fisher's Test Approach and Generalizations*, lecture notes in economics and mathematical systems, Berlin: Springer-Verlag.

Fisher, I., assisted by H.G. Brown (1913). *The Purchasing Power of Money*, rev. 2nd edn, New York: Macmillan; also repr. with same page numbering in id. (1977), *The Works of Irving Fisher*, vol. 4, ed. W.J. Barber et al., London: Pickering & Chatto.

Fisher, I. (1921). "The Best Form of Index Number," *Quarterly Publications of the American Statistical Association* 17: 533–551 (including discussion by W.C. Mitchell, W.M. Persons, C.M. Walsh, and reply by Fisher).

——— (1922). *The Making of Index Numbers*, Boston: Houghton Mifflin, for Pollak Foundation for Economic Research.

——— (1923a). "Professor Bowley on Index Numbers," *Economic Journal* 33: 246–251 (with reply by A.L. Bowley, 251–252).

——— (1923b). "Professor Young on Index Numbers," *Quarterly Journal of Economics* 37: 742–755.

——— (1923c). "Comment on Review of Fisher's *The Making of Index Numbers*," *American Economic Review* 13: 652–654.

——— (1924). "Mr. Udney Yule on Index Numbers," *Journal of the Royal Statistical Society* 87: 89–98.

——— (1927a). *The Making of Index Numbers*, 3rd edn, Boston: Houghton Mifflin, Riverside Press, for Pollak Foundation for Economic Research.

——— (1927b). "The 'Total Value Criterion': A New Principle in Index Number Construction," *Journal of the American Statistical Association* 22: 419–441.

——— (1928). *The Money Illusion*, London: Allen & Unwin.

——— (1997). *The Works of Irving Fisher*, 14 vols, ed. W.J. Barber assisted by R.W. Dimand and K. Foster, consultant ed. J. Tobin, London: Pickering & Chatto.

Foster, W.T. and W. Catchings (1923). *Money*, Boston: Houghton Mifflin, Riverside Press, for Pollak Foundation for Economic Research.

——— (1925). *Profits*, Boston: Houghton Mifflin, Riverside Press, for Pollak Foundation for Economic Research.

Frisch, R. (1930). "Necessary and Sufficient Conditions Regarding the Form of an Index Number Which Shall Meet Certain of Fisher's Tests," *Journal of the American Statistical Association* 25.

——— (1934). "Reply to Mr. Subramanian's Note," *Journal of the American Statistical Association* 29: 317.

——— (1936). "Annual Survey of General Economic Theory: The Problem of Index Numbers," *Econometrica* 4: 1–38.

Hastings, H.B. (1923). *Costs and Profits: Their Relation to Business Cycles*, Boston: Houghton Mifflin, Riverside Press, for Pollak Foundation for Economic Research.

Hawtrey, R.G. ([1930] 1951). "Money and Index-Numbers," *Journal of the Royal*

Statistical Society 93: 64–85, as repr. in F.A. Lutz and L.W. Mints (eds), *Readings in Monetary Theory*, New York: Blakiston, 129–155.

Jasny, N. (1972). *Soviet Economists of the Twenties*, Cambridge: Cambridge University Press.

Jazairi, N.T. (1972a). "Fisher's Ideal Index Reformulated," *International Statistical Review* 40: 47–51.

——— (1972b). "Note on Fisher's Ideal Index," *Journal of the Royal Statistical Society*, set. C, 21: 89–92.

Jevons, W.S. (1884). *Investigations in Currency and Finance*, ed. H.S. Foxwell, London: Macmillan.

Keynes, J.M. (1983). *Collected Writings*, vol. 11, ed. Donald E. Moggridge, London: Macmillan, and New York: Cambridge University Press, for the Royal Economic Society.

Klezl, F. (1924). "Methods of Calculating Index Numbers," *International Labour Review* (August): 236–262.

Konüs, A.A. ([1924] 1939). "The Problem of the True Index of the Cost of Living" (in Russian), *Economic Bulletin of the Institute of Economic Conjuncture* 9–10: 64–71, tr. *Econometrica* 7: 10–29.

Konüs, A.A. and S.S. Byushgens (1926). "K probleme pokupatelnoi cili deneg [On the problem of the purchasing power of money]," *Voprosi Konyunkturi* 2:1 (supplement to *Economic Bulletin of the Institute of Economic Conjuncture*): 151–172.

Meeker, R. (1921). "On the Best Form of Index Number," *Quarterly Publications of the American Statistical Association* 17 (September): 909–915.

Mises, Ludwig von ([1912] 1934). *Theory of Money and Credit*, London: Routledge.

Persons, W.M. (1921). "Fisher's Formula for Index Numbers," *Review of Economic Statistics* 3: 103–113.

Pigou, A.C. (1912). *Wealth and Welfare*, London: Macmillan.

——— (1920). *The Economics of Welfare*, London: Macmillan.

Serletis, A. (1997). "Index Numbers," in D. Glasner (ed.), *Business Cycles and Depressions: An Encyclopedia*, New York: Garland, 323–325.

Snyder, C. (1923). "Fisher's *The Making of Index Numbers*," *American Economic Review* 13: 416–421.

Subramanian, S. (1934). "On a Certain Conclusion of Frisch's," *Journal of the American Statistical Association* 29: 316–317.

Swamy, S. (1965). "Consistency of Fisher's Tests," *Econometrica* 33: 619–623.

Vogt, A. and J. Barta (1997). *The Making of Tests for Index Numbers* ("published in honour of the 50th anniversary of the death of Irving Fisher"), Heidelberg: Physica-Verlag.

Wald, A. (1937). "Zur Theorie der Preisindexziffern," *Zeitschrift für Nationalokonomie* 8: 179–219.

Walsh, C.M. (1901). *The Measurement of General Exchange-Value*, New York: Macmillan.

——— (1921). *The Problem of Estimation*, London: P.S. King.

Young, A.A. (1923). "Fisher's *The Making of Index Numbers*," *Quarterly Journal of Economics* 37: 342–364.

Yule, G.U. (1923). "Review of Fisher, *The Making of Index Numbers*," *Journal of the Royal Statistical Society* 86: 424–430.

10

FRANK KNIGHT'S POSITION ON CAPITAL AND INTEREST

Foundation of the Knight/Hayek/Kaldor debate

Avi J. Cohen

INTRODUCTION

Frank Knight's position on capital and interest was developed in a large scattering of articles (1916, 1925, 1931, 1932, 1933, 1934, 1935a, 1935b, 1935c, 1935d, 1935e, 1935f, 1936a, 1936b, 1937, 1938, 1941, 1944, 1946) between 1916 and 1946. Many of his articles are criticisms of others' points of view, and he never lays out a clear, definitive statement of his own position. Coupled with his often opaque writing style and sometimes contradictory statements, it is difficult to explain his position. Even Lutz (1968: 104), who provides the best summary of Knight on capital and interest, begins with the caveat that he "can claim no more than an earnest effort to understand" Knight's position.

Knight's position on capital and interest was the focal point of the 1930s debate between Knight, Hayek, and Kaldor. As a necessary prelude to analyzing that debate, I shall attempt in this chapter the most comprehensive articulation of Knight's position to date. I do not intend to defend or to criticize Knight, but simply to try to understand his position. While there is no judgment of Knight in this chapter, two interesting issues emerge from clarifying Knight's position. There is surprising heterogeneity among the early neoclassical capital theorists, Clark, Fisher, and Knight. Furthermore, there are remarkable similarities between Knight's views on methodology and capital, and those of Joan Robinson regarding the Cambridge capital controversy.

My effort to understand Knight will place his theory in a broader context before focusing on his specific models. First, I briefly situate Knight's capital and interest theory in the context of his general price theory. Second, I provide historical context by tracing the major theoretical influences on Knight, particularly from J.B. Clark and Irving Fisher. These contexts make it easier to understand Knight's unique contributions to the theory of capital and interest and his models of interest determination. Out of his numerous publications and critiques, his positive models are developed in a few key articles (1931, 1936a, 1936b, 1944) which warrant and receive extra attention in the final major section of the chapter.

PRICE THEORY

Knight begins with a traditional neoclassical approach to price theory, grounding the explanation of price in tastes and technology. He views diminishing marginal utility as a law of human nature, and diminishing returns as a law of nature.[1] The nontraditional part of his approach begins with his view that the two laws are not symmetrical. Knight places more emphasis on the physical law of diminishing returns, claiming that it is "more universally and accurately in conformity with the facts, more dependable, than its psychological counterpart" (1921: 96–97).

The basic principle determining all prices is opportunity cost. The "cost of . . . any commodity is the non-production of a determinate amount of other commodities" (1935a: 23). Knight rejects explicitly the dominant alternative principles for determining price–pain cost (labor theory of value) and pleasure (utility theory of value).[2] He also rejects the traditional Marshallian approach to price theory, describing one of his articles (1931: 176) as "directed primarily against the generally accepted 'eclectic' or 'equilibrium' statement of general price theory, according to which demand and supply are 'like the two blades of a pair of scissors.'" Prices, for Knight, "are typically 'determined' by conditions outside the exchange itself, namely, in the conditions of production" (1931: 181). The opportunity cost principle applies also to the determination of factors prices, which Knight (1935b: 171) sees as a corollary of the general determination of prices in the process of resource allocation.

J.B. CLARK INFLUENCES

All capital theories must address the tension between the dual nature of capital as both (1) heterogeneous, concrete capital goods, and (2) a monetary fund of value which is homogeneous, malleable, and perfectly mobile. Clark emphasized capital's role as a permanent or perpetual fund of value. Knight's position is almost identical to Clark's, emphasizing capital as a fund of value, its permanence, and the resulting synchronization of production and consumption.[3]

Knight defines capital as "a *claim or title to a fixed amount of wealth, not involving the ownership of any particular piece or kind of property*. In the strict sense, *capital is value*" (1916: 282). Knight acknowledges explicitly that his own capital concept "is clearly what is meant (though not said) by Professor J.B. Clark, who considers it as a sort of metaphysical essence persisting through changing material forms" (1916: 282 n.). The distinction between capital value and capital goods corresponds to a distinction between interest and rent: "Interest is the payment for the use of free capital; for the use of capital goods when employed by another than their owner, the payment is a *rent*" (1921: 328).

Knight considers this interest-generating fund of value to be permanent or perpetual: "All capital is, in a growing society, inherently immortal" (1933: 338). He rejects the empirical possibility of any serious reduction in the quantity of social (value) capital (1934: 265), despite writing in the middle of the Depression. There are a number of implications that flow from the idea of permanence.

First, there is no difference between the replacement of a capital good and its maintenance. "[A]ll capital is inherently immortal. . . . If a particular capital instrument 'wears out,' . . . its replacement . . . is to be taken for granted as a technological detail. In accounting terms there is no difference between replacement and maintenance, 'eventual' replacement being included in maintenance as a matter of course" (1934: 264).

Second, abstinence is the origin of permanent capital. Knight asserts, like Clark, that "Men save in large measure with no thought of ever consuming the capital, or *even the income* which it yields. For this reason the older term 'abstinence' [is] far more descriptive than its modern substitute 'waiting. . . .' Capital formation is the result of abstinence rather than waiting" (1921: 133 n.). Since abstinence, or saving, is not undertaken for future consumption, interest is neither the reward for abstinence nor compensation for positive time preference. As we shall see in discussing Fisher's influence, Knight rejects the idea of inherent, psychological, positive time preference.[4]

Third, the permanence of capital reflects the stationary-state underpinnings of Knight's analysis. Knight has a sophisticated understanding of the limitations of equilibrium analysis, and recognizes that there can be no change either in the value or form of the capital stock in the stationary state. Nonetheless, like Clark, he ignores these limitations and allows the form of the capital stock to change:

> The notion of an economy stationary in the sense that productive equipment is changed in form but quantitatively maintained without increase gives rise, indeed, to difficulties. But we undoubtedly have to recognize the conceptual validity of the idea, even if we never could precisely describe or identify the reality.
>
> (1936a: 456 n.)

The final implication of the permanence of the fund of capital is the concept of production and consumption as synchronized (Clark's term) or simultaneous (Knight's term). According to Knight (1933: 339): "In a stationary economy there is no interval between production and consumption. The rendering of service and enjoyment of service rendered are simultaneous and equal." This concept is the same one behind Clark's (1899: 313) example of the stationary-state forest, where "[t]he planting and the cutting are . . . simultaneous." Once the permanent fund of capital is established, the simultaneous nature of production and consumption eliminates all waiting in equilibrium.

A less capital-specific influence of Clark appears in Knight's symmetrical treatment of all factors of production. For Clark, the single principle of rent explains all factor returns. Knight argues that all factors of production can be viewed as "a pure quantity of capital" (1934: 258). In the extreme case of what he calls a "completely economic" (1935a: 22) society, where all factors, including human beings, could be freely bought and sold, capital would be the only factor of production.[5]

With capital as the only factor of production, Knight rejects the classical distinctions (adopted by Böhm-Bawerk) between primary and secondary factors, or between produced and nonproduced factors. He allows that

> The distinction between human beings and property and that between personal and real property are important in law and human relations, but no fundamental economic differences correspond to them. The original fallacy was probably rooted in the "moral prejudices" that only labor is really productive, and that land is a gift of nature. Realistic economic analysis must avoid any general classifications of productive agents and. . . . [instead] speak of the yield and "hire" of productive agents, irrespective of kind.[6]
>
> (1946: 394–395)

Given Knight's views on the simultaneous nature of production and consumption, and his rejection of distinctions between primary and secondary factors, it is not surprising that he rejects totally the Austrian concept of a period of production. Knight identifies the classical assumption that labor is a primary factor of production that produces capital (with the cooperation of land), as the "essential fallacy of the Ricardo–Jevons–Böhm-Bawerk theory (developed and much refined by Wicksell)" (1936a: 453). Once the fund of value capital is in place and production and consumption are simultaneous, the period of production "is a mere technical detail" (1934: 267). Knight believes that the length of the production process has nothing to do with theories of capital and interest, and has no real meaning at all. On top of these theoretical reasons for rejecting the concept of the period of production, Knight (1934: 262 n.) also rejects it on empirical grounds, claiming that no capital goods are actually produced by labor alone.

IRVING FISHER INFLUENCES

Fisher's influences on Knight were both positive and negative. Knight adopts some of Fisher's ideas, but also articulates his own position *in opposition* to Fisher. The most important positive Fisherian influences on Knight are the concept of the (discounted) income stream and the attempt to bypass a theory of capital in determining the interest rate. The crucial Fisherian concept Knight opposes is the role of time preference in determining the interest rate.

Fisher viewed his concept of an income stream as his most important and unique contribution to the theory of capital and interest. Knight (1935a: 12–13) also views the concept of an income stream as crucial: "Perpetual service income is the primary magnitude in economic analysis." The value of capital is the discounted stream of future income services.

Fisher uses the income stream concept to develop the traditional neoclassical theory of interest as determined by the "two blades of the scissors"—subjective impatience and objective investment opportunities. Knight accepts Fisher's argument that in equilibrium, the interest rate "measures" or "equals" the rate of time preference, as well as the productivity of capital/investment opportunities. But Knight rejects the role of impatience in the theory of interest, claiming that time preference "has little or nothing to do with 'determining' the rate" (1931: 176, 201).[7] What is the reasoning behind Knight's position?

Knight begins by dismissing the idea that positive time preference is an inherent characteristic of human nature. Instead of a preference for present over future goods, Knight believes that the norm is a preference for a uniform consumption stream through time. Since his views are quite unorthodox, they are worth quoting at length:

> There is literally no "sense" in the notion of an inherent reluctance to postpone, or preference of present to future enjoyment, as a general principle embedded in human nature. . . . No one wants his present or immediately prospective enjoyment all transferred to the future, but no more does anyone want all his future enjoyment transferred to the present. There is no presumption, *a priori*, as to which a normal human being would choose if compelled to consume both to-day's and to-morrow's rations of food either to-day or to-morrow. Either alternative would in general mean a sacrifice in comparison with consuming to-day's rations to-day and to-morrow's rations to-morrow. . . . The permanent and cumulative saving and investment we . . . find in the world cannot be explained . . . through comparison between present and future enjoyment, or "waiting" and being paid for waiting.
>
> (1934: 272 n.)

In equilibrium, time preference is positive and equal to the rate of interest, but Knight argues that individuals prefer a dollar today to a dollar tomorrow *because* the interest rate is positive and they can earn interest on today's dollar.[8] In Knight's (1916: 287) words: "To attribute interest to the discount of the future is . . . to commit the fallacy of interchanging cause and effect." The productivity of capital makes more available in the future than in the present, and it is this alteration of the income stream that causes positive time preference to emerge (1936b: 636).[9] In Böhm-Bawerk's terminology, Knight is accepting the first cause of interest (relative underprovision in the present) and the third (productivity), while rejecting the second cause (pure time preference).

Knight's position denies time preference as a determinant of savings decisions, so he provides an alternative explanation. Saving, for Knight, is determined by social, rather than economic, motives: "A realistic discussion of the motives involved in decisions as to saving would run rather in terms of interest in security and power, of living standards, of forms of social emulation, and of similar facts of social psychology and culture history" (1932: 263).[10]

The final positive Fisherian influence on Knight is the attempt to bypass a theory of capital in determining the interest rate. Knight (1935a: 16 n.) recognizes the circularity problems flowing from the fact "that capital quantity itself involves the interest rate." But he believes that "the rate can be derived very simply in terms of perpetual income without reference to capital quantity. . . . [T]he rate of interest . . . is the ratio of the additional perpetual income creatable by investing a one-year segment of any given perpetual income to the given income itself."

This strategy of determining the interest rate as the ratio of additional income generated by a one-time investment is very Fisherian, and continues an interest theory tradition that extends to Solow's (1963) version of the same strategy.[11] Fisher tried to overcome the interdependence problems between the measurement of capital and the interest rate by focusing on the rate of return of an investment yielding a stream of future profits. Fisher also attempted to sidestep capital theory by utilizing a partial equilibrium framework to explicitly avoid the interdependence between the interest rate and all prices, including the prices of capital goods. Knight does not explicitly address the partial/general equilibrium question. His supply and demand models seem to involve aggregate capital, and he recognizes the resulting interdependence between curves which makes their use problematic. The difficulties with Knight's strategy will emerge in examining the methodological issues of his specific models.

KNIGHT'S MODELS OF INTEREST DETERMINATION

Even in Knight's specific models of interest determination, it is difficult to explain his position. First, the models change over time. Knight (1916, 1931, 1936a, 1936b, 1944) develops a sequence of differing and contradictory static equilibrium models. Second, Knight views interest rate determination as part of the capital accumulation process, and recognizes the limitations of static equilibrium models for analyzing such out-of-equilibrium processes. Knight's articles often contain an equilibrium model, a critique of the model, and unorthodox modelling techniques that attempt to address the critique. The result is often dizzying puzzlement for the reader as to why Knight is plunging ahead with a model he has just criticized as inadequate for its task.

To try and make sense of these models, it is first necessary to sketch Knight's general methodological concerns. That will be followed by a summary of the contents *common* to (if not explicitly present in) all of the differing models—the equilibrium determination of the rate of interest. Only then can we sensibly proceed to the sequence of individual models.

Methodology

By 1936, Knight divided economic analysis into three categories: statics, dynamics, and historical/evolutionary economics. Statics examines equilibrium under given conditions. This is the only realm of normal price theory.

Dynamics also presumes stationary conditions, but examines "the process by which . . . equilibrium is established" (1931: 181). More generally, dynamics concerns "movement under given conditions . . . whether or not it tends toward equilibrium" (1931: 210 n.). Normal price theory cannot explain dynamics. "Normal-price reasoning makes no pretence of explaining . . . the price which would obtain . . . during the interval in which the economic system was in the process of readjustment toward general equilibrium; it relates only to the price after the establishment of equilibrium" (1936b: 615).

Historical/evolutionary economics examines "[c]hanges in . . . given conditions (wants, resources, and technology)" (1935a: 20 n.). According to Knight, economic statics and dynamics have close analogues in mechanics, but changes in given conditions "are analogous with nothing dealt with in the science of mechanics, and should be designated . . . as 'historical' or 'evolutionary' economics" (1935a: 20 n.). Again, equilibrium-based price theory is of no use: "long-run historical changes must be faced as problems of historical causality and treated in terms of concepts very different from those of given supply and demand functions and a tendency toward equilibrium under given conditions" (1931: 210).

Equilibrium determination of the interest rate

The main propositions common to all of Knight's models of capital and interest are clear and easily summarized (1934: 260–261). Knight continues Fisher's tradition of the equilibrium determination of the interest rate by a set of simultaneous equations.[12] The price of a capital good is equal to both its discounted future yield and its cost of production (construction costs plus carrying charges). The interest rate, the discount rate, and the carrying charge rate are all equal and represent the maximum possible return given technical conditions. These equations can be solved for the interest rate, which can then be used to value the capital good:

> [S]et up an equation expressing the equality of the two values of any wealth item, one the discounted value or present worth of the stream of services it will yield . . . and the other the cost of producing any new item yielding an equal stream of perpetual money income. Both sides of the equation involve the rate, and the equation is to be solved for the rate as the unknown. The rate of interest being known, the quantity of wealth, represented by any source of a known money value, is then found by the operation of "capitalization."
>
> (1935a: 14)

If there is a discrepancy between the discounted present value of a capital good and its cost of production, competition will force the present value back to cost of production:

> If the capitalized value of any [capital good] is more than the known cost of producing items yielding an equivalent income stream, people will instead of purchasing the existing items set about producing new income-yielding goods and these will sell not at their capitalized value but at the lower level set by cost of production. Conversely, no new wealth will be produced for the future unless the capitalized value of the expected income is greater than the cost of production. Hence . . . all . . . wealth must sell under competitive conditions for precisely the cost of producing items of any physical type yielding the same income (after all deductions necessary for perpetual maintenance).
>
> (1932: 259)

In equilibrium, the interest rate is "set by the productivity of the increment of investment about to be made" or, as Knight also puts it, the interest rate is "the marginal productivity of capital" (1935a: 16 n.).[13] This is where Knight clearly departs from Fisher, denying any role for subjective impatience. Instead, objective cost conditions are paramount: "The rate of interest is essentially 'determined' by 'cost of production' in the only sense in which cost is ever said to determine price, i.e. 'alternative cost'" (1933: 335).

Knight's (1931) vintage model

Knight's 1931 model of interest determination (see Figure 10.1) is a modification of his earliest (1916) supply and demand model. Knight drops the upward-sloping supply curve of savings from the 1916 model, citing empirical evidence showing that the supply of savings is uncorrelated with changes in interest rate. In its place he substitutes a vertical supply curve of capital, arguing that at a moment in time "supply is an almost completely fixed quantity" (1931: 203). The downward-sloping demand curve is derived from J.B. Clark's decreasing marginal productivity of additional capital "dosing."

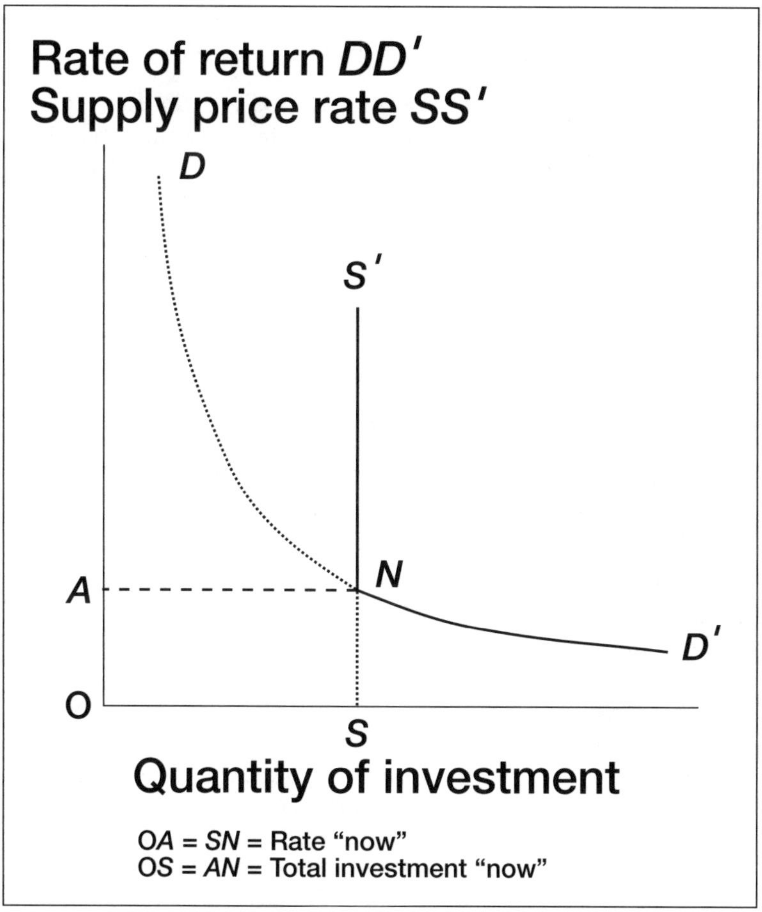

Figure 10.1 Model of interest determination (*Source:* Knight 1931: 207)

Knight describes saving and investment as a "cumulative process" of growth, lying "outside the framework of the conventional 'static' economic system" (1931: 206). Nonetheless, Knight plunges ahead with a conventional supply and demand diagram, albeit with unorthodox modifications that reflect his concerns about the limitations of the diagram. He eliminates the demand curve above the existing interest rate *OA*. That portion of the curve would involve removal of existing capital, and Knight is uncertain how that would work out quantitatively. Similarly, it is uncertain what would happen to the existing stock of capital if the interest rate fell below the current rate *SN*.

Saving, or the real production of capital, shifts the vertical supply curve to the right. At the same time, "social progress in . . . other phases than capital accumulation moves the demand curve for capital upward . . . so that there is no clear vertical drift of the intersection point" (1931: 210).[14]

Knight's (1936a, b) vintage model

Knight's 1936 articles, "The Quantity of Capital and the Rate of Interest: I and II," bear remarkable similarities to Joan Robinson's ([1953–4] 1980) article, "The Production Function and the Theory of Capital." Like Robinson, Knight begins with a classic statement of the circularity problem in the determination of interest and capital value:[15]

> The problem of capital as a quantity is obviously another view of the problem of the rate of interest. Difficulty and complexity arise because the relation between capital and interest takes different forms and especially because of the danger of circular reasoning. On the one hand, capital is usually and properly defined as "income" "capitalized" at some "rate of return." But the interest rate is usually thought of as the ratio between a net annual yield and a quantity of capital. On the face of it, this is a vicious circle; interest cannot be a rate of return, i.e., a ratio to a principal, unless the terms of the ratio are definable independently of the rate of return itself, yet in the same units for both numerator and denominator.
>
> (1936a: 433)

Knight's aim is to show that "the vicious-circle difficulty is spurious" and that the interest rate can be determined by "a relation between an instantaneous rate of investment and a resultant instantaneous rate of growth in potential income," "without reference to capital quantity" (1936a: 434). The ratio of the rate of growth in potential income to the rate of investment that produces it, for Knight, is "the real rate of interest," which he also defines as "the marginal productivity of new investment" (1936a: 462).

Knight had much earlier worked out his response to the vicious-circle criticism of his interest rate theory:

> The correct statement of the productivity theory . . . sidetracks the objection . . . that the product of capital is not homogeneous with the capital, and that consequently no such ratio can exist until the capitalization process has been applied to the capital itself. Before the investment is made the capital and its anticipated product are quite homogeneous [value in dollars], and it is in the market for capital not yet invested that the interest rate is determined. Capital goods once created are, of course, valued by capitalization; this operation presupposes an interest rate, which is therefor in no wise affected by the relation between capital goods and their income.
>
> (1921: 167 n.)

Knight's solution, where the interest rate is determined as a value ratio of expected dollar return to the dollar amount about to be invested, is consistent with his emphasis on capital as a fund of value.

Even Robinson would agree that, *in equilibrium*, Knight's determination of the interest rate is logically correct: "In a position of equilibrium all three evaluations [a who's who of heterogeneous capital goods, net present value, and cost of production] yield equivalent results; there is a quantity which can be translated from one number to another by changing the unit. This is the definition of equilibrium" (Robinson [1953–4] 1980: 118).

The real difficulties arise in extending the analysis to out-of-equilibrium situations, whether dynamic adjustments to equilibrium, or historical changes in conditions associated with accumulation and growth. Knight recognizes these difficulties, admitting that his equilibrium solution to the circularity problem does *not* cover the establishment of equilibrium from a disequilibrium situation. He criticizes his own model as "unsatisfactory" in this regard.[16] He identifies clearly the limitations of price theory for analyzing these difficulties:

> Normal-price reasoning makes no pretence of explaining . . . the price which would obtain . . . during the interval in which the economic system was in the process of readjustment toward general equilibrium; it relates only to the price after the establishment of equilibrium.[17]
>
> (1936b: 615)

Dynamic analysis is always more difficult than static analysis. What makes the problem more serious and important for Knight is his belief that "normal-equilibrium price analysis has no application to a situation of . . . the capital market" (1936b: 614). Because the stock of capital can grow or fall "without a definite prospect of coming to a stationary level" (1936b: 616), equilibrium price theory is inapplicable. What is needed instead is "a special methodology" that can deal with "historical changes" (1936b: 617).

Despite these misgivings, Knight again moves on to present an equilibrium supply and demand model for interest determination (see Figure 10.2). The quantity of capital is the independent variable measured on the *x*-axis, and the interest rate is measured on the *y*-axis. He assumes that there is "some measure of increasing quantities of capital invested," but identifies this measure as "one of the most serious difficulties" that must be dealt with later. Point *P* is a "starting-point" or the "here and now" and assumes long-period equilibrium; "capital has been so invested as, in the absence of further accumulation, to leave no incentive to make any change" (1936b: 620).

The downward-sloping demand curve reflects "the tendency of interest to fall as investment increases under given conditions." Knight believes only the portion near *P* has any quantitative meaning, hence the dashed curve further down to the right. Points on the demand curve up and to the left of *P* involve social disinvestment and are "clearly inadmissible" because they violate *ceteris paribus* conditions. Knight argues that the process of investment could never "be reversible over any considerable segment of the demand curve, or that capital originally invested could be recovered without loss" (1936b: 621).

The vertical supply curve of capital (*QS*) represents the existing capital stock. Although Knight draws the vertical curve, he contradicts his diagram

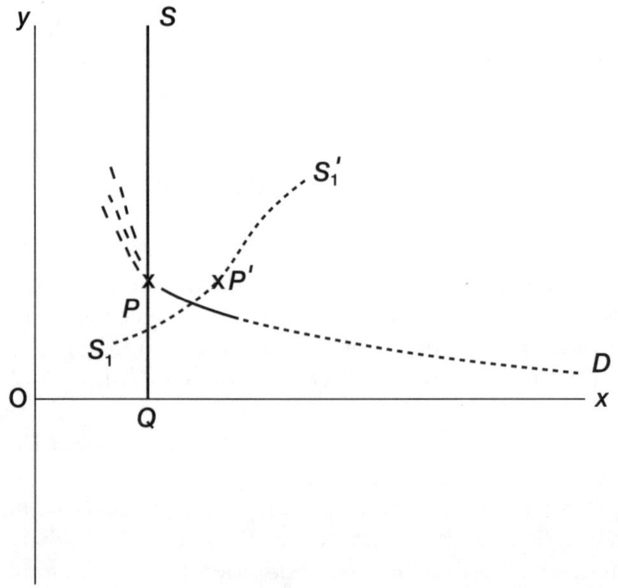

Figure 10.2 Model of equilibrium supply and demand (*Source:* Knight 1936b: 620)

by saying that the supply curve applicable to the momentary situation "is restricted to a single point" (1936b: 628). This restriction is necessary because at different rates of interest, the quantity (in value terms) of the existing capital stock changes due to price–Wicksell effects.

In "a short-period situation," Knight allows this diagram to determine the interest rate, "which is always the marginal demand price of the momentary supply" (1936b: 629). The situation is not stationary, however, because saving and capital accumulation are occurring continuously.

To model the passage of time and the accumulation of capital, Knight shifts the vertical supply curve to the right, with an apparent decrease in the marginal productivity of new investment. But this is not a once-over comparative statics exercise. Knight believes that *ceteris paribus* does not hold in the capital market and that shifts of the supply and demand curves are interdependent. Increased saving and investment "will lead to social changes" (1936b: 629) such as the stimulation of invention and the development of new wants, that "act as a cause in the historical sense" (1936b: 622) and prompt a rightward shift of the demand curve. Knight also believes that as accumulation progresses, the *ceteris paribus* conditions for supply "cannot possibly remain unchanged" (1936b: 627). "The act of making any addition (however small) to the supply of capital . . . necessarily changes the conditions . . . under which any further addition will be made to total supply" (1936b: 628).

This conception of the cumulative effect of saving and investment leads Knight to two conclusions about the capital market. First, the net empirical effect on interest of increasing supply and demand is unclear. The forces of decreasing marginal productivity of capital (from increasing supply) and increasing demand for capital (from increasing income, saving, invention, and wants) work in opposite directions. Citing Taussig (1908, 2: 32), Knight (1936b: 630) claims that " 'the rate of interest for long periods . . . depends on a race between accumulation and improvement.' " Second, Knight concludes that "it is wholly illicit to argue that the process of capital accumulation moves toward saturation and a final equilibrium" (1936b: 628).

Knight ends the 1936b article with a section titled "The Meaning of a Changing Quantity of Capital." He returns to the measure of capital, which he calls "the knottiest question of all," with "no unique solution." He recognizes that only under conditions of general equilibrium does the "quantity of capital in an economic system ha[ve] definite meaning" (1936b: 639). Knight describes the out-of-equilibrium measurement problem as the question of

> whether or not we are constantly to recapitalize previous investment at the changing interest rate—the rate being presumed to fall in consequence of the diminishing return from further investment. To do so apparently yields a spurious growth in the quantity of capital.

> Yet in some connections this must rather obviously be done, and the limitation simply kept in mind.
>
> (1936b: 641)

Knight shows here an understanding of price–Wicksell effects as yet another complication of using an equilibrium model to analyze the capital market. Once again, despite these complications, he insists on pressing on with the analysis. Knight, I believe, would agree with Robinson's ([1953–4] 1980: 129) statement that "the assumptions of equilibrium become entangled in self-contradictions if they are applied to the problem of accumulation going on through time with a changing factor ratio." But, unlike Robinson's abandonment of her early (1956, 1962) equilibrium-based models of capital and interest, he kept searching for some modification of the equilibrium method that would allow him to continue on while "keeping in mind" its limitations.

Knight's (1944) vintage model

Knight's final capital and interest model eliminates supply and demand curves altogether, and with them many of the unresolved methodological problems of using an equilibrium model to analyze nonstationary accumulation processes. This is the famous "Crusonia plant" model. In the hypothetical economy of Crusonia, there is

> only one "want" . . . that . . . is gratified by a single productive agent or resource. The resource must, of course, be of the nature of capital. . . . We may think of our Crusonia as living on the natural growth of some perennial which grows indefinitely at a constant (geometric) rate, except as new tissue is cut away for consumption. We assume that it requires no cultivation or other care. . .
>
> (1944: 30)

Capital is the only factor of production. The only allocation decision is how much of the plant to consume. If the rate of consumption is identical to the rate of plant growth, there is a stationary state with constant capital and income. If the rate of consumption is less than the growth rate, the "saving" is automatically added to capital, increasing future income.

Capital is measured as "a potential perpetual stationary rate of consumption." The rate of return on capital investment is the natural growth rate of the plant. Investment can only take the form of sacrificed consumption, and the rate of return can be measured as a ratio of "the rate of growth in the capital (potential, permanent, and constant consumable income) . . . to the rate of consumption sacrificed for the sake of investment" (1944: 31). There are no diminishing returns from investment since there are no fixed factors.

The Crusonia plant model is remarkable, not only for the way in which it sidesteps methodological problems, but for the way in which it incorporates so many of the fundamental themes and characteristics of Knight's theory of capital and interest. As a one-commodity model, all of the measurement problems of capital disappear—interdependence between capital value and interest, Wicksell effects, potential divergence between cost of production and discounted future earnings of capital goods. Knight (1944: 31) notes that "there is no problem of measurement with respect either to the amount of investment (its cost) or its yield. Both may be taken as physical quantities . . . of 'nutritive material.'" The rate of return, as in Fisher's rate of return over cost, is a purely physical ratio. Since the rate of return is constant, and all savings are automatically reinvested at that rate, the economy is always in equilibrium. There are no out-of-equilibrium situations to complicate the analysis.

The Crusonia plant continues a long tradition of models of production as organic growth, going back to Wicksell, to Clark's forest, and to Fisher's orchards. Fisher emphasized the concept of investment opportunities given by nature—Knight's actual production is by nature. Clark's forest still required the planting of trees—Knight's Crusonia plant is self-perpetuating. The homogeneous Crusonia plant, as capital, is self-perpetuating and permanent, incorporating Clark's concept of capital as a homogeneous, permanent fund of value. Production and consumption are simultaneous, and without any inputs there is no period of production.

Capital is the only factor of production, and the rate of interest is determined entirely by technical conditions; the marginal productivity of capital. Subjective factors like utility, time preference, impatience, or abstinence, play no role.[18] The interest rate can also be conceived of as a ratio of two rates of change—an increase in income relative to a sacrifice in consumption—without any reference to a quantity of capital. Finally, the constant rate of interest in the model is consistent with the empirical evidence of relatively constant historical real rates of interest.

CONCLUSION

Frank Knight's position on capital and interest is difficult to synthesize because it is teeming with unresolved tensions. There is the basic tension underlying all capital theories between the dual nature of capital as both (1) heterogeneous, concrete capital goods, and (2) a monetary fund of value which is homogeneous, malleable, and perfectly mobile. Knight follows Clark in emphasizing capital as a fund of value, its permanence, and the resulting synchronization of production and consumption. But Knight sidesteps the heterogeneous nature of capital with his one-commodity Crusonia plant model. Knight takes from Fisher the concept of a discounted income stream and the attempt to bypass a theory of capital in determining the interest rate, but rejects any role for time preference.

Within his own sequence of models, Knight never reconciles their difference and contractions. Most importantly, he never resolves the tension between his continued attempts to use equilibrium models of capital accumulation and interest rate determination, and his sophisticated understanding of their limitations for analyzing such out-of-equilibrium processes. This tension is reminiscent of Joan Robinson's early attempts (1956, 1962) to develop an equilibrium-based theory of capital and interest, while Knight's criticisms of equilibrium methodology are remarkably similar to criticisms made by Robinson in the Cambridge capital controversies (see Cohen 1984, 1993b).

Despite these tensions, Knight's position does have coherence, which is most evident in the Crusonia plant model. The concepts that recur throughout Knight's writings and find their clearest expression in the Crusonia plant model are: production as organic growth, capital as a homogeneous, permanent fund of value, the simultaneity of production and consumption, and interest determined entirely by the marginal productivity of capital without reference to either the measurement of capital or time preference. These concepts are central to the 1930s debate between Knight, Hayek, and Kaldor.

NOTES

1 The law of diminishing returns "is a generalization from the facts of physical nature as the [law of diminishing utility] is a generalization from the facts of human nature" (1921: 96).

2 Knight (1931: 211 n.) believes "in extinguishing both the doctrine of pain cost [of production] and that of utility as determinants of price in general."

3 Knight identifies the issues in the 1930s capital controversy as the same as those of the Böhm-Bawerk/Clark controversy. He describes the Austrian theory as "the view that capital consists of things, 'capital goods,' which are periodically worn out and reproduced; while the productivity theorists, notably represented by J.B. Clark, have held that capital is essentially a continuing fund, persisting through changes in the capital goods in which it is embodied. The general issue in the two controversies is the same, namely, the meaning of a quantity of capital and of the yield of capital, and the connection between the two."

4 Knight's position on abstinence and replacement is the same as Clark's. This is the position that Taussig (1908), as described in Cohen (1993a), criticizes so effectively.

5 "'Capital' is the ideal 'factor of production' and is 'theoretically' (meaning in a society completely economic) all-inclusive" (Knight 1935a: 22).

6 Knight wavered throughout his career on the validity or usefulness of the conventional tripartite classification of factors as land, labor, and capital. In (1928) he advocated discarding outright the classification. In (1944: 33 n.) he is more willing to allow the classification "for expository purposes, unrealistic as it is." He says, "There is some 'sense' in the view of land as fixed in supply, of capital goods as freely producible under 'economic' conditions, and of labourers as variable in

supply, but with changes controlled mostly by 'social forces' or human interests of a 'noneconomic' character. . . . However, the least critical examination largely destroys the validity of these distinctions" (1944: 33).

7 Knight (1941: 411) does not mince words in stating "that the literature on economic thought hardly contains an error more egregious or palpable than the time-preference theory of interest."

8 According to Knight (1921: 131), "where interest can be obtained it is natural that men should esteem a present dollar equally with its amount at the current interest rate at a future date, since one can be freely exchanged for the other."

9 "It is neither true nor false, but simply unmeaning, to say, as Böhm-Bawerk so often does, that 'present goods are as a rule worth more than future goods of like kind and number'. . . . Professor Fisher rightly recognizes that the time-shape of the income-stream is the significant matter" (Knight 1916: 287 n.).

10 "[T]he saving of capital is not to any considerable extent a matter of doing without a certain quantity of consumption over a limited period of time in order to consume the resultant capital with its increase during some later interval. Investment is generally made with a view to permanence, i.e., perpetual maintenance in some form." Then, in a footnote, Knight says: "This is the essential fallacy in Professor Fisher's theory of impatience as the basis of interest and of Professor Fetter's time-preference theory" (1936b: 634–635).

11 Elsewhere, Knight (1933: 335) defines interest as "the ratio by which [perpetual] income can . . . be increased by investing instead of consuming."

12 Lutz (1968: 108–112) concisely presents Knight's equations.

13 Elsewhere, Knight (1916: 294) says: "the productivity of capital is not merely the indispensable condition of interest, it *is* the rate of interest."

14 Knight (1934: 277 n.) says that his 1931 article "contains errors, which the writer hopes to take up and correct in the near future, but the main argument on interest theory is still believed to be sound." However, Knight never explicitly identifies those errors.

15 Robinson ([1953–4] 1980: 115) says: "When we know the future expected rate of output associated with a certain capital good, and expected future prices and costs, then, if we are given a rate of interest, we can value the capital good as a discounted stream of future profit which it will earn. But to do so, we have to begin by taking the rate of interest as given, whereas the main purpose of the production function is to show how wages and the rate of interest . . . are determined by technical conditions and the factor ratio."

16 Knight (1936b: 612) acknowledges that his analysis does *not* cover "the establishment of an equilibrium . . . beginning with a system in some other condition than that of equilibrium and, holding other things equal, including the quantity of capital, while the capital is shifted about between different modes of investment. In this sense the treatment is unsatisfactory. . ."

17 Knight's understanding of the limitations of equilibrium theory are similar to Robinson's ([1953–54] 1980: 120) claim that to analyze equilibrium is not the same thing as analyzing a tendency toward equilibrium: "The neoclassical economist thinks of a position of equilibrium as a position towards which an economy is tending to move as time goes by. But it is impossible for a system to *get into* a position of equilibrium, for the very nature of equilibrium is that the system is already in it, and has been for a certain length of time."

18 A utility analysis could be consistently added to Knight's model, but it would play no determining role. He (1944: 32) notes that the physical magnitudes involved in the calculation of the interest rate (nutritive plant material gained and sacrificed) can also be evaluated in subjective terms of satisfaction, but "any

change which may occur in the relation between intensity of satisfaction and time rate of physical consumption enters in the same way into both the numerator and denominator" and hence cancels out.

REFERENCES

Clark, J.B. (1899). *The Distribution of Wealth*, New York: Macmillan.

Cohen, A.J. (1984). "The Methodological Resolution of the Cambridge Controversies," *Journal of Post-Keynesian Economics* 6 (Summer): 614–629.

——— (1993a). "The Mythology of Capital or of Equilibrium?: The Böhm-Bawerk/Clark Controversy." Department of Economics Working Papers no. 93–7, April, Toronto: York University.

——— (1993b). "Does Joan Robinson's Critique of Equilibrium Entail Theoretical Nihilism?" in G. Mongiovi and C. Rühl (eds.), *Macroeconomics Theory: Diversity and Convergence*, Aldershot: Edward Elgar, 222–239.

Knight, F.H. (1916). "Neglected Factors in the Problem of Normal Interest," *Quarterly Journal of Economics* 30 (February): 279–310.

——— (1921). *Risk, Profit and Uncertainty*, Boston: Houghton Mifflin.

——— (1925). "A Note on Professor Clark's Illustration of Marginal Productivity," *Journal of Political Economy* 33 (March): 550–553.

——— (1931). "Professor Fisher's Interest Theory: A Case in Point," *Journal of Political Economy* 39 (March): 196–212.

——— (1932). "Interest," in E.R.A. Seligman (ed.), *Encyclopedia of the Social Sciences*, vol. 7: 251–276.

——— (1933). "Capitalistic Production, Time and the Rate of Return," in *Essays in Honour of Gustav Cassel*, London: Allen & Unwin, 327–342.

——— (1934). "Capital, Time and the Interest Rate," *Economica*, n.s., 1 (August): 257–286.

——— (1935a). "The Ricardian Theory of Production and Distribution," *Canadian Journal of Economics and Political Science* 1 (February): 3–25.

——— (1935b). "The Ricardian Theory of Production and Distribution," *Canadian Journal of Economics and Political Science* 1 (May): 171–196.

——— (1935c). "Professor Hayek and the Theory of Investment," *Economic Journal* 45 (March): 77–94.

——— (1935d). "Comment," *Journal of Political Economy* 43 (August): 625–627.

——— (1935e). "The Period of Production: A Final Word," *Journal of Political Economy* 43 (October): 808.

——— (1935f). "The Theory of Investment Once More: Mr. Boulding and the Austrians," *Quarterly Journal of Economics* 50 (November): 36–67.

——— (1936a). "The Quantity of Capital and the Rate of Interest: I," *Journal of Political Economy* 44 (August): 433–463.

——— (1936b). "The Quantity of Capital and the Rate of Interest: II," *Journal of Political Economy* 44 (October): 612–642.

——— (1937). "Note on Dr. Lange's Interest Theory," *Review of Economic Studies* 4: 223–230.

——— (1938). "On the Theory of Capital: In Reply to Mr. Kaldor," *Econometrica* 6 (January): 63–82.

——— (1941). "Professor Mises and the Theory of Capital," *Economica*, n.s., 8 (November): 409–427.
——— (1944). "Diminishing Returns from Investment," *Journal of Political Economy* 52 (March): 26–47.
——— (1946). "Capital and Interest," in *Readings in the Theory of Income Distribution*, Homewood, Ill.: Irwin, 384–417.
Lutz, F.A. (1968). "Frank H. Knight," in id., *The Theory of Interest*, Chicago: Aldine Publishing Company, 104–123.
Robinson, J. ([1953–54] 1980). "The Production Function and the Theory of Capital," in id., *Collected Economic Papers*, 5 vols, Cambridge, Mass.: MIT Press, 2: 114–131.
——— (1956). *The Accumulation of Capital*, London: Macmillan.
——— (1962). *Essays in the Theory of Economic Growth*, London: Macmillan.
Solow, R.M. (1963). *Capital Theory and the Rate of Return*, Amsterdam: North-Holland.
Taussig, F. (1908). *Principles of Economics*, 2nd edn, 2 vols, New York: Macmillan.

Part IV

INSTITUTIONAL ECONOMICS

11

EUROPE IN AMERICA

Veblen and his Canadian connections[1]

Robin Neill

INTRODUCTION

America is part of Euro-American civilization, and American intellectual history is part of Euro-American intellectual history, and cannot be understood apart from it. As an element in this general hypothesis I conjecture that John Rae, Thorstein Veblen, and Harold Innis cannot be understood apart from the content of Common Sense Scottish Philosophy. Their environment in America occasioned new departures, and controlled what they accepted from Europe, but what they accepted was from Europe, and their new departures were from a European base.

John Rae, Thorstein Veblen, and Harold Innis were heretical economists. All three were deeply concerned with scientific method, rejecting classical and neoclassical economics on that ground. Innis explicitly drew on the work of Veblen (Innis 1929; Baragar 1996), and it has been suggested that Veblen drew on the work of Rae (Spengler 1959a: 35–38; Edgell and Tilman 1991), so it is reasonable to speculate on the nature of the intellectual connections between all three. The nature of these connections throws light on the place of European thought in American intellectual history, and on the meaning of the doctrines of all three men.

JOHN RAE

Introduction

There were three grounds on which Rae criticized Adam Smith and the classics: the ground of scientific method, the ground of human motivation, and the ground of human epistemology and psychology. The first of these was drawn directly from Francis Bacon's *Novum Organum*. The second turned on whether or not humankind acted out of selfishness or benevolence (altruism), and what the consequences of these motivations might be. The third turned on whether humankind was anything more than a receiver of information, and a fixed set of emotional responses to information, or whether human understanding brought something to what was received from environment, something that would allow it to rise above a preprogrammed response, that is, that would allow it to rise into creative action. Rae was a radical empiricist in science. His psychology, however, was that of a subgroup of that broader grouping of scholars whose work can be taken as the product of the late eighteenth-century Scottish Enlightenment: David Hume, Thomas Reid, and Dugald Stewart. For Rae, influenced by the Common Sense epistemology of Reid and Stewart, human agency was as much motivated by altruism as by selfishness, and it was characterized by initiative and creativity as much as by derivative response to outside forces.

Baconian science

Rae's economics was the consequence of his critique of the work of Adam Smith, in particular, but it used and criticized the work of others: J.B. Say, H. von Storch, David Ricardo, and J.R. McCulloch. Rae's critique was motivated explicitly by an appeal to Baconian empiricism.

In Baconian science unbiased observation was assumed to be possible, given sufficient self-discipline, and conceptualization was supposed to have followed upon exhaustive, disciplined investigation. In Bacon's view, science in his time departed from this empiricist ideal in ways which he categorized under four headings: the Idols of the Tribe, the Idols of the Cave, the Idols of the Market, and the Idols of the Theatre. Lapses in scientific method listed under these headings were different aspects of one basic epistemic flaw, and Rae selected one category of problems, the Idols of the Theatre, to serve in his elaboration of the effects of that flaw on the validity of the conclusions of contemporary political economy.

The Idols of the Theatre were propensities of the mind that produced premature conceptualizations, impatient imputations of regularity, which then were taken as givens of nature. Finding roots in the biases of language, common usage, previous education, and personal circumstance and interest, these propensities produced a superficial systematization of objects of common observation, rather than explanations of the fundamental causes and characteristics of phenomena. Having roots in such samsaric soil, what passed for science, according to Bacon (and his disciple, Rae), was not science, but an illusion based on "the narrowness and darkness of a few experiments" that lent "a mischievous authority to a few commonly accepted notions and to superstition" (Bacon 1960: 62–63).

Armed with this mind-set, Rae attempted to discredit the economics of Adam Smith:

> His [Smith's] objective being everywhere to build common facts and familiar observations into a system, not to enquire into the causes and real laws from which they spring, he takes these things for granted which would present themselves to the inductive enquirer as phenomena, the principles of which his manner of philosophizing would call on him to investigate. . . . In the *Wealth of Nations* terms like "capital" [are not founded on] the general laws of a system, but [on] the usual expected results of those laws. They do not answer the question, what is it, in the nature of money and matter, that makes anything constitute a capital, or yield a profit.
>
> (Rae 1834: 334–335, 341)

For Rae it was the physical productivity of physical instruments, determined by the knowledge embodied in them, that was the essence of capital [stock] (Rae 1834: 80–90). In this, Rae asserted what Veblen later called "the technological view of capital" (Veblen [1908a] 1934).

Epistemology and psychology

The general thrust of change in the informational environment of the eighteenth century in Europe was away from a paradigm rooted in the revelations of the Christian religion, toward one rooted in observation of natural phenomena. There was a passage from superstition to science; though that puts it too simply, because the line between what was superstition and what was true but not provable in the confines of defined science, and between what was scientifically provable and what was read into putative science by the operation of Bacon's Idols, was virtually undrawable. Indeed, if Flower and Murphey (1977) have it right, nineteenth-century American philosophy was driven by a perceived need to draw that line: that is, to define the boundaries of the paradigm shift from revelation and intuition to observation and reason.

At the beginning of this period, John Locke wrote *An Essay Concerning Human Understanding*. It was Locke's view of human understanding that everything in the mind was derived from perceptions, that is, pure, unalloyed or unadulterated perceptions of some external reality. Any general or abstract ideas were a consequence of repeated association of particular pure perceptions. Thus, for example, the idea of causality was a derivative of repeated particular perceptions of one thing following upon another. David Hume accepted this general idea, and James Mill embodied it in his 1829 book, *Analysis of the Phenomenon of the Mind*. James Mill, however, under the influence of Jeremy Bentham's utilitarianism, added another dimension to the matter.

Bentham portrayed humankind as individuals responding to the stimulus of pleasure and pain associated with perceptions of external reality. He construed rational behavior as an enlightened approach to maximizing pleasure for the greatest possible number of people. What caused pleasure was useful. It produced "utility." Rationality, in this dimension of human experience, was defined as maximization of utility. Rationality was enlightened hedonism, and the Associationist psychology–epistemology of Locke and Hume was a cognate, natural (not-revealed) intellectual foundation for this hedonistic ethic.

In general, focusing on what was new in the works of Locke, Hume, Bentham, and Mill senior, humankind was portrayed as a group of individuals responding to, and totally subject to, external stimuli.

That all of these elements in the information environment (individualism, empiricist Associationist psychology–epistemology, rationalism, and hedonism) came together to produce a dominant paradigm, in the Kuhnian sense, we have the authority of Joseph Schumpeter:

> First, the historical origin of all social science is in the concept of Natural Law. . . . Second, . . . Utilitarianism was a natural-law system. Like all natural-law systems, it was all embracing in principle and very nearly so in actual practice. It was conceived as a unitary social science that was both normative and analytic. . . . Third, we know that this unitary social science of Utilitarianism was individualist, empiricist, and "rationalist." . . . Individualism does not necessarily involve empiricism or rationalism in this sense; empiricism does not necessarily involve individualism, and rationalism in this sense does not necessarily involve individualism and empiricism. But . . . so powerful a synthesis as Bentham's was bound to create, in the minds of foes as well as friends, an association between all the elements that enter into it which gave the impression of logical connection even where none existed.
>
> (Schumpeter 1954: 428–429)

Just as Rae's Baconian view of science led him to reject the systematizing approach of the classical economists, particularly insofar as it terminated in the Wages Fund Doctrine of capital, so his Common Sense epistemology led him to reject the notion that all motivation was individualist and selfish. He argued that national and individual interests were not identical (Rae 1834: 9–77); he rejected the Locke–Hume idea "that the human mind was a mere bundle of sensations" (Rae 1834: 348); and he built his theory of capital on the proposition that humankind advanced in consequence of its subjectively applied creativity. Rae listed the motivations of human agency to be: (1) idle curiosity (Rae 1834: 212); (2) the instincts to invent and copy (Rae 1834: 215); and (3) "social and benevolent affections" (Rae 1834: 222). While admitting that less admirable, selfish, and grasping motives were also present, he associated economic innovation and accumulation with the three listed (Rae 1834: 222, 224–264). On this basis, Rae spelled out the benefits and costs of particular policies in particular cases, rejecting the unrelieved laissez-faire position of the classical economists (Rae 1834: 358–385). Indeed, he looked on the Lockean empiricist, individualist, rationalist paradigm, and its issue in capital theory, as "a sort of practical demonstration *ad absurdum* of some fundamental fallacy in the science" of the then prevailing school of political economy (Rae 1834: 348).

On the sources of Rae's thought

Warren James has pointed out that there is a gap in our knowledge of Rae's education, and, consequently, the sources of his ideas have to be deduced from his writings (James 1965: 8–16). This is not an impossible task, however, because Rae was not reluctant to credit those from whom he had learned.

Rae had read Dugald Stewart's *Account of the Life and Writings of Adam Smith, LLD* (Stewart 1853), and he cited it at least four times in his own *Statement* (Rae 1834: 78, 332, 348, 358), each time favorably. Much of the general nature of Rae's criticism of Adam Smith seems to have been drawn from Stewart. His rejection of the idea of economic man as "a mere bundle of sensations" was supported by reference to Stewart's (1792) *Elements of the Philosophy of the Human Mind*, in which Stewart asserts, against Locke and Hume, that the mind cannot be reduced to a mere receptacle, a "*tabula rasa*" (Stewart 1792: 99). The importance for Rae's *Statement* cannot be overstressed, because the distinctive basis of Rae's economics was an assertion of the creativity of the economic agent in matters both technical and institutional.

Rae's allegation that Adam Smith's doctrines were mere systematizations, rather than explanations based on empirically derived laws, was an echo of Stewart's reference to Smith as being a master of "*Theoretical or Conjectural History*" (italics in original) (Stewart 1853: xxxv). Rae's advocacy of the possible usefulness of the "operations of the legislator" was foreshadowed in Stewart's "Life of Adam Smith," where Stewart asserts that

> the capacity of a people to exercise political rights with utility to themselves and to their country, presupposes a diffusion of knowledge and good morals, which can only result from the previous operation of laws favourable to industry, to order, and to freedom.
>
> (Stewart 1853: 1)

It was also foreshadowed by Stewart's statement that the prime usefulness of free-trade doctrines lies in their "flattering the indulgence of statesmen" and absolving them from all responsibility (Stewart 1853: lvii).

These parallels between the doctrines of Rae and Stewart do not indicate that Rae derived his economics from Stewart. Rae's contribution to capital theory had no precedents. The parallels and citations show only that the two held a common set of ideas. They locate Rae in a particular informational environment, and expose the epistemological and psychological roots from which he drew inspiration. Rae begins his *Statement* with an appeal to Baconian method, against the mere systematizing of contemporary political economy. Stewart begins his critique of the materialism and skepticism of Locke and Hume, on the one hand, and of Berkeley's "reveries," on the other, with the same appeal to Baconian method. Stewart and Rae inhabit the same intellectual space.

More than to Bacon, Dugald Stewart refers approvingly to Thomas Reid (Stewart 1792: 3, 7, 15, 95, 97, 112, 160, 162, etc.). It was Reid who had shown that it was as "unphilosophical" to attempt "an explanation of perception, or of the association of ideas on mechanical principles, as it would be to explain gravitation by supposing the particles of matter to be animated with principles of motion" (Stewart 1792: 14). Reid and his Common Sense Philosophy provided the epistemological root of Rae's economics.

Conclusion: Rae

From Rae's standpoint, the conclusions of classical economics were a mere systematization, a consistent intellectual organization, of the workaday perceptions of the landowners, merchants, manufacturers, and bankers of the time (Rae 1834: 341–342). The effective dynamic of mechanical inventiveness, physical productivity, and institutional formation had no place in the resulting system. Indeed, any empirical fact related to these matters that contradicted the assertion of scientific validity for the so-called laws of political economy (Rae 1834: 42–43) was dismissed, ignored, or explained away by contemporary theorists.

The epistemological roots of Rae's economics were European. Rae was Europe in America. The Upper Canadian frontier supplied him with observations. It may be that his theory of banking owed much to the process of institutional formation on the frontier. His economics was consistent with his American circumstance. The main lines of his thought, however, and his principal subject, capital theory, owed nothing to America. His "friends" in Upper Canada, with the possible exception of Hugh Bowlby Wilson (Goodwin 1961: 133), seem to have been a hindrance rather than a help to him as he worked out his *Statement* (James 1965, 1: 438–439). He influenced economic thought in Canada, but there was no economic thought in Canada that influenced him (Goodwin 1961: 56–57).

JOHN RAE AND THORSTEIN VEBLEN

Parallels: capital theory

Capital theory in Rae and Veblen had two common roots. The first was the notion that orthodox capital theory was based on the common-sense, day-to-day perceptions of the business world, and, for that reason, was not scientific. The second was the notion that scientific capital theory had to do with mechanical productivity, that it was, at base, an engineering phenomenon. For Rae, capital theory based on common perceptions was a mere systematization, not a product of inductive, Baconian science. For Veblen, capital theory based on common perceptions described the redistributive activities of business practice, not its productive process. The great difference between Rae and Veblen lay in the uses they made of this distinction. Rae simply stated that classical capital theory was systematized, but not understood, common observation. Veblen had two theories of capital: one, a "technological view of capital," focused on production (Veblen [1908b] 1961); the other, a monetary view of capital, focused on the distribution of wealth (Veblen [1908c] 1961). Veblen saw the importance of what Rae simply dismissed as incorrect. Perhaps Veblen was wrong in assigning a largely dysfunctional role to activities involving ownership of assets denominated in money, but he did clearly see the two functions of two kinds (aspects?) of capital.

It is possible to cite Rae and Veblen to show the similarities in their treatments of capital. First [with conscious repetition], Rae:

> His objective being everywhere to build common facts and familiar observations into a system, not to enquire into the causes and real laws from which they spring, [Smith] takes these things for granted which would present themselves to the inductive enquirer as phenomena, the principles of which his manner of philosophizing would call on him to investigate. . . . In the *Wealth of Nations* terms like "capital" [are not founded on] the general laws of a system, but [on] the usual expected results of those laws. They do not answer the question, what is it, in the nature of money and matter, that makes anything constitute a capital, or yield a profit.
>
> (Rae 1834: 334–335, 341)

In this passage, Rae has distinguished between business practice and a false theory of capital based on it, on the one hand, and productive physical "instruments" and a true theory of capital based on that concept, on the other. Veblen, in turn, offers a more advanced statement distinguishing two kinds of capital, technological and monetary, and two kinds of theory:

> What has been said . . . applies to "capital goods," so called, and is intended to apply to these in their character of "productive goods" . . . what is had in mind is the industrial and technological efficiency . . . of the material means of production. . . . In modern business practice, [however], capital is distinguished into two coordinate categories of assets, tangible and intangible. "Tangible assets" is here taken to designate pecuniarily serviceable capital goods, considered as a valuable possession yielding an income to their owner. . . . "Intangible assets" . . . are also assets to the amount of their capitalisable value, which has commonly little, if any, relation to the industrial serviceability of these items of wealth considered as factors of production.
>
> (Veblen [1908c] 1961: 352–353)

The distinction between scientific and systematic capital theory (Rae), and between technological and monetary capital theory (Veblen), depended on capital being viewed as an engineering or a monetary thing. Rae criticized Smith, saying: "Capital is uniformly treated of in the *Wealth of Nations*, as a thing homogeneous in its nature, having always the same qualities (according to the definition of Mr. Say, an amount of values) and any increase or diminution of it, as a mere alteration in quantity" (Rae 1834: 354). Veblen allowed that the arguments of J.B. Clark "will hold good if 'productive goods' are rated by bulk, weight, number, or some such irrelevant test, instead of by their productivity" (Veblen [1908d] 1961: 199). For neither Rae nor Veblen was capital just a sum of monetary value. Capital was defined as a quality imparted to something physical by virtue of the human agency associated with it.

Parallels: human agency

Of greater importance for the role of European ideas in the formation of American economic thought is the common root of Rae's and Veblen's economics in a specific notion of man, or, as in the following citations, in their rejection of a particular notion of human agency.

Rae, seeking the underlying problem in the economics of Adam Smith and his followers, stated the following:

> Dugald Stewart has a remark on the abstract philosophy of David Hume, that seems not inapplicable to this, so termed, abstract science [Political Economy]. It is well known, that the sceptical philosopher deduced, pretty clearly, from Mr. Locke's principles, that the human mind was a mere bundle of sensations. The professor [Dugal Stewart] observes, that, before any formal refutation of the doctrine appeared [from the pen of Thomas Reid], it might have been

> sufficient answer to it, that it was so contrary to the experience of every one, as to make it more reasonable to suppose an error, either in the premises or deduction, though that error might not be discoverable, than to believe that the metaphysicians were right, and all the rest of mankind wrong. Such an answer is, I suspect, that which is now present to the minds of very many, in regard to the strange dogmas of the prevailing school of political economy. They regard them as a sort of practical *demonstratio ad absurdum* of some fundamental fallacy in the science.
>
> (Rae 1834: 348)

It is possible to construe this statement in such a way as to disassociate the notion of man in Rae's economics from that implied to be correct by Dugal Stewart. It is not possible to interpret the "Introduction" to Rae's treatment of "The Operation of the Legislator on National Stock," which also begins with a citation from Dugald Stewart on the nature of man, as anything but a rejection of the passive role set for human agency in the economics of the proponents of laissez-faire (Rae 1834: 358–368).

Veblen, seeking the underlying problem in the economics of Karl Menger, stated the following:

> The reason for the Austrian failure seems to lie in a faulty conception of human nature—faulty for the present purpose, however adequate it may be for any other. In all the received formulations of economic theory, whether at the hands of English economists or those of the Continent, the human material with which the inquiry is concerned is conceived in hedonistic terms; that is to say, in terms of a passive and substantially inert and immutably given human nature. The psychological and anthropological preconceptions of the economists have been those which were accepted by the psychological and social sciences some generations ago. The hedonistic conception of man is that of a lightning calculator of pleasures and pains, who oscillates like a homogeneous globule of desire of happiness under the impulse of stimuli that shift him about the area, but leave him intact. He has neither antecedent nor consequent. He is an isolated, definitive human datum, in stable equilibrium except for the buffets of the impinging forces that displace him in one direction or another. Self-imposed in elemental space, he spins symmetrically about his own spiritual axis until the parallelogram of forces bears down upon him, whereupon he follows the line of the resultant. When the force of the impact is spent, he comes to rest, as a self-contained globule of desire as before. Spiritually, the hedonistic man is not a prime mover. He is not the seat of a process of living, except in the sense that he is

> subject to a series of permutations enforced upon him by circumstances external and alien to him.
>
> (Veblen 1898: 73–74)

Veblen goes on to give a positive description of the self-determining, purposive, and inventive nature of man as conceived in contemporary psychology and sociology.

These statements, drawn from Rae and Veblen, indicating the nature of human agency that would make either money or machinery into capital, expose the common epistemological and psychological roots of their economics.

The common epistemological and psychological root

There is an unbroken descent from the Scottish Common Sense Philosophy to American pragmatism. At every point in this descent, according to Flower and Murphey (1977), the important stimulant was transference of European thought to America.

The content of the Scottish Common Sense Philosophy emerged from the conflict of faith and science at the time of the Scottish Enlightenment (1730–1830). Its transmission to America was related to the controversies sown by the Enlightenment within the Scottish Church. Names associated with the genesis of the doctrine, in its narrowest sense, were Thomas Reid (1710–1796), Dugald Stewart (1753–1828), and Thomas Brown (1778–1820). Names associated with its transmission were Francis Hutcheson (1694–1746), John Witherspoon (1722–94), and James McCosh (President of Princeton, 1868–88). Both Witherspoon and McCosh emigrated from Scotland to make their careers at Princeton, but Princeton was not the only school influenced by the Common Sense Philosophy. According to Flower and Murphey, teachers of the doctrine and books influenced by it were pervasive in America. It was an important element conditioning the reception of other doctrines from Europe (Flower and Murphey 1977, 1: 268–278).

Thomas Reid was the first to state the Common Sense Philosophy. Stewart and Brown may have improved the statement, but they added nothing of substance. Reid took his cue from the problem of knowing as it appeared in the works of Locke, Berkeley, and Hume. Rejecting the four extremes of idealism (it is all in our heads), materialism (it is all external to our heads), of skepticism, and of direct perception of truth, Reid made some common-sense assertions. There exists a real world external to our minds. There is a self, that is, a knowing subject. The external world is perceived by the self. In this interaction there are objective and subjective causes. The human mind is active in the knowing process. In some substantive way, it makes what it knows. It is not just a receiving *tabula rasa*. Knowledge so gained is cumulative, sufficent to govern action, and corrigible in the light of action's results. Human activity is not just reactive. It is purposive. It has ends set by the actor. With this knowing process, humans generate science, and the achievements of science are valid. According to Flower and Murphey, Reid's position was very close to what was to be the position of William James (Flower and Murphey 1977, 1: 247–253).

By the middle of the nineteenth century the Common Sense Philosophy had suffered a decline in popularity, its strong originators not being able to reproduce themselves. Thereafter, in part because of the "unfortunate" character of McCosh's book, *The Scottish Philosophy*, which abetted the attacks of British empiricists and idealists (Flower and Murphey 1977, 1: 242), further decline set in. At this same time philosophic discourse was enlivened by the idealist contributions of Kant and Hegel, in Germany, and subjected to the empiricizing influence of Darwin's *The Origin of Species* (1859), and Herbert Spencer's "Social Darwinism." These European intrusions entailed, again, a separation of idealism and realism, as they had been separated at the time of Berkeley and Locke. American pragmatism, according to Flower and Murphey, bridged this gap, as Scottish Common Sense had bridged it earlier.

Pragmatism was a product of the philosophy of C.S. Peirce. It was launched into the information environment from seminars at Harvard and Johns Hopkins. At Harvard, Peirce interacted with William James, O.W. Holmes, John Fiske, and others; at Johns Hopkins, with John Dewey, Thorstein Veblen, and others.

According to William James:

> Men are knowers and doers—not simply receivers of stimuli from outside. . . . [Experience] is a dynamic learning, cumulative and self-correcting and, above all, systematic. . . . Human organisms are selective and adaptive. They pursue ends preferentially and behave purposively.
>
> (Flower and Murphey 1977: 640–642)

According to Thorstein Veblen, who stood alongside of other pragmatists (White 1973: 55–63):

> The later psychology, reinforced by modern anthropological research, gives a different conception of human nature. . . . According to this view, human activity, and economic activity among the rest, is not apprehended as something incidental to the process of saturating given desires. The activity is itself the substantial fact of the process, and the desires under whose guidance the action takes place are circumstances of temperament which determine the specific direction in which he is engaged. But, in view of the science, they are elements of the existing frame of mind of the agent, and are the

> outcome of his antecedents and his life up to the point at which he stands. They are the products of his hereditary traits and his past experience, cumulatively wrought out under a given body of traditions, conventionalities, and material circumstances; and they afford the point of departure for the next step in the process. The economic life history of the individual is a cumulative process of adaptation of means to ends that cumulatively change as the process goes on, both the agent and his environment being at any point the outcome of the last process. . . . What is true of the individual in this respect is true of the group in which he lives.
>
> (Veblen 1898: 66–67)

However much the pragmatic synthesis was an American phenomenon, it was a synthesis depending on European thought transferred to America. At the root of the synthesis lay the Common Sense conception of knowing and acting. This was the connection between Rae and Veblen, and it explains the similarities between their economics. Others who have given consideration to the sources of Veblen's economics (Dorfman 1958; Daugert 1950) have approached this view, but, not having the assistance of Flower and Murphey, they have not quite come to it. More recently, looking at the matter from the point of view of Rae's contribution, Douglas Mair sensed the substantial similarity between Rae and Veblen, but failed to trace its roots in intellectual history and did not elaborate on his intuition (Mair 1990: 282–283).

Veblen, having read Rae?

Whatever may be said of the European roots of the connection between Rae and Veblen, it remains true that Veblen was directly aware of Rae, and expressed flattering disapproval: "Nor should that remnant of the classical school which has not yet given its adherence to the marginal utility doctrines readily find fault with an exposition which finds its foundations in so good and authentic a utilitarian theorist as John Rae" (Veblen [1909] 1934: 238). Further, there is a story repeated by Dorfman (1973: 30–31) that Veblen at one point suggested, in conversation, that someone said he had copied his doctrines, or part of his doctrines, from Rae. Against these veiled suggestions there is the evidence that Veblen had his own definition of capital before Rae was "discovered" in America (Spengler 1959b), and that he did not change his definition in consequence of his becoming aware of Rae.

Veblen's comment on Rae

Veblen classified Rae as a classical economist and a utilitarian. What he meant by this should be seen in the light of his elaboration of the preconceptions of economics, particularly his comments on the classical school (Veblen

1899a, 1899b). That Veblen should classify Rae with the classical, as opposed to the neoclassical, school seems straightforward. Rae wrote in the 1830s. The neoclassical "marginalists" appeared on the scene in the 1870s. Two outstanding marginalists, Böhm-Bawerk and Fisher, claimed to have seen their insights in Rae, but Rae was not a marginalist. Neither the term nor the idea appears anywhere in his writings. It was only by looking back on Rae with marginalist eyes, that anyone could read a degree of marginalism into his economics. Goodwin has grasped the situation in his comment that Rae "was groping for a concept of the margin" (Goodwin 1961: 124). He was groping for it blindly, in the sense that he himself did not see his doctrine as needing some concept that he could not find. Rae was not neoclassical, so he could be listed as classical, and Veblen so listed him.

That Veblen classified Rae as a utilitarian is less easy to understand. When Veblen pointed out the distinctive characteristics of utilitarian doctrine he stated that it takes effort and value in exchange, rather than productiveness, as a determinant of value (Veblen 1899b: 135):

> The shifting of the point of view that comes into economics with the acceptance of utilitarian ethics and its correlate, the Associationist psychology, is in great part a shifting to the ground of causal sequence, as contrasted with that of serviceability to a preconceived end . . . the utilitarian economists make exchange value the central feature of their theories, rather than the conduciveness of industry to the community's material welfare.
>
> (Veblen 1899b: 136)

Veblen was simply wrong about Rae in this matter, because Rae made it very clear that conduciveness to the community's material welfare was the cardinal element in value, in his view (Rae 1834: 265–299), and that, particularly in capital theory, this could not be measured by relative value, that is, value in exchange (Rae 1834: 193–197). Veblen's description of Rae as a classical, utilitarian economist could be taken as proof that Veblen had not actually read Rae. The similarities between the economics of the two, then, would be entirely the result of their common roots in the Scottish Common Sense Philosophy.

Veblen's view independent of Rae

There can be no doubt that there is some progression in Veblen's definition of capital. In his 1892 comment on Böhm-Bawerk's definition, Veblen makes no reference to the state of the industrial arts, that is, the technological sophistication of society. The distinction he offers is the distinction between the process of production and that of consumption, and correlatively, between wages as earnings and wages as consumption. Veblen's goal, in this comment, is to show that the wages fund controversy turns on the points of view taken by the respective sides (Veblen 1892). In his own definition of capital, some sixteen years later, Veblen focused on a distinction between capital goods as the embodiment of a state of the industrial arts, what he called a "technological view of capital," on the one hand, and on a "pecuniary" view, that is, a monetary and ownership view, on the other. The production–consumption distinction can be seen as embryonic to the technological–monetary view, but there is a difference. This difference generates the possibility that Veblen's definition of capital changed as a result of his reading Rae.

The focus of Veblen's attention changed over time. His first extended treatment of technology appears in *The Theory of Business Enterprise* (1904). It does not feature *improvement* in the industrial arts, and it is largely preliminary to the main point of the book. His definition of capital, in 1908 and in his subsequent works, turns on a distinction between a "technological view" and a "pecuniary view" of capital, and his elaboration of the technological view of capital involves considerable discussion of improvement in the industrial arts. Further, as time passed, Veblen gave increasing attention to the institutional aspect of his analysis. Still, the dual aspect of capital, whether production and consumption or technological and monetary, is not abandoned; in fact, the latter duality can be interpreted as a development of the earlier.

It was, then, during the period in which he was disputing capital theory with Irving Fisher, when Fisher was elaborating the theories that he, Fisher, attributed to Rae, that Veblen elaborated his distinction between technological and monetary capital.

Veblen's distinction is reminiscent of propositions in Rae's *Statement*. The critical element in the technological view of capital, according to Veblen, is "a matter of knowledge, usage, habits of life . . . a body of technological knowledge" ([1908b] 1961: 325). This knowledge is said to be embodied in equipment, and a list of pieces of such equipment is given, echoing Rae's list of "instruments" (Veblen [1908b] 1961: 329; Rae 1834: 86–89). Veblen asserts that "the technological situation is primary in the production process" as opposed to the distribution process, where property rights and money values are primary (Veblen [1908b] 1961: 340). He regards the traits of human nature, and the strength of the propensity to dissipation, as matters of great importance for the state of the arts and the material wellbeing of any civilization. For anyone who has read Rae this is *déjà vu* (Rae 1834: 18, 119–129, 260).

Still, the Rae–Veblen parallel is by no means complete. Veblen's primary concern is the dysfunctional nature of the institutions and practices of "business enterprise." Rae, at times, is concerned with business institutions, particularly banking institutions, but his concern is with their function as aids to industrial advance. In Veblen's definition of capital, business enterprise is designed for nothing but acquisition of wealth. Veblen refers to technological advance, but is not concerned with the process by which it takes place. That he leaves to instinct. He focuses on the way in which institutional structure impinges on technological advance through the operation of "predatory," that is, acquisitive, behavior. Rae, on the contrary, focuses on the processes of invention and innovation, which, for him, are a consequence of purposive behavior. He proposes policies and institutions that will foster invention and innovation.

The difference between Rae and Veblen is most evident in their accounts of "primitive accumulation," that is, their choice of the fundament of economic progress. Veblen lists the theories of "primitive accumulation" (Veblen [1908b] 1961: 342). For Karl Marx, it is a matter of force and fraud. For Werner Sombart, it is "from landed wealth." For the critics of Sombart, it is from usury and petty trade. Omitting Smith's theory that it is a matter of saving from current revenues, and Rae's theory that it is a matter of technological progress, Veblen selects "the gains of business, that is to say, . . . the gains of advantageous bargaining" (Veblen [1908b] 1961: 342) as the fundamental element in accumulation.

Given Veblen's perspicacity, had he known of Rae's view on primitive accumulation, and reflected on it, he would have seen that all theories of primitive accumulation, excluding Rae's, turn on the distribution of wealth. To be consistent with his own view on the dysfunctionality of the distribution system with respect to advance in the industrial arts, Veblen should have allowed that only Rae had a theory of primitive accumulation that dealt directly with the production of a surplus to be subsequently distributed according to property rights. In the light of these differences between Rae and Veblen, it is difficult to believe that Veblen had read Rae with any degree of concentration, if he had read him at all.

The clinching argument may be that Veblen never cited Rae. While Veblen gave up citations, except for a few sources on factual matters, after 1914, and *The Theory of the Leisure Class* (1899c) is devoid of citations, *The Theory of Business Enterprise* (1904) and *The Instinct of Workmanship* (1914) have extensive citations, particularly citations to members of the German School of Historical Economics. "On the Nature of Capital" (1908b, 1908c) has citations, though not extensive citations. It cannot be said that "Veblen never cited anyone but himself." Indeed, that would give a very wrong impression of Veblen. Still, his only published mention of Rae is his comment, in his critique of Fisher's theory of interest and capital, that Rae was a good utilitarian theorist.

Conclusion: Veblen

J.J. Spengler and others notwithstanding, it is unwarranted to conclude that Veblen had read Rae and was aware of the substance of Rae's economics. Any parallel between Veblen and Rae has to be accounted for by their common root in the Scottish Common Sense Philosophy. Indeed, in Veblen's case, it has to be accounted for by the rebirth of the substance of the Common Sense Philosophy in American pragmatism. Unlike Rae, who was intellectually European, Veblen was intellectually a first-generation American.

THORSTEIN VEBLEN AND HAROLD INNIS

Introduction

There is no evidence that John Rae was known to Harold Innis, or to any Canadian economist, in the first half of the twentieth century.

Much has already been said about the contribution of Innis to economics in Canada (Neill 1972, 1988, 1991). What is needed here is a demonstration that Innis was influenced by Veblen, and, for all intents and purposes, by no one else. To do this it will be necessary to show that it is unlikely that the general influence of European thought, in the form of the Scottish Common Sense Philosophy, or in the form of historical economics, can account for the content of Innis's economics. In particular, it will be necessary to show that Innis, like Veblen and consciously following Veblen, attempted unsuccessfully to square the circle of theory by making it "evolutionary."

Philosophy in Canada

Innis was certainly interested in philosophical questions. Even as he pursued his later studies in communications he was conscious of attempting to answer a question raised by James Ten Broeke, who had taught him philosophy when he was an undergraduate at McMaster: "Why do we attend to the things to which we attend?" Still, there is little likelihood that Ten Broeke was expounding the Scottish Common Sense Philosophy in its original form, let alone in its pragmatist American reincarnation. There is even less likelihood—indeed, there is no evidence at all—that Innis moved from philosopy to a critique of neoclassical theory that paralleled or followed Veblen's. He spent no time critiquing theory, but, alleging Veblen to have completed that task, moved immediately to history (Innis 1929: 22–26).

Ten Broeke, who influenced Innis in his early contact with philosophy, probably taught no particular doctrine. Innis described him as "by far the most heretical thinker in the University," and said that he taught the subject in such a way as to free anyone who wanted from the confines of any school of thought. In Canada in general, moreover, anyone remaining in the confines of a particular school of thought most probably followed John Watson, who, in turn, followed the English Idealists. Watson's influence was pervasive (McKillop 1994: 187–193; Armour 1981). The Scottish Common Sense Philosophy "lost its centrality in English Canadian Universities" following

Watson's arrival in 1872. American pragmatism had no effect on philosophy in Canada until the 1930s (Armour 1981: 405).

Innis's adoption of the historical approach in economics was, no doubt, in some degree, a consequence of his subjective disposition. It was facilitated by the general bias of "social scientists" in the Ontario Universities (McKillop 1994). But Innis's pursuit of history was not consequent upon reading Europeans. His only reference to the German historical economists that is significant with respect to the sources of his thought appears in his assessment of Veblen's work. The "lines along which" he pursued history were determined by what he judged to be Veblen's positive contribution, and by the material offered him as the stuff of Canadian history.

Innis can be cited in support of this contention:

> It is to be hoped that economic theory will not disappear through neglect or through the deadening influence of specialization, and that Veblen's attempt at synthesis may be revised and steadily improved. The conflict between the economics of a long and highly developed country such as England and the economics of the recently industrialized new and borrowing countries will become less severe as the study of cyclonics [J.M. Clark's "non-Euclidean economics," Veblen's "evolutionary economics"] is worked out and incorporated in a general survey of the effect of the industrial revolution such as Veblen has begun and such as will be worked out and revised by later students.
>
> (Innis 1929: 26)

In a letter to L.C. Marshall, who was still at Chicago in 1927, Innis wrote:

> In Canada we have assumed economic importance largely through the export of staple products. Consequently we have approached the general subject of economic history from the standpoint of the large and basic industries. We have tried to work out the significance of these industries (beginning with the fur trade) from an institutional standpoint following the work which was suggested in a vague way in Veblen's Instinct of Workmanship and more precisely in Ogburn's "Social Change" and in Whissler's "Relation of Man to his Environment." In other words there appears to be excellent material for the determination of certain phases of cultural growth. . . . making some advance along the line of studying the relationship between technology and industry. It is exactly the problem which is facing us in an attack on economic history.

There is no problem here in recognizing that Innis saw others doing in a better way, what Veblen had suggested. Innis included a long list of such fellow workers in his article on Veblen's contribution. Further, with respect to the emphasis on "staple" products, we have the comment by Allan Gruchy, in the middle of his description of Veblen's theory of economic growth:

> Veblen points out that after 1875 a new dual or hybrid economy made its appearance. As technology improved and the scale of industrial operations was enlarged, a cluser of "primary," "staple," or "key" industries developed in the industrial firmament. And around this central cluster or "tactical center" were the consumer goods industries and agriculture, in which technological progress and capital accumulation played less important roles.
>
> (Gruchy 1958: 165)

Innis followed Veblen by working out the institutional consequences of the advance of European technology in the northern half of the North American continent. His results were the same as Veblen's insofar as neither he nor Veblen was successful in working out an "evolutionary economics," or as Innis put it, in developing a "theory not only of dynamics but of cyclonics."

The constructive part of Veblen's work, according to Innis, was an elaboration of the effects of the industrial revolution. Several of Veblen's works focus explicitly on the effects of the industrial revolution on the institutionalization of business enterprise. Much, if not all, of Veblen's work turned on the distinction between technical production, on the one hand, and the distributional (acquisitional) function of business enterprise in the market (price) system, on the other.

There were several works, however, as Carter Goodrich has pointed out, that dealt with the matter historically: *Imperial Germany and the Industrial Revolution* (1915a), *Absentee Ownership and Business Enterprise in Recent Times* (1923), and "The Opportunity of Japan" (1915b). Carter Goodrich was one of a small group of students and faculty at Chicago who formed around discussion of Veblen's work. Others were Frank Knight, Morris Copeland, J.M. Clark, and Innis. Goodrich's selection of these works is of great significance with respect to Innis's interpretation of Canadian economic history.

Imperial Germany presented the cases of England and Germany, and a sketch of the case of America (Veblen [1915a] 1964: 332–340). In England, technological advance proceeded slowly, so that the organization of business enterprise, embodying the constraining consequences of acquisitiveness, developed *pari passu* with productivity. In Germany, technology was imported (borrowed) in an advanced form, so that the institutions of business enterprise were slow in catching up and developed differently. *Imperial Germany* presented a historical description of what these developments were. The article on Japan presented the case of that country in consequence of late, rapid borrowing of advanced technique: the institutional and political consequences. *Absentee Ownership* was a presentation of "the case of America" (Goodrich 1958: 119–201) with respect to the advance of technology and the formation of business enterprise, in which Veblen focused on the institutional consequences of the acquisitive appropriation of open access resources.

In his turn, Innis presented the consequences of "wholesale borrowing" of advanced technology in the geographical and institutional circumstances of the Canadian case. As in Veblen's cases, attention was turned to the effects of technological change on the organization of both private and public enterprise. Innis's great staples studies, *The Fur Trade in Canada*, *Settlement and the Mining Frontier*, and *The Cod Fisheries*, were studies of the borrowing of advanced technology in a new country (Neill 1972: 36–49). The similarity between Innis's and Veblen's case studies is more transparent, however, in Innis's shorter works, such as "Industrialism and Settlement in Western Canada" (Innis 1930), "Government Ownership in Canada" (Innis 1931), and "Government Ownership and the Canadian Scene" (Innis 1933).

Similarities reveal differences. Veblen contrasted the engineer and the price system as agents of production and acquisition, respectively, and tended to stress the dysfunctional nature of the price system with its roots in acquisitive distribution ("predation"). Innis, looking at the Canadian case, pointed to waste generated by the engineer in the public sector, freed from the constraints of the price system. There are traces of Veblen's disparagement of the price system and its correlative, price economics, in Innis's early works. His repeated references to the advance of an "acquisitive" society in *The Fur Trade in Canada*, and his own disparagement of "price economics" (Neill 1972: 40–41), are evidence, but that sort of evidence disappears very early in Innis's career.

Innis received Veblen mediated by the people he met at Chicago, but he showed himself capable of an independent interpretation. Innis drew the idea of "cyclonics" directly from Veblen, and he developed it further. The most advanced statement of this "economic dynamics" appeared in "The Penetrative Powers of the Price System" (Innis 1938), some ten years after publication of his review of Veblen's contribution (Innis 1929). Cyclonics was not theory, however, except as a historian might see theory (Neill 1991: 131–132). Knight and Clark accommodated what they took from Veblen to neoclassical theory. Innis, like Veblen, did not produce a body of theory.

J.M. Clark's Veblenian influence on Innis is evident in Innis's contribution to studies produced to explain the severity of the depression in Canada, all of which turned on the economics of overhead costs: *Problems of Staple Production in Canada* (1933), *The Canadian Economy and its Problems* (1934), *Essays in Political Economy in Honour of E.J. Urwick* (1938), and especially in his article "Unused Capacity as a Factor in Canadian History" (Innis 1936).

F.H. Knight's Veblenian influence expressed itself in Innis's concern with "Discussion in the Social Sciences," beginning in the early 1930s and continuing in his discussion of "The Economic Significance of Culture" (Innis 1944), "Industrialism and Cultural Values" (Innis 1951), and in his later communications studies. In this aspect of his work, Innis was more inspired or stimulated by Knight to pursue a particular line of thought, because, in these studies, Innis drew directly on Veblen's treatment of the impact of technological change on habits, values, and institutions, and on the effect of these on economic activity.

Conclusion: Innis

It seems fair to conclude that Innis was influenced directly by North American elements in the information environment. The bias toward history that marked Canadian social science in the first half of the twentieth century had its roots in European historical economics. This generated the tolerance that Innis needed, but he, himself, drew on American sources, specifically Veblen and some of those interested in Veblen. Of the three—Rae, Veblen, and Innis—Innis least represented Europe in America.

VEBLEN AND HIS CANADIAN CONNECTIONS

In examining the relationship between Veblen and his Canadian connections, John Rae and Harold Innis, it becomes evident that they were all influenced by European thought and by the historically different conditions of the America they observed. Abstracting from their different historical contexts, they differed from one another in their intellectual proximity to European thought.

Rae was the very embodiment of European thought in America. The doctrines he used to produce his own economics, drawn from Scottish Common Sense Philosophy, were as European as those he criticized, and those he criticized were European. His work was American only insofar as he was in America when he produced it, and insofar as it was consistent with his American circumstance. Rae's economics was a European immigrant in America.

Significant elements of Veblen's thought can be found in the economics of John Rae, but Veblen developed these elements independently of Rae. Like Rae, Veblen was an embodiment of European thought in America. Still, there was a difference. Veblen's use of European doctrines was mediated by pragmatism, a uniquely American synthesis of a number of streams of European thought. Because pragmatism had something substantial in common with Scottish Common Sense Philosophy, there was much in Veblen that was reminiscent of Rae. Veblen's economics, like Rae's, was American because it was produced in America, but further, it grew out of an American information environment. Veblen's economics was first-generation American.

Harold Innis was a generation removed from European thought. The information environment in which he worked was receptive to his doctrine, or at least to his approach to economics, because particular elements of European thought were present in it. His doctrine itself, however, was a derivative of Veblen's economics, and of the discourse of a small group of Americans who were interested in Veblen's economics. Innis's economics was second-generation American.

NOTE

1 I acknowledge the assistance of Malcolm Rutherford, whose knowledge of the literature on Veblen and Rae is more thorough than mine.

REFERENCES

Armour, L. (1981). *The Faces of Reason*, Waterloo, Ont.: Wilfrid Laurier University Press.

Bacon, F. (1960). *The New Organon and Related Writings*, ed. F.H. Anderson, New York: Liberal Arts Press.

Baragar, F. (1996). "The Influence of Thorstein Veblen on the Economics of Harold Innis," *Journal of Economic Issues* 30: 667–683.

Daugert, S.M. (1950). *The Philosophy of Thorstein Veblen*, New York: King's Crown Press.

Dorfman, J. (1958). "The Source and Impact of Veblen's Thought," in D.F. Dowd (ed.), *Thorstein Veblen: A Critical Reappraisal*, Ithaca, NY: Cornell University Press.

——— (1973). "New Light on Veblen," in J. Dorfman (ed.), *Essays Reviews and Reports*, New York: Augustus M. Kelley, 5–362.

Edgell, S. and R. Tilman (1991). "John Rae and Thorstein Veblen on Conspicuous Consumption: A Neglected Intellectual Relationship," *History of Political Economy* 24: 731–743.

Flower, E. and M.G. Murphey (1977). *A History of Philosophy in America*, 2 vols, New York: G.P. Putnam & Sons.

Goodrich, C. (1958). "The Case of New Countries," in D.F. Dowd (ed.), *Thorstein Veblen: A Critical Appraisal*, Ithaca, NY: Cornell University Press.

Goodwin, C.D.W. (1961). *Canadian Economic Thought*, Durham, NC: Duke University Press.

Gruchy, A. (1958). "Veblen's Theory of Economic Growth," in, D.F. Dowd (ed.), *Thorstein Veblen: A Critical Reappraisal*, Ithaca, NY: Cornell University Press.

Innis, H.A. (1929). "The Work of Thorstein Veblen," *Southwestern Political and Social Science Quarterly* 10: 56–68.

——— (1930). "Industrialism and Settlement in Western Canada," *Report of the Proceedings of the International Geographical Congress*, Cambridge, July, 1928: 369–376.

——— (1931). "Government Ownership in Canada," *Schriften des Vereins für Sozialpolitick* 176: 241–279.

Innis, H.A. (1933). "Government Ownership and the Canadian Scene," *Canadian Problems: As Seen by Twenty Outstanding Men of Canada*, Toronto: 69–90.
——— (1936). "Unused Capacity as a Factor in Canadian Economic History," *Canadian Journal of Economics and Political Science* 2: 1–15.
——— (1938). "The Penetrative Power of the Price System," *Canadian Journal of Economics and Political Science* 4: 299–319.
——— (1944). "On the Economic Significance of Culture," *Journal of Economic History* (supplement) 4: 80–97.
——— (1951). "Industrialism and Cultural Values," *American Economic Review*, papers and proceedings, 41: 201–209.
James, R.W. (1965). *John Rae: Political Economist*, Toronto: University of Toronto Press.
Mair, D. (1990). "John Rae: Ugly Duckling or Black Swan?" *Scottish Journal of Political Economy* 37: 275–287.
McKillop, A.B. (1994). *Matters of Mind*, Toronto: University of Toronto Press.
Mixter, C.W. (1902). "Böhm-Bawerk on Rae," *Quarterly Journal of Economics* 16: 385–412.
——— (ed.) (1905). *A Sociological Theory of Capital*, New York: Macmillan.
Neill, R. (1972). *A New Theory of Value: The Canadian Economics of H.A. Innis*, Toronto: University of Toronto Press.
——— (1988). "Rationality and the Informational Environment: A Reassessment of the Work of Harold Adams Innis," *Journal of Canadian Studies* 22: 78–93.
——— (1991). *A History of Canadian Economic Thought*, London: Routledge.
Rae, J. (1834). *Statement of Some New Principles on the Subject of Political Economy, Exposing the Fallacies of the System of Free Trade, and of some other Doctrines Maintained in the "Wealth of Nations*," Boston: Hiller Gray & Co.
Schumpeter, J.A. (1954). *History of Economic Analysis*, New York: Oxford University Press.
Spengler, J.J. (1959a). "Veblen and Mandeville Contrasted," *Weltwirtschaftliches Archive* 82: 3–67.
——— (1959b). "John Rae on Economic Development: A Note," *Quarterly Journal of Economics* 73: 393–406.
Stewart, D. (1792). *Elements of the Philosophy of the Human Mind*, London: A. Strahan & R.T. Cadwell.
——— (1853). "Account of the Life and Writings of Adam Smith, LLD," reprinted as "Introduction," *Theory of Moral Sentiments* by Adam Smith, London: Henry G. Bohn.
Veblen, T.B. (1892). "Böhm-Bawerk's Definition of Capital," *Quarterly Journal of Economics* 6: 247–250.
——— (1898). "Why Is Economics Not an Evolutionary Science?" *Quarterly Journal of Economics* 12: 373–397.
——— (1899a). "The Preconceptions of Economic Science: I," *Quarterly Journal of Economics* 13: 121–150.
——— (1899b). "The Preconceptions of Economic Science: II," *Quarterly Journal of Economics* 13: 396–426.
——— (1899c). *The Theory of the Leisure Class*, New York: Viking Press.
——— ([1904] 1932). *The Theory of Business Enterprise*, New York: The New American Library.

——— ([1908a] 1934). "Fisher's Capital and Income," in id., *Essays in Our Changing Order*, ed. L. Ardzrooni, New York: Viking Press, 148–172.

——— ([1908b] 1961). "On the Nature of Capital: I," in id., *The Place of Science in Modern Civilization*, New York: Russell & Russell, 324–351.

——— ([1908c] 1961). "On the Nature of Capital: II," in id., *The Place of Science in Modern Civilization*, New York: Russell & Russell, 352–386.

——— ([1908d] 1961). "Professor Clark's Economics," in id., *The Place of Science in Modern Civilization*, New York: Russell & Russell, 180–230.

——— ([1909] 1934). "Fisher's Rate of Interest," in id., *Essays in Our Changing Order*, ed. L. Ardzrooni, New York: Viking Press, 137–147.

——— ([1914] 1964). *The Instinct of Workmanship and the State of the Industrial Arts*, New York: W.W. Norton.

——— ([1915a] 1964). *Imperial Germany and the Industrial Revolution*, New York: Augustus M. Kelley.

——— (1915b). "The Opportunity of Japan," *Journal of Race Development* 6: 23–38.

——— (1923). *Absentee Ownership and Business Enterprise in Recent Times: The Case of America*, New York: Viking Press.

White, M. (1973). *Pragmatism and the American Mind*, New York: Oxford University Press.

12

MARSHALL, VEBLEN, AND THE SEARCH FOR AN EVOLUTIONARY ECONOMICS

Neil B. Niman

Neoclassical and institutional economics are often described as representing opposite ends of a broad spectrum of different "kinds" of economics. The conventional wisdom places Alfred Marshall firmly in the camp of the neoclassicals and Thorstein Veblen with the institutional economists. While the followers of each of these thinkers went on to develop independent schools of thought that have little, if anything, in common, closer examination of their work reveals a tremendous amount of commonality between these two historic figures.

Both Marshall and Veblen were grappling with the difficulties surrounding a desire to bring economics into the ranks of the "modern sciences." In doing so, both were highly influenced by Darwin's theory of evolution and the evolutionary ideas of Herbert Spencer (Niman 1991; Edgell and Tilman 1989). But the similarities do not just end with a common set of influences, for both men to a greater (in the case of Veblen) and lesser (in the case of Marshall) degree attempted to create a framework suitable for capturing the characteristics of an "evolutionary economics."

In trying to identify the similarities between two historic figures, there is a natural tendency to base a comparison on the contributions of each person. Unfortunately, Marshall, for the most part, only promises that he will develop an evolutionary economics and Veblen left behind nothing more than a montage of ideas.[1] While it would be easier to draw comparisons between two well-defined and fully articulated theoretical constructs, it is by no means an impossible task. Both men, prolific writers in their own right, have left behind enough clues that it becomes possible to identify a great deal of common ground.

Commonality between the ideas of Marshall and Veblen can be found in their shared criticism of the classical school, their belief that economics would be better served from an evolutionary approach, and a deep-rooted conviction that businessmen may not always act in the best interests of society. By exposing these points of agreement, the conclusion will be reached that while the followers of Marshall and Veblen have found them to be at odds, it is not because these two figures failed to see eye-to-eye on those matters *they* deemed important.

SHARED CRITICISM OF THE CLASSICALS

Both Veblen and Marshall embraced Darwinian ideas as a critical tool for structuring their own, very idiosyncratic interpretations of economic reality. The appeal of Darwinism for Veblen was that it provided justification for dispensing with an economics riddled with too many reminiscences of the "natural" and the "normal," of "verities" and "tendencies," of "controlling principles" and "disturbing causes" (Veblen 1898: 64). This meant overthrowing the classical conception of a "natural order" so that it could be replaced with a richer framework for understanding social phenomena (Hodgson 1992).

Marshall, on the other hand, did not want to dispense with such ideas as orderliness, social progress, or goal-directed change. He merely wanted to substitute the values inherent in what Bowler (1988) has termed the "non-Darwinian revolution" in social thought for those eighteenth-century ideas that continued to dominate economic thinking. Thus the value of Darwinism (as it was interpreted by Herbert Spencer) was found in its suitability as a vehicle for promoting moral advancement (Levitt 1976).

To promote their own personal agendas, each scholar took the classicals to task on the very same grounds. Whether it was the classicals' reluctance to incorporate the more modern advances of the other sciences, their rigid adherence to a natural order, or their failure to use economic analysis to explain real events, both men found the classical approach to be inadequate. This inadequacy stemmed to a large extent from the inability to graft the Darwinian concept of evolution on to a rigid classical structure that all but precluded change.

This may come as a surprise because, at first glance, one may be tempted to draw the conclusion that Marshall (the great conciliator) and Veblen (the consummate critic) have vastly different views of the classical economists. After all, Marshall was interested in demonstrating that his work in the *Principles* was, if nothing else, consistent with the broad foundations laid by the classicals. Veblen, on the other hand, found little if anything of redeeming value in the work of the classicals. However, if one goes beneath the surface and addresses specific criticisms, the gulf between Marshall and Veblen seems to be surprisingly narrow.[2]

The classicals' failed to keep pace with other sciences

In order to embrace Darwinian ideas, both scholars realized that they would have to push forward and develop a more modern approach to economic analysis. For both scholars, it was the adoption of the evolutionary point of view and not some fundamental revision in the theory of value that distinguished the work of the classicals from those who are engaged in a more "modern" economics.

From Veblen's perspective, economics was helplessly behind the times and unable to handle its subject matter in a way that would enable it to stand as a modern science. This, in part, stems from Veblen's belief that classical economics was hopelessly mired in an "hedonistic-associational psychology" (1900: 242). As a result, Veblen concludes: "Economics is not an evolutionary science—by the confession of its spokesmen; and the economists turn their eyes with something of envy and some sense of baffled emulation to these rivals that make broad their phylacteries with the legend, 'Up to date' " (1898: 374–375).

For Veblen, the failure of economics to keep pace with the times implied that economic agents are nothing more than passive participants who react rather than enact change within the strictures of a natural order. However, "it is the characteristic of man to do something, not simply to suffer pleasures and pains through the impact of suitable forces" (1898: 390). To broaden the conception of human nature and to be able to investigate more closely the myriad of forces that mold and shape behavior, Veblen needed to do away with the hedonistic-associative psychology of the classicals.

Take the case of pecuniary emulation, a key component in Veblen's *Theory of the Leisure Class*. Here, the possession of wealth is viewed as a meritorious act that confers honor on its possessor and provides the measuring stick for comparing oneself to one's neighbors. The desire to build esteem relative to others directs human beings who strive to improve their station in life, rather than passively sitting still and blindly responding to a given set of conditions.

In order for emulation to occur, differences must exist or there is no basis for striving to mimic one's own neighbors. Comparisons cannot be made if everyone is the same, and it is variation in the population that provides the basis for explaining the competitive struggle for survival that creates the need for selection. Selection is important because it guides the unfolding process of change.

Such a concept of struggle provides the mechanism for explaining social change in *The Theory of the Leisure Class*. For Veblen, the economic process "bears the character of the struggle between men for the possession of goods," but it is not a "struggle for subsistence" or one prompted by the "niggardliness of nature" ([1899] 1979: 24). Rather, it is a struggle for esteem: that is, to gain distinction by achieving material success relative to others. It is the desire for and pursuit of social esteem that drives economic change.

Marshall also relies on Darwin in his shared criticism that the classicals were "behind the times." Marshall (in agreement with Veblen) felt that the fundamental problem with the classicals was their inability or unwillingness to adopt a broader and more realistic conception of human behavior. As Marshall contended:

> While the earlier economists argued as though man's character and efficiency were to be regarded as a fixed quantity, modern economists keep constantly in mind the fact that it is a product of the circumstances under which he has lived. This change . . . is partly due to . . . the indirect influence of a similar change in some branches of natural science.
>
> ([1920] 1979: 631)

In doing so, Marshall also breaks with the "hedonistic-associative psychology" of the classicals otherwise known as utilitarianism. His dissatisfaction with utilitarianism and his desire to see the construction of a more "dynamic" conception is found in a series of letters written to Edgeworth in 1880 where Marshall reveals: "I have still a hankering after a mode of exposition in which the dynamical character of the problem is made more obvious; which may in fact represent the central notion of happiness as a process rather than a statical condition." When queried about what he meant by dynamical, Marshall responds: "I think there is room for question whether the Utilitarians are right in assuming that the end of action is the sum of the happiness of individuals rather than the vigorous life of the whole" (Whitaker 1996a: 124–125).

The Darwinian concept of a selection process based on a competitive struggle is appealing for Marshall because struggle connotes work and work builds character.[3] As Marshall writes:

> The truth seems to be that as human nature is constituted, man rapidly degenerates unless he has some hard work to do, some difficulties to overcome; and that some strenuous exertion is necessary for physical and moral health. The fullness of life lies in the development and activity of as many and as high faculties as possible.
>
> ([1920] 1979: 112)

From character springs social progress and thus the underlying Darwinian framework enables Marshall to argue for a better tomorrow. After all, for Marshall, "Work is not punishment for fault: it is a necessity for the formation of character and, therefore, for progress" (Pigou 1966: 367).

The classical reliance on natural order

If the modernization of economics is truly important for the development of meaningful economic analysis, why did the classicals blindly sit by and refuse to draw from the evolutionary approach found in the natural sciences? One possible explanation stems from the fact that much of classical economics is a reflection of an eighteenth-century natural philosophy designed to explain individual freedom (O'Brien 1978: ch. 2). Thus resistance to evolutionary ideas might emerge from the fear that the adoption of a nineteenth-century evolutionary philosophy would subjugate individual action to a much larger force of nature, so challenging individual freedom. Alternatively, if the process of evolution is constantly changing the world, is it possible to speak of an unchanging natural order that resists the pull of such a powerful force?

For Veblen, the failure of the classicals to adopt an evolutionary perspective stems from the fact that they were "content to occupy themselves with repairing a structure and doctrines and maxims resting on natural rights, utilitarianism, and administrative expediency" (1898: 374). As a result, the classicals were forced to justify their theories not on the basis of fact or economic process, but rather, "it is for the scientific purpose an imputation of spiritual coherence to the facts dealt with" (1898: 379). One which promotes an "uncritical conviction that there is a meliorative trend in the course of events, apart from the conscious ends of the individual members of the community" (1900: 242–243).

Why was it so important that Veblen should eliminate the classical conception of a natural order? For Veblen, acceptance of the classicals' natural order was tantamount to acknowledging the existence of their "law of the conservation of economic energy" where "the economic income and outgo balance one another" ([1901] 1969: 281). In such a natural order where the distribution of income is tied to productivity, it becomes all but impossible for a leisure class to emerge. It also deprives Veblen of the basis for his business cycle which is found in the tension between those who strive for industrial efficiency and those who restrict output to maximize profit.

As importantly, adherence to some notion of natural order implies that action is teleological and directed toward the achievement of some end (Veblen 1898). Darwinian evolution, on the other hand, contends that there is not some ultimate cosmic goal at the end of the evolutionary process. Change is not directed toward some final resting place. In order to use Darwinian ideas to talk about the process of change, Veblen therefore must dispense with the notion of a natural order.

The importance of Darwin in challenging the classical view with respect to the existence of a natural order is also found in Marshall. The classicals' adherence to a natural order forced them to attribute "to the forces of supply and demand a much more mechanical and regular action than is to be found in real life: and they laid down laws with regard to profits and wages that did not really hold even for England in their own time" ([1920] 1979: 630). Thus Marshall contended:

> The laws of economics are to be compared with the laws of the tides, rather than with the simple and exact law of gravitation. For the actions of men are so various and uncertain, that the best statement of tendencies, which we can make in a science of human conduct, must needs be inexact and faulty.
>
> ([1920] 1979: 26)

Why is it so important for Marshall to argue against the existence of a natural order and what role does Darwin play in the process? Marshall felt that there was a direct connection between industrial conditions and the corresponding ethical beliefs and development of a society. Ethics are something that are not only socially determined by the underlying production conditions, but also change as those conditions change. Marshall's fascination with Darwin stems in part from his interest in reforming human nature and advancing ideas leading to a more moral and ethical society.[4]

What Darwinism meant to Marshall was not the competitive struggle for existence, but rather (as he reveals in a letter to Benjamin Kidd) "the dominance of sacrifice for future generations as an or even *the* essential element of progress" (Whitaker 1996b: 385)—a theme that is reinforced in Marshall's *Principles* where he writes at length:

> But deliberate, and therefore moral, self-sacrifice soon makes its appearance; it is fostered by the far-seeing guidance of prophets and priests and legislators, and is inculcated by parable and legend. Gradually the unreasoning sympathy, of which there are germs in the lower animals, extends its area and gets to be deliberately adopted as a basis of action: . . . The races in which these qualities are the most highly developed are sure, other things being equal, to be stronger than others in war and in contests with famine and disease; and ultimately to prevail. Thus the struggle for existence causes in the long run those races of men to survive in which the individual is most willing to sacrifice himself for the benefit of those around him; and which are consequently the best adapted collectively to make use of their environment.
>
> ([1920] 1979: 202–203)

Self-sacrifice for Marshall is both a necessary condition for social survival, and an outcome that raises the ethical and moral character of civilization. Self-sacrifice and the struggle for existence enables Marshall to argue that the world is truly becoming a better place to live where individuals are able to achieve a higher level of happiness.

Classical theory was too abstract

The reliance on a natural order and the inability or unwillingness to modernize economics contributed to a heightened level of abstraction. The conquest of the deductive method embodied in the Ricardian "vice" had distracted economics from its primary concern of offering insights about actual problems based upon fact. Regardless of whether or not theoretical abstractions about basic principles are of value, both men agreed that how you choose to look at the economy only has validity if it is grounded in the reality of the times.

As Veblen wrote: "In the days of the early classical writers economics had a vital interest for the layman of the time, because it formulated the common sense metaphysics of the time in its application to a department of human life. But in the hands of the later classical writers it has lost much of its charm in this regard" (1898: 69). Compare this with Marshall who expressed the view that "The chief fault, then, in English economists at the beginning of the century was . . . that Ricardo and his followers neglected a large group of facts, and a method of studying facts which we now see to be of primary importance" ([1885] 1966: 154).

This interest in the facts stems, in part, from the interest both scholars have in Darwinism. After all, the Darwinian process of selection is based not on representative agents, but rather, on a diverse population. Thus, while a generalized principle such as natural selection can explain how change occurs, the actual changes themselves depend upon the composition of actual populations. Without an understanding of the facts as they exist in all of their complexity, it becomes impossible not only to discuss change, but also to interpret the changes that actually occur.

COMMON FOUNDATIONS FOR AN EVOLUTIONARY SYSTEM

To advance their ideas, Marshall and Veblen not only had to break from the classical tradition, but had also to develop new foundations for an evolutionary economics. The cornerstone of their new approach rested on the belief that human action leading to the creation of knowledge is the principal engine for setting in motion a chain of events leading to real economic change.

Process analysis

Obsessed with the concept of a natural order and ignorant of the facts of everyday life, the classicals were hopelessly behind the times. For both Veblen and Marshall, a new approach was called for that would focus on process rather than the "codified rules of the game of causation" (Veblen [1908a] 1969: 38).

From Veblen's perspective, "modern science is becoming substantially a theory of the process of consecutive change, which is taken as a sequence of cumulative change, realized to be self-continuing or self-propagating and to have no final term" ([1908a] 1969: 37). Rather than focusing exclusively on cause (as did the classicals), a modern science centers on how things work themselves out from cause to effect. These processes (influenced by the Darwinian principle of selection from a diverse population) imply that an outcome can only be determined after the process unfolds. From such a perspective, anything becomes possible because outcomes are in part determined by random occurrences (mutations) that contribute to the diversity of a population subject to the selection process.

For Marshall, abandonment of the classicals' emphasis on prior causes and adoption of a process-type of analysis stems from the fact that "the actions of men are so various and uncertain, that the best statement of tendencies, which we can make in a science of human conduct, must needs be inexact and faulty" ([1920] 1979: 26). As a result, "for dealing with most modern problems it is modern facts that are of the greatest use" ([1920] 1979: 33). Thus Marshall also moves away from the view of a natural order that predefines outcomes. However, where Marshall differs from Veblen, is in his desire to believe that while outcomes are not determined, they lead to the betterment of humanity.

The importance of human action

Regardless of whether you are looking at Marshall or Veblen, the starting point for the development of an evolutionary conception of economics begins with human action. The action of human beings becomes the change agent for an economy subject to Darwinian forces of competition and selection. Given that human nature itself is the subject of change, it also becomes the basis for change by providing the needed diversity for selection to become a discriminating force in the overall process of change.

For Veblen:

> It is in the human material that the continuity of development is to be looked for; and it is here, therefore, that the motor forces of the process of economic development must be studied if they are to be studied in action at all. Economic action must be the subject-matter

> of the science if the science is to fall into line as an evolutionary science.
>
> (1898: 72)

Thus, in contrast to the classicals who viewed humanity in hedonistic terms where people are viewed as a "lightning calculator of pleasures and pains," Veblen advocated the adoption of a more modern view where a human being "is not simply a bundle of desires that are to be saturated by being placed in the path of the forces of the environment, but rather a coherent structure of propensities and habits which seeks realisation and expression in an unfolding activity" (1898: 74). This led him to the conclusion that "The economic life history of the individual is a cumulative process of adaptation of means to ends that cumulatively change as the process goes on, both the agent and his environment being at any point the outcome of the last process" (1898: 74–75).

The idea of human action as the basis for economic change is also found in Marshall. For Marshall, the evolutionary theory of Darwin has led to "the discovery that man himself is in great measure a creature of circumstances and changes with them; and the importance of this discovery has been accentuated by the fact that the growth of knowledge and earnestness have recently made and are making deep and rapid changes in human nature" ([1885] 1966: 153–154). Why for Marshall is human action so important? It is because economics is the "science of activities and not that of wants" ([1920] 1979: 76–77).

Knowledge as a driving economic force

If human action forms the basis for economic change, how does this action lead to change? What is the cause and effect relationship between the two? Once again, we find that both Marshall and Veblen share a common point of view. The answer resides in the role of knowledge.

For Marshall and Veblen, knowledge rather than labor or plant and equipment is the dynamic element present that brings about change. It is knowledge leading to the development of new methods of production that provides the needed linchpin between human action as the cause and cumulative economic change as the effect.

As Veblen commented, knowledge is important because capital assets such as plant and equipment

> are facts of human knowledge, skill, and predilection; that is to say, they are, substantially, prevalent habits of thought, and it is as such that they enter into the process of industrial development. The physical properties of the materials accessible to man are constants: it is the human agent that changes,—his insight and his appreciation of what these things can be used for is what develops.
>
> (1898: 71)

This view was shared by Marshall who contended that "Capital consists in a great part of knowledge and organization. . . . Knowledge is our most powerful engine of production. . . . Organization aids knowledge. . . . It seems best sometimes to reckon Organization apart as a distinct agent of production" ([1920] 1979: 115). Thus for Marshall, "In a sense there are only two agents of production, nature and man" ([1920] 1979: 116).

SIMILAR EVOLUTIONARY SYSTEMS

From these common foundations, it remains to be seen whether these two scholars construct consistent frameworks leading to a shared understanding of the driving forces found in a capitalist economy. It is perhaps easy to argue that Marshall only talks about developing an evolutionary economics while Veblen actually delivers. But what is it that Veblen delivers? More importantly, how different is this from what Marshall promises?

Veblen's view of capitalism

While Veblen did not leave a single piece that summarizes his conception of what exactly it means to develop an "evolutionary economics," it is possible to construct a broad synthesis that captures the essence of Veblen's ideas. This simple characterization can be found in Figure 12.1.

In the evolutionary theory of Veblen, human behavior is motivated by inborn instincts such as workmanship, idle curiosity, and the urge to care for others. These instincts lead to the formation of habits of thought that form the basis for social institutions. These institutions provide the cultural context that guides human behavior.

Within this basic framework, Veblen tries to articulate a theory of cumulative change for a capitalist economy. Under capitalism, the instincts of workmanship and curiosity lead to the development of new technologies, thereby becoming the driving force for change. However, the existing set of institutional arrangements pit the businessman's desire for pecuniary gain against the technician's desire for industrial efficiency.

It is the actions of businessmen who harness the efforts of technicians in an effort to gain a pecuniary advantage. However, while the businessman sets into motion those forces that lead to change, he also engages in competitive strategies that disrupt industrial efficiency, thereby inhibiting the ability to change.[5] Therefore, "under the rule of pecuniary standards and management—circumstances make it advisable for the business man at times to mismanage the processes of industry, in the sense that it is expedient for pecuniary gain to inhibit, curtail, or misdirect industry, and so turn the community's technological proficiency to the community's detriment" ([1908b] 1969: 359). For Veblen, the pace of change is therefore regulated

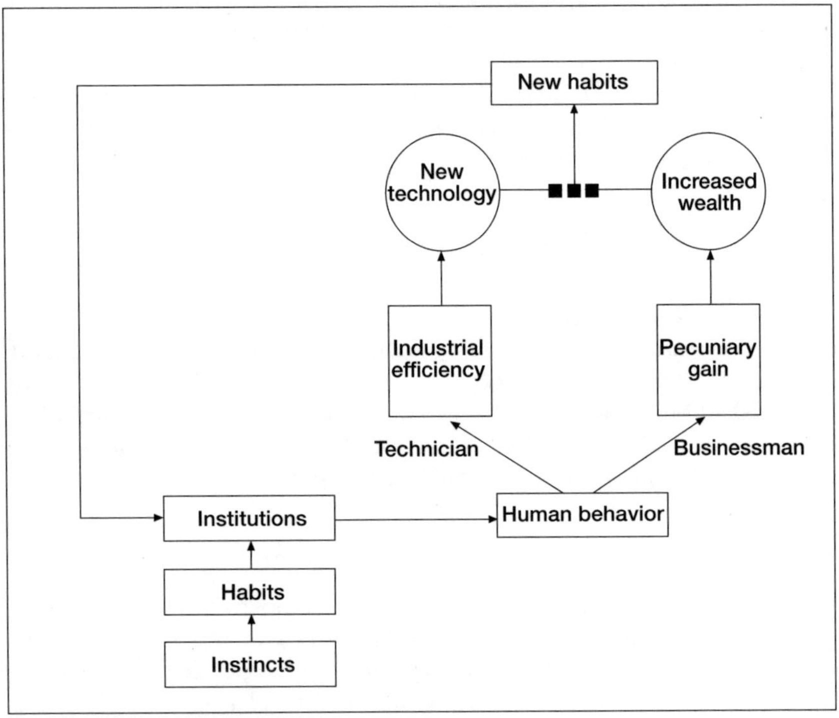

Figure 12.1 Veblen's view of capitalism

by the balance of power between those who promote change by creating new technology and those who stand in its way in their pursuit of greater wealth.

Marshall's evolutionary approach

A similar tension can be found in the evolutionary ideas of Marshall. However, just as Veblen did not leave a single piece of work that offers a comprehensive framework, the same holds true of Marshall. Clearly, the *Principles*, an exercise in the development of foundations for economics, does not contain a fully developed evolutionary economics. But various bits and pieces can be found both in the *Principles* and in some of Marshall's (1897, 1898) other writings. A thumbnail sketch of Marshall's evolutionary approach can be found in Figure 12.2.

In the writings of Marshall, industrial organization owes a debt to biology for having illustrated "a fundamental unity of action between the laws of nature in the physical and in the moral world." This central unity is set forth in the general rule "that the development of the organism, whether social or physical, involves an increasing subdivision of functions." By promoting "the

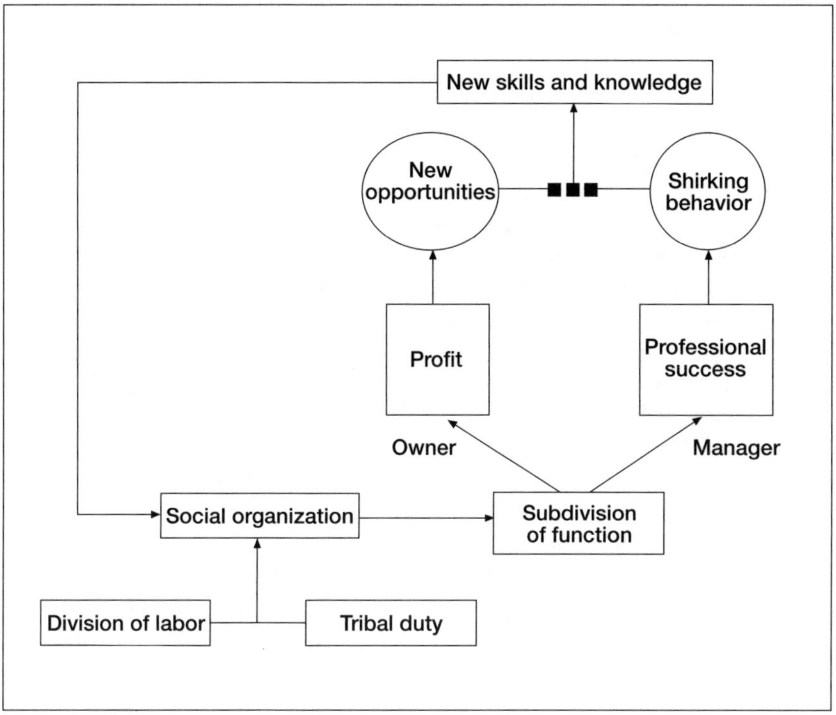

Figure 12.2 The Marshallian evolutionary approach to economics

development of specialized skill, knowledge and machinery," the subdivision of function enhances the development of the social organism and hence maximizes the likelihood for survival in the "struggle for existence" ([1920] 1979: 200–201).

The subdivision of function springing forth from Adam Smith's concept of the division of labor, however, while a necessary, is not a sufficient condition for survival. Marshall points to the duty one has to family and race (the tribe) as determining whether survival is assured for a particular group. Only when "tribal affection" gradually grows into a "noble patriotism" and the "unreasoning sympathy" for others becomes the "basis for action" does a race become strong enough to survive and "ultimately prevail" ([1920] 1979: 202).

Thus, from a social perspective, it is both the division of labor and the sense of "tribal duty" that lead to the creation of social organizations.[6] The firm, as one of these organizations predicated on the subdivision of function, provides the key for understanding Marshall's immature theory of institutional change. For Marshall, the subdivision of functions within the context of the firm is determined by the "employer of labour" who is both "a merchant and organizer of production" and a "natural leader of *men*" ([1920] 1979: 248). It is through the actions of this individual that a firm is able to grow like "the young trees of the forest as they struggle upwards through the benumbing shade of their older rivals" ([1920] 1979: 263). But soon, as the firm grows larger, it begins to stagnate.

Why does a firm stagnate? When a firm reaches a certain size, there is a "consequent transference of authority and responsibility from the owners of each business to its salaried managers and officials" ([1897] 1966: 307). For Marshall, this separation between ownership and control creates a moral hazard problem. Seeking to take advantage of new opportunities created by something like a change in technology, the manager is forced to bear all of the risks without being able to share fully in the rewards.[7] If the change fails, he is to blame, while if it succeeds, the owner of the firm enjoys the lion's share of the rewards. For the manager, "the path of least resistance, of greatest comfort and least risk to himself is generally that of not striving for improvement himself, and of finding plausible excuses for not trying an improvement suggested by others, until its success is established beyond question" ([1897] 1966: 307).

It is this tension between the owner who strives for greater success through the creation of new opportunities and the manager who, motivated by professional success, shirks from his responsibilities that determines the strength of those forces leading to change. Marshall believed these "bureaucratic habits of shirking troublesome initiative" left without adequate checks might lead to the "ossification of the social organism" as society is deprived of the advantages associated with the new change ([1897] 1966: 308).

Comparing the two frameworks

Both Veblen and Marshall undertake the difficult task of developing evolutionary theories of the economy that attempt to at least pay lip service to Darwinian principles. In attempting such a difficult task, the principal obstacle that must be overcome is addressing the issue of how to reconcile human and social behavior that is both biologically and culturally determined. To ignore culture is tantamount to arguing that social institutions are irrelevant. On the other hand, to ignore the fact that economic agents are indeed human beings subject to the same evolutionary principles as any other living organism is the equivalent of "throwing the baby out with the bath water."

Similarities in the human component can be found in the instincts for workmanship and family found in Veblen and the need for energetic work and the tribal sense of duty in Marshall. The human characteristics that both agree upon are those that contribute to the formation of a social identity—one that is required to ensure survival against the ravages of the "struggle for existence."

To nurture these human characteristics and promote their development, social institutions create structures that shepherd the production of goods and services in the economy. The ability to harness the industrial arts and direct them to where they can be utilized best for both Marshall and Veblen takes place in the context of the firm. Within the firm, human nature is molded into a tool that helps ensure the survival of society.

For both Marshall and Veblen, the industrial revolution and the corresponding increase in the division of labor offer the potential for greater efficiencies, but at the cost of harmony within the firm. The need to separate tasks in response to the increased size of the modern business enterprise leads to the formation of groups whose interests do not necessarily coincide. In the work of Veblen ([1904] 1965), this is manifested in the growing separation of pecuniary and technological matters leading to a conflict between the businessman and the technician who find themselves at odds over the value of industrial efficiency.

In the world of Marshall ([1875] 1975), the restlessness, self-confidence, and need to prove oneself that was reflected in the American character, finds its way to England with the increase in the growth of the size of the firm and the consequent transfer of authority to a professional group of managers (Marshall [1897] 1966). With the emergence of the professional manager, the economic fabric underlying the British economy begins to break down as long-held associations based upon reputation rather than money (Marshall [1889] 1966) cannot withstand the driving force of the industrial revolution. As a result, the cadre of young professional managers find themselves at odds with the owners of the business who are, themselves, products of a past where cooperation rather than competition was the rule of the day. An era that, for Marshall, found cooperation to be a useful tool for minimizing what he considered to be "the great waste product" resulting from the squandering of the higher abilities of the working class ([1889] 1966: 229).

The "hero" for both Veblen and Marshall is that group whose allegiance is tied to the past where the needs and interest of society take precedence over those of the individual. Whether it is the emergence of the businessman who squanders industrial efficiency for the sake of pecuniary gain or the manager who wastes the talents of the working class in the pursuit of professional success, the hero is the group that stands firm in the traditions of the past. These conflicting groups oversee a process that promotes change by creating new opportunities based on new technology (Veblen) or new forms of knowledge (Marshall)—change that ultimately leads to the formation of new institutions or substantial modification in existing ones.

VEBLEN ON MARSHALL

To this point it has been argued that the similarities between Veblen and Marshall with respect to their views on classical economics, evolutionary change, and the structure of capitalist economies are strikingly similar. However, the fact remains that Veblen was not ignorant of Marshall's work. Veblen's faint praise of Marshall's "most effective modernised classical economics" (1900: 263) may lead one to argue that despite such similarities, the two were cut from very different bolts of cloth.

While the followers of Marshall for the most part ignored his proclamation that "biology is the mecca of economics" ([1920] 1979: xii),[8] the significance of evolutionary themes for Marshall was not missed by Veblen. In commenting on Marshall's work, Veblen writes: "His insistence on the continuity of development and of the economic structure of communities . . . [a]ll gives an air of evolutionism to the work. Indeed, the work of the neoclassical economics might be compared, probably without offending any of its adepts, with that of the early generation of Darwinians" (1900: 265).

From Veblen's perspective, Marshall's work had only an "air of evolutionism" because of his overdependence on the use of statical concepts to describe economic phenomena. Such a "taxonomic" approach is inconsistent with Veblen's view of what constituted a modern evolutionary economics. Concepts such as supply and demand or competitive equilibrium appeared to be mired in a pre-Darwinian classical tradition that relied on similar devices.

In fact, it was the liberal sprinkling of abstract theoretical devices throughout the *Principles* that have led many to believe that Marshall's contribution to the history of economic thought lies in the area of abstract theory. Doing so, however, would conflict with Marshall's own stated views on the importance of economic theory. In a letter written to F.Y. Edgeworth in 1902, Marshall commented:

> In my view "Theory" is essential. . . . But I conceive no more calamitous notion than that abstract, or general, or "theoretical" economics was economics "proper." It seems to me an essential but a very small part of economics proper: and by itself sometimes even—well, not a very good occupation of time. . . . Economic theory is, in my opinion, as mischievous an impostor when it claims to be economics *proper* as is mere crude unanalysed history. Six of ye one, ½ dozen of ye other!
>
> (Pigou 1966: 437)

Marshall viewed his *Principles of Economics* as a modest effort to lay out the foundations for economic analysis. These foundations were to be a starting rather than an ending point in his intellectual thought (Niman 1991). Fearing just such a misinterpretation, Marshall contended:

> it is especially needful to remember that economic problems are imperfectly presented when they are treated as problems of statical equilibrium, and not of organic growth. For though the statical treatment alone can give us definiteness and precision of thought, and is therefore a necessary introduction to a more philosophic treatment of society as an organism, it is yet only an introduction.
>
> ([1920] 1979: 382)

Marshall realized that "the predominant attention paid in the present volume to the normal conditions of life in the modern age, has suggested the notion that its central idea is 'statical,' rather than 'dynamical,' . . . but in fact it is concerned throughout with the forces that cause movement and its key-note is of dynamics, rather than statics" ([1920] 1979: xii–xiii).

Clearly, Marshall and Veblen would dispute the value of such "foundations" even if they represented only a modest starting point for the subsequent development of a more accurate representation of real economic phenomena. Yet, to condemn or criticize Marshall from doing just that is to misunderstand his use of theory. Marshall was, in his own way, an early proponent of the notion of bounded rationality (Simon 1955). For Marshall, the complexities of the real world make it virtually impossible for any single individual to grasp problems in their totality. Theory is helpful as a tool for breaking the whole into a series of parts that can be easily dissected and understood before reassembling the whole once again. Theory is not a means for hiding from the complexity of the real world or an escape from having to explain actual economic problems.[9]

If Marshall's views about his own work are to be accepted, then Veblen's criticism of Marshall is only partially valid. True, the economic system that Marshall offers in the *Principles* is, at best, a modernized classical system. That is not the same thing as saying that Marshall himself was a classical economist.

Why then is what is commonly referred to as Marshallian economics so different from the institutional economics of Veblen? The answer resides in Marshall's inability to produce the second volume to his *Principles*. A second volume would perhaps look Veblenian, but without its existence we will never know. Why then, if Marshall was committed to an evolutionary approach, did he fail to complete his self-assigned task?

One possible explanation stems from his psychological makeup. After describing all of the starts and stops in Marshall's publishing odyssey, Whitaker (1990) concludes (along with Keynes (1924)) that the problem to a large degree revolved around a psychological propensity toward perfection. "Give Marshall a deadline and he would produce a short vigorous piece, which he would then proceed to grumble at and denigrate . . . but allow him to operate without limitation on time or space and incessant fruitless recasting would inhibit his progress, leading often to a virtual paralysis" (Whitaker 1990: 221).

Another explanation stems from Marshall's position as Professor of Political Economy at Cambridge University. As the chief spokesperson for the study of economics in Britain, Marshall spent a great deal of his time on the backroom politics necessary to establish economics as an independent field of study. The battle chronicled in Whitaker (1996b) clearly took its toll on Marshall. In addition to the effort expended establishing a separate tripos for economics within the confines of Cambridge, Marshall took it upon himself to salvage economics from disgrace in wider British scientific circles (Coats 1967). As a result, Marshall found himself spending ever greater amounts of time trying to raise the professional standing of economics (Maloney 1985). The net result was that Marshall, a man plagued by health problems, found himself having to devote a great deal of his limited energy to ensuring that the study of economics would grow and flourish.

IS THERE REALLY A DIFFERENCE BETWEEN MARSHALL AND VEBLEN?

Conventional wisdom aside, there does exist a symmetry between the ideas and aspirations of Marshall and Veblen. Both view the firm as an institution run by businessmen whose interests do not foster technological advancement and ultimately economic change.[10] For Veblen, these institutions are bound to habits, while for Marshall, to the division of labor. It is at this juncture that those who might like to see such a comparison between these two great thinkers argue that habits and the division of labor are two distinct concepts that are inherently irreconcilable. After all, the division of labor is an idea wedded in classical economics, a point of view that both Marshall and Veblen would argue is inconsistent with an evolutionary point of view. However, as Jones (1985: 1052) points out, if Darwin indeed was inspired by the classicals, then Darwinian evolution becomes an "unsuitable club with which to beat classical economics, since the former evolves from the latter."

Since evolutionary science is a theory of cause and effect based on cumulative causation, any theory that shares these principles is evolutionary regardless of whether or not they are based on ideas that have been embodied in a pre-Darwinian theory. Thus, while Marshall and Veblen may differ in terms of how they might explain the foundations for an evolutionary economic theory, it is important to note that in terms of the expressed desire to explain change, and the identification of what drives change, the two are similar in their respective points of view.

NOTES

1 In commenting on the lack of a single coherent statement of Veblen's system, Walker remarks: "There is no study in the past literature that shows the economic system that Veblen constructed, perhaps because of the difficulty of discerning its outlines in the many pages of his verbose and discursive works. Veblen himself never provided an outline of it, nor even considered it explicitly as a subject" (1977: 213–214).

2 One may use Marshall's admonition that "there has been no real breach of continuity in the development of the science" ([1920] 1979: v) to conclude that he paid only "lip service" to the promise of an evolutionary economics. Alternatively, one could argue as does Veblen that continuity is important to the development of scientific thought (1900: 242).

3 The importance of this passage is revealed by Marshall in a letter he wrote to Benjamin Kidd where he states: "thus the brief hint as to my ethical position given in Book IV CH. VIII of my Principles seemed to me to [be] mere Darwini-anism" (Whitaker 1996b: 385).

4 Marshall's desire to do good and his emphasis on ethical values is the theme of Reisman's (1990) book. As Reisman concludes: "Alfred Marshall, anxious to do good, made it his mission to contribute what little he could to that improvement and that betterment which in his view tended to convert the dismal science of self-centered cost-accounting into the ethical science of hope through change" (1990: 265).

5 According to Veblen, "it happens so frequently that it might fairly be said to be the common run that business interests and undertaker's maneuvers delay consolidation, combination, coordination, for some appreciable time after they have become patently advisable on industrial grounds" ([1901] 1969: 300).

6 The role the division of labor plays as an organizing principle is developed in detail in Limoges and Menard (1994).

7 Also, Marshall notes the growing scientization of managers: "for business experts are getting more and more into the habit of writing and reading specialist journals, of holding congresses, and in other ways coming under the judgment of one another. The old thankless task of attempting an improvement which may after all turn out badly, and to which a man's official superiors and the public at large may be indifferent, assumes a new shape when it is like you to be judged by a critical and appreciative audience who knows the technical difficulties of the problem" ([1897] 1966: 308).

8 Gerald Shove hypothesized that the loss of interest in biology stemmed from "the fact that among the natural sciences physics has once more taken over the lead from biological studies" (1942: 323).

9 As Marshall remarked: "The only resources we have for dealing with social problems as a whole lie in the judgment of common sense. For the present, and for a long time to come, that must be the final arbiter. Economic theory does not claim to displace it from its supreme authority, nor to interfere with the manner nor even the order of its work, but only to assist it in one part of its work. For common sense does not deal with a complex problem as a whole. Its first step is to break the problem up into its several parts; it then discusses one set of considerations after another, and finally it sums up and gives its conclusions. . . . Having done its work it [theory] retires and leaves to common sense the responsibility of the ultimate decision; not standing in the way of, or pushing out any other kind of knowledge, not hampering common sense in the use to which it is able to put

any other available knowledge, nor in any way hindering; helping where it could help, and for the rest keeping silent" ([1885] 1966: 164–165).

10 In criticizing Veblen, Malcolm Rutherford (1984: 338) comments that "the difficulty with Veblen's treatment is not that there is no theory of innovation, but that he provides almost no examples of the conflict between industrial and pecuniary efficiency which relate specifically to new technology." However, it is precisely at this juncture that Marshall's rather underdeveloped theory of institutional change can be used to supplement the evolutionary theory of Veblen.

REFERENCES

Bowler, P. (1988). *The Non-Darwinian Revolution*, Baltimore: Johns Hopkins University Press.

Coats, A.W. (1967). "Sociological Aspects of British Economic Thought (CA. 1880–1930)," *Journal of Political Economy* 75: 706–729.

Edgell, S. and R. Tilman (1989). "The Intellectual Antecedents of Thorstein Veblen: A Reappraisal," *Journal of Economic Issues* 23 (December): 1003–1026.

Hodgson, G. (1992). "Thorstein Veblen and Post-Darwinian Economics," *Cambridge Journal of Economics* 16 (September): 285–301.

Jones, L. (1985). "The Institutionalists and *On the Origin of Species*: A Case of Mistaken Identity," *Southern Economic Journal* 54 (April): 1043–1055.

Keynes, J.M. ([1924] 1966). "Alfred Marshall 1842–1924," repr. in A.C. Pigou (ed.), *Memorials of Alfred Marshall*, New York: Kelley.

Levitt, T. (1976). "Alfred Marshall: Victorian Relevance for Modern Economics," *Quarterly Journal of Economics* 90: 425–443.

Limoges, C. and C. Menard (1994). "Organization and the Division of Labor: Biological Metaphors at Work in Alfred Marshall's *Principles*," in P. Mirowski (ed.), *Natural Images in Economics*, New York: Cambridge University Press.

Maloney, J. (1985). *Marshall, Orthodoxy and the Professionalisation of Economics*, Cambridge: Cambridge University Press.

Marshall, A. ([1875] 1975). "Some Features of American Industry," repr. in J.K. Whitaker (ed.), *The Early Economic Writings of Alfred Marshall, 1867–1890*, vol. 2, London: Macmillan.

——— ([1885] 1966). "The Present Position of Economics," repr. in A.C. Pigou (ed.), *Memorials of Alfred Marshall*, New York: Kelley.

——— ([1889] 1966). "Co-operation," repr. in A.C. Pigou (ed.), *Memorials of Alfred Marshall*, New York: Kelley.

——— ([1897] 1966). "The Old Generation of Economists and the New," repr. in A.C. Pigou (ed.), *Memorials of Alfred Marshall*, New York: Kelley.

——— ([1898] 1966). "Mechanical and Biological Analogies in Economics," repr. in A.C. Pigou (ed.), *Memorials of Alfred Marshall*, New York: Kelley.

——— ([1920] 1979). *Principles of Economics*, 8th edn, Cambridge: Macmillan.

Niman, N. (1991). "Biological Analogies in Marshall's Work," *Journal of the History of Economic Thought* 13: 19–36.

O'Brien, D.P. (1978). *The Classical Economists*, Oxford: Clarendon Press.

Pigou, A.C. (ed.) (1966). *Memorials of Alfred Marshall*, New York: Kelley.

Reisman, D. (1990). *Alfred Marshall's Mission*, New York: St. Martin's.

Rutherford, M. (1984). "Thorstein Veblen and the Processes of Institutional Change," *History of Political Economy* 16: 331–348.

Shove, G. (1942). "The Place of Marshall's *Principles* in the Development of Economic Theory," *Economic Journal* 52: 294–329.

Simon, H. (1955). "A Behavioral Model of Rational Choice," *Quarterly Journal of Economics* 69: 99–118.

Veblen, T. (1898). "Why is Economics not an Evolutionary Science?" *Quarterly Journal of Economics* 12: 373–397.

——— ([1899] 1979). *The Theory of the Leisure Class*, New York: Penguin Books.

——— (1900). "The Preconceptions of Economic Science, III," *Quarterly Journal of Economics* 14: 240–269.

——— ([1901] 1969). "Industrial and Pecuniary Employments," repr. in *The Place of Science in Modern Civilization*, New York: Capricorn.

——— ([1904] 1965). *The Theory of the Business Enterprise*, New York: Kelley.

——— ([1908a] 1969). "The Evolution of the Scientific Point of View," repr. in id., *The Place of Science in Modern Civilization*, New York: Capricorn.

——— ([1908b] 1969). "On the Nature of Capital," repr. in id., *The Place of Science in Modern Civilization*, New York: Capricorn.

——— ([1919] 1969). *The Place of Science in Modern Civilization*, New York: Capricorn.

Walker, D. (1977). "Thorstein Veblen's Economic System," *Economic Inquiry* 15: 213–237.

Whitaker, J. K. (1990). "What Happened to the Second Volume of the *Principles*? The Thorny Path to Marshall's Last Books," in id. (ed.), *Centenary Essays on Alfred Marshall*, Cambridge: Cambridge University Press.

——— (ed.) (1996a). *The Correspondence of Alfred Marshall Economist*, vol. 1, Cambridge: Cambridge University Press.

——— (ed.) (1996b). *The Correspondence of Alfred Marshall Economist*, vol 2, Cambridge: Cambridge University Press.

13

COMMONS VERSUS VEBLEN ON THE PLACE OF THE INDIVIDUAL IN THE SOCIAL PROCESS

A case of methodological divergence

Philippe Broda[1]

INTRODUCTION

Institutionalist thought must not be considered as monolithic. As Rutherford says, it is composed of two main research programs (Rutherford 1994: 1–2). The first branch, whose founding father is Thorstein Veblen, puts a strong emphasis on the presumed dichotomy between business and industry. Its framework is cultural. The second, whose leader is John R. Commons, puts its emphasis on the legal aspects of the economic system. Their theoretical divergences have already been pointed out by Endres (1985: 637–649), but in order to understand their difference concerning the place of man in the social process, theory is not enough. We have to refer to their methodological positions. Although the orthodox economists who usually see the individual only through his action on the market are an obvious target of attack for both Veblen and Commons, each takes a different path when presenting their own positions on the subject.

In the first part of this chapter, their respective conceptions will be described. According to Veblen, man is not a "lightning calculator of pleasures and pains" but a "bundle of instincts" (Veblen [1919] 1990: 73). From his theory of instincts, it is possible to see that individual conduct can be almost reduced to cultural conditioning. In Commons's model, although social actors are also "institutionalized minds," their behavior is not so strongly shaped. In a kind of dualism, it mixes the tendency to conditioned behavior with a capacity for creativity. Commons ascribes an important role to the people able to display such inventiveness. Therefore, if we examine the extreme case of great men, the divergence between Commons and Veblen is striking.

In the second part, the methodological roots of this contrast will be dealt with. According to Veblen, the criterion of modern science is that it is marked by a Darwinian logic. This means that its investigations must be "matter-of-fact." This is taken as true for any scientific field. In the social sciences, the consequence is that the process of social evolution is presumed to be "blind," devoid of the intentions expressed at the individual level. On the other hand, thanks to the concept of "willingness," Commons asserts the uniqueness of the data in social sciences. He carries this premise throughout his thinking; the meaning that men impute to their economic situation becomes decisive and the collective dimension integrates this element of volition. Commons then develops arguments which are close to some pragmatist ideas. There, normative and positive aspects cannot be easily dissociated. Commons himself admits that his purpose has always been to save capitalism by making it better.

THE PLACE OF THE INDIVIDUAL

The capitalist system is based on exchange. This is why its supporters present hypotheses concerning individual behavior whose properties are expressed in a market structure. As for the institutionalists, they take the market as an institution among others. Accordingly, their conception is different. Instead of focusing on the intelligence underlying actions, Veblen underlines institutional influences. He does not deny the existence of intelligence, but he submits it to institutions. With respect to Commons, he makes this quality relative too, but, in his analysis, human conduct integrates intelligence with elements of institutional conditioning.

Veblen: institutional determination

Veblen's central assertion concerning the individual is that he is a "coherent structure of propensities and habits which seeks realisation and expression in an unfolding activity" (Veblen [1919] 1990: 74). Veblen thinks that "activity itself is the substantial fact of the [economic] process" (Veblen [1919] 1990: 74). In this way, he intends to reverse the orthodox perspective in which, according to him, man is passive (Veblen [1919] 1990: 157). To this end, he proposes a theory of instincts whose connotations, which are rather negative today, may lead to misunderstanding of his views.

The study of the instincts in Veblen's system allows the claim that his perception is not mechanical and does not neglect the intelligent dimension of the human behavior. Yet, with that observation, it is also possible to see that this intelligence is finally submitted to cultural factors.

The theory of the instincts

Since the time of James, Loeb, and MacDougall, much change has occurred in the analysis of the instincts.[2] Nowadays, any reference to them in the field of social sciences is indisputably out of fashion. It could be tempting to use the obsolescence of these pioneers, who left an obvious stamp on Veblen,[3] to reject the whole of the Veblenian logic. This is why Ayres, an avowed disciple of Veblen, tried to put forward a new interpretation of the theory of the instincts in the thought of his predecessor (Ayres 1958: 25–37). Nevertheless, Veblen's original model is less unfit and inconsistent than is sometimes argued.[4]

First, Veblen himself does not find the word "instinct" very satisfactory (Veblen [1914] 1990: 2–3). Thus, Edgell notes that he frequently uses substitutes such as "spiritual endowment," "hereditary traits," or "proclivities" (Edgell 1975: 271). Moreover, his definition is deliberately vague and is not integrated into a biological perspective. It conveys a cultural sense. For Veblen, the instincts are the "innate and persistent propensities of human nature" (Veblen [1914] 1990: 2) which, combined with external circumstances, orientate the process of institutional evolution. According to Veblen, this process can give rise to other instincts. We may remark that, strictly speaking, these derivations should not be called instincts since they are not innate, but this is what Veblen calls them.

Be that as it may, the relative plasticity of the concept must not incite the belief that Veblen's thinking is confused. In any case—primitive instinct or derivation—instinctive conduct involves an aim and a consciousness of the objective from the social actors. In this, it is distinguishable from tropismatic action, direct and immediate, symbolized by the reflex. Veblen admits it can be difficult to define the border between instinct and tropism. An instinctive action which is considered "lower" is so simple and requires so little human deliberation that it may also be ranked among the "half-tropismatic" actions. However, in the last analysis, man is different from animal mainly by the fact he is able to think and reflect upon his behavior.

The diversity of the goals that motivate the actions of individuals allows for the delimitation of the instincts. For example, the instinct of "idle curiosity" does not answer to the same expectations as the "parental bent." This does not prevent these human drives from influencing and "contaminating" each other. Yet, if every instinct is normally characterized by the end it is destined to reach, there is an instinct, the "instinct of workmanship," which appears to differ from this pattern. Among the three primitive instincts which are the starting point of Veblen's reasoning—the two others are idle curiosity and parental bent—it is certainly the most fundamental (Veblen [1914] 1990: 25). Its function is auxiliary, at the service of the other instincts. This is what makes it so important. While the others provide men with their ends without helping them about the way to follow, the instinct of workmanship focuses exclusively on the means. It is here that the intelligence of individuals intervenes. Their reflections, their solutions, are guided by this instinct, whose usual expression is the contempt of waste. Where human deliberation is diminished, this peculiar instinct is not on favorable ground: "response to the direct call of such half-tropismatic, half-instinctive impulses as hunger, anger, or the promptings of sex, is little if at all troubled with any sentimental suffusion of workmanship" (Veblen [1914] 1990: 29). On the other hand, from the moment it is a question of more complex instincts, its role appears to be essential. The quest of efficient means is indeed gratifying. It can even become the real end itself. So, it is certain that Veblen does not conceive of the human creature as an automaton.

Of course, the desire to optimize the use of resources is not alien to the plans of *homo oeconomicus* as described by the orthodoxy. In spite of this, Veblen's instinct of workmanship cannot be compared to the orthodox conception because, finally, it reflects "a proclivity for taking pains" (Veblen [1914] 1990: 33). In standard microeconomics, work is just a necessity which men are compelled to do in a logic of personal income, never an end in itself. More generally, Vinokur observes that the Veblenian theory of instincts is constructed to disclose a view opposite to that of orthodox hedonism (Vinokur 1969: 82).

However, Veblen is not simply critical and negative. He also tries to rebuild economics on new foundations, and his theory of the instincts is used as a basis for this project. As far as *homo oeconomicus* is a fundamental hypothesis in the orthodox model, it is a postulate which is disconnected from any reality. It is true that Veblen takes his inspiration from scientific works which are contemporary to him, but his thinking on the instincts is completely idiosyncratic. As Mayberry rightly argues, "he is not making statements which a psychologist can refute, because he is not making empirical statements at all" (Mayberry 1969: 318). His instincts are categories so flexible that they could be made consistent with almost all the discoveries in the field of psychology (Mayberry 1969: 318). He does not expect confirmation or denial of them. Therefore, the idea that man is active, that he is a bundle of instincts, represents an abstraction suited to the modern scientific criteria. And since, according to Veblen, the approach in social science must be cultural, it is interesting to analyze what happens to these instincts and to the human intelligence in this perspective.

A twofold submission

We could expect problems of social coordination between individuals whose penchant for activity is so firmly stated. But these are overcome owing to the Veblenian theory of "habituation."[5] This coordination is affirmed *a priori*. Institutions are defined as "habits of thought" and it is their structure that governs the behavior of individuals so that they are made compatible. Man and his instincts are actually drowned in their own cultural milieu. The propensities for activity on the part of individuals are, in a sense, made uniform. This institutional conditioning operates, at the same time, on the ends of the community and on the means they use to pursue them.

Concerning the ends, a rapid historical flashback illustrates that one instinct or another is favored depending on the character of the institutional framework. During the primitive era, called "savagery," the parental bent and the instinct of workmanship find expression and selfish conduct is scarce. But, after an improvement in living conditions, the egoistic and emulative tendencies find a more fertile ground. The "instinct of sportsmanship" and the practice of conquest replace the instinct of workmanship and peaceful production. Consequently, the development in the industrial arts is obstructed.[6] The institution of private property is a symbol of these "barbarian" days. Solidarity even appears as a dangerous anachronism in this epoch of rapacity.

During the "handicraft" era, which comes after this age of predation, the new ways and customs privilege less violent methods of appropriation. It is a matter of producing for oneself and not of extorting goods from others. The instinct of workmanship is rehabilitated, although it still remains in the service of the disposition to emulation. Gradually, mechanization increases the size of the firms, until, with advent of the "machine" era, production and acquisition become dissociated and, to a certain extent, antagonistic. The best way to amass pecuniary values is not to produce more but to control strategic positions in the production process, even if it disturbs its functioning.[7] It follows that the rapacious tendencies again find expression while the instinct of workmanship atrophies. The two tendencies are opposed anew, while the parental bent is not valorized more than during the previous period.

We are thereby able to remark on the perfect subordination of the instinctive actions to the institutional framework: The objectives pursued consciously by man, the rationalizations he elaborates for his own conduct, are a product of his socialization. The instinct of workmanship cannot develop without an inducement from the customs of the epoch. It is the institutional environment which decides which instincts blossom and which do not.

But institutional conditioning does not concern only the ends; it also affects the means that men use to accomplish them. This is important since human intelligence is expressed through these means. To see how the thoughtful conduct is made conventional, an examination of the "contamination" of the instincts is required. Veblen considers that the dispositions of individuals interfere with one another in a process of "crossing and grafting." Lines of behavior constantly repeated under the impulse of a specific instinct become habitual and can end up shaping conduct directed at many different ends.

The instinct of workmanship is then perceived as the contaminating instinct above all, due to its auxiliary character. The requirement of efficiency that it stimulates finds itself at the confluence of all human activities. Those of production, which are indispensable to the survival of mankind, are based continually on this instinct hostile to waste. The norms which develop in this activity spread to the rest of the society through the instinct of workmanship. The less vital activities both refer to the instinct directly and are contaminated by the norms of behavior associated with the activity of production. In this manner, Veblen's so-called materialism is directly linked to the instinct of workmanship.

Even "idle curiosity," which is disconnected from material considerations, does not escape this contamination. This point deserves to be noted particularly because scientific knowledge, which stems from it, epitomizes the best achievements of human intelligence. Notwithstanding, it is the instinct of workmanship that "affords the norms, or the scheme of criteria and canons of verity, according to which the ascertained facts will be construed and connected up in a body of systematic knowledge" (Veblen [1918] 1954: 5).

From this, it is clear that the means that men use in order to succeed in their aims are, themselves, subjected to institutional conditioning. Thus the meaning of intelligence is limited to an adaptation of means and ends to institutions. It is not supposed to be able to modify them deliberately. Things are different with Commons.

The road to "reasonableness"

Like Veblen, Commons does not accept the fundamental assumptions of the orthodox economists about individual action. He criticizes the idea of rationality. He even announces that men are "stupid" in that they are usually reluctant to change their behavior when the circumstances demand it. They find it difficult to get rid of obsolete routines which ensure their "security of expectations." This means, again like Veblen, that Commons assigns an important place to institutions.

Nevertheless, his position diverges seriously from Veblen's, and not only because he attaches only an anecdotal interest to the theory of instincts.[8] He introduces the concept of "reasonableness" and he indicates "a slow infiltration of reason provoked by uncomfortable experiences" (Commons [1934b] 1990: 846). The social process discloses a kind of dualism through individual conduct: human action is often customary, but it also can be clever. Commons appreciates all the manifestations of intelligence, especially with great men, whereas even in this case, Veblen reduces them to their institutional environment.

Stupidity and intelligence

The march of society toward "reasonableness" is possible because, although institutions, through their "working rules," condition individual conduct, they do not shape it entirely. Institutions promote the emergence of "habitual assumptions," but a degree of discretion is inherent in human action. The norms in force provide security of expectations to the individual, but they are sufficiently flexible and evolutionary to offer a margin for maneuver.

In Commons's logic, the notion of choice is very wide: "such a will never chooses between acting and not-acting—it always chooses between two degrees of power in acting" (Commons [1924] 1959: 72). All the time, individuals engage in a multitude of choices. A large part of them are made on the basis of habit and are devoid of real deliberation. But others are real choices. Everything depends on how agents assess the nature of the transactions in which they are participating. When they grant them a special importance, they are more inclined to think than when they merely consider them as ordinary: their "crucial choices are conscious, perhaps deliberative" (Commons [1924] 1959: 72). Commons distinguishes "strategic" from "routine" transactions. According to him, it is the former which give rise to reflection. As Biddle explains: "Commons believed that the ability to consistently identify and respond correctly to the strategic transactions was a rare talent" (Biddle 1990b: 6).

This individual margin of maneuver is the area of discretion that is creative of new norms. For, in the scarcity context underlying Commons's analysis, innovative conduct is frequently the source of new conflicts between individuals. Hence, the necessity for the representatives of the "going concerns" in which men are members (state, firm, and so on) to find new solutions and resolve these conflicts in a manner consistent with their estimation of what is in the collective interest. In this, the role of law is peculiarly significant at the level of the state, the going concern which encompasses all the others. From this it is easy to understand the attention that Commons devoted to the judgments delivered by the courts and that he analyzed in his *Legal Foundations of Capitalism* (1924).

In the United States, the courts are called to settle disputes between social actors. In this they use the method of "exclusion and inclusion." According to Commons:

> by this is meant that a meaning given in a former decision may have been too broad or too narrow to fit the issue in the instant case. If too broad, then the precedent from the precedent case does not apply. . . . This is the process of "exclusion." If the former meaning was too narrow, then that precedent can be extended to furnish the rule of the instant case. . . . This is the process of "inclusion."
>
> (Commons 1935: 140)

Ultimately, judges make the law. This is what leads to the working out of new social norms.

For Commons, social coordination is not simply presumed, it is also constructed by man. Of course, the American judge is also an "institutionalized mind"and his decisions are relative to the socioeconomic environment in which he lives. Nonetheless, the direction he gives to the evolution of social norms is not definitively imposed by these considerations. Thus the judge can endorse or oppose the abuses of capitalism. Besides, the process is endless. New rules shift the margins for individual maneuver but they do not abolish them. Therefore, new individual initiatives—arising from the creativity and discretion allowed in the new institutional context—are likely to cause new types of social conflicts and then new judgments. Although judicial decisions may entail unanticipated consequences, institutional evolution does not take place in a hazardous way. It integrates human "willingness."

The stress that Commons lays on the threat of social chaos confirms the fact that institutional coordination is constructed and that it is open to change. In *Institutional Economics* ([1934b] 1990), a warning is sounded: the population might prefer an economic system like communism or fascism in order to get a livelihood in preference to "savage capitalism."[9] Here we grasp Commons's attempt to reconcile economics, law, and ethics through his unit of analysis, the "transaction." The ethical question, the concern for justice, is represented in the agreement of individuals with the working rules of the going concern to which they belong. The concept of going concern is relevant only "as long as there are expectations" (Commons [1934b] 1990: 620) that the concern is fulfilling. When the concern stops fulfilling the expectations of its members, it will cease to exist. Then, individuals will organize their relationships differently. Men come and go, but the concern "goes on," if not in one form then in another (Commons 1951: 34).

The existence of both human intelligence and human stupidity is particularly interesting in the context of Commons's reform outlook. If individuals did not behave with reference to "habitual assumptions," there would be disorder. The existing rules would be inefficient, unable to fashion human activity, but it would be impossible to appraise the possibility of establishing new rules that might work better. It is fortunate that men do conform to "habitual assumptions." Instead of complaining about it, Commons prefers to make use of it as a tool, in order to gauge the distance between his goal and the current situation. If the capacity to adapt is not overtaxed by the reform, stupidity may be considered as allowing a change of working rules.[10] In addition, once internalized, the new norms ensure a degree of stability for the new order.

However, the "reasonableness" Commons longs for is not merely what is customary practice, but "the *highest* degree . . . that the nature of the industry or employment would *reasonably permit*" (Commons 1934a: 155). Therefore, it is essential to check if certain measures adopted at an individual level can be generalized to the whole society.[11] It is obviously human intelligence which is the driving force of Commons's theory—and, on that point, its divergence from Veblen's seems to be clear enough.

Great men and social evolution

In the Veblenian perspective, the institutional process is "blind." It does not show the least sign of human design. Even great men are not supposed to be able to guide the evolution of institutions. Veblen is convinced that the transformation of, for example, German institutions finds its explanation "in the material situation of the German peoples rather than in their diplomatic history" (Veblen 1915: 145). In other words, it is not the stature of men like Bismarck that must be invoked to account for the formation of the German empire. In his typical style, Veblen writes that

> In their absence their room would probably have been so nearly filled by convenient understudies that none but a very critical historical audience would have detected a false line or gesture. . . . Did not the rôle create the personage out of commonplace plastic material, rather than the personage create the rôle?
>
> (Veblen 1915: 146–147)

He does not call into question the qualities or the influence of these great men. According to him, they stem from the fact that they were extraordinarily adapted to the institutional framework of their time. Germany was characterized by barbarian institutions. It was a dynastic state, very hierarchical and greedy for conquests. The possession of high performance technology aroused the empire's rapacity and bestowed the means for such a program. Then, it was almost inevitable that within the Junker class, individuals motivated by the idea of constructing an empire would emerge. The Prussian hegemony occurred "not because these personages were exceptions, but because they were not" (Veblen 1915: 148).

It is important to keep in mind that, despite this determinism, the cultural process has no visible end. The development of the empire was an eventuality among others, even if it was not the most improbable. It is possible to conceive of alternative scenarios. For example, the habits of thought related to mechanization could have dashed the dynastic temptation, but this did not happen.

In Veblen's theory, there are indeed cases of people escaping the hold of their institutional conditioning, but their situation is exceptional. The case of the Jews illustrates this exception (Veblen 1934: 219–231). First, the Jewish culture is supposed to be so "archaic" that it has limited ability to condition habits of mind. Moreover, the gentile culture does not accept Jews without difficulty. Therefore, the Jews are often pulled this way and that, wandering between several cultures, without taking root anywhere. Their spirit tends to become more independent. Nevertheless, their case is the exception proving the rule of the conditioning of human spirit by its institutional structure. Besides, being outside of an institutional configuration does not mean being able to control its evolution.

As for Commons, he does not hide his admiration for great men. He thinks that the creativity of great men is able to counterbalance the inclination to customary behavior. Even in *Social Reform and the Church* (1894), he praises some aspects of the philosophy of capitalism. It allows the expression of individual talents and differences.[12] Commons pays compliments to men like Carnegie, the most powerful businessman in the steel industry in the United States, and Dill, the inventor of the holding company.[13]

But excesses may also come out of capitalism, and other men have striven to correct them. They worked to make it "reasonable" in Commons's sense. Accordingly, he cannot help but congratulate individuals like Governor La Follette, who tried to give shape to progressive ideals in the state of Wisconsin, the unionist Gompers, and Beatrice and Sidney Webb.[14] His interest in reform leads him to this. Innovation occurs frequently enough to alter existing practices. As they are generalized they take on the status of norms, as indicated in his notion of "reasonableness."

In conclusion, Commons does not underestimate the role of great men, in fact of all men who use their creative discretion. They start new lines of conduct which may be adopted by the whole society. Hence, it is in individual behavior, even though institutionalized, that Commons finds the source of institutional change. In order to explain this difference between Veblen and Commons, recourse to methodological arguments is fruitful.

SOME METHODOLOGICAL EXPLANATIONS

Veblen and Commons, each in his own way, acknowledge the twofold dimension of human behavior: it can be as deliberative as customary. This does not prevent them from analyzing the place of the individual in the social process quite differently. This theoretical divergence stems from personal choices, namely, Veblen's decision to focus on the notion of habit in contrast with Commons's emphasis on the idea of intelligence. In order to understand their respective positions on the subject, it is necessary to examine the reasons for these choices: in other words, their methodological conceptions. One fact is certain, both of them felt it important to justify their economic theory in terms of a more general view of the requirements of research in social science.

In tackling methodological considerations, the intention is not to explain the discrepancy at stake between Commons and Veblen through influences that might have shaped their ideas outside their consciousness. It is well known that, among the streams of thought which fed the institutionalist tradition at the end of the nineteenth and at the beginning of the twentieth centuries, evolutionary theories and pragmatism are usually mentioned. Thus it might be possible to wonder if, for example, despite his conspicuous criticism of pragmatism (Veblen [1919] 1990: 5–13), Veblen did not fall under its influence.[15] Such an approach is not taken here. Attention is turned exclusively to the arguments that they themselves invoked when they considered the methodology of the social sciences.

Veblen locates his investigation in the perspective of what he considers to be the Darwinian revolution. Commons does not contest the scope of Darwinism but he refers more readily to pragmatism. Behind these preferences is the fact that, for Veblen, any inquiry conducted in the social sciences must conform to the criteria of validity used in other scientific fields, even if that demands forsaking the idea of teleology. This is not without consequence for social science. In contrast, Commons dwells on the specificity of social sciences, which requires a particular point of view. He argues that the "volitional" dimension of human behavior is a foundation of social sciences, even if the effect of purposeful individual action is the generation of unanticipated social consequences.

Veblen's Darwinism

Veblen's most important articles about scientific methodology were gathered in *The Place of Science in Modern Civilization and Other Essays* in 1919, a time when the key components of his work had been completed. But these articles, which were often very critical of orthodox economics,[16] had been written earlier, at the time Veblen was beginning his more constructive work. Thus, his "Why Is Economics Not an Evolutionary Science?" (Veblen [1898] 1990), an article that contains, in a sense, the foundation of his methodological position, is older than his first book *The Theory of the Leisure Class* (1899). This allows us to see that his theory, as it was developed, was articulated around his own conception of the proper nature of the discipline of economics.

Here epistemology and methodology are a little interwoven. Before discussing the implications of adopting a Darwinian methodology in social sciences, the reason why Veblen believes so firmly in the similarity of approach, whatever the scientific field may be, must be examined. This demands a quick look at the question of how men gain knowledge.

A "matter-of-fact" requirement

It has been shown that the instinct of workmanship pervades all the spheres of human behavior, including scientific research. Idle curiosity depends on it.

This means that the canons of science originate from the cultural milieu, that they force themselves upon men. They are not immutable, as in different periods they respect different rules of "dramatic consistency." In fact, they evolve with the institutional framework and with how men get their livelihood. In the savage era, knowledge is built around the ideas of birth, growth, and death. During the barbarian epoch, it is no longer biological notions but relations of domination which provide these preconceptions. Later, with the advent of handicraft, the interpretative systems abandon the metaphor of a sovereign ruling by means of decrees for the idea of a clockmaker divinity. Lastly, with the machine era, the criteria of scientificity become more sophisticated, less anthropomorphic. Owing to mechanization, man becomes conscious of his smallness and gets rid of many teleological expressions linked to his "personal equation" in his scientific discourse. Research is now conditioned by the idea of change, of process (Veblen [1919] 1990: 33). There is no presumed direction to this movement. The Darwinian revolution is supposed to symbolize this new way to do science and Veblen uses it as a "catch-word."

According to Veblen, the main feature of Western culture lies in this modern approach to knowledge, called "matter-of-fact," which benefits technological development because "it implies a close contact, if not coincidence, of reality with fact" (Veblen [1919] 1990: 46). If one agrees with Veblen that the salvation of a cultural pattern depends closely on its material subsistence, his obvious liking of technological efficiency and current scientific criteria is easily comprehensible. However, this "matter-of-fact" knowledge does not represent an absolute requirement of scientificity. The incommensurability of the successive paradigms is clearly evident in his reading of the history of economic thought. Thus he does not reproach previous writers for inconsistency, but for obsolete preconceptions. The Veblenian conception is utterly relativist.[17]

Veblen is aware, of course, that the various sciences apply to different objects. This does not prevent him from drawing the principal dividing line between pre-Darwinian and Darwinian science, not between the diverse sciences. The problem that he claims to observe is that "matter-of-fact" preconceptions have not spread equally to all fields of scientific investigation. Present in the natural and physical sciences, they seem to be missing in social sciences. There, the canons of the previous era, which correspond to what is commonly called Newtonianism, still prevail. Veblen does admit that progress has been made in that domain since Smith's days, thanks to men like Cairnes and John Stuart Mill (Veblen [1919] 1990: 68–70, 159–171), but he argues that it is generally insufficient. Therefore, it is to comply with the spirit of his time that he advocates the adoption of a Darwinian methodology in social sciences. It remains to be seen in what way the analysis of economic questions is affected by this demand for modernity.

Application to social science

Veblen's Darwinism amounts to a rejection of any preconceptions in which the idea of normality, of a natural course of events, is taken as underlying the operation of the economic system. Thus laws of production or of markets are dismissed. In Veblen's model, the mistake comes from the fact that the capitalist system must not be considered as given. The nature of economic relations has to be perceived in the perspective of constant change. Expressed in an exaggerated way, the law is that there is no law.

The need to study economic matters from the angle of process is connected to the cultural approach. This can be seen in Veblen's definition of an evolutionary economics as "the theory of a process of cultural growth as determined by the economic interest, a theory of a cumulative sequence of economic institutions stated in terms of the process itself" (Veblen [1919] 1990: 77). This Darwinian methodology supposes an extension of the economic field to its cultural dimension. This sheds light on why he neglects the intelligent aspects of human conduct, while admitting they exist. The contrast between Veblen and mainstream economics is clear. In the Veblenian cultural approach, individual intentions are reduced to their institutional conditioning and it is the analysis of institutions that becomes fundamental. In the orthodox camp, individual preferences are taken as fundamental and institutional factors are presumed to be exogenous. According to Veblen's terminology, this opposition can be summarized in the difference between two processes of investigation: the method of "sufficient reason," which focuses on purpose and intent, and the method of "efficient cause," which focuses on the sequence of cause and effect, without any teleological bias.

It is enough to quote Veblen to see the implications of his Darwinian methodology for the place given to the individual in the socioeconomic process:

> now it happens that the relation of sufficient reason enters very substantially into human conduct. It is this element of discriminating forethought that distinguishes human conduct from brute behavior. . . . But while modern science at large has made the causal relation the sole ultimate ground of theoretical formulation; and while the other sciences that deal with human life admit the relation of sufficient reason as a proximate, supplementary or intermediate ground, subsidiary and subservient to the argument from cause to effect; economics has the misfortune—as seen from the scientific point of view—to let the former supplant the latter.
>
> (Veblen [1919] 1990: 238)

It is possible to check that Veblen actually adopts this attitude of neutralization of the individual because he believes that the new criteria of scientificity constrain him to do so. Veblen takes great pains to argue that the deliberative aspects of human action are not discernible at the cultural level, since the process examined must be "blind." Accordingly, "it is at the same time no less true that human conduct, economic or otherwise, is subject to the sequence of cause and effect, by force of such elements as habituation and conventional requirements" (Veblen [1919] 1990: 239).

It is here that the difference between Veblen and Commons is perhaps the most marked, since the author of *Institutional Economics* argues that the intentions expressed at the individual level are perceptible at the institutional level, and that developing economic analysis without taking that fact into account is not acceptable.

Commons's pragmatism

Unlike Veblen, Commons's views on the methodology to follow in social sciences were developed rather late, and do not occupy the same place as for Veblen. According to Gonce, Commons's first systematic study on that subject was published in 1925 (Gonce 1971: 93 n. 57), one year after *Legal Foundations of Capitalism*, a key book in his career.

In his early writings, Commons wished that churchmen would base their ideas about social matters on the scientific discoveries in that field.[18] Since then, reformist plans and attempts to be close to concrete problems were always fused together in his investigations.[19] This continuity characterizes Commons's work and suggests that his methodological arguments constitute a simple external stratum, a veneer that does not fundamentally modify his views. His methodological ideas do have value, however, as they provide his perception, in retrospect, of his own approach.

Commons may not deny the merits of Darwinism, but there is no comparison with the meaning that Veblen confers on it. For Commons, it is pragmatism that is the key reference. It is from his affirmation of the peculiarity of social sciences, through the notion of "willingness," that his use of pragmatism is justified. In addition, needless to say, it is also consistent with his reformist activity.

The specificity of social science

Commons often draws analogies between the various sciences. For example, he finds in each one a unit of activity. This is why he tries to identify what in economics corresponds to molecules in physics, atoms in chemistry, planets and stars in astronomy, and even what is the unit correlating economics, law, and ethics, in the same way as the "interactions of corpuscular wave-lengths" is the common unit to physics, chemistry, and astronomy (Commons [1934b] 1990: 55–56). Yet, he recognizes that the differences between scientific fields are significant enough to make it unwise to push the comparison too far. In each science, the principles guiding the investigation change.

It is the varied nature of the data that commands this dissociation. First, there are the physical sciences, which deal with lifeless matter. There, the concept of mechanism is central and the principle of energy is unifying. Newton's world illustrates this configuration in which the ideas of equilibrium and normality are recurrent. Next, the natural sciences deal with data as living bodies. It is a question of organism, not of mechanism. Likewise, the principle of scarcity is substituted for that of energy. The Darwinian theory of natural selection symbolizes this kind of development. Such a perspective is new. As Gruchy has stated: "the concept of mechanism emphasizes the notion of repetitivity, but the organism draws special attention to the phenomena of change" (Gruchy 1940: 825).

It is worthwhile to note that, for Commons, the Newtonian and Darwinian patterns share the particular feature of making intentionality inoperative. In the former case, it retreats in front of the prodigious efficiency of the presumed mechanism. In the latter, its vain feature appears as soon as "blind causation" and unanticipated changes become keys to understand the phenomena. Then Commons turns to the social sciences. The contrast between them and the two previous approaches is obvious. They take into account human conduct. Their data are perceived as the outcomes of choices.

It is above all because of the unifying principle of "willingness" that human behavior and social sciences are supposed to be distinguished from the Newtonian and Darwinian frameworks. The idea of purpose becomes a central element in the process that is examined. In order to take decisions, men must have different options, otherwise they would be exclusively coerced and it would be incorrect to talk about choices. These possibilities are factors of uncertainty. Here, we meet again the problem of the "security of expectations." Thus the unit of activity relevant for the social sciences must be "one whose repetitions are expected by the participants to continue in the future substantially similar to what they are in the present and have been in the past" (Commons 1935: 125).

In the context of scarcity that Commons describes, the plans of any individual interfere with the intentions of others. So, his unit of activity, the "transaction," contains in itself the three principles of conflict, dependence, and order. When he investigates the historical foundations of one of its components, the "bargaining transaction," he indicates that the courts have elaborated an ethical standard of "willing buyer" and "willing seller" (Commons [1934b] 1990: 61). Somehow or other, willingness is the essential point.[20] In this regard, Commons argues that "the meaning of Willingness is the inseparable activity of meaning, valuing, transacting, and governing" (Commons [1934b] 1990: 96). Thus:

> value and economy become verbs instead of nouns. Value becomes *valuing*; economy becomes *economizing*. Economizing becomes the

> operation of rules of conduct in the nation or the business concern. . . . Value and economy become millions of people valuing and economizing through billions of transactions in conformity to numberless working rules over a stretch of time that has no beginning and no ending.
>
> (Commons [1924] 1959: 8)

This opens the door to the introduction of pragmatist references.

Thought and action

Commons justifies explicitly his connection with pragmatism only in the following passage: "we investigate how our minds and the world about us actually behave in a society of human beings whose future is frankly recognized as unpredictable but which can be controlled somewhat by insight and collective action" (Commons [1934b] 1990: 107). However, as already said, even before putting forward methodological arguments, Commons's use of pragmatist ideas was central in his thinking. The attention that he devoted to judicial decisions, his development of "Negotiational Psychology,"[21] and, for that matter, the great bulk of his work, show his interest in how individuals perceive their situation and how they subscribe to institutional norms.

Peirce is a pioneer of American pragmatism and, according to Commons, his conception of the active mind remedies the shortcomings of the theory of ideas proposed by Locke and then Hume.[22] But it is James and Dewey whose views are crucial for social science: "we use the term 'pragmatism' always in the scientific sense of Peirce as a method of investigation, but we consider that Peirce used it only for the physical sciences where there is no future and no purpose, while Dewey and James used it always for the human sciences, where the subject-matter itself is a pragmatic being always looking to the future and therefore always motivated by purposes" (Commons [1934b] 1990: 655).

Commons prefers Dewey's pragmatism as it integrates a social dimension and it is close to the way the courts work.[23] It also conforms to Commons's refusal to separate thought from action. Commons displays hostility against the scientists lost in their abstractions and remaining far from the concrete problems. He argues that "what business men, laboring men, courts, executives, politicians, and so on, really mean is not what they say, nor even what they think, but what they *do*" (Commons [1934b] 1990: 24–25). Action takes its sense in a particular context, or more precisely, the meaning that an individual gives to his situation depends on the environment he belongs to. And since the will is connected to the sense that man ascribes to events, he attacks the old theories of the will which "may be described as the *will-in-vacuo*, instead of the *will-in-action*" (Commons [1924] 1959: 69). He assumes that every choice, every expression of power over nature or other individuals, is a three-dimensional act. These three dimensions break down human action into what is performed, what is avoided, and what is the limit placed on this performance (Commons [1924] 1959: 69–79).

In Dewey's mind, from the moment the frontier between facts and values disappears, the one between normative and positive points of view becomes, at the very least, blurred. And this applies also to Commons. His case is particularly significant. In the introduction to *Institutional Economics*, he defines himself as a participant and an observer of social life. This is interesting because it is especially difficult to identify what pertains exclusively to his reformist action and what relates only to his thought. Both spheres are mingled. In other words, he himself may be considered as an "active mind." His ideas evolved as his personal experiences, which themselves were linked to his conceptions, went by.[24] This evolution occurred even if his overall project did not change, namely, to save capitalism by making it good.

Commons's "Negotiational Psychology" is a wonderful example of this proximity between thought and reform. His psychology of transactions is their "scientific understanding." From here, the transition to his reformist ambition is not too complicated. From the behavior of individuals during their transactions, through the meaning they give to them, nothing prevents a valuation of their adaptation to the desired plan.

In order to conclude on this point, it must be said that, although he believes that such a reformist approach is preferable to a utopian scheme, Commons does not think that it can ensure absolute and perfect results. He does not neglect the idea that individual actions are able to generate unexpected consequences. Moreover, "Reasonableness" is different from "Reason." It consists in finding satisfactory answers to social problems, answers that are intermediary between reality and ideal. In Commons's logic, it is a question of an experimental process, made of trials, errors, and corrections. This model puts the emphasis on the acceptability of the reforms by the social actors. Thus his defense of a proposition about unemployment insurance was not motivated only by arguments of constitutionality: there "was an appeal to individualism *through* collective action" (Commons [1934b] 1990: 843). For all these reasons, a connection between Commons and Simon is possible.[25] Their common pragmatist foundations could confirm it.

CONCLUSION

The place that Veblen and Commons grant to the individual in the analysis of social phenomena is appreciably different. It is worth showing that the differences between them on that subject may be explained by methodological arguments. Both of them, indeed, admit the intelligent nature of human behavior and the role of institutional influences in shaping the same human behavior. Moreover, in their respective perspectives, individual conduct brings about unintended social effects. Thus it is their methodological approach to social science which is able to account for the fact that Veblen is particularly interested in the inertia of institutions and the role of habituation, while Commons cannot omit the volitional aspects of human behavior.

Veblen and Commons defend *a priori* methodological positions that disclose some similarities. Each in his own way is very critical toward orthodox theory that both judge to be too disconnected from economic reality. Veblen refers to "matter-of-fact" knowledge as the criterion of modernity drawn from the Darwinian revolution. As for Commons, he draws on pragmatism to expose this idea. Yet their methodological choices also contain areas of disagreement. Invoking his Darwinian methodology, Veblen expels the teleological dimension of human action from his field of investigation. On the contrary, and despite a late formulation, Commons makes it the starting point of his research. This explains his proximity with pragmatism. Veblenian attitude of scientific neutrality and Commons's active reformism are also related to this same methodological difference.

NOTES

1 I am indebted to Professor Rutherford and Professor Samuels for their stimulating comments. Any errors remain my own responsibility.

2 See Lorenz (1974: 9–69).

3 This is established not only in the secondary literature (e.g., Daugert 1950: 72–73, 89) but also by Veblen's rare citations.

4 Such negative reading may be illustrated by Seckler, who describes Veblen as hesitating between "humanism" and "behaviorism" (Seckler 1975: 55–63, 78–99).

5 With respect to that, Rutherford mentions: "habituation is frequently utilized by Veblen as a substitute for a proper analysis of how institutions change base and of how a new consensus is formed and extended, elaborated, and given concrete expression" (Rutherford 1984: 347).

6 See, for illustration, Veblen (1914: 168–169).

7 *The Theory of Business Enterprise* (Veblen [1904] 1988), ch. 3, is eloquent on the subject.

8 Thus he compares the "expected orderly repetition" of his "managerial transaction" to Veblen's instinct of workmanship (Commons [1934b] 1990: 658).

9 See the last chapter of *Institutional Economics* (Commons [1934b] 1990) entitled "Communism, Fascism, Capitalism."

10 For example, Harter describes meticulously the context and the mechanics of the program for compensating injured workers in which Commons was very active (Harter 1962: 100–114).

11 This had been a constant preoccupation during his career, even before he thought about the concept of "reasonableness." See his examination of the Amana Society of Communists in Iowa (Commons 1895: 561–574).

12 See, for instance, Commons ([1894] 1967: 9–10, 34). As to its results, Commons

writes: "unquestionably the corporations have made possible the present marvellous development of industry" (Commons [1894] 1967: 126).

13 Biddle makes this point too (Biddle 1990a: 26).

14 On these cases, see Commons ([1934a] 1990). It must be added that Commons even wrote a paper about Gompers, "The Passing of Samuel Gompers" (Commons 1925).

15 Relevant arguments have been advanced, whether for or against this influence. According to Corei, for instance, Veblen's ideas are grounded on pragmatist views about meaning (Corei 1995: 18–26). In the same connection, Ayres's works suggest a real complementarity between Veblen and Dewey. On the opposite side, Dugger notes that any instrumentalist conception of knowledge seemingly leaves no room for Veblen's idle curiosity (Dugger 1979: 427).

16 To such a point that Knight considered his contribution as mainly "destructively valuable" (Knight 1920: 519). He was not (and is not) the only one.

17 On that point, see Samuels (1990: 695–718).

18 For illustration, see Commons ([1894] 1967: 19–22, 75–76).

19 On these points, Ely's influence is indisputable.

20 The subtitle of Ramstad's paper, "Theoretical Foundations of a Volitional Economics," underscores that fact—and its content too (Ramstad 1990).

21 Biddle is enlightening on that (Biddle 1990b: 1–25).

22 See, for illustration, Commons ([1934b] 1990: 150–155).

23 See Commons (1924), ch. 9, especially section 4. In fact, it is true not only for the courts, but also for any authority playing a role in the determination of social working rules.

24 For illustration, Chasse shows that the transformation of Commons's position about the nature of reform, including state intervention, is related to his own reformist activities (Chasse 1986: 762–767).

25 It is obviously Parsons's opinion (Parsons 1985: 774). For further developments, see my Ph.D. dissertation (Broda 1996: 132–137).

REFERENCES

Ayres, C.E. (1958). "Veblen's Theory of Instincts Reconsidered," in D.F. Dowd (ed.), *Thorstein Veblen: A Critical Reappraisal*, New York: Cornell University Press, 25–37.

Biddle, J.E. (1990a). "Purpose and Evolution in Commons's Institutionalism," *History of Political Economy* 22 (spring): 19–47.

——— (1990b). "The Role of Negotiational Psychology in J.R. Commons's Proposed Reconstruction of Political Economy," *Review of Political Economy* 2 (March): 1–25.

Broda, P. (1996). *Marché et institutions chez les institutionnalistes américains: Le cas de Veblen et de Commons*, Ph.D. dissertation: University of Paris I.

Chasse, J.D. (1986). "John R. Commons and the Democratic State," *Journal of Economic Issues* 20 (September): 759–784.

Commons, J.R. ([1894] 1967). *Social Reform and the Church*, New York: Kelley.

——— (1895). "Progressive Individualism," *The American Magazine of Civics* 6 (June): 561–574.

——— ([1924] 1959). *Legal Foundations of Capitalism*, Madison: The University of Wisconsin Press.

——— (1925). "The Passing of Samuel Gompers," *Current History* 21 (February): 670–676.

——— (1934a). *Myself*, New York: Macmillan.

——— ([1934b] 1990). *Institutional Economics: Its Place in Political Economy*, New Brunswick, NJ: Transaction.

——— (1935). "The Problem of Correlating Law, Economics and Ethics," in *Mélanges Geny*, Paris: Sirey, 124–144.

——— (1951). *The Economics of Collective Action*, New York: Macmillan.

Corei, T. (1995). *L'Economie institutionnaliste: Les fondateurs*, Paris: Economica.

Daugert, S. (1950). *The Philosophy of Thorstein Veblen*, New York: King's Crown Press.

Dugger, W.M. (1979). "The Origins of Thorstein Veblen's Thought," *Social Science Quarterly* 60 (December): 424–431.

Edgell, S. (1975). "Thorstein Veblen's Theory of Evolutionary Change," *American Journal of Economics and Sociology* 34 (July): 267–280.

Endres, A.M. (1985). "Veblen and Commons on Goodwill: A Case of Theoretical Divergence," *History of Political Economy* 17 (winter): 637–649.

Gonce, R.A. (1971). "John R. Commons's Legal Economic Theory," *Journal of Economic Issues* 5 (September): 80–95.

Gruchy, A.G. (1940). "John R. Commons' Concept of Twentieth-Century Economics," *Journal of Political Economy* 48 (6): 823–849.

Harter, L.G. (1962). *John R. Commons: His Assault on Laissez-Faire*, Corvallis, Ore.: Oregon State University.

Knight, F.H. (1920). "Book Review of *The Place of Science in Modern Civilization*," *Journal of Political Economy* 28 (6): 518–520.

Lorenz, K. (1974). "Sur la formation du concept d'instinct," in id., *Trois essais sur le comportement humain*, Paris: Points Seuil, 9–69.

Mayberry, T.C. (1969). "Thorstein Veblen on Human Nature," *American Journal of Economics and Sociology* 28 (July): 315–323.

Parsons, K.H. (1985). "John R. Commons : His Relevance to Contemporary Economics," *Journal of Economic Issues* 19 (September): 755–778.

Ramstad, Y. (1990). "The Institutionalism of John R. Commons: Theoretical Foundations of a Volitional Economics," *Research in the History of Economic Thought and Methodology* 8: 53–104.

Rutherford, M. (1984). "Thorstein Veblen and the Processes of Institutional Change," *History of Political Economy* 16 (fall): 331–348.

——— (1994). *Institutions in Economics: The Old and the New Institutionalism*, Cambridge: Cambridge University Press.

Samuels, W.J. (1990). "The Self-Referentiability of Thorstein Veblen's Theory of the Preconceptions of Economic Science," *Journal of Economic Issues* 24 (September): 695–718.

Seckler, D. (1975). *Thorstein Veblen and the Institutionalists*, Boulder, Colo.: Colorado Associated University Press.

Veblen, T. ([1898] 1990). "Why is Economics Not an Evolutionary Science?" in id. ([1919] 1990), *The Place of Science in Modern Civilization and Other Essays*, New Brunswick, NJ: Transaction, 56–81.

——— ([1899] 1994). *The Theory of the Leisure Class*, New York: Dover Publications.

——— ([1904] 1988). *The Theory of Business Enterprise*, New Brunswick, NJ: Transaction.

Veblen, T. ([1914] 1990). *The Instinct of Workmanship and the State of the Industrial Arts*, New Brunswick, NJ: Transaction.
——— (1915). *Imperial Germany and the Industrial Revolution*, New York: Huebsch.
——— ([1918] 1954). *The Higher Learning in America: A Memorandum on the Conduct of Universities by Businessmen*, Stanford, Calif.: Academic Reprint.
——— ([1919] 1990). *The Place of Science in Modern Civilization and Other Essays*, New Brunswick, NJ: Transaction.
——— (1934). *Essays in Our Changing Order*, ed. L. Ardzrooni, New York: Viking Press.
Vinokur, A. (1969). *Thorstein Veblen et la tradition dissidente dans la pensée économique américaine*, Paris: Pichon et Durand-Auzias.

Part V

AMERICAN ORIGINALS

14

PEIRCE'S ECONOMIC REASONING IN HIS METHODOLOGICAL ESSAY, "ON THE LOGIC OF DRAWING HISTORY FROM ANCIENT DOCUMENTS ESPECIALLY FROM TESTIMONIES"[1]

James R. Wible

INTRODUCTION

The pragmatist philosopher, Charles Sanders Peirce, had a lifelong interest in economics and economic aspects of scientific methodology. Although he wrote mostly in the natural sciences, mathematics, and philosophy, there are several significant essays with economic themes. Two of his writings were quite mathematical and would have qualified as state of the art contributions in his time. One of his essays created a mathematical–utility model of the economics of greater precision in empirical scientific research (Peirce 1879). Another was a mathematical model of monopoly with an addendum on consumer theory which included a statement of the axiom of transitivity (Peirce [1874] 1982). Besides these two obvious economic essays, there is a third piece which exhibits an extensive amount of economic reasoning. This third piece exceeds seventy pages in published form and contains several pages and a schematic graph on economic aspects of scientific methodology. The long title to this piece will be abbreviated as "The Logic of History" (Peirce [1901] 1958).

What makes "The Logic of History" so compelling is the sheer scope and magnitude of Peirce's vision of science. In order to critique the reconstruction of the works of Aristotle by German scholars, Peirce creates what amounts to a new scientific method. This new method is intended as a replacement for existing conceptions of science rooted in the empiricism of David Hume. Peirce patently rejected positivism and his new scientific method clearly contains many aspects of what subsequently became late twentieth-century philosophy and methodology of science. Furthermore, economics is a key part of Peirce's scientific method. Toward the end of the essay, there is an extensive discussion and analysis of the economic aspects of hypothesis formation and evaluation. Peirce maintains that the most relevant and least costly evidence supports his theory of the reconstruction of the works of Aristotle. He believes that the German scholars have been inefficient and wasteful in their recognition and use of facts and in their appraisal of competing hypotheses. Thus Peirce's rejection of the position of the German scholars is in a significant way economic. In Peirce's view of scientific method, economic considerations can play a decisive role in appraising competing hypotheses. For Peirce, economic factors seem to be an important aspect of the growth of scientific knowledge.[2]

PEIRCE'S BACKGROUND AND PREVIOUS WORKS IN ECONOMICS

Retrospectively, Charles Sanders Peirce is now recognized as an intellect of the first rank, having made major contributions to philosophy, mathematics, astronomy, geology, semiotics, and other fields.[3] These contributions were known to others who were able to benefit from Peirce's keen analytical and philosophically interpretative mind. In contrast to his superior intellectual gifts, in his personal life, Peirce was a tragic figure who at times existed on the margin of poverty. He was a fugitive from the law and homeless for a time, and he benefited in his last years from funds William James was able to arrange for his basic support.[4] Kevin Hoover (1994: 287) has remarked that "Peirce was a polymath and a frustrated genius." But Peirce's interest in and writings about economics largely have remained unknown to the economics profession. Peirce's mathematical manuscripts and papers on economics would have been major contributions when they were written in the late nineteenth century. However, as a historical matter, it appears that Peirce's writings and his conception of a mathematical political economy had no impact on the subsequent development of economic ideas. Thus Peirce cannot be portrayed as a long forgotten figure whose rediscovery reveals the impact of an otherwise unknown great mind who has significantly affected the history of economics. Peirce's writings on economics apparently had no contemporaneous impact on the development of the theory and practice of economics.[5]

The case for Peirce is a contemporary one and has two aspects. First, the problems of philosophy which so preoccupied Peirce and the other pragmatists have again taken center stage. Questions about truth, objectivity, meaning, communication and discourse, and the role of science in relation to the preceding issues are again some of the most important problems of philosophy.[6] Presently, there appears to be a genuine revival of interest in the contributions of the pragmatists, and particularly Peirce. Second, as this chapter is being written, there appears to be an accelerating revision, if not reconstruction, of neoclassical economics. This mechanistic, Walrasian, and neoclassical paradigm appears to be giving way to an analytical evolutionary economics.[7] What Peirce gives us is an analytical evolutionary view of the world, science, and the economy. Thus attention given to Peirce's economics and philosophy could help us further develop a post-Walrasian conception of economic science.[8]

As mentioned previously, Charles Sanders Peirce had a continuing and fundamentally conceived interest in economics. Economics was central in his conception of the world. Early in his career, the philosopher Max Fisch (1982) reports that Peirce drew some graphs for a lecture his father gave on political economy. The father was Benjamin Peirce, professor of mathematics at Harvard, a founder of the U.S. Coast Survey, and America's foremost mathematician in the mid to late nineteenth century. Peirce the son continued to be fascinated with economics, even as he was preoccupied with difficult scientific research and original contributions to mathematical logic, astronomy, semiotics, and philosophy. Peirce seems to have read many of the great economists of his time, although he seems to be unaware of Jevons's work on mathematical economics.

Other than correspondence in letters and graphs for a lecture given by his father, Peirce's (1874) first contribution to mathematical political economy can be found in his short manuscript titled, "On Political Economy," by the editors of Peirce's paper. This manuscript contains two parts. The first part is a mathematical model of the profit-maximizing monopolist.[9] The second part is a discussion of the theory of demand which contains the axiom of transitivity. The model of monopoly reflects Peirce's early concern for formulating a mathematical political economy. Before writing "On Political Economy," Peirce included mathematical formulations of competition and monopoly in two letters. In correspondence with the astronomer Simon Newcomb, who also wrote a handbook on political economy, and in a letter with an attorney Abraham Conger, Peirce (1871, 1873) presented the core first-order conditions for profit maximization under conditions of monopoly. Peirce focused on monopoly because it was one of the main subjects in Cournot's ([1838] 1929) *Researches into the Mathematical Principles of the Theory of Wealth*. At the time Peirce was writing, Cournot's work was the most advanced work of mathematical political economy that Peirce seemed to know. The details of the mathematics of Peirce's correspondence and "On Political Economy" have been discussed previously in Wible (1995b), so a detailed presentation will not be given here.

The second part of "On Political Economy," which is one page in length and constitutes about one-fourth of the published version of the manuscript, is on the theory of demand. Both the theory of monopoly and the page on consumer theory were written on the same day, September 21, 1874. At the beginning of this part of the manuscript, about a third of a page is devoted to Peirce's general view of political economy. Peirce summarizes his view this way:

> Thus the facts of political economy are of three categories:
> I Dependence of demand on price
> II Dependence of cost on demand
> III Dependence of price on demand and cost, or other circumstances.
> (Peirce [1874] 1982: 176)

Then Peirce pens a short paragraph on the theory of demand. In the first sentence of this paragraph, Peirce asserts that he will state the dependence of demand on price as a proposition. The second sentence summarizes marginal utility theory for a single individual. Peirce restates in words that an individual will choose an alternative which gives the greatest additional satisfaction or marginal utility. Then the last sentence reformulates marginal utility theory in logical form as the axiom of transitivity:

> The dependence of demand on price arises from this fundamental proposition. The desire of a person for anything has a quantity of one dimension, and a person having a choice will take that alternative which gives him the greatest satisfaction. In other words *if a person prefers A to B and B to C he also prefers A to C. This is the first axiom of Political Economy* (italics added for emphasis).
> (Peirce [1874] 1982: 176)

Following this statement of the axiom of transitivity, Peirce briefly explores two ideas: alternative product choices in consumer demand, and diminishing marginal utility. It is worth noting that another statement of transitivity in economic theory does not come until half a century later. So Peirce was quite extraordinary in realizing that the theory of consumer demand could be reformulated axiomatically.

A few years later, Peirce wrote his second substantive piece on economics. In comparison to the manuscript on monopoly which remained unpublished until the late twentieth century, Peirce's (1879) "Note on the Theory of the Economy of Research" was published in government documents as a U.S. Coast Survey Report. In this paper, Peirce presents the formal mathematics of a utility model for research project selection in science. A much longer discussion can be found in Wible (1994). What concerned Peirce was the greater precision in measurement which could be obtained from providing more funding for a research project. Realizing that resources were limited, Peirce first created a multiple project version of the model with mathematical equations. In the model, a ratio of marginal utility of greater precision to its marginal cost for each project was created and then the inference was drawn that this ratio should be equated for all projects. Then Peirce presented a graphical version of the special case for two projects. For one project, the ratio of marginal utility to marginal cost for increasing precision reads in the typical Cartesian fashion from left to right. For the other project, Peirce reversed the horizontal axis and the ratio reads from right to left. In both cases the ratio of marginal utility to marginal cost for greater precision declines as more resources are devoted to either project. Consequently, given the way the graph is constructed, the plot of the ratio for each project would intersect. The intersection point provides a theoretical answer to how funds should be allocated between projects in the two-project case.

The note on research project selection encapsulates Peirce's idea that resource constraints affect scientific inference. The note still ranks as one of the most direct and forthright statements of the role of economic factors in the scientific process. The note is written in an inferential rather than a descriptive manner. This gives the note a self-referential quality of drawing a scientific inference about scientific inference and, even more specifically, a meta economic inference about the nature of economic inference. Other innovative aspects of the note are its dependence on the equality of ratios, which circumvents problems with the measurability of cardinal utility, and the graph for the two-project case is quite novel for its time.[10]

THE METHODOLOGICAL CONTRIBUTIONS OF "THE LOGIC OF HISTORY"

Introduction

While his writings on monopoly, transitivity in consumer choice, and the economy of research demonstrate an unusual level of technical competence in economics for his day, Peirce's interest and reliance on economic notions is much broader and more fundamental than these technical contributions alone would suggest. A concern for economic aspects of many forms of inquiry seems to pervade Peirce's thought. One of the longest and most unusual discussions of economic aspects of inquiry is presented in the context of a dispute over ancient manuscripts. Because this discussion is so far removed from the traditional domains of economics, mathematics, logic, and the sciences to which Peirce made so many contributions, "The Logic of History" illustrates how broadly Peirce applied his concern for the economic aspects of inquiry.

Around the turn of the century, German historical scholars were working on manuscript fragments of Aristotle's writings. Peirce was unhappy with the method of induction being used by those attempting to compile a unified collection of the philosopher's writings. He thought their conception of the nature of scientific inference was flawed. In elaborating his alternative conception of scientific inference, Peirce again returned to economic issues and wrote several pages to explain economic aspects of scientific methodology. He maintained that these same concerns also affected critical, historical investigation of these ancient documents. Peirce maintained that his own theories of repetitive characteristics in Aristotle's manuscripts were more economically testable than those of the Aristotelian scholars in Germany.

The next few sections of the chapter are intended as a reader's guide to Peirce's ([1901] 1958) "The Logic of History." For the most part, the essay will be considered in the same order as it is presented in the Harvard edition. Many of the most important philosophical and methodological issues will be highlighted first. Then the economic aspects of the argument will be presented in the subsequent sections. There will be extensive quotations to illustrate the points being made by Peirce. Peirce's writings are notoriously difficult to read and to understand. However, there are many places where his comments are brilliant, provocative, prophetic, and occasionally humorous. Thus his writings deserve extensive quotation. Again, my apology is offered to those who may grow impatient with so much direct quotation. Such readers may wish to cover the material at a faster pace. My hope is to present systematically and efficiently the most important contributions of the essay and give the reader a representative sampling of Peirce's own words.

Other than the economic aspects of scientific inquiry, "The Logic of History" is notable for its philosophical and methodological positions. These positions are much more extensive than those usually associated with Peirce and his well-known pragmatic maxim. Peirce's scientific methodology offers perspectives on the nature of science that are similar to those views which came after the decline of positivism, also known as the received view in the 1950s and 1960s. Although it was the economics of science which initially drew my attention to Peirce's methodology, it is striking how contemporary Peirce's view of science appears to be. The methodological innovations of Peirce's "The Logic of History" appear so extensive that they deserve a separate listing. There may be others who no doubt held similar views. But the length of the list, their similarity to late twentieth-century conceptions of science, and the importance given to economic factors, makes "The Logic of History" a truly extraordinary piece. Some of the major issues raised by Peirce in this essay are:

1 A rejection of Humean empiricism.
2 A discussion of the extremely long-run time horizon needed for scientific progress.
3 A discussion of truth as the goal of science.
4 An awareness that an explicit scientific method makes science more efficient or less wasteful.
5 A concern for the role of error in the psychology of discovery.

6 A discussion of logic, explanation, and prediction.
7 An assertion of the abstract and theoretical nature of facts.
8 A rejection of nominalism and positivism.
9 A discussion and comparison of deduction and induction.
10 An awareness of the costly nature of experimentation.
11 A discussion of types of induction, both mathematical and scientific.
12 An awareness of the logic of falsification.
13 A discussion of hypothesis formation.
14 A discussion of economic aspects of hypothesis formation and evaluation.
15 An encapsulation of the new scientific method as rules of inquiry.
16 A conception of scientific decision-making as a method of inference.
17 An awareness that scientific discovery is mostly evolutionary, rather than revolutionary.
18 An awareness that economic factors may be used in deciding between competing hypotheses.

Obviously, this is quite a list, and it is unfortunate that "The Logic of History" heretofore has not received the recognition it no doubt deserves. However, these are the issues selectively presented below.

An outline of Peirce's essay "The Logic of History" is presented in Table 14.1. In the Harvard edition of Peirce's writings, the essay is presented in a sequence of ten sections. The major division headings were added by this writer to simplify the presentation and discussion of the essay. The first of the ten sections is a brief abstract obtained from the records of the meeting where the paper was presented. The first major subdivision of the essay,

Table 14.1 An outline of Peirce's essay "On the Logic of Drawing History from Ancient Documents"

	1	Abstract
Part I	*A presentation and critique of the method of likelihoods*	
	2	The theory of balancing likelihoods
	3	Criticism of the theory of balancing likelihoods
Part II	*Peirce's new logical theory of the proper method of science*	
	4	The logic of science
	5	Regularity and explanation
	6	Abduction, induction, and deduction
	7	Three kinds of induction
	8	Abduction
Part III	*An application of Peirce's new method to the works of Aristotle*	
	9	The logic of history
	10	Application of the method

Note: This outline incorporates the section titles from the Harvard edition and the major subdivision headings were added by this author to simplify the presentation and discussion of the essay.

Part I, presents and critiques an antiquated method of empirical scientific thinking that Peirce calls the theory of balancing likelihoods. It consists of sections 2 and 3 of the essay. Part II is an elaboration and discussion of Peirce's alternative view of scientific method; it contains sections 4–8 of the essay. Part III applies Peirce's conception of scientific method to hypotheses and arguments about the reconstruction of the ancient manuscripts of Aristotle; it contains sections 9 and 10.

The abstract

An appropriate way to begin a discussion of "The Logic of History" is with excerpts from the abstract. The abstract is the very first section of the essay. It comes from a report of a meeting of the National Academy of Sciences in November 1901. It is unclear whether Peirce wrote the abstract. The abstract is two paragraphs in length and appears to be about twice the length of a more modern scientific abstract. However, given the fact that the manuscript is 75 pages in its recently published version, the abstract does not seem inappropriately long. Some of the most important comments from the abstract are reproduced below:

> Mr. C.S. Peirce gave an abstract of a long paper on the logic of the process of drawing history from ancient testimonies. He endeavored to show that the method of balancing the veracity of a witness against the improbability of his narrative, although it may be defended upon principles of the calculus of probabilities under certain conditions, is nevertheless in the great majority of cases illogical, because there is not the roughest approximation to fulfillment of those conditions. For the testimonies are seldom even approximately independent and still seldom independent of the antecedent probability of the narrative . . . the probabilities upon which the critics of history rely are not objective, but are mere expressions of their preconceived notions, than which no guide can be less trustworthy.
>
> Mr. Peirce then undertook to develop the principles upon which ancient historical research ought to proceed in order to be scientific. He pointed out that the logic of scientific investigation, in which a conclusion is not established for many years, perhaps not for generations, cannot be assumed to be the same as the proper logical procedure for an individual who seeks a practical basis for present action. . . . This scientific procedure consists, according to Mr. Peirce, in carefully framing a hypothesis, in tracing out the experimental consequences of that hypothesis, and in testing those consequences by comparison with facts not taken into account in the formation of the hypothesis. If the facts refute the hypothesis, it must

> be abandoned and another substituted; but if the predictions based upon it are verified, it will be entitled to be received as a scientific result until we find deductions from it which are contrary to the facts.
>
> (Peirce [1901] 1958: 89–90)

Peirce's critique of Hume's theory of testimony and likelihoods

Part I of the paper follows the abstract and consists of sections 2 and 3. As suggested in Table 14.1, this part of the essay presents the method of likelihoods and Peirce's critique of that method. Peirce began the manuscript proper with an account of the theory of literary criticism for appraising ancient documents discovered by archaeologists. Supposedly, the historical critics based their interpretations on David Hume's theory of testimony. According to Peirce, Hume's view of the validity of a witness depended on a doctrine of probabilities which required a balancing of likelihoods of favorable and unfavorable arguments. The likelihood of favorable arguments being true and unfavorable arguments being false was compared to the converse, namely, the likelihood of favorable arguments being false and unfavorable arguments being true. These probabilities were to be the objective basis of the validity of testimony given by a witness. After providing an analytical presentation of the argument with ratios of the approximate probabilities, Peirce remarks:

> This is *Hume's Theory Improved*, by merely being disembarrassed of blunders. If we strip the mathematics from it, we have the simple *theory of balancing likelihoods*, which is the theory that Hume undertook to elaborate and to render scientific. It really hardly differs from Hume's Theory Improved except in its vagueness. At any rate, it involves the notion that the different arguments have likelihoods, that they are quantities upon an algebraic scale, and that they are to be combined as independent.
>
> (Peirce [1901] 1958: 92–93)

Hume's method of balancing likelihoods in Peirce's eyes is an inadequate method for historical inquiry. The criticism is developed in two ways. First, Peirce maintains that the German critics of ancient history misused Hume's method. Second, Hume's method is flawed when applied to questions from ancient history.

Regarding the first point, Peirce's critique of the German critics has several aspects. One aspect concerned the use of the word "proof." While Hume apparently took care to avoid the use of that term in his historical research,

Peirce thought that "the word 'proof' is continually in their mouths" (Peirce [1901] 1958: 93). He believed the German critics were discontented with the idea of probability, searching for an argument whose conclusion is established as a matter of necessity. Peirce also thought that the critics were prone to reject views based on the evidence and to favor views "which reject all of the historical evidence" (Peirce [1901] 1958: 93). The consequence was that their views seemed to be unduly arbitrary and quite subjective.

Moving to a critique of Hume's method, Peirce maintained that the theory of balancing likelihoods was a bad method for treating ancient documents. The method of likelihoods is based on a notion of independence. Peirce discussed the "time honored urn from which balls are drawn at random and thrown back after each drawing" (Peirce [1901] 1958: 94). The difficulty with problems studied from ancient history is that for the sources of historical information the conditions of independence typically are not fulfilled. Peirce ([1901] 1958: 99) makes the argument in the following way:

> Passing now to the objections to the method of balancing likelihoods in the study of ancient history, the most obvious, perhaps, although not the most important, is, that the different testimonies and other arguments, are not commonly even in a rough sense independent, as the only rational basis for the method requires that they should be. Circumstantial evidences are, no doubt, often sufficiently independent; but direct testimony seldom is so. The same circumstances which lead one witness into error are likely to operate to deceive another. . . . The method of balancing likelihoods not only supposes that the testimonies are independent but also that each of them is independent of the antecedent probability of the story; and since it is far more difficult to make allowance for a violation of this requirement than of that of the independence of the testimonies, it becomes a much more serious matter.

Peirce's methodology of science and testimony

Part II of "The Logic of History" presents Peirce's alternative theory of scientific method as a replacement for the late nineteenth-century version of Humean empiricism which he believes should be rejected. Part II consists of sections 4–8. Section 4 is titled "The Logic of Science." In the very first sentence, Peirce indicates that his aim is to create a "new logical theory of the proper method of dealing with ancient testimonies" (Peirce [1901] 1958: 107). But the title of the section suggests a much broader scope than a new method for documentary criticism of ancient manuscripts. In this part of the essay, Peirce proposes what amounts to a new methodology of science. What Peirce wants to focus on are those methodological principles which lead to scientific progress in the long run. The long-run focus appears early in this discussion of scientific method and includes a brief mention of the issue of cost:

> With science it is entirely different. A problem started today may not reach any scientific solution for generations. The man who begins the inquiry does not expect to learn, in this life, what conclusion it is to which his labors are tending. Strictly speaking, the inquiry never will be completely closed. Even without any logical method at all, the gradual accumulation of knowledge might probably ultimately bring a sufficient solution. Consequently, the object of a logical method is to bring about more speedily and at less expense the result which is destined, in any case, ultimately to be reached, but which, even with the best logic, will not probably come in our day.
>
> (Peirce [1901] 1958: 108)

This is shortly followed by a simple statement of the focus of his conception of the methodology of science: "The question of what rules scientific inference ought to follow in order to accelerate the progress of science to the utmost is a comparatively simple one, and may be treated by itself" (Peirce [1901] 1958: 108).

In the next paragraph, Peirce raises the issue of the purpose of science. He maintains that "Science seeks to discover whatever there may be that is true" (Peirce [1901] 1958: 109). Truth is further elaborated as a principle which would prevent us from being surprised by a future fact. Truth is a matter of conditionally predicting a future fact. In his conception of science, mathematics is considered partly scientific. The spirit and purpose of mathematics is quite similar to the spirit and purpose of science. However, mathematical propositions do not correspond to "perceptual facts." What science is interested in are not the abstract ideas and images that may be independent of experience. Science is interested in the "solid truth or reality," but not the existential reality of the whole perceptual and conceptual world of the mind (Peirce [1901] 1958: 109). Two pages later, Peirce provides an overview of his theory of truth:

> Then, as to the word "true," I may be asked what this means. Now the different sciences deal with different kinds of truth; mathematical truth is one thing, ethical truth is another, the actually existing state of the universe is a third; but all those different conceptions have in common something very marked and clear. We all hope that the different scientific inquiries in which we are severally engaged are going ultimately to lead to some definitely established conclusion, which conclusion we endeavor to anticipate in some measure. Agreement with that ultimate proposition that we look forward

> to,—agreement with that, whatever it may turn out to be, is the scientific truth.
>
> (Peirce [1901] 1958: 111)

Truth is also a matter of inference. The perceptions which appear in ordinary experience are not to be accepted at face value. An inference is a conclusion which is a consequence of a long process of deliberation:[11]

> Confining ourselves to science, inference, in the broadest sense, is coextensive with the deliberate adoption, in any measure, of an assertion as true. For the deliberation implies that the adoption is voluntary; and consequently, the observation of perceptual facts that are forced upon us in experience is excluded.
>
> (Peirce [1901] 1958: 110)

Peirce also speculates about what was later called the psychology of discovery in science. A new branch of science originates when a surprising error is found. A surprise requires a context for the formation of an expectation. In Peirce's view, a scientist begins inquiry with a "theory of the universe" (Peirce [1901] 1958: 111). This theory forms the basis of an expectation. When an expectation is contradicted by a surprising fact, an error has been discovered. The scientist must then try to reconcile an existing theory with the newly discovered error.

Proceeding from broader statements about science, scientific methodology, and the psychology of discovery, Peirce takes up the issue of scientific explanation. For an explanation to occur, regularity must exist, and to be discovered, it must be a surprising regularity. The first instance of a newly experienced phenomenon is a surprise which invites inquiry, theoretical speculation, and the subsequent formulation of an expectation. An explanation takes the form of a proposition and its content states a conditional prediction. The prediction could be one which is stochastic rather than a deterministic certainty. A phenomenon which is conditionally predictable is one which Peirce also called rational.[12]

Near the end of the discussion of the nature of explanation, Peirce takes time to explore the nature and role of the conception of a fact. He criticizes Venn's assertion that the isolation of facts needs explanation. Peirce maintains that facts are both connected and separated. He even suggests that separation is a kind of connection. However, even more importantly, Peirce takes time to criticize what later became the logical positivist view of facts, namely, that facts are ultimate building blocks for the logic of inference in science. As mentioned previously, Peirce conceived of facts as abstractions, a position somewhat contrary to the doctrines of positivism. In "The Logic of History," he restates his opposition to the nominalism most often associated with the positivist school:

> Mr. Venn belongs to a school which considers the logical process as starting at the percepts, if not at impressions of sense. Mr. Venn is himself so candid and so acute that he may perhaps have seen the error of this. But supposing that he has followed his school, the discrepancy between him and me would easily be accounted for, because there can be no doubt that every *percept* does involve elements that call for explanation. But I maintain that logical criticism cannot go behind *perceptual facts*, which are the first judgements which we make concerning percepts. A perceptual fact is therefore an abstract affair. Each such fact covers only certain features of the percept.
>
> (Peirce [1901] 1958: 117)

In section 6 in Part II, Peirce focuses on three aspects of the scientific process: abduction, induction, and deduction. Abduction is the process of finding, suggesting, and adopting a likely hypothesis. Abduction is the search for a plausible explanation and prediction of observed facts. The mere adoption of a hypothesis by abduction is a beginning rather than an end. The abducted hypothesis could be in error and should "only be adopted on probation and must be tested" (Peirce [1901] 1958: 122). A further restriction which is often imposed on the process of abduction is discovered and rejected by Peirce. A rule has been suggested by Auguste Comte that metaphysical hypotheses should be excluded from science. Peirce defines a partially metaphysical hypothesis as one with some consequences which are and others which are not possible in experience. After expressing some sympathy with Comte's rule, Peirce notes that its practical effects are quite limited because it is impossible to construct a wholly nonmetaphysical hypothesis:

> I have no particular objection to Comte's rule. Indeed, I think it would obviously be fully justified by a consideration of the purposes of hypothesis. Only I beg to remark that its positive utility is limited by the circumstance that such [a] thing as a hypothesis which is either wholly or partially metaphysical cannot be constructed.
>
> (Peirce [1901] 1958: 123)

After the provisional adoption of a hypothesis by a process of abduction, the next step is deduction. Through deduction the implied consequences of a probational hypothesis can be derived. Peirce believed that his view of deduction was in harmony with Kant's, that deduction explicates what is implicitly assumed in the premises of the hypothesis. However, Kant's view is qualified in an important way from Peirce's intimate knowledge of mathematics. The idea of a mathematical corollary most closely approximates the idea of truth as deduced implications from a proposition. The proof of a major theorem is more complicated: such a proof often requires a lemma. A lemma is a demonstrable proposition which is outside the domain of inquiry.

So the notion of truth as a deduced implication from a hypothetical proposition is a very limited view of the nature of deduction. Peirce hoped that all of mathematics would be reformed so that every asserted proposition would be supported by a properly established postulate.

Having presented discussions of abduction and deduction, Peirce next considers the process of induction. Comments on economic aspects of scientific inquiry precede his characterization of induction:

> We proceed to test the hypothesis by making the experiments and comparing those predictions with the actual results of the experiment. Experiment is a very expensive business, in money, in time, and in thought; so that it will be a saving of expense, to begin with that positive prediction from the hypothesis which seems least likely to be verified. For a single experiment may absolutely refute the most valuable of hypotheses, while a hypothesis must be a trifling one indeed if a single experiment could establish it.
>
> (Peirce [1901] 1958: 125)

Then without so much as a brief transition, Peirce characterizes induction in the following way:

> When, however, we find that prediction after prediction, notwithstanding a preference for putting the most unlikely ones to the test, is verified by experiment, whether without modification or with a merely quantitative modification, we begin to accord to the hypothesis a standing among scientific results. This sort of inference it is, from experiments testing predictions based on a hypothesis, that is alone properly entitled to be called *induction*. . . . Induction, on the other hand, is not justified by any relation between the facts stated in the premisses and the fact stated in the conclusion; and it does not infer that the latter fact is either necessary or objectively probable. But the justification of its conclusion is that that conclusion is reached by a method which, steadily persisted in, must lead to true knowledge in the long run of cases of its application, whether to the existing world or to any imaginable world whatsoever. Deduction cannot make any such claim as this; since it does not lead to any positive knowledge at all, but only traces out the ideal consequences of hypotheses.
>
> (Peirce [1901] 1958: 125)

Section 7 of the essay contains a rather detailed discussion of three different types of induction. First, there are quantitative inductions which are drawn from collections with a predesignated character. In this part of the discussion, Peirce explores aspects of set theory introduced by himself, Dedekind, and Cantor relating to numerability of a collection of objects and how conceptions of sets relate to induction. Second, there are also quantitative inductions for which it is difficult to discover a frequency ratio. For this type of collection, an established principle appears to hold all of the time. One break in the pattern would be sufficient to demonstrate an error with the accepted principle. Such a break is difficult to predict and would be wholly unexpected. However, errors in induction will be corrected through time. The third type of induction is qualitative rather than quantitative. This type of induction occurs when an aggregate cannot be considered as a collection. Its elements or unity are not capable of being measured or counted according to Peirce. Instead, the qualitative distinction much and little is drawn. Qualitative predictions are made on the basis of a hypothesis suggested by cases which have been observed in the past. This process does not constitute a random sample. Hypotheses need to be corrected and modified to better accord with the facts. Qualitative induction proceeds slowly compared to quantitative induction. Peirce remarks: "Discovery instead of being shot like a bolt out of the blue, creeps upon us as a dawning day" (Peirce [1901] 1958: 136). Peirce also tells us of his reluctance to set forth his theory of three types of induction. He warns of possible oversights in his theory, but he feels the need to publish it anyway (Peirce [1901] 1958: 126).

THE ECONOMIC CONTRIBUTIONS OF "THE LOGIC OF HISTORY"

In section 8 of "The Logic of History," Peirce again reconsiders the process of preparing an initial hypothesis which he calls abduction. Here is found a clearer statement of abduction and its relation to induction:[13]

> Abduction makes its start from the facts, without at the outset, having any particular theory in view, though it is motived by the feeling that a theory is needed to explain the surprising facts. Induction makes its start from a hypothesis which seems to recommend itself, without at the outset having any particular facts in view, though it feels the need of facts to support the theory. Abduction seeks a theory. Induction seeks for facts. In abduction the consideration of the facts suggests the hypothesis. In induction the study of the hypothesis suggests the experiments which bring to light the very facts to which the hypothesis had pointed.
>
> (Peirce [1901] 1958: 137)

The purpose of section 8 is to consider those principles which should guide the search for a theory to explain the facts. An abduction is nothing more than a guess at an explanation that might rationalize the facts at hand. Peirce maintains there are three things which need to be considered in choosing a hypothesis as a basis for further inquiry. The chosen hypothesis: (1) needs to "be capable of being subjected to experimental testing," (2) it needs to "explain the surprising facts we have before us," and (3) there must be "the consideration of economy" because of "the enormous expensiveness of experimentation in money, time, energy, and thought" (Peirce [1901] 1958: 138).

At the beginning of the next section of the paper, Peirce provides a schematic chart of those factors which affect the selection of a hypothesis. The chart is reproduced as Table 14.2. It is more helpful to present it here than with the next section where it serves as nothing more than an introduction. The upper category of entities for determining the merit of a hypothesis has been explained in previous sections. These concern the ability of the hypothesis to explain the facts. The lower part of Table 14.2 contains the "economical considerations" which Peirce discusses on six of the eight pages of section 8 which concerns the process of abduction.

In Peirce's theory of hypothesis formulation as indicated in Table 14.2, there are three major categories of economic factors: (1) cost, (2) value, and (3) the effect of a hypothesis on other scientific projects and hypotheses. Cost is a relatively simple matter. Hypotheses which are inexpensive or "cheap" to test should be given priority in the scientific process. Peirce puts it this way:

> Under the head of cost, if a hypothesis can be put to the test of experiment with very little expense of any kind, that should be regarded as a recommendation for giving it precedence in the inductive procedure.
>
> (Peirce [1901] 1958: 139)

Table 14.2 Two categories of considerations in hypothesis selection in Peirce's methodology of science

Experiential character of the hypothesis		
Its explaining all the facts	As natural concomitants	
	As deductions	Corollarial
		Theorematic
Economical considerations	Cheapness	
	Intrinsic value	Naturalness
		Likelihood
	Relation of hypotheses	Caution
		Breadth
		Incomplexity

Source: Peirce ([1901] 1958: 146).

After a brief consideration of cost, the next topic is value. For Peirce, the value of a hypothesis depends on how close it is to the truth. A good hypothesis sets up an expectation that it may be true. Peirce seems to be something of an extraordinary optimist because he believes that the human mind is very good at guessing a correct hypothesis. The guessing takes the form of a process where initial guesses are replaced by better guesses. In this regard, the guessing processes of the human mind, particularly if they are theoretically and economically guided, are quite superior to random guesses. The economic value of theoretically guided guessing is expressed in the following way by Peirce:

> We cannot go so far as to say that high human intelligence is more often right than wrong in its guesses; but we can say that, after due analysis, and unswerved by prepossessions, it has been, and no doubt will be, not very many times more likely to be wrong than right. . . . Still science will cease to progress if ever we shall reach the point where there is no longer an infinite saving of expense in experimentation to be effected by care that our hypotheses are such as naturally recommend themselves to the mind, and make upon us the impression of simplicity,—which here means facility of comprehension by the human mind,—of aptness, of reasonableness, of good sense.
>
> (Peirce [1901] 1958: 140)

Having made his case with positive arguments, Peirce restates economic aspects of abduction in negative terms:

> But experience must be our chart in economical navigation; and experience shows that likelihoods are treacherous guides. Nothing has caused so much waste of time and means, in all sorts of researches, as inquirers' becoming so wedded to certain likelihoods as to forget all the other factors of the economy of research.
>
> (Peirce [1901] 1958: 140)

The third category of economic factors in addition to cost and value is the relation of a hypothesis to other research projects. This relational category is further subdivided into the topics of "Caution, Breadth, and Incomplexity" (Peirce [1901] 1958: 141). Caution returns to the theme that the human mind is an efficient guesser. Here Peirce considers the game of twenty questions. A skilled guesser is allowed to ask a sequence of twenty questions that will each be given an answer of yes or no. The aim is to guess the subject or thought in the other game player's mind. This game could go in 2^{20} different directions. A good game player might become quite efficient in guessing the unknown thought or subject. The economic efficiency of a skilled game of twenty questions needs to be operative in science:

> Thus twenty skillful hypotheses will ascertain what two hundred thousand stupid ones might fail to do. The secret of the business lies in the caution which breaks a hypothesis up into its smallest logical components, and only risks one of them at a time. What a world of futile controversy and of confused experimentation might have been saved if this principle had guided investigations into the theory of light!
>
> (Peirce [1901] 1958: 141)

A concern for the breadth of a hypothesis is the second aspect of the economic factors. Here Peirce is concerned with using the most general hypothesis because it represents an economy of explanation and may save some repetitious work. Again in Peirce's own words, we have the best expression of this aspect of the economics of hypothesis selection:

> While if we find there is but one cause, we at once reach a wide generalization which will save repetitious work. It is, therefore, good economy, other things being equal, to make our hypotheses as broad as possible.
>
> (Peirce [1901] 1958: 142–143)

The last aspect of the economic relational factors is "incomplexity" or just simplicity. Peirce compares fitting a set of data using linear or quadratic functional forms. Even though the quadratic form may be closer to the truth, it may be easier to begin with the linear version as a provisional hypothesis. Thus Peirce recommends simplicity as a consideration in the economics of hypothesis selection.

AN APPLICATION OF PEIRCE'S SCIENTIFIC METHOD AND THE ECONOMICS OF HYPOTHESIS FORMATION TO THE WORKS OF ARISTOTLE

Part III of "The Logic of History" contains an application of Peirce's theory of scientific method to ancient historical manuscripts. It is written as two separate sections of the essay. Section 9 enumerates six rules for a scientific interpretation of ancient manuscripts. These rules immediately follow the schematic summary of the principles which were presented in Table 14.2 and discussed previously. The second and last rules explicitly suggest an economic dimension. In condensed form, Peirce's ([1901] 1958: 146–147) six rules for inquiry regarding ancient manuscripts are:

1 A hypothesis should explain all of the related facts.
2 The first hypothesis to be tested should be that the "principal testimonies" are true. Peirce argues that it is "wasteful" to abandon the most plausible hypothesis early in the process of investigation.
3 Probabilities, although not conclusive, should help influence a preference for one hypothesis rather than another.
4 A hypothesis should be divided into component parts so that parts of the hypothesis can be tested separately, if possible.
5 When there is doubt about two competing hypotheses, the field of facts should be enlarged.
6 Preference should be given to a hypothesis which has a lower cost of inquiry when some aspects of testing can be shared with a previously tested hypothesis.

Although not listed as an enumerated rule for interpretation, Peirce again suggests that an element of surprise is the key to a process of testing. How well a hypothesis accords with the facts tells us little. What is interesting are unlikely or surprising consequences when the hypothesis may not be true.

In the last section of the essay, Peirce applies his scientific method, its six rules of inquiry, and its economic implications to the works of Aristotle. He begins with the facts and a narrative as suggested by rule one. The facts tell us about the large number of works in the late nineteenth-century edition of Aristotle and the large number of manuscripts and manuscript fragments which are listed in a catalogue of Aristotle's writings. At the time Peirce wrote "The Logic of History," he estimates that there were 46 works containing a million words in the published edition of Aristotle's writings. A catalogue of Aristotle's works mentioned 146 titles, which suggests that the total volume of Aristotle's writings was three times that of the published edition. Other scholars listed some 600 fragments. Also listed among the facts are stylistic aspects of Aristotle's writings. The writings were repetitious, more Roman than Greek, and often contained many cross-references (Peirce [1901] 1958: 149 ff.).

The narrative is Peirce's brief story of what happened to the manuscripts of Aristotle from the time of his death in 322 BC until they passed into the hands of an editor in the century before the birth of Christ. Peirce calls this the Scepsis story because it is the place which seems to have affected the physical deterioration of the manuscripts the most (Peirce [1901] 1958: 163). Originally the manuscripts were located at Aristotle's school in Athens. After his death, the manuscripts were kept by Aristotle's successor, Theophrastis, for about thirty-five years. Upon his death, they were given to a friend Neleus whose heirs kept Aristotle's books in a damp cellar for more than a century and a half. Neleus lived at a place called Scepsis in Aeolis in Asia Minor. In Scepsis, Peirce speculates that the manuscripts suffered "from damp and insects, and were in places illegible" (Peirce [1901] 1958: 151).

After Scepsis, the books were carried to Rome and then to Rhodes, where a later editor attempted to arrange the papers, correct the text, and publish a new edition.

At this point Peirce, following rule two, interrupts the Scepsis narrative to state his hypothesis quite succinctly and directly. Rule two asserts the primacy and efficiency of the "principal testimonies" of the Scepsis story:

> The hypothesis that this story is true is so natural, and it ought to be so easily refuted if it is not true, that I am strongly inclined, in spite of the jeers of all the great German critics, to admit it on probation.
>
> (Peirce [1901] 1958: 151)

Then the narrative continues with some difficult facts which the hypothesis should address. Subsequently, he returns to the notion of deducing the consequences of his hypothesis and remarks:

> Having thus reviewed all the supposed difficulties of this hypothesis and having found that they are not serious, we may admit it upon probation, and proceed to trace out its consequences.
>
> (Peirce [1901] 1958: 153)

On a later page he lists some of the deduced implications of the hypothesis and their likely probabilities according to rules three and four in his methodology:

> At any rate, some of the phenomena to which our hypothesis points as probable are as follows:
>
> 1st, strange stupidities, or commonplaces, where what went before, led us to think that a remarkable idea was to be developed.
>
> 2nd, stupidities, commonplaces, and puzzling places occurring toward the ends of books at intervals of about 70 Berlin lines or multiples thereof; at least when Aristotle's autographs and not copies were there.
>
> 3rd, the appearance of transpositions of passages of about 70 Berlin lines, under the same limiting condition.
>
> 4th, omissions of matter which it was in the line of Aristotle's highly systematic thought to insert, and which he would probably have treated in about 70 Berlin lines or a multiple.
>
> (Peirce [1901] 1958: 157)

From here, Peirce proceeds to examine one of the books of Aristotle's writings, the *Prior Analytics*, in great detail. Here he is enlarging the field of facts as suggested by rule five. Indeed, what are found are many of the phenomena which Peirce predicted based on his general knowledge of the works of Aristotle. Peirce speculates there is a missing treatment of syllogisms which are truisms. He also reviews some of Aristotle's discussion of syllogisms in relation to geometry. Then he presents an interpretation of Aristotle's view of the logic of induction. Here Peirce suggests that Aristotle had a conception of abduction. One gets the impression that Peirce's view of abduction is thought by Peirce to be implicit in Aristotle's writings, although Peirce does not directly make that claim.

At this point, Peirce believes that he has inferentially established his view of what had happened to the manuscripts of Aristotle in the early centuries of their existence. Following rule six, he argues that the Scepsis narrative is a better hypothesis:

> I think, then, that my interpretation of the passage, considering its being what the current of thought demands . . . comes within a tolerably close approach to certainty. If we accept it, it affords a remarkable confirmation of the Scepsis story; because of the bold insertion it supposes to have been made in the text
>
> (Peirce [1901] 1958: 163)

And then he adds a rejection of the German scholars:

> All of the best critics of Germany, on the other hand, utterly reject the Scepsis story. Their reasons I have already indicated. They are so weak that I think I am justified in surmising that the real motive of their rejection is a reluctance to accepting any ancient testimony without dressing it up and putting a new face upon. At any rate, their general principle . . . seems to me to amount to believing whatever they are inclined to believe.
>
> (Peirce [1901] 1958: 164)

With regard to the economic aspects of the argument, rule six suggests that a hypothesis should be adopted which has the lower cost of inquiry. Peirce criticized the German scholars for their inefficiency:

> But especially in ancient history, where the only facts we have are, in most cases, testimonies, the extremely bad economy of supposing those testimonies false, before we have first thoroughly tried the hypothesis that they are true, and have found it quite inadmissible, is so obvious, that it is difficult to repress a certain contempt for the reasoning powers of those critics who are given to this procedure.
>
> (Peirce [1901] 1958: 147)

CONCLUSIONS

In his essay "The Logic of History," the pragmatist philosopher Charles Sanders Peirce has created a philosophically and economically innovative methodology of science. The purpose of Peirce's innovative method of science was to provide a context for criticizing and rejecting the reconstruction of Aristotle's works by German scholars. Peirce wanted the history behind the interpretation and recognition of Aristotle's writings to be as scientifically based as possible. To that end, Peirce provided a long discourse on the analytical, inferential, and evolutionary nature of scientific methodology. Philosophically, Peirce's new method portrayed a conception of science which appears to be almost a century ahead of its time.[14] Peirce rejected positivism and Humean empiricism. Among other things, Peirce held that facts are theoretical abstractions, that science is a rule-governed process of inference, that science is partly metaphysical, and that science slowly makes progress in the very long run. Economically, Peirce integrates economic factors into his conception of scientific method. Economic concerns play an important role in the creation and testing of competing hypotheses. Economic arguments are used to criticize and reject the views of the German scholars. More generally, Peirce argues that a process of rule-governed inference in science is more efficient than other methods of scientific inquiry.

NOTES

1 I would like to thank Kevin Hoover, Lawrence Boland, Wade Hands, and two anonymous referees for helpful comments in revising this chapter.
2 Another version of "The Logic of History" can be found in Eisele (1985: 705–800). This version omits the application to Aristotle. Instead it focuses on a reconstruction of the events of the life and writings of Plato.
3 Wiener (1958: ix) remarks that Peirce was "the most versatile, profound, and original philosopher that the United States has ever produced." A similar view is held by the contemporary German philosopher Karl-Otto Apel (1995: xix) who says: "Charles Sanders Peirce is considered by many to be America's most original and greatest philosopher."
4 Details of Peirce's life can be found in a scholarly, provocative, and entertaining biography of the life of Peirce by Joseph Brent (1993).
5 Except for a few articles and the contributions of philosophers Nicholas Rescher (1976, 1978, 1989), Carolyn Eisele (1979b, 1979c), William Brown (1983), and W.C. Stewart (1991), the economic aspect of Peirce's philosophy has been ignored.
6 Apel (1995), Diggins (1994), and Rorty (1982) discuss the place of contemporary versions of pragmatism in the context of modern philosophy. Such concerns are also evident in the mainstream literature in philosophy of science.
7 One new school of economics which fits within this description is known as the New Institutional Economics. It began with Ronald Coase's (1937) theory of the firm and finds Oliver Williamson (1985) among others as a leading proponent.

This literature is further appraised and criticized in Rutherford (1989) and Wible (1995a). Other examples of evolutionary economics are Nelson and Winter (1982) and Georgescu-Roegen (1971).

8 This theme was explored by Colander (1995). Wade Hands (1994) also has reviewed this contribution of Peirce's.

9 Peirce's ([1874] 1982) "On Political Economy" may be the densest piece of mathematical writing in the nineteenth century. In three pages of text there are nineteen interrelated equations and on the fourth page is found the axiom of transitivity.

10 There is a dialectical quality to the "Economy of Research." On the surface it is about measurement in the natural sciences or the search for more refined cardinal measures of natural properties. But the theory is qualitative and makes relational inferences about how resources should be allocated among research projects. Thus we have an ordinally developed economic theory of cardinal measurement in the natural sciences.

11 Kuklick (1977: 117–123) maintains that Peirce's conception of truth is incompatible with his pragmatic maxim quoted above in the text. The reason is that it is impossible to imagine conceivable consequences of an infinite future.

12 In his own words, he elaborates on the nature of scientific explanation: "Now what an explanation of a phenomenon does is to supply a proposition which, if it had been known to be true before the phenomenon presented itself, would have rendered that phenomenon predictable, if not with certainty, at least as something very likely to occur. It thus renders that phenomenon rational,—that is, makes it a logical consequence, necessary or probable" (Peirce [1901] 1958: 113).

13 Harris and Hoover (1980) provide an analysis and discussion of Peirce's theories of abduction and induction. Their essay appears not to include the specifics of "The Logic of History." However, Peirce repeated the general aspects of his views in many different writings.

14 Readers may find it useful to note that I studied American pragmatism and Peirce while a graduate student at Penn State with the noted Peirce scholar Carl Hausman. Hausman (1993) has recently published a monograph on Peirce's evolutionary philosophy. Other than those references already mentioned, additional works which are worth consulting on Peirce are Thayer (1981), Murphey (1993), Rosenthal (1994), and Hookway (1985). There have been hundreds of articles on Peirce which have appeared in the relatively new journal, *Transactions of the Charles S. Peirce Society*.

REFERENCES

Apel, K.-O. (1995). *From Pragmatism to Pragmaticism*, repr. of 1981 edn, trs. J.M. Krois, New Jersey: Humanities Press.

Brent, J. (1993). *Charles Sanders Peirce: A Life*, Bloomington, Ind.: Indiana University Press.

Brown, W.M. (1983). "The Economy of Peirce's Abduction," *Transactions of the Charles S. Peirce Society* 19 (fall): 397–411.

Coase, R.H. (1937). "The Nature of the Firm," *Economica*, n.s., 4: 366–405.

Colander, D. (1995). "Marshallian General Equilibrium Analysis," draft of a presidential address to the Eastern Economic Association, March 17, Roosevelt Hotel, New York City.

Cournot, A. ([1838] 1929). *Researches into the Mathematical Principles of the Theory of Wealth*, trs. N.T. Bacon, New York: Macmillan.

Diggins, J.P. (1994). *The Promise of Pragmatism*, Chicago: University of Chicago Press.

Eisele, C. (1979a). *Studies in the Mathematical Philosophy of Charles S. Peirce*, ed. R.M. Martin, New York: Mouton Publishers.

——— (1979b). "The Correspondence with Simon Newcomb," in id., *Studies in the Mathematical Philosophy of Charles S. Peirce*, ed. R.M. Martin, New York: Mouton Publishers, 52–93.

——— (1979c). "The Mathematics of Economics," in id., *Studies in the Mathematical Philosophy of Charles S. Peirce*, ed. R.M. Martin, New York: Mouton Publishers, 251–254.

——— (ed.) (1985). *Historical Perspectives on Peirce's Logic of Science*, Berlin: Mouton Publishers.

Fisch, M. (1982). "The Decisive Year and Its Early Consequences," introduction to *Writings of Charles S. Peirce: A Chronological Edition*, vol. 2, 1867–1871, ed. E.C. Moore et al., Bloomington, Ind.: Indiana University Press, xxi–xxxvi.

Georgescu-Roegen, N. (1971). *The Entropy Law and the Economic Process*, Cambridge, Mass.: Harvard University Press.

Hands, D.W. (1994). "The Sociology of Scientific Knowledge and Economics: Some Thoughts on the Possibilities," in R. Backhouse (ed.), *New Perspectives on Economic Methodology*, London: Routledge, 75–106.

Harris, J.F. and K.D. Hoover (1980). "Abduction and the New Riddle of Induction," *The Monist* 63 (July): 329–341.

Hausman, C.R. (1993). *Charles Peirce's Evolutionary Philosophy*, Cambridge: Cambridge University Press.

Hookway, C. (1985). *Peirce*, London: Routledge & Kegan Paul.

Hoover, K.D. (1994). "Pragmatism, Pragmaticism and Economic Theory," in R. Backhouse (ed.), *New Perspectives on Economic Methodology*, London: Routledge, 286–315.

Kuklick, B. (1977). *The Rise of American Philosophy: Cambridge, Massachusetts, 1860–1930*, New Haven: Yale University Press.

Murphey, M. (1993). *The Development of Peirce's Philosophy*, Indianapolis: Hackett Publishing.

Nelson, R.R. and S.G. Winter (1982). *An Evolutionary Theory of Economic Change*, Cambridge, Mass.: Harvard University Press.

Peirce, C.S. ([1871] 1968), "Letter to Simon Newcomb," in W.J. Baumol, and S.M. Goldfeld (eds), *Precursors in Mathematical Economics: An Anthology*, London: London School of Economics and Political Science, 186–187.

——— ([1873] 1982). "Letter, Peirce to Abraham B. Conger," in *Writings of Charles S. Peirce: A Chronological Edition*, vol. 3, 1872–1878, ed. C.J. Kloesel et al., Indianapolis: Indiana University Press, 109–110.

——— ([1874] 1982). "[On Political Economy]," in *Writings of Charles S. Peirce: A Chronological Edition*, vol. 3, 1872–1878, ed. C.J. Kloesel et al., Indianapolis: Indiana University Press, 173–176.

——— (1879). "Note on the Theory of the Economy of Research," *United States Coast Survey* for the fiscal year ending June 1876, U.S. Government Printing Office 1879, repr. in *Operations Research* 15 (1967): 642–648; and in *The Collected Papers of Charles Sanders Peirce*, vol. 7, ed. A.W. Burks, Cambridge, Mass.: Harvard

University Press, 1958, 76–83; and in *The Writings of Charles S. Peirce: A Chronological Edition*, vol. 4, 1879–1884, ed. C.J. Kloesel et al., Indianapolis: Indiana University Press, 1986, 72–78.

——— ([1901] 1958). "On the Logic of Drawing History from Ancient Documents Especially from Testimonies," repr. in *The Collected Papers of Charles Sanders Peirce*, vol. 7, ed. A.W. Burks, Cambridge, Mass.: Harvard University Press, 89–164.

Rescher, Nicholas (1976). "Peirce and the Economy of Research," *Philosophy of Science* 43: 71–98.

——— (1978). *Peirce's Philosophy of Science*, Notre Dame, Ind.: University of Notre Dame Press.

——— (1989). *Cognitive Economy: The Economic Dimension of the Theory of Knowledge*, Pittsburgh: University of Pittsburgh Press.

Rorty, R. (1982). *Consequences of Pragmatism*, Minneapolis: University of Minnesota Press.

Rosenthal, S.B. (1994). *Charles Peirce's Pragmatic Pluralism*, Albany, NY: State University of New York Press.

Rutherford, M. (1989). "What is Wrong with the New Institutional Economics (and What is Still Wrong with the Old)?" *Review of Political Economy* 1 (November): 299–318.

Stewart, W.C. (1991). "Social and Economic Aspects of Peirce's Conception of Science," *Transactions of the Charles S. Peirce Society* 27 (fall): 501–526.

Thayer, H.S. (1981). *Meaning and Action: A Critical History of Pragmatism*, 2nd edn, Indianapolis: Hackett Publishing.

Wible, J.R. (1994). "Charles Sanders Peirce's Economy of Research," *Journal of Economic Methodology* 1: 135–160.

——— (1995a). "The Economic Organization of Science, the Firm, and the Marketplace," *Philosophy of the Social Sciences* 25 (March): 35–68.

——— (1995b). "Peirce's Mathematical Note 'On Political Economy' and the Axiom of Transitivity," paper presented at the History of Economics Society Meetings, Notre Dame.

Wiener, P.P. (1958). "Introduction," in id. (ed.), *Values in a Universe of Chance: Selected Writings of Charles S. Peirce*, Garden City, NY: Doubleday Anchor.

Williamson, O. (1985). *The Economic Institutions of Capitalism*, New York: Free Press.

15

THE SOCIAL CONSCIENCE OF AN AMERICAN ECONOMIST

Alvin S. Johnson as advocate/reformer

Jerry L. Petr[1]

INTRODUCTION

Alvin Saunders Johnson (1874–1971) was a noteworthy twentieth-century American economist. As one who wrote his doctoral dissertation at Columbia under John Bates Clark, later supervised the dissertation of Frank H. Knight at Cornell (a dissertation that became *Risk, Uncertainty and Profits*), and served as president of the American Economic Association (AEA) in 1936, Alvin Johnson can be placed squarely in the American neoclassical economic mainstream. He attained high position in a fundamentally conservative discipline that prided itself on its scientific prowess, and that, frequently, celebrated the laissez-faire implications of its analytical models. Yet, in important respects, Johnson was not representative of the stereotypical dispassionate scientist, absorbed in manipulation of deductive models (under the cloak of scientific detachment) to the neglect of pressing social issues (that would have required "normative" emotionalism). Defiant of any disciplinary dogma that relied on the logical beauty of hypothesized market outcomes to achieve a social optimum, Johnson stands as an intriguing intellectual puzzle. He was both a master of the disciplinary core of equilibrium analysis, and a servant to humanitarian values—values which drove him to innovative and interventionist policy prescriptions that ranged far beyond the antiseptic analysis of his disciplinary home.

One purpose of this chapter is to illuminate that contrast between the professional activism of Alvin Johnson as advocate/reformer versus the frequently venerated model of the dispassionate scientific investigator of economic phenomena. At the height of Johnson's professional power, the more conventional posture of analytical detachment was well represented by Frank Fetter, who had preceded Johnson in the AEA presidency by a quarter of a century (in 1912). Fetter celebrated the maturation of American economics in terms of its development, at the end of the nineteenth century, into a "finer, abstract, disinterested type of pure economics." He cited Johnson's mentor, Clark, as the best example of this superior "scientific spirit" which, Fetter asserted, was particularly difficult in economics "where thought is so easily colored with human interest, with selfishness and with prejudice" (Hollander 1927: 363).

Johnson would not easily have worn the labels of "selfish" or "prejudiced," but neither was he content that he or his colleagues should be abstractly disinterested in the face of human problems. In fact, his brief presidential address to the American Economic Association in 1936 was an activist call to arms and a not-so-gentle chiding of the profession for its posture of detached bemusement during the Great Depression. Johnson lamented the fact that "the economist has not been active enough, responsible enough, well enough organized, to bring forward his findings . . . before the moment for action has gone by." He rejected the dominant ethic of individualistic scholarly effort, called for collective action to meet society's needs, and concluded that "the time has come when the economists need to organize themselves to do the work which society may reasonably require of them," and to "use our organized moral forces to encourage the full employment of [our professional] resources for the general good" (Johnson 1937: 2–3).

Contemporary observers also identified a contrast similar to that highlighted in this chapter. Rexford Tugwell, while advocating empirical and problem-oriented disciplinary innovation and policy development, attacked the "laissez-faire milieu" of his neoclassical colleagues (Krohn 1993: 42). The dominant position of the American economics profession, at the time of great national crisis, seemed to be opposed to any economic innovation, wedded to deductive models, and critical of the policy activism of either the Keynesians or the American institutionalists (Krohn 1993: 39–40). In contrast, Alvin Johnson articulated his "interventionist" posture (ironically in the same volume of tributes to J.B. Clark from which the Fetter position is cited) as follows:

> It is not by any law of nature, but because of a lazy habit of mind that assumes that if laissez-faire and free movement serve well to govern the traffic in peanuts and popcorn, gimcracks and gewgaws, therefore they must also serve well to govern the exchange of lands and homes, the price men pay for the right to produce a people's bread, the price they may exact of others when they in turn choose to shift to the urban side of the national economic equation.
>
> (Johnson 1927: 228)

It is this willingness to impose his "normative" will on what many economists like to call a "positive" science that illustrates Joseph Dorfman's observation that "Johnson illustrates vividly the paradox of the brilliant codifier of the classic school being driven by his humane interests into innovation" (Dorfman 1949: 433). This chapter explores the origin and nature of those "humane interests" and considers their "innovative" consequences, for the profession and for the larger society. This then is the tracking of the normative wanderings of a scientist squarely in the middle of the neoclassical paradigm during the first half of this century.

BIOGRAPHICAL SKETCH[2]

Alvin S. Johnson was the Nebraska-born son of Danish immigrants. Intellectually precocious (reminiscent of J.S. Mill) he was, while enrolled at the University of Nebraska, a student of the classics, reading both Greek and Latin as well as German and Sanskrit. He avoided "courses in economics and political science, as ruling class apologetics" (Finkelstein 1948: 41). As he neared graduation he was offered a "teaching fellowship in Greek, Latin, or Germanics" (p. 100). He chose Greek. At that time he also had a book contract to "bring out a Comparative grammar of Greek, Latin, Sanskrit, and Gothic" (p. 99).

Johnson had come to the university self-taught in Latin. As a child he had been mostly "home schooled," observing that his "early [formal] schooling interfered very little with my education" (p. 40). As a young boy he read aloud to his mother "most of the novels of Dickens, half of Thackeray, a third of George Eliot, Hugo's *Les Miserables*, Tolstoi's *Anna Karenina* and the *Kreutzer Sonata*" (p. 46). By age 13 he had read Herbert Spencer and had come "to the conclusion that the great philosopher was after all a damn fool" (p. 24). He also read history and law in the treasured library of an intellectual uncle. Johnson and his wife, Margaret Edith Henry Johnson (Ph.D., Columbia), later home-schooled their own seven children (Johnson 1936: 15).

Before attending college, at age 16 he had been elected "lecturer" for the local Farmers' Alliance Lodge, and had developed his first economic policy platform. This included planks calling for government regulation of railway rates, abolition of trusts, a graduated income tax, pensions to support the aged and disabled, government storage of agricultural imperishables with warrants against the value of the stored products circulating as legal tender, and guaranteed bank deposits (p. 64). That was in 1890! In a foreshadowing of his later career, he also called for expanded adult education (Finkelstein 1948: 40).

Despite Johnson's success and talent in classical studies, his pragmatic concern with future professional opportunities redirected his academic pursuits more toward the public policy agenda of the Farmers' Alliance platform. After completing his bachelor's and master's degrees (his MA was in Greek) at the University of Nebraska, and his military service during the Spanish–American War, Johnson enrolled in the School of Political Science at Columbia University for his doctoral work. There he studied economics with, among others, E.R.A. Seligman and John Bates Clark. Clark supervised Johnson's dissertation "Rent in Modern Economic Theory."

Johnson's talent in economics launched him on an auspicious and prestigious academic track. He received his Ph.D. from Columbia in 1902, and between 1900 and 1912 he held teaching positions at Columbia, Bryn Mawr, Nebraska, Texas, Chicago, Stanford (head of department), and Cornell. Later, in 1938–39, he was on the faculty at Yale. "By moving," he noted, "a body greatly increases its visibility" (p. 177). He prided himself on his pursuit of truth regardless of prevailing opinion and, while teaching at Texas, bought a Missouri farm that, to him, "represented a sheet to windward if ever a storm of academic persecution should blow up" (p. 201). He was skeptical of colleagues' confidence that threats to academic freedom were a thing of the past, noting that "American history has proved to me that persecution for opinion lies deep in the mores of America. It may slumber for a time, but on the first occasion it leaps into savage life" (p. 201).

During this time he established a solid publication record as he wrote on rent, trade, labor, taxation, minimum wages, economic theory, and economic freedom. His work appeared in the *American Economic Review*, the *Quarterly Journal of Economics*, and the *Political Science Quarterly*, as well as in popular journals.

However, just as he earlier had concluded that study of the classics was not a growth industry with strong career possibilities, so Johnson, before age 40, found himself at another professional crossroads. He viewed himself as primarily an economic theorist, but believed that "economic theory by 1912 had fought itself to a virtual standstill." It had built up a "competent and consistent picture of an economic world based on perfect competition" which seemed, to Johnson, increasingly unrealistic. He acknowledged the developing work in imperfect competition (citing J.M. Clark) and in empirical analysis (crediting W.C. Mitchell), but, for him, "economic science was drifting farther away from the comprehension of the intelligent laymen, for whom Adam Smith, Ricardo, Malthus, and John Stuart Mill wrote their powerful books" (p. 225). Frustrated by his conviction that "the divorce between academic economics and the intelligent public was nearly complete" (pp. 225–226), he determined to address the needs of the intelligent public and to subordinate his academic role.

When reflecting on his days at Columbia, Johnson reported that "the scholar who won my unreserved admiration and loyalty was John Bates Clark" (p. 123). Therefore, it is not surprising that when, in 1912 while teaching at Cornell, Johnson received an invitation from Clark, now head of the division of economics and history at the Carnegie Endowment for International Peace, to become his editorial secretary, Johnson accepted and a new phase of his career began.

From that point, Johnson's career was "triple-tracked." One major track, continuing from his Carnegie Endowment editorial work, featured the creation or assembly of written materials for public enlightenment. This track eventually included principal roles with journals of opinion, most notably the editorship of the newly created *New Republic*, distinctive contributions to *The Unpopular Review*, editorial work with the *American Journal of Adult Education*, *Social Research*, *The American Scholar*, and the *Yale Review*, and, ultimately, the working editorship of the first *Encyclopedia of the social sciences* (under the general editorship of E.R.A. Seligman). One observer later called the encyclopedia "the United States' most distinguished contribution to international scholarship" (Colm 1968: 261).

A second track was directed at Johnson's commitment to adult education, or, as Johnson put it, "continued education for the educated" (p. 274). The main fruit of this effort was his collaboration with James Harvey Robinson, Charles Beard, Thorstein Veblen, Herbert Croly, and others in the foundation of the New School for Social Research. The School opened its doors in 1919, and Johnson was soon to become its Director, a position he held until his "retirement" in 1945. During the 1930s, the New School's graduate faculty, as a "University in Exile," became a haven for European scholars fleeing Nazi persecution.

Finally, Johnson continued to practice "policy economics," with an emphasis on issues of land reclamation, community development, and antidiscrimination policy. His pen was his weapon in many other economic policy debates, and his popular writing was consistently on the side of humane reform.

In addition to his editorial and commentary work, his dedication to adult education, and his economic policy contributions, this remarkable individual also had a "second life" as a writer of fiction. He published two successful novels and three collections of short stories. All these works, in some way, address elements of his fundamental social concerns. One of his novels, *Spring Storm*, was published by Knopf in 1936, the year of his AEA presidency. His autobiography, *Pioneer's Progress*, was published in 1952 (when Johnson was 78 years old), and two collections of his short stories were published in the 1960s. One of these, *The Battle of the Wild Turkey and Other Tales*, was published to critical acclaim in 1963 when Johnson was 89. Alvin Johnson died in 1971 at the age of 96.

JOHNSONIAN ECONOMICS

As noted above, Alvin Johnson was, among other things, a codifier of the conventional economic wisdom of the first quarter of the twentieth century. Dorfman notes the "high regard" in which he was held "by circles representing the dominant viewpoint of formal economic theory" (Dorfman 1949: 420), and credits him with being "one of the keenest and most effective expositors of marginalist doctrine of the type formulated by John Bates Clark" (Dorfman 1959: 272). Yet, like Mill and Marshall, he was also extraordinarily creative in wielding the tools of economic analysis in unconventional ways to accomplish his "reformist" objectives. He was obviously unsatisfied by many of the conventional answers to economic and social problems. Gerhard Colm, a European émigré who served as a faculty member at the New School and later as head of the National Planning Association, has suggested that "in economics, Johnson might be characterized as a neo-classicist with strong social and institutional undertones" (Colm 1968: 260). This is not the place for a complete presentation of Johnson's economic ideas, but a few elements may illustrate his disciplinary ideas as well as his moral stance.

Although he was a master of conventional economics when operating within its formal boundaries, Johnson refused to be confined within those boundaries in his social commentary or policy analysis. He was consistent in his concern with the broader community impact of economic policy actions, his insistence on the importance of institutional factors in understanding economic outcomes, and his stress on the importance of dynamic factors.

For example, at the national level, he did, on occasion, advocate a kind of neomercantilism in his support of "protectionism as an instrument of nationalism." Acknowledging the economic cost of such a policy, he asserted it to be "an expense very often worth assuming, if it is a part of a systematic development policy" (Dorfman 1949: 422). In his work with the Bureau of Reclamation (he never did entirely break free from his rural roots), he argued similarly that "it may be worth while to spend public money lavishly on building an organic community of healthy, happy Americans, enjoying an American standard of living, and exciting emulation in social organization among other rural communities," while refusing "one dollar's subsidy" if the only result was "thousand-acre fields of sugar beets with migratory Mexican labor" (Dorfman 1959: 274). He was not anti-Mexican, but he was in favor of violating market allocational decisions only in cases where he could identify a positive social benefit. Johnson also utilized the concept of externalities (or Clark's "inappropriables") to justify public expenditure projects, such as railway construction, again in the service of community building (Dorfman 1949: 425).

Other examples of his awareness of the importance of social and institutional factors in economic outcomes abound. In one paper he dismissed liberal condemnation of slum landlords with the suggestion that one look at the "chain of institutional causes typified by scarcity of land, high prices of building materials, the incapacity of a raw immigrant population to pay for better habitations or to appreciate the need for light and air" that led to the emergence of such urban predators (Johnson 1954: 31).

Johnson's concerns also reached into the area of income distribution. Johnson's conviction was that "the daily earning of every able-bodied and willing worker shall be sufficient to satisfy all reasonable desires" (Dorfman 1949: 422–423)—a position not exactly consistent with his mentor, Clark's, normative interpretation of marginal productivity theory. Similarily to Veblen, he differentiated "productive" (obtained from production) from "exploitative" (resulting from distribution) income flows (Dorfman 1949: 421). In other policy areas, Johnson supported a minimum wage (to be adopted state by state), progressive income and inheritance taxes, trade unionism, and some government price regulation (such as railway rates). He distinguished between intra-industry competition (often lacking) and interindustry competition (frequently substantial).

Even in conventional price analysis, Johnson often found that "prevailing economics offered only a formal solution for much of the phenomena in the field of commodity values." Analytical problems could, of course, be cast in terms of supply and demand, "or into the 'more seductive terms of a balancing of utility and cost'," but such procedure "excluded from analysis 'all the problems of value and distribution that are refractory to the supply and demand analysis, that persist in all their original perplexity despite their subjugation under supply and demand equations'" (Dorfman 1949: 423). Johnson occasionally felt more comfortable with the Veblenian rhetoric of "fashionable consumption" than with more conventional analytic terms.

Perhaps Johnson's most succinct summation of his broad analytical approach is his observation that "[John Bates] Clark's system . . . was essentially static. . . . I was convinced that pure economics could offer no realistic theory of economic dynamics. In that, I believed, one had to go back to the underlying motives of men, through psychology and sociology and to the social-economic-historical forces underlying technical progress" (Johnson 1952: 154). In addition to this, and surprisingly for a mainstream codifier and eventual AEA president, Johnson understood capitalism to be a productive but transitory system of class relationships between "a class that rules and a class that is controlled" (Johnson 1954: 3). He astutely commented that "what the orthodox economists failed to observe is that so-called 'economic conduct' is class conduct. It is confined to the merchants and manufacturers of a competitive regime, whose daily life consists in the manipulation of exchange values" (Johnson 1954: 4). While Johnson admired the economic freedom that accompanied capitalism, he also argued that "the worker has paid for his freedom with increased insecurity of his lot" (Johnson 1954: 9). He saw government as the appropriate vehicle to restore some of that security.

Perhaps Johnson's economics was implicit in his youthful experiences in rural Nebraska. He exhibited, at an early age, a quite holistic understanding of both the benefits and costs of "economic progress." In his autobiography he distinguished between a "way-of-life" farm, which he loved, and a "cash farm," about which he was much more skeptical (Johnson 1952: 68–69). Or, more simply put, "as it was then, before the high prices of wheat and corn wrecked the landscape, the place was very charming" (Johnson 1952: 25). Market economics conferred benefits, but there was a social price to be paid.

ADVOCACY AND REFORMISM

The fact that Alvin S. Johnson was an extraordinarily bright person who became a skilled economist and held progressive policy views is interesting, but hardly unique. The most riveting facet of this remarkable career is the energetic and creative activism that brought Johnson's intelligence and morality directly to bear on significant social issues. There are few examples of persons so deeply enmeshed in the world of the academy who also establish such a strong record of activism. It is that record of social achievement that occupies much of the remainder of this chapter.

In his autobiography, Johnson reveals the motivation for his activist posture. "I felt," he wrote, "that I was my brother's keeper—a feeling that has been with me through life, with the concept of brotherhood expanded to include anyone needing help that I could give" (Johnson 1952: 32). This spirit imbued much of the work that Johnson undertook with great passion as well as talent. His advocacy and reformist activities flowed in several directions, but a predominant theme was a very broadly conceived "adult education" for a democratic society. A second important theme was the protection of human rights.

A central tenet of the Johnsonian faith was commitment to liberal democracy or democratic liberalism. "To me," he wrote, "liberal democracy affords the most favorable seedbed for the development of the individual, who is in the last analysis the source of all values, all true progress" (Johnson 1946: 9). He further argued that the satisfactory functioning of liberal democracy is dependent on two conditions. The first is "a peace that is not merely absence of war but an acceptance of the rights of other peoples and persistent effort to understand them and to cooperate with them in the work of civilization." Second, is "education not limited to the early years but continuing throughout active life" (Johnson 1946: 10). Such continuing education, and efforts toward international peace, established much of Johnson's activist agenda.

Commitments such as editorship of the *Encyclopedia of the Social Sciences*, or column writing for the *New Republic*, can be understood as educational ventures, broadly defined. But the institutional centerpiece of Johnson's dedication to adult education, and the focal point of much of his mature professionalism, was the foundation and direction of the New School for Social Research. The New School opened in 1919 as the result of the work of Johnson, Herbert Croly, James Harvey Robinson, Charles A. Beard, Thorstein Veblen, Mrs. Willard Straight, Mrs. George Bacon, "and other liberals" (Johnson 1952: 167). John Dewey, Harold Laski, Wesley C.

Mitchell, and Franz Boas are also frequently cited as participating founders (Krohn 1993: 60).

During the First World War, Croly and Johnson had discussed the establishment of an intellectually free American center for adult education on the model of the London School of Economics. The LSE, noted Nebraskan Johnson, "was not handicapped by mobs of beef-devouring alumni, passionate about football and contemptuous of scholarship" (Johnson 1952: 292). The discussion was given greater impetus to action in 1917 when Robinson and Beard both resigned from Columbia in protest over the dismissal of two colleagues who were seen to be insufficiently supportive of the U.S. war effort by university president Nicholas Murray Butler. The editorial offices of the *New Republic* quickly became the planning grounds for a new, independent, social science institution. Influenced by the ideas of John Dewey and Thorstein Veblen, it was not to be an undergraduate degree-granting college, but rather a center for social science research and adult education (Rutkoff and Scott 1986: 1–18). "[I]nternational understanding and a critical analysis of society were to be the guiding principles of the curriculum" (Krohn 1993: 60).

The history of the New School, with its illustrious faculty, novel mission, and provocative output, is itself a remarkable story that has been informatively chronicled elsewhere (Rutkoff and Scott 1986; Krohn 1993). Our purpose here is briefly to extract a sense of Alvin Johnson's reformist activism as reflected in that institution.

The more practical aspect of that activism involved Johnson as the administrative builder of the New School. Within a few years of its idealistic founding, the New School was floundering in practical difficulties. In 1922, Johnson was called upon to assume its directorship and to lead it to maturity. During his 23 years of official leadership he offered a blend of imagination, energy, and managerial skill that resulted in the expansion of program, broadening of curriculum, spread of influence, and construction of a Manhattan campus. The New School added degree programs, achieved accreditation, and was recognized as the leading adult education institution in the country. Johnson remained actively involved in New School activities well beyond his official retirement in 1945.

The more inspiring and humanistic side of Johnson's New School activism was his leadership in conceiving and implementing the "University in Exile" at that institution. As a result of his work in editing the *Encyclopedia of the Social Sciences*, Johnson had become familiar with leading scholars worldwide, and particularly in Europe. As the Nazi threat to the European intellectual community became increasingly apparent in the early 1930s, he mounted a massive effort to rescue threatened scholars and government leaders by finding them positions in "safe havens," many of them at the New School. Against massive apathy, Johnson raised both consciousness and money that facilitated the emigration of dozens of eminent scholars and their relocation at the New School and elsewhere. In so doing, he was able not only to save individuals, but also to preserve the German tradition in various areas of social science research. He was interested both in the lives and contributions of individual scholars, and in providing a beachhead for intellectual viewpoints counter to an American tradition that he believed to be overly narrow and constrained (Krohn 1993: 59–63).

The scholars brought to the New School's "University in Exile" in 1933 became the "New School Graduate Faculty in Political and Social Science" in 1934 (The New School 1963: 4). The "honor roll" list of "European Scholars and Artists Helped by the New School for Social Research between 1933 and 1945" (with substantial help from the Rockefeller Foundation) includes more than 180 names. A few of these are Paul Baran, Gerhard Colm, Mario Einaudi, George Katona, Emil Lederer, Claude Lévi-Strauss, Rudolf Littauer, Adolph Lowe, Bronislaw Malinowski, Jakob Marschak, Franco Modigliani, Hans Staudinger, Leo Strauss, and George Szell (Krohn 1993: 205–210).

A more modest, and less successful, extension of the "Johnson Rescue Effort" was the establishment of the "Alvin Corporation" in North Carolina. Despite its modest size and short existence, it reinforces the image of the "scholar/activist."

The Alvin Corporation took root at the confluence of two streams of Johnsonian interests, agricultural development and human rights. Drawing upon his Nebraska roots, Johnson, throughout his life, was interested in agricultural development and land reclamation projects. As noted earlier, he was interested in reclamation as an avenue to community development, which he saw as a sort of "externality" to successful farming.[3]

His commitment to human rights, liberal democracy, and non-discrimination—a consistent theme through all of Johnson's ventures—was particularly outraged by the Nazi persecutions in Europe. Johnson had been involved for a number of years with a group of Southern business, government, and agricultural innovators in a project designed to establish several cooperative agricultural communities in North Carolina.[4] The project met modest agricultural success, and, in the late 1930s, triggered in Johnson's head the idea to do something similar in order to resettle Jewish refugees from Europe. Johnson did the fund-raising, bought the land from one of his North Carolina collaborators, recruited the tenants, hired the manager, and brought the refugee truck farm into existence for ten families in 1940.

Now, more than fifty years later, a review of the Johnson files on the Alvin Corporation conveys the depth of his dedication to this project and to the people it was designed to benefit. Johnson, director of the New School, head of the New York "Committee Against Discrimination in Employment," and national economic and educational leader, was, nevertheless, intimately involved with the functioning of the 200-acre refugee farm. His correspondence with the farm managers covered such matters as details of fertilizer application, timely ditch-cleaning, disciplining of troublesome settlers, and securing appropriate agricultural advice. He also continued to be involved with fund-raising and public relations, and wrestled with the pain of extended economic losses from the project as farm conditions and product markets proved more troublesome than anticipated. Improved national economic conditions, which attracted some of the settlers into urban jobs, and continued farm losses finally resulted in cessation of the experiment in 1946.

Johnson, ever the Nebraska farm boy, surmised, "if I could have lived with the community I think it would have succeeded. . . . I could come down only at infrequent intervals, and when I came I was desolated by gardening tricks the settlers had missed" (Johnson 1952: 365). Nevertheless, he consoled himself with the observation that "morally, I think it paid. From first to last it has built ten families into the American structure." Unfortunately, he noted, "morality pays no dividends" (Johnson 1945).

The final aspect of Johnson's advocacy/reformism to be discussed here is his role in the passage of the first statute in this country prohibiting discrimination in employment. Because of Johnson's demonstrated dedication to civil rights and nondiscrimination, New York Governor Dewey asked him to chair that state's "War Council Committee Against Discrimination in Employment" in 1943. The committee had been established primarily to promote nondiscriminatory hiring in war-related industries. Johnson immediately seized upon it as a vehicle to promote nondiscrimination in all industries after the war, forcefully lobbied for greater budget, staff, and mandate, and, after years of political in-fighting and hard knocks, was able to celebrate the passage of the Ives–Quinn Bill which "barred discrimination in employment on account of race, color, creed or national origin" (The New School 1963: 5).

Subsequently, Johnson was asked to serve as a commissioner on the New York "Temporary Commission on a State University," and to chair the "Committee for Equality in Education" to root out discrimination in the New York public system of higher education. These efforts, reported Johnson, were "in large part animated by the outraged feelings of the Jewish intellectual public over the intrusion into American educational life of Old World antisemitism and its institution of the *numerus clausus*" or quota system (Johnson 1952: 392). These efforts also were successful, leading "to a law barring discrimination in student admissions to non-sectarian institutions of higher learning in New York State. This law, too, has been emulated by other states" (The New School 1963: 6).

There is more to recount, but limited space for recounting. There was work on child welfare, on international peace, a major study on prostitution in New York, and a study of library operations for the Carnegie Corporation. Is it any wonder that, in January 1946, Max Lerner opined in his column in *The Nation* that "on my select list of Americans of first-rate stature I cherish the name of Alvin Johnson" (Lerner 1946)? At that point Johnson still had twenty-five years of contribution ahead of him!

FINAL THOUGHTS

What conclusions can be drawn from this brief excursion into the social conscience of an American economist? Perhaps that economics, as a social science, is committed by human beings. Those human beings are particular products of nature and nurture whose value systems intrude upon their work—some perhaps more transparently than others. Alvin Johnson, very much like Mill and Marshall before him, exemplifies the intellectual who masters the intricacies of his science and who also understands the difference between disciplinary rectitude and social policy evaluation. Economic theory, for Johnson, was an intriguing and challenging intellectual puzzle to which he brought extraordinary mental power. Social policy required a broader evaluative perspective to which he brought the vision of his heart. In his eagerness to apply that vision to his policy work he differed from the more restrained enthusiasms of many of his professional colleagues.

With an insight again reminiscent of J.S. Mill, Johnson viewed industrial capitalism as an instrumental but transitory phase of human civilization. In one of his best-known essays, "The Soul of Capitalism," Johnson presented his evolutionary notion of the economic system, celebrated capitalism's contributions to human freedom and material well-being, acknowledged its "ugly" materialism, and predicted its demise—to be succeeded by an order in which "unbridled individualism" will be overtaken by a "spirit of fraternity . . . [that] will carry the principle of cooperation to lengths beyond present dreams" (Johnson 1954: 1–16). Perhaps his predictive powers are suspect; but his work, his reformist advocacy, was consistent with his vision.

Johnson understood and contributed to the internal logic of an economic system that led to "efficient" allocation and distribution outcomes, and he valued the institutional structure of an economic system that protected and extended human liberty. But he was always considerate of larger issues of costs and benefits as he weighed social policy actions in the community he inhabited. In a self-reflective short piece he prepared after his official "retirement," he commented on his long relationship with Justice Louis Brandeis. Johnson reported: "I was strongly attracted to Brandeis, and to the end of his life I never visited Washington without managing to wheedle an hour or two out of Brandeis. . . . [He] was for government by the people, at whatever necessary cost in efficiency" (Finkelstein 1948: 51). Johnson understood his own priorities.

Alvin Johnson's archived files at the University of Nebraska contain a revealing exchange of letters between himself and John Maurice Clark, a former student of Johnson's at Columbia, on the issue of Johnson's "Committee for Equality in Education" in 1947. Johnson had obviously written to solicit Clark's support for the Committee. Clark's response was masterful in its academic evasiveness, wondering about his own qualifications due to residence, expressing his own lack of specific information about the issues of discrimination, worrying about the intrusion of bureaucracy and regulation on processes of "slow, evolutionary development," and finally reminding Johnson of the "wertfrei" nature of economics (which he admitted could be an "unwarranted belief"). In any case, he verbosely demurred.

Johnson's reaction was a model of clarity and directness. "Of course," Johnson agreed, "you are the sole custodian of your own time, and if you haven't time to look into educational discrimination in the State of New York, and assure yourself whether it is a serious evil or not, I have no right to ask you to take the time." He continued, "I am a bit astonished that you have to 'assume' that there is discrimination. You must have heard of quota systems, of the requirement on college applications to supply also the mother's maiden name—in case the father's name is Fitzpatrick and the mother's name was Cohen. The technique of discrimination developed rapidly after the rise of Hitler," he instructed Clark. "As for the slow process of evolutionary development, this is as likely to work balefully as beneficially." Finally, Johnson concluded, "that the educational institution should be free to apply a flexible judgment I agree. But it isn't free when it is chained to a quota system, or hamstrung by racialism criteria" (Clark 1947; Johnson 1947).

There you have it. Johnson's voice seems to say: "I am who I am; I believe what I believe; my values influence my work. I can understand and replicate your theoretical formulations, but I must decide how and when they are appropriate for decisions about how human societies operate. Our human frailties may result in erroneous or misguided judgments, but I cannot pretend to leave my conscience at the door. I am intelligent enough to have some understanding of the world, and I am humane enough to want to try to make it better."

This chapter concludes with two observations about Johnson's autobiography, one omission and one inclusion. In his 400 pages of self-description, Johnson omits the fact that he attained the presidency of the American Economic Association. But he does let the reader know that, when he taught at the University of Nebraska in the first decade of this century, the economics department chair, W.G. Langworthy Taylor, "used as a text Mill's *Principles*, expurgated by J. Laurence Laughlin of all Mill's lapses into humanity" (Johnson 1952: 171–172). Johnson, throughout his career, was intent on putting them all back in.

NOTES

1 This chapter is a revision of a paper presented at the meetings of the History of Economics Society, Vancouver, BC, June, 1996. The author expresses appreciation to A. W. (Bob) Coats and Robin Neill for their helpful comments on an earlier draft, and to anonymous referees for thought-provoking suggestions. None of them bears responsibility for remaining clumsiness of thought or expression.

2 Most of the factual information in this section is drawn from Johnson's auto-

biography, *Pioneer's Progress* (Johnson 1952). All page references in this section not otherwise attributed refer to that volume.

3 In a letter to a potential supporter of the Alvin Corporation, Johnson noted that "in the Far West the railways figure that every new farmer is worth $1000 to them. He is worth at least another thousand to the local towns" (Johnson 1939).

4 Some of his proposals for agricultural cooperative communities appear in his 1932 article, "Relief from Farm Relief" (Johnson 1932).

REFERENCES

Clark, J.M. (1947). Letter to Alvin Johnson, September 7, Johnson Papers, University of Nebraska Library.

Colm, G. (1968). "Johnson, Alvin," *International Encyclopedia of the Social Sciences*, New York: Macmillan and Free Press, 260–262.

Dorfman, J. (1949). *The Economic Mind in American Civilization*, vol. 3, *1865–1918*, New York: Viking Press.

——— (1959). *The Economic Mind in American Civilization*, vols 4–5, *1918–1933*, New York: Viking Press.

Finkelstein, L. (ed.) (1948). *American Spiritual Autobiographies: Fifteen Self-Portraits*, New York: Harper.

Hollander, J. (ed.) (1927). *Economic Essays Contributed in Honor of John Bates Clark*, New York: Macmillan.

Johnson, A. (1927). "The Farmers' Indemnity," in J. Hollander (ed.), *Economic Essays Contributed in Honor of John Bates Clark*, New York: Macmillan, 215–228.

——— (1932). "Relief from Farm Relief," *Yale Review* 22 (September): 52–64.

——— (1936). *An Autobiographical Note: Alvin Johnson*, New York: Knopf.

——— (1937). "The Economist in a World in Transition," *American Economic Review* 27 (March): 1–3.

——— (1939). Letter to Mrs. Vincenza Coster, February 15, Johnson Papers, University of Nebraska Library.

——— (1945). Letter to Mr. Joseph Halle Schaffner, July 17, Johnson Papers, University of Nebraska Library.

——— (1946). *The Clock of History*, New York: Norton.

——— (1947). Letter to J. M. Clark, September 10, Johnson Papers, University of Nebraska Library.

——— (1952). *Pioneer's Progress*, New York: Viking Press.

——— (1954). *Essays in Social Economics*, New York: New School for Social Research.

Krohn, C. (1993). *Intellectuals in Exile: Refugee Scholars and the New School for Social Research*, Amherst, Mass.: University of Massachusetts Press.

Lerner, M. (1946). "Homage to Alvin Johnson," *The Nation*, January 5.

The New School for Social Research (1963). "Alvin Johnson: A Biographical Sketch," mimeo, Johnson Papers, University of Nebraska Library.

Rutkoff, P. and W. Scott (1986). *New School: A History of the New School for Social Research*, New York: Free Press.

16

ROBERT A. HEINLEIN AND ISSUES IN AMERICAN ECONOMICS

Robert P. Rogers

INTRODUCTION

Robert A. Heinlein is considered one of the premier science fiction writers of the twentieth century. Along with John W. Campbell, Isaac Asimov, Arthur C. Clarke, Theodore Sturgeon, A.E. Van Vogt, L. Sprague de Camp, and Lester del Ray, Heinlein laid the foundations of science fiction as we know it today. In Heinlein's fiction, one finds many of the issues with which twentieth-century mainstream American economists have grappled concerning government, money, scarcity, and production. The very plots of major stories and books such as "Life-Line" (1987a), *Waldo* (1950), *Magic, Inc.* (1950), *The Moon is a Harsh Mistress* (1966), and "The Roads Must Roll" (1987a) involve people facing these problems when obtaining their livelihood. In fact, Heinlein coined one of the most celebrated economic expressions of the twentieth century: "There ain't no such thing as a free lunch (TANSTAAFL)" (Heinlein 1966: 129).

Heinlein's views are consistent with much in mainstream American economics. Most American economists believe in a market-centered economy, the main differences among them being how much government intervention is needed for its efficient and equitable operation. Like many economists, Heinlein is a supporter of a market-centered economy in that he has a preference for the pursuit by individuals of their own goals in market settings.

Also like many American economists, Heinlein had a skeptical view of government manipulation of the economy. In Heinlein's works, governments are usually depicted as inefficient and often malevolent enterprises, frequently run for the benefit of their controllers. While these views definitely put Heinlein in agreement with the more conservative mainstream economists, the views are not all that inconsistent with most of the profession in America. Even very interventionist American economists insist on the demonstration of a costly externality before taking government action (Stiglitz 1988: ch. 3).

In his stories and novels, however, Heinlein reveals an element that contradicts much in the ideas of conservative and/or libertarian American economists. His works often seem to imply a need for and the ability of one individual to benignly manage and manipulate a whole economy. He seems to believe that market-centered societies with minimal government intervention do not arise and cannot continue without the heroic exertions of some all-knowing and all-wise individual.

In much of Heinlein, a presumption exists that one individual—computer if not human—has the ability to plan the future of a sophisticated technological economy. Apparently, Heinlein is unfamiliar with the problems created by the dispersed and subjective nature of economic information. The data needed to manage a modern economy are scattered among people throughout society, and gathering it in time for planners to make rational decisions is impossible. Furthermore, since much of this information involves consumer tastes and preferences which are difficult to ascertain and new technologies which are not clearly understood, it has a subjective and uncertain quality. This problem was first pointed out by the Austrian School of economics (see Vaughn 1980; Murrell 1983). Ironically, Heinlein, a free market advocate, makes the same mistake about information dispersal and scarcity that the early socialist planners did. Even one of his most libertarian novels, *The Moon is a Harsh Mistress*, seems to miss this aspect of the basic economic problem in that a computer successfully runs the Moon economy.

In contrast, American economists of almost all political views are acutely aware of this problem. Most assert that only a decentralized market economy can assimilate and deploy the information necessary to use a complicated technology producing billions of products to efficiently cater to the wishes of millions of people (e.g., see Colander 1995: 850–855).

To see how Heinlein's economic views might have developed, let us look first at a short biographical sketch. We shall then scrutinize the author's views as they are revealed in five of his important stories and novels: *Magic, Inc.*, *Stranger in a Strange Land* (1987c), *The Moon is a Harsh Mistress*, *Time Enough for Love* (1973), and *The Cat That Walks Through Walls* (1985). Examining how Heinlein confronts various economic situations gives the reader an indication of how well the core principles of economists are correlated with his views. Heinlein's major difficulty is his misunderstanding of the information problem. Even with his feel for microeconomic trade-offs and his comprehension of business problems, Heinlein fails to see how the dispersed and subjective nature of economic data can frustrate the efforts of a central planner.

In the concluding section of this chapter we shall attempt to show how this oversight occurred. We shall hypothesize that, first, the experience of the United States during Heinlein's life and, second, the limitation of the economist's view of human nature explain the tension between Heinlein's belief in market-centered economies and his partiality toward the all-powerful individual who can benevolently rule and manipulate whole societies.

HEINLEIN'S LIFE

Born in 1900, Heinlein spent most of his boyhood in Kansas City with summer vacations in the small town of Butler, Missouri, his birthplace. His grandfather in Butler was a country doctor and he strongly influenced the boy. His father, Rex Ivar Heinlein, was a salesman who, over time, sold an assortment of products, including farm machinery and greeting cards. While Rex Heinlein never became wealthy, he did rise far enough in society to be well connected to the local Democrat Party political machine, the Pendergast Organization. This connection would later give his son his first chance of fame and fortune.

Heinlein did well in school, being a high-ranking student who started junior college at a time when most people did not graduate from high school, let alone go on to college. It was in his second year of college that Rex Heinlein's political connections benefited Robert by securing him an appointment to Annapolis, America's elite naval officers' academy. Graduating twentieth in a class of 243, Robert Heinlein seemed set on a promising career in the Navy. After serving as a line officer on destroyers and battleships, he was assigned to one of the first Second World War-type aircraft carriers, the *Lexington*. On this ship, Heinlein worked on the development of a radical new technology, the flying of aircraft off of ships. But illness intervened, and Heinlein was medically retired from the Navy due to chronic tuberculosis.

After the Navy, he attempted several careers. Health prevented him from pursuing graduate school in physics and mathematics, and for medical reasons he moved to Colorado. There, he engaged in a number of businesses including mining, architecture, and real estate. He also made one run for political office. It was from his many experiences in his early manhood—the Navy, business, and politics—that Heinlein derived many of the future ideas for his fiction.

In 1939, in response to an advertisement for a writing contest, he wrote a science fiction short story, "Life-Line" (1987a). On finishing the story, he submitted it to *Astounding Science Fiction*, a somewhat more prestigious magazine than the one running the ad. The story was accepted, and following this initial success, Heinlein spent two prolific years writing and publishing short stories and serialized novels. Essentially, he had found his economic and social niche—within the science fiction community, he was considered among the best.

The Second World War cut short his rise in that field, but it certainly helped him with later works. With his background and training, he was assigned as a civilian to research at the Naval Air Materials Command in Philadelphia. In this work, Heinlein was joined by other science fiction writers and technocrats; among them were Isaac Asimov and L. Sprague de Camp. Probably most important to Heinlein's future in this group was a naval officer and engineer named Virginia Gerstenfeld. After a postwar divorce from his first wife, Heinlein married Gerstenfeld. She did much to further his career, first, by keeping him healthy enough to do his work and second, by developing his ideas.

Heinlein's subsequent (postwar) career can be divided into two periods (see also Franklin (1980) and Thorner (1989) for alternative divisions of his literary life). In the first period, Heinlein wrote in several genres, which included novels and short stories for science fiction specialty magazines and also for large general circulation publications such as the *Saturday Evening Post* and *Boy's Life*. His stories in *Boy's Life* were about youth in an interplanetary future. During this time, Heinlein not only reinforced his position of preeminence in science fiction, but also enjoyed a modicum of financial success.

His financial success was, in fact, one of the foundations for his second postwar period, lasting from 1960 until his death in 1988. In this period, he was able to concentrate mainly on novels. Generally very successful financially, these novels also became conduits for his ideas on society, in contrast to his earlier works in the 1940s and 1950s, which, while often presenting his particular views on society, were primarily motivated by financial and artistic goals.

It was with the 1959 dispute over publication of the novel *Starship Troopers* (1987b) that Heinlein began to concentrate on works expressing his own particular ideas. *Starship Troopers* was originally one of a series of works for youth contracted with the publisher, Scribner's. Positing that the voting franchise should only come with some form of governmental (usually military) service, the novel ran against the prevailing views of both the American intelligentsia and people. Scribner's rejected the book because of this apparently militaristic message, but Heinlein found another publisher. In spite of its politically incorrect premises, the book enjoyed both critical and financial success, winning the *Hugo* Award for the Best Science Fiction of the Year in 1959.

After his success with *Starship Troopers*, Heinlein published a book on which he had been working for some time, *Stranger in a Strange Land*. With this book, Heinlein broke through to a very wide audience. Its basically libertarian message seems to be at considerable odds with *Starship Troopers*. While the latter glorifies the military, or at least the infantry troopers, *Stranger in a Strange Land* celebrates an alternative life-style similar to those of the 1960s counterculture. Like *Starship*, *Stranger* enjoyed both critical and financial success, also winning the *Hugo* Award. However, just as the message of the first novel was roundly denounced by many literary critics, so the plot and character development of the later work was also attacked.

Nevertheless, the success of these two novels gave him the freedom to devote his full attention to other novels that express his often idiosyncratic views, and the last twenty-eight years of his career were devoted to writing such books. Among them are three of the five works on which we will concentrate in this chapter: *The Moon is a Harsh Mistress*, *Time Enough for Love*, and *The Cat That Walks Through Walls*.

ECONOMICS, GOVERNMENT, AND THE GREAT LEADER

Magic, Inc.

In this section, we examine the economic views expressed in five of Heinlein's stories and novels starting with the novella, *Magic, Inc.* This work exposes some of Heinlein's early views on the working of the capitalist system, revealing not only Heinlein's sympathy toward the entrepreneur, but also his views on the role of government in the system. In this story, first published in 1940, one can see ideas resembling the public choice school of economics. In fact, it could serve as an illustration of the public choice model of government regulation, often called rent-seeking (see Buchanan, Tollison, and Tullock 1981).

The narrative takes place in a middle-sized western American city with an economic organization and political system typical of early twentieth-century America. The *Magic, Inc.* society, however, is different in one way: in addition to the conventional technology, much of the construction, manufacturing, and, by implication, other economic activity is performed by way of magic. Through spells and conjurings, magicians, wizards, and witches build houses, make dresses, and provide other goods and services. Nonetheless, these spells and conjurations are not free goods, and they co-exist in competition with more conventional economic activity.

Businessmen thus employ magic in roughly the same way as they utilize other resources and technologies. If costs of magic are lower and the resulting product superior, they use it; if not, they obtain their goods through conventional means. Magic is an alternative part of the economic system, just like skilled workers, machine tools, and trucks. As with any other economic activity, there arises a perceived need—or, more accurately, demand—for regulation.

The story starts with the main protagonist, a building contractor called Archibald Fraser, receiving a visit from an unsavory character who threatens "bad luck" or "Nasty Business" if Fraser does not patronize a certain group of magicians. This group of magicians is headed by a Mr. Ditworth who had earlier approached Fraser to encourage him to join an association of businessmen who would buy only from magicians approved by and/or members of that association. Ditworth's ostensible goal is to raise the standards of the magic practice.

On the day following the threat, Fraser finds his office gutted, apparently by magic actions. Consulting Joe Jedson, a friend in the clothing business who uses magic somewhat more intensively, Fraser investigates the occurrence and tries to undo it through hiring some other magicians. At first, his efforts succeed, but later he finds that most of the magicians in the city have been forced into Ditworth's group. In addition, he learns that they have presented to the state legislature a bill that would give their association control of the magicians' trade. This bill would set up a board controlled by the association which would run a licensing procedure controlling entry into the magician market. This type of bill was and is very common in American state government. Similar legislation has been passed for trades such as veterinarians, optometrists, morticians, TV repairmen, car dealers, and, in one state, rock concert promoters. Thus it does not stretch our credibility that magicians would seek such legislation—providing, of course, that you can accept the idea of magic to begin with.

The plot follows the efforts of Fraser and his friends, who include Jedson and two independent magicians, Amanda Jennings and Joe Bodie, to block the legislation. In spite of their efforts, the bill passes and the expected results ensue. Higher magic prices drive the magician-dependent Jedson to bankruptcy. Fraser still has some ways of substituting for magic, and consequently he just manages to survive in his business.

An irresistible business opportunity involving magic folding umbrellas leads Fraser and his associates finally to foil Ditworth through the "Other World" from which the magic comes to earth. In their efforts, they are aided by a federal agent, Bill Kane, who had been investigating Ditworth for antitrust violations. Without Ditworth, the state law regarding the magicians' trade is revoked, and Fraser goes on to ultimate success in both the umbrella and contracting businesses.

In this story, Heinlein's sympathetic treatment of, first, the state governor and, secondly, the federal agent Kane, indicates that he still has some faith in the working of government. This book was written in 1940, and at that time Heinlein was still the left-wing Democrat who probably remembered that his education had come via the Pendergast machine. However, at least a hint of skepticism toward government action reveals itself in his account of Ditworth's machinations before the state legislature. A good indication of Heinlein's view of government—and that of many Americans (including some economists)—is betrayed in Fraser's observation on the state capital building:

> It gave me a warm feeling to climb up the big wide steps of the statehouse. The old ugly mass of masonry seemed to represent something tough in the character of the American people, the

> determination of free men to manage their own affairs. Our own current problem seemed a little smaller, not quite so overpoweringly important—still worth working on, but simply one example in a long history of the general problem of self-government.
>
> I noticed something else as I was approaching the great bronze doors; the contractor for the outer construction of the building must have made his pile; the mix for the mortar was not richer than six to one!
>
> (Heinlein 1950: 244–245)

Stranger in a Strange Land

In the novel, *Stranger in a Strange Land*, Heinlein comes closest to a view of the economy consistent with a market-centered economy. Heinlein's main protagonists in this book, however, view the market as merely a means of actuating people's desires rather than as an ideal social organization.

It is not so much in this novel's overall plot that Heinlein's economic ideas are revealed, but in the opinions expressed in certain subsidiary discussions. Nonetheless, a summary of the plot is necessary to put these discussions in context. Michael Smith is the love child of two astronauts on Earth's first voyage to Mars, but disaster strikes this expedition and he is left as the sole survivor. He is rescued and brought to Earth twenty years later by the second Earth-to-Mars expedition. In the meantime, he has been cared for and raised by the natives of Mars, the "Old Ones." These "Old Ones" are an omnipotent race of beings who have extraordinary physical and mental powers, some of which have been conveyed to Smith.

When Smith comes to Earth, the World Government tries to hold him in communicado because of his legal claim through a certain obscure law to all the resources of Mars and a large amount of other valuable property. However, he is rescued again by a number of characters who distrust the World Government. The principal of these characters is Jubal Harshaw, a physician, lawyer, novelist, and general manipulator of the social system. Out of kindness, Harshaw takes Smith in and then arranges with the government a modus vivendi that allows Smith his basic freedom and access to some of his wealth, while also satisfying the various rival factions within the government.

Once free from both imprisonment and economic worry, Smith sets out to find his goal in life. After some adventures with a carnival and a fundamentalist religious group called the Fosterites, Smith organizes his own religious group, to whom he teaches some of the physical and mental abilities that he had learned from the "Old Ones." This group becomes an extended family that is united not only by close friendship and love, but also often by what most people would call promiscuous sexuality. Smith's community from this novel thus became a model for many of the hippie communes of the 1960s and 1970s.

With his organization, Smith sets out to change the basic nature of Earth's society. Smith sees himself and his disciples as totally changing society, due primarily to the amazing abilities learned by Smith from the "Old Ones." One Smithite describes his views as follows:

> "This Setback is only apparent [the burning of Smith's principal temple building]," Sam assured him. "The egg was ready to hatch and now we'll spread out. Of course we'll go on having trouble—because no society will allow its basic concepts to be challenged with impunity. And we are challenging everything from the sanctity of property to the sanctity of marriage."
>
> (Heinlein 1987c: 400)

In spite of this almost anarchistic declaration, the Smithites are not against the market as much as they are against the present social and technical structure of society. In fact, they use the market to obtain what they want. The same Smithite, Sam, continues:

> "What happens to the market when illuminati know which stock will move?"
>
> "Do you know?"
>
> Sam shook his head. "Not interested. But Saul over there—that other big Hebe, my cousin—gives it grokking, with Allie. Michael has them be cautious, no big killings and they use a dozen dummy accounts—but any of the disciplined can make any amount of money at anything—real estate, stocks, horse races, gambling, you name it—when competing with the unawakened. No, money and property will not disappear—Michael says that both concepts are useful—but they're going to be turned upside down and people will have to learn new rules (the hard way, just as we have) or be hopelessly outclassed."
>
> (Heinlein 1987c: 400)

It is ironic that a book that was a cult classic in an era when the capitalist system was roundly denounced did not advocate changing this system, but actually suggested using the market. Most—though by no means all—of the 1960s radicals viewed the market as the core of a corrupt establishment. In contrast, Smith saw it merely as a tool through which his group could obtain their legitimate goals.

The passage quoted from above goes on to state that many special interest groups will be weakened or even destroyed by the extraordinary powers wielded by Smith and his group:

> What happens to the cloak and suit industry when clothing isn't necessary and women aren't so engrossed in dressing up (they'll never lose interest entirely)—and nobody gives a damn if he's caught with arse bare? What shape does "the Farm Problem" take when weeds can be told not to grow and crops can be harvested without benefit of International Harvester?
>
> (Heinlein 1987c: 400)

Here Heinlein presents a very good description of the dynamic nature of a market economy. Smith and his group, who set out to change totally the nature of society, see the market as merely a mechanism with which they can work—not as something that must be destroyed. (This is a view similar to that of Schumpeter (1962).) It is with this set of ideas that Heinlein comes closest to an adherence to a market-centered libertarian economy.

The Moon is a Harsh Mistress

Ironically, with *The Moon is a Harsh Mistress*, which of all Heinlein's novels most concerns the economic system, the author moves away from an unqualified belief in the market-centered society. In this novel, Heinlein reveals the contradiction between his views on the market-centered economy and on the need for one omnipotent and all-knowing individual to manipulate and control the whole of society. On the one hand, he portrays a Moon community which may be his ideal libertarian society where almost anything goes in the way of social and economic relationships. On the other hand, the lunar economy is almost totally controlled by Mike, a self-aware supercomputer. Mike not only administers the economy for the Earth-dominated colonial government but also operates many of the big businesses such as the telephone company.

As if running the economy and the phone company is not enough, Mike, along with his philosophical cohort, Dr. Barnardo LaPaz, carefully orchestrates a sequence of events that leads to the overthrow of the colonial government. It is this orchestration of events that reveals Heinlein's faith in the ability of certain individuals to comprehensively control a complicated human society. These two individuals, one electronic and one organic, are capable of both dealing with any contingency and influencing the actions of their enemies. Thus the lunar society presents a contradiction between the market-centered economy idealized by libertarians and the central core of this economy administered by an all-knowing computer.

To fully understand the contradiction that Heinlein displayed in this novel, one should examine first its setting and then its plot. The story begins with the Moon society (called Luna) as a penal colony, exporting hydrophonically grown food to a not overpopulated but inefficiently managed Earth. The population of Luna is made up of either convicts or the progeny of convicts. Due to differences in gravity, living on the Moon changes physiology so much that it is nearly impossible for a Moon native or a long-time resident to return to Earth. While the government pays only monopsonistic prices to the people growing the foodstuffs sent to Earth, the colonial administration—called the Authority—generally allows the "Lunies" to manage their own personal lives.

The result is a free-ranging society where conventions are derived very directly from present or recent conditions. For instance, polyandrous marriages exist because of the disproportionate number of males in the community. With only a few women present, polyandry seems a rational and fair way of dealing with the sexual and procreative desires of individuals. From this institutional setting, however, arise some rather interesting consequences. The men and women in these polyandrous relationships develop into closely knit and rather stable extended families, which provide for the young and the elderly, and also do much to promote the careers of adults.

The economic life of Luna is carried out by a variety of businesses, ranging from one-person contractors to an organization, owned and controlled by the Authority, which exports the food. Between those two extremes are a heterogeneous group of firms, varying greatly in size and type, and including extended family farms. Technology and history seem to dictate the curious organization of this economy.

While the Authority buys the foodstuffs exported to Earth, the actual growing of the food is done by small enterprises that combine the characteristics of the family farm and the American West mining prospector. In this story, water exists on the Moon in underground deposits, and the "farmers" exploit this resource by excavating large caves in which the light generated from the Sun is combined with the water and waste materials from the colony to produce the food. In these enterprises, there is an element of risk and a lack of scale economies that dictate rather small enterprises.

In contrast, scale economies seem to dictate the industrial organization of the export Authority. To propel the food to Earth, the Authority, after purchasing the produce, operates a gigantic slingshot capable of handling all the food traffic. This slingshot is what American antitrust authorities define as an "Essential Facility."

Often, the idiosyncratic organization of Luna's large collection of enterprises is due not so much to technology as to the peculiar institutional history of the Moon colony. For instance, the insurance industry—instead of being a group of staid private bureaucracies—consists of a profusion of small "bookies" willing to make odds on most any event. Apparently, these "bookies" arose from the prison conditions of the first arrivals on the Moon.

On Heinlein's Luna, a larger share of the economy is run by the private sector than is the case either on our present-day planet or on the Earth in the novel. When not provided by the extended family, education is offered by groups of private competing companies: for example, Professor LaPaz is one of these education entrepreneurs. In addition, law and order is predominantly enforced by a set of private judges responding to citizen arrests. Disputes are also handled by a private mediation industry. Violence in the form of duels is sanctioned. However, uninvited assaults are a rarity; assaults on women especially are swiftly punished by the predominantly male population, by whom women, being few in number, are highly valued. As H. Bruce Franklin states, "[Luna] embodies many features of Heinlein's anarchist utopia" (Franklin 1980: 162).

Even though the Authority pays the Lunies only a monopsonistic price for the Earth-bound foodstuffs, lunar society is reasonably stable. The Lunies grumble, realizing that they are being economically exploited, but they also see that compared to past societies and even to their contemporary Earth they are, in fact, quite affluent. Thus little impetus exists for change, even though the Authority is neither particularly popular nor very strong militarily.

What leads to change is the recognition by Professor LaPaz that the lunar economic and ecological situation is not stable. The export of foodstuffs by the Authority is depleting nonreplaceable resources on the Moon. The nutrients provided by biological waste materials, the lunar soil, and the underground water are all being sent to Earth and not returned. LaPaz predicts that the system will eventually break down.

Mike, the computer, confirms Professor LaPaz's analysis and estimates that this drain on resources will lead to a breakdown in the lunar economy in about seven years. Realizing that the Authority, an agent of the nations of Earth, will never stop the export of food, a small group plans to overthrow the Authority and set up an independent lunar government which would stop this exportation. The group consists of Mike, LaPaz, and two other protagonists, Manuel Garcia O'Kelly, the narrator—who stumbles into the plot as a computer programmer—and Wyoming Knott, an attractive female associate of LaPaz. (How Mike, the main computer of the Authority, becomes a revolutionary is detailed in the story.)

The group follows an elaborate strategy developed by LaPaz and Mike. A mixture of political intrigue, diplomatic maneuvering, and military action takes place that eventually leads to the replacement of the Authority by an independent lunar government and the recognition of that government by the Earth nations. Most of the novel describes the implementation of the scheme conceived by Mike and LaPaz.

At the end of the novel, however, LaPaz dies within sight of victory, and unascertained battle damage to the facility where he is housed causes Mike to lose his self-awareness. After the loss of these individuals, the newly independent lunar government moves toward the semisocialized regime that Heinlein portrays on Earth—and implicitly asserts is everywhere.

In *The Moon is a Harsh Mistress*, Heinlein describes what many consider his ideal society, offering maximum social and economic freedom for the individual. Yet the action in the novel implies that the society cannot exist without an all-powerful, all-knowing, and almost dictatorial leadership. Ironically, it seems that only under the guidance of the omnipotent Mike can the ideal libertarian lunar society exist.

Time Enough for Love

In the fourth work examined here, *Time Enough for Love*, Heinlein describes the life of Lazarus Long, the character with whom he most closely identifies. Many of his basic views on life, philosophy, and economics are revealed in the actions, attitudes, and opinions of Lazarus Long. An examination of the plot for this novel reveals much about Heinlein's views on the economy, the government, and the individual.

As of the year 4272, when *Time Enough for Love* opens, Lazarus Long is the "Senior," the oldest living member of the human race. In that year, Lazarus Long secretly checks into a fleabag hotel on the planet, Secundus, in order to die by slow starvation. But his plans are interrupted by Ira Weatheral, the head of the planet. Secundus is the home planet of the Howard families, a group of people who have been bred for long life and of which Lazarus Long is of course the oldest member.

To put these actions in context, the history of the Howard families as shown in an earlier work, *Methuselah's Children* (1986), should be examined. The families arose out of the Howard Foundation established in the late nineteenth century by Ira Howard, a tycoon who died an early death. Desiring that others should not have the same problem, Ira Howard left his fortune to a foundation whose objective is to develop longevity.

The method chosen by the Foundation to achieve their aim was selective breeding to encourage long life. The Foundation searched out families characterized by longevity and arranged for them to introduce their children to the children of similar families. If these children were married, the Foundation would pay the couple quite a large sum of money for each child. Thus, through these introductions and the child subsidy, the Howard Foundation bred a group of long-life families. Over time, this process expanded the average life of the Howard family members to well over 150 years.

In the twenty-fourth century, this longevity leads to difficulties with the rest of the population. As documented in *Methuselah's Children*, the general public believes that the longevity of the Howard families is due to secret medicines hoarded by the families. In popular argot, the members of the families are called "Methuselahs." In truth, however, the Howard families' longevity is due solely to interbreeding. *Methuselah's Children* describes how the Howard families are rescued from persecution and possible pogrom by a group of supremely competent people (with the connivance of one sympathetic prominent figure in the government). Essentially, the group steals an interstellar spaceship in order to move the families off of the earth. After a number of adventures with alien life-forms, the families then return to Earth where they find that longevity remedies have been discovered. Consequently, the envy and persecution of the Howards is no longer an issue.

One of the main characters in *Methuselah's Children* is Lazarus Long, born Woodrow Wilson Smith, one of the very early Howard family members, in 1912. He has managed to live on into the twenty-fourth century, and now, during the next 1,800 years, he goes on to many other adventures. Thus part of this next novel, *Time Enough for Love*, narrates in flashbacks several of these adventures, while the other strand, interspersed with these flashbacks, carries on the story of the Senior after his rescue from suicide by Ira Weatheral. At this time, not only can people live a very long time indeed, but also it is possible to rejuvenate people to a younger and healthier biological age.

Lazarus Long, the Senior, having gone through the rejuvenation process many times before, chooses not to subject himself to it again basically because he sees no further reason for living. His attitude is not that life is bad, but rather that he has experienced all that life has to offer and cannot see any point in living on. When Weatheral and his associates interfere with his planned death, the Senior is piqued and demands that he be allowed the suicide option which is part of the standard rejuvenation contract.

Weatheral and his associates first prevent Lazarus Long from exercising that option by means of an elaborate scheme of trickery. Then they persuade Long to reconsider rejuvenation if they can find for him some suitable endeavor that will keep him occupied and enthusiastic. Many ideas are discussed, including the possibility of transforming the Senior into a woman, and developing from that idea, a project which involves presenting Lazarus with two female clones.

Finally, Weatheral and his sensate computer, Minerva, propose a tripart program for Lazarus. The first part is colonizing another planet where Lazarus Long and his friends can run matters more or less as they please. Ira Weatheral, being a rarity among humans—a head of state who does not really like his job—joins them. The second part of the Weatheral–Minerva program to keep Lazarus Long alive is to surround him with women; though not explicitly stated, the plot makes this second ploy obvious. The third part is a new avocation for Lazarus, time travel, the objectives of which are not entirely clear.

Subsequently, Long does go on a time-travel voyage—to the time of his childhood, the 1910s. He meets his grandfather, mother, and his earlier five-year-old self. He falls in love with his mother, Maureen, and consummates an oedipal affair, but at a very high cost. His love for his mother and regard for his grandfather lead him to enlist in the First World War American army. He is almost killed, but just in time is rescued by his time-traveling female clones.

Like *Stranger in a Strange Land*, the economic environment in *Time Enough for Love* is secondary to Heinlein's exposition on personal life. The economic views that come through, however, are almost identical to those in *The Moon is a Harsh Mistress*. There exists the same dichotomy between a libertarian society and the need for the benevolent controlling individual. Heinlein expresses a desire for a nonintrusive government which allows individuals to do most of what they want. Nevertheless, such a government does not seem to exist in his novels without being manipulated by some omniscient ruler.

This incongruity is illustrated by the political regime on Secundus at the time when the Senior is rescued from his own suicide. Ira Weatheral is the absolute ruler of this world by authority of the charter of the Howard Foundation which originally owned the planet. Weatheral abides by the dictum that "The government that governs best is the government that governs least." Early in the book, he expresses these feelings about his job:

> Despite what I told the Senior, my ancestor Grandfather Lazarus, I work hard in governing Secundus. But only in thinking about policy and in judging the work of others. I don't do donkey work; I leave that to professional administrators. Even so, the problems of a planet with more than a billion people can keep a man busy, especially if his intention is to govern as little as possible—as that means he must keep a sharp eye out and his ear tuned for signs that subordinates are doing unnecessary governing. Half my time is used in the negative work of plucking such officious officials and ordering that they never again serve in any public capacity. Then I usually abolish their jobs, and all jobs subordinate to them. I have never noticed any harm from such pruning.
>
> (Heinlein 1973: 47)

Even with this attitude, however, Weatheral sees problems for the government that most advocates of a market-centered economy and certainly libertarians would eschew:

> This leaves me too little time for my prime work: thinking about policy. The purpose of my government is never to do good, but simply to refrain from doing evil. This sounds simple but is not. For example, although prevention of armed revolution is obviously part of my main duty, i.e. to keep order, I began to have doubts about the wisdom of transporting potential revolutionary leaders years before Grandfather Lazarus called it to my attention. But the symptom that roused my worry was so null that it took ten years for me to notice it: During those ten years there was not one attempt to assassinate me. By the time Lazarus Long returned to Secundus for the purpose of dying this disturbing symptom had continued twenty years. This was ominous, and I realized it. A population of one billion-plus so

> contented, so uniform, so smug that not one determined assassin shows up in a double decade is seriously ill no matter how healthy it looks.
>
> (Heinlein 1973: 47–48)

Apparently Ira Weatheral seems to believe that a function of government is to alter the nature of the population instead of merely serving it. This exhibits Heinlein's belief in the ability of one or a few humans to calculate the good of a population, a view that is contrary not only to libertarians but also to thinkers and economists of many other persuasions. Most American economists as well as many others are skeptical about, and often afraid of, attempts by government to change the basic nature of the population. Eventually, however, Weatheral decides that the problem of a too complacent population is beyond his or his computer's competence, and so he joins Lazarus Long on another planet where his type of human is more prevalent.

The subsequent experience on Secundus illustrates Heinlein's conviction that a good strong leader is necessary for optimal, nonintrusive government. Ira Weatheral's successor, Arabelle Foote-Hedrick, is a meddlesome busybody who insinuates government into all areas of people's lives. (Heinlein makes it clear that it is not Arabelle's gender but her character that is objectional. Apparently, she is not the choice of Ira Weatheral and his faction, which now includes the Senior. They wanted another woman, Susan Barstow, to be the chief on Secundus.)

This view is buttressed by Heinlein's excursion into monetary matters in one of the flashback episodes in *Time Enough for Love*. At a time much earlier in his life than Ira Weatheral's era, Lazarus Long, under the name Ernest Gibbons, is the leader of the colonists on an unsettled planet called New Beginnings. Long/Gibbons chooses not to be the political leader of the colonists, but instead becomes a small town merchant banker. In addition to owning the local trading post, which sells supplies and buys agricultural produce for export (to where is not clear from the text), he owns the local bank. Along with doing the usual banking services, loans, and deposits, this bank maintains the local currency or money supply. Gibbons manipulates and stabilizes the currency's unit of account by tying it to the price of wheat. Thus he creates a commodity currency similar to the gold standard.

Eventually, people become dissatisfied and demand that the government take control of the currency and the bank. Long/Gibbons, foreseeing this outcome, has hedged himself. When the actual demand is made, therefore, he quickly and willingly turns control of the bank over to the local government, who have no idea what to do. Presumably, the currency then goes to pieces, but before that happens Long/Gibbons goes on to other adventures.

Again, this episode demonstrates Heinlein's concept that good government, a stable currency, and presumably a stable economy can only be achieved by the all-wise, all-knowing individual. Essentially, even a commodity-based currency can only be operated by such an omnipotent individual.

This experience contradicts many free-market monetary thinkers, ranging from gold standard advocates (Mises 1949: 418) to Milton Friedman (Friedman 1956; Friedman and Schwartz 1963), who argue for their particular monetary regimes on the basis that such systems are invulnerable to tinkering by government or any central authority. Their goal is a stable monetary system that can be maintained, even though the political structure may be controlled by fools. Heinlein seems to believe that this aim is impossible to achieve, at least on planet New Beginnings.

The Cat That Walks Through Walls

In *The Cat That Walks Through Walls*, we are first shown the ultimate contradiction between Heinlein's views of the economy and of society in general, and then we learn how he resolves that contradiction. First, Heinlein and his chief protagonist, Richard Ames, born Colin Campbell, believe that society should be organized in a way which allows individuals to fulfill their economic and personal goals. Conversely, Heinlein also believes that an elite group has the ability—and, possibly, a duty—to manipulate society and, ultimately, reality in order to maximize some idea of the social good. Furthermore, he seems to posit that participation in such an enterprise may be the supreme fulfillment for the individual.

To understand this contradiction, an examination of Campbell/Ames's character and the novel's plot and setting is necessary. The chief character, Colin Campbell, like the author, is a partly (but far from totally) disabled veteran. Campbell, however, has had a more colorful military career than Heinlein. During the battle in which he is wounded, Campbell had been accused of committing cannibalism, and even though he and his colleagues had been cleared of that charge, he now chooses to live under a pseudonym as Richard Ames. To make a living, Campbell/Ames writes science fiction adventure stories in which he exhibits very much Heinlein's ideals and those of the twentieth-century American: He believes in self-sufficiency and self-fulfillment, and he is very much against the government providing for the individual and protecting him from the consequences of his or her own actions (see Heinlein 1985: 190 and 197–199 for Campbell's treatment of the hanger-on, Bill).

The plot starts when Campbell/Ames's theater date with Gwen Novak is later interrupted by an unwelcome visitor at their dinner table. Campbell/Ames lives in the universe described in the earlier novel, *The Moon is a Harsh Mistress*, but 100 years after the revolution. Given his social and philosophical predilections, it is not surprising that Campbell/Ames is a naturalized citizen of the Moon. However, he lives in a man-made satellite of the Moon, called the Golden Rule habitat. This habitat seems even more in line with Campbell/Ames's social views than the Moon. The government of this habitat is a private for-profit corporation which makes its money by renting the space in the habitat to people and businesses, most of whom earn their income from exporting their goods and/or services. Campbell/Ames, an author catering for an audience spread throughout the solar system, is fairly typical.

The unwelcome visitor is a nondescript character named Enrico Schultz, who then proceeds to be murdered. Following this murder, the habitat administration, in spite of its philosophical agreement with Campbell/Ames, no longer finds him welcome in its domain. Campbell/Ames and Gwen Novak therefore leave the habitat for the Moon, where they have a series of misadventures. From much of the action and Campbell/Ames's comments, it is obvious that conditions on the Moon have deteriorated since the revolution described in *The Moon is a Harsh Mistress*. Anyway, the upshot of this series of misadventures is that Campbell/Ames comes into the world of Lazarus Long and the Time Corps.

Headed by Long, his relatives, and other cohorts, the Time Corps is an organization that operates in a multiverse where a large number of parallel universes or realities coexist, and people journey from one reality to another in various vehicles. People can also travel between points in time within one universe as well as between different universes. Long's cohorts consist not only of his friends and relatives from the world of *Time Enough for Love*, but also of characters from other Heinlein novels. Among them are mathematicians, Hilda and Jacob Burroughs, from *The Number of the Beast* (1980), Jubal Harshaw from *Stranger in a Strange Land*, and computer wizard Manuel Garcia O'Kelly from *The Moon is a Harsh Mistress*. Furthermore, Gwen Novak turns out to be Hazel Stone, a young girl at the center of the earlier lunar revolution and now an agent of the Time Corps.

The Time Corps is engaged in changing the sequence of events in the various universes in ways that improve human welfare. Long and his colleagues encounter two difficulties in this task.

In the first place, there exist two types of people or beings who seem out to thwart the efforts of the Time Corps. Type one beings oppose the Time Corps either because they have different conceptions of social welfare or simply because they are evil. Groups in this type work for their own purposes, which are generally opposed to the objectives of the Time Corps. (Indeed, one of their actions precipitated the plot of the earlier novel, *The Number of the Beast*. In that novel, one of these groups recognized that the work of mathematician, Jacob Burroughs, would give humans access to the multireality multiverse. In spite of the efforts of this group, Lazarus Long and his relatives from *Time Enough for Love* are already in this multiverse. In *The Number of the Beast*, Burroughs and Long's group became allies.)

Type two of those bent on thwarting the Time Corps are authors who created universes in their works of imagination. In Heinlein's multiverse, the very act of artistic creation can lead to the settings of the works becoming actual universes. Apparently the creation of these universes can affect other realities in the multiverse, and thus create implementation problems for the Time Corp. (There is definitely an element of surrealism in Heinlein's later novels.)

The second major difficulty for the Time Corps is that it does not have sufficient information to predict the consequences of its actions. In several episodes, Time Corps' actions actually lead to a deterioration in the conditions it had been attempting to improve. Here, the Time Corps leadership fails to recognize something that Austrian economists pointed out to the Socialists (Vaughn 1980; Murrell 1983), namely, that in a complicated environment no one can totally predict the consequences of one's actions. The Austrian economists concluded that it was beyond the ability of any one individual or small group to gather and process the information needed to make comprehensive plans directing a complex society. The Time Corps could opt for the Austrian solution to the problem which would entail introducing an element of laissez-faire into their operations.

Instead the Corps decides that an all-knowing superthinker is needed to see into the future sufficiently to be able to estimate the consequences of their actions. Consisting of mathematicians and historians in addition to supreme people of action like Lazarus Long, it is not surprising that the Time Corps would try to totally control the situation. Their research on the history of their various universes indicates that Mycroft Holmes or Mike, the computer that orchestrated the lunar revolution in *The Moon is a Harsh Mistress*, was such an individual before he lost his consciousness. According to Gwen/Hazel, the computer is actually asleep and needs only to be awakened.

The Time Corps' plan to rescue Mike the computer leads to the involvement of Colin Campbell and the series of events in the novel. For reasons not apparent to me or, more importantly, to the character himself, the Time Corps badly needs Colin Campbell to effect the violent rescue of Mike. Much of the novel narrates the attempts of the Time Corps personnel to persuade Campbell to participate in this rescue. Campbell is skeptical, but his love for Gwen/Hazel and his sense of adventure prevail over his feeling that the Time Corps has not presented a sufficiently compelling case for his participation. The book ends with the rescue of Mike the computer.

This description of the novel's setting reveals much about Heinlein's basic economic and social views, but perhaps more emphasis is needed to better highlight the issues which concerned Heinlein. Thus the story begins in the type of environment that Heinlein would want to live in. On the Moon, a market economy thrives, though with an undesirable growth in government involvement. On the Golden Rule habitat, the market seems all-pervasive, but external forces intrude and destroy Campbell/Ames's place in this world.

He is then thrown into the multiverse milieu of Lazarus Long, Hilda, and Jacob Burroughs, where one can enjoy the libertarian—and libertine—

life-style of the Longs with their extended marriages, ubiquitous sexual contacts, and apparently immense wealth. In this world, however, there is again danger from the outside, and an overwhelming responsibility not only to react to this danger, but also to remedy the situation. In this setting, the Time Corps both protects the worlds and realities of the Longs and the Burroughs, and also tries to improve the environment of other universes.

HEINLEIN'S VIEWS AND HIS EXPERIENCE

An interesting analogy can be made between the Time Corps in *The Cat That Walks Through Walls* and United States foreign policy in the twentieth century. It may explain much about Heinlein's discrepant views on economics and government. Ostensibly, early twentieth-century United States, like Campbell, was merely attending to its own affairs. Yet outside forces led to it becoming involved in world politics. First, the United States protected its close kindred nations from imperial Germany, which arguably led in turn to its having to protect itself from the Nazis. These actions led to a further impulse to manipulate the rest of the world in such a way that it was better off, at least by American standards. Some assert that it was this impulse and not the need for protection that led to the U.S. difficulties initially with imperial Japan and latterly with communist Russia.

Impacting on our analysis of Heinlein, what is interesting about American foreign policy is not the nature of American action in the world but its influence on individual lives. The war-making and peace-making efforts of the United States involved many of its citizens in very interesting and often heroic situations. In this environment, Heinlein spent what were probably many of the happier years of his life—in the Navy and in the Second World War research at the Philadelphia shipyard. Individual effort in great social enterprises such as the U.S. involvement in the World Wars and in the Cold War may well be Heinlein's idea of supreme individual fulfillment.

This idea of service to a greater cause realizing personal fulfillment seems also consistent with the theme of many of Heinlein's works. In *Starship Troopers*, the heroes are cast in the role of super infantrymen in a space-age fighting force. Since this force is fighting an only cryptically described enemy, the major emphasis of the book is on the character of the troopers. In *Time Enough for Love*, when Lazarus Long is presented with the option of going into the First World War, there is not even an intellectual argument—only the loss of his contacts with his family and oedipal lover, Maureen. Having come from the future, he knows well the dubious outcome of that conflict, and therefore some internal desire or need must lead Long into this precarious endeavor.

In *The Cat That Walks Through Walls*, again a conflict exists between the individual and the society that wants him to participate in its great social enterprise. Colin Campbell resists until the last moment the efforts of Lazarus Long and the Time Corps to entice him into the Mike rescue effort. It is not clear that intellectually he is ever convinced that it is a worthwhile endeavor. As with Long and the First World War, Campbell apparently has an internal need to be part of the great heroic enterprises such as the Time Corps.

What arguably is more important to Heinlein, therefore, is less the ultimate goal of great social enterprises such as war than the self-fulfillment that participation gives to individuals. This may explain the contradiction in his economic views. While he favors a market economy and its social milieu, his characters ultimately gravitate toward great social enterprises such as the First World War and the endeavors of the Time Corps.

Emerging continually from Heinlein's work is that contradiction between his belief in a market-centered society and his ideal of the omnipotent all-knowing individual. On the one hand, he believes that the market-centered libertarian society is the best economic and social environment for most humans. On the other hand, he seems to believe that ultimate personal fulfillment only comes from engaging in enterprises that would not occur in a smoothly running market society. Moreover, he seems to posit that only through the intervention of an omnipotent individual can a market-based libertarian society survive.

One might surmise that such a contradiction in Heinlein indicates how uninfluential the insights from economics have been for the rest of society. Another conjecture, however, may better explain the contradiction. Perhaps, the difference arises less from Heinlein's lack of economic awareness and more from the limitation of the economic worldview. Most economic analyses assume that men and women are selfish maximizers working at the margin. This paradigm view presents men and women as boring, banal, calculating machines.

In contrast, Heinlein sees humans as noble creatures searching for the greater fulfillment that comes only with heroic exertions—a concept that can be seen most vividly in the life of Lazarus Long. Many times Long had the opportunity to settle into a quiet bourgeois life. For instance, he had a standing offer to be the head of the quiescent planet, Secundus. Even when he was Ernest Gibbons on New Beginnings, he could easily have prevailed on the disaffected population to allow him to continue managing the bank and its money supply. Instead, he moved on to further adventures, eventually leading the Time Corps.

Thus the difference between Heinlein's market ideal and the prevalence of the omnipotent and omniscient hero in his works may indicate as much a shortcoming in the economic worldview as any deficiency in Heinlein's perception. While the economic model is adequate for the day-to-day life of most people, it is inadequate for the total self-fulfillment exemplified by Heinlein's heroes. Contrast Ira Weatheral running his complaisant planet with Professor LaPaz in *The Moon is a Harsh Mistress* struggling to save lunar society. Which one seems more interesting and heroic, and which constitutes a better story?

REFERENCES

Buchanan, J.M., R.D. Tollison, and G. Tullock (1981). *Toward a Theory of the Rent-Seeking Society*, College Station, Tex.: Texas A&M Press.

Colander, D.C. (1995). *Economics*, 2nd edn, Chicago: Irwin.

Franklin, H.B. (1980). *Robert A. Heinlein: America as Science Fiction*, Oxford: Oxford University Press.

Friedman, M. (1956). *Studies in the Quantity Theory of Money*, Chicago: University of Chicago Press.

Friedman, M. and A.J. Schwartz (1963). *A Monetary History of the United States, 1867–1960*, Princeton: Princeton University Press.

Heinlein, R.A. (1950). *Waldo* and *Magic, Inc.*, 1 vol., New York: Ballantine Books.

——— (1966). *The Moon is a Harsh Mistress*, New York: Putnam.

——— (1973). *Time Enough for Love*, New York: Ace Books.

——— (1980). *The Number of the Beast*, New York: Ballantine Books.

——— (1985). *The Cat That Walks Through Walls*, New York: Ace Books.

——— (1986). *Methuselah's Children*, Riverdale, NY: Baen Publishing Enterprises.

——— (1987a). "Life-Line" and "The Roads Must Roll," in *The Past Through Tomorrow*, New York: Ace Books, 15–33.

——— (1987b). *Starship Troopers*, New York: Ace Books.

——— (1987c). *Stranger in a Strange Land*, New York: Ace Books.

Mises, L. von (1949). *Human Action: A Treatise on Economics*, New Haven: Yale University Press.

Murrell, P. (1983). "Did the Theory of Market Socialism Answer the Challenge of Ludwig von Mises? A Reinterpretation of the Socialist Controversy," *History of Political Economy* 15: 92–105.

Schumpeter, J.A. (1962). *Capitalism, Socialism and Democracy*, 3rd edn, New York: Harper Torchbooks.

Stiglitz, J.E. (1988). *Economics of the Public Sector*, 2nd edn, New York: Norton.

Thorner, J.L. (1989). *A Guide Through the Worlds of Robert A. Heinlein*, New York: Gryphon Books.

Vaughn, K.I. (1980). "Economic Calculation under Socialism: The Austrian Contribution," *Economic Inquiry* 18 (October): 535–554.

Part VI

AMERICAN ECONOMISTS AND THE WORLD

17

THE INTERNATIONAL DIMENSION OF AMERICAN ECONOMICS[1]

Craufurd D. Goodwin and Stephen Meardon

THE EARLY YEARS: TURNING INWARD

Before the American Revolution, economic thinkers in the American colonies necessarily thought in global terms. After all, they were part of the British Empire, which was present on all the continents, and as it prospered so might they. They argued against a variety of imperial policies that seemed inimical to their local welfare, such as the Navigation Acts, metropolitan monopolies in the sale of such goods as tea, and taxation without representation. But always these were disputes within an imperial family on which, it must be remembered, the sun never set.

Benjamin Franklin, a leading example of an enlightened North American Mercantilist writer, was highly optimistic about the ultimate place of America within the British Empire. He saw the old world nearly fully populated and the new as brimming with undeveloped resources and opportunities. It was necessary in America mainly to think of how best to exploit the open spaces. Franklin was confident that the imperial center of gravity would ultimately shift westward and that even the seat of government would move from London to America. The implication of this train of thought was that the colonists for their own good needed to stay well informed both about the economic details of the empire and about the prevailing state of thinking in Britain about economic policies (see Dorfman 1966: 178–206).

The new conception articulated during the second half of the eighteenth century, and epitomized in Adam Smith's *Wealth of Nations*, of a world economy made up of freely interconnected national markets and with interference from government mainly to assure peace and justice, could be welcomed by colonists whether or not they understood the theoretical underpinnings of the policy conclusions. Franklin, for example, applauded the writings of Smith and the Physiocrats while still thinking in Mercantilist categories. After all, notions like laissez-faire and extension of the market leading to improved division of labor were wholly consistent with the colonists' longstanding arguments that they should be afforded the benefits of empire without the extraction of so many rents, upon which the imperial authorities were insistent.

This habit of thought began to change in the years surrounding the Revolution, as American economic thinkers became increasingly disgusted and dismayed by British colonial policy. They concluded that the practices of interfering with and restraining colonial markets could be justified neither through enlightened Mercantilist thinking nor with the market analysis of Smith and Quesnay. Americans needed to break free not only politically, but also intellectually, from Britain and the European continent.

Thomas Jefferson developed this idea to some length. Only in the representative government of a republic, Jefferson claimed, might reason be expected to prevail. Since all of the rest of the world suffered under some comparable despotism to that of Britain, the new United States was the only nation that might yield rational thinkers and sensible policy. Indeed, the correct path for the United States to follow at the moment was to isolate itself from the intellectual corruption all around it and demonstrate in its own thought and actions what might be accomplished from an uncontaminated approach to issues:

> Let us, then, with courage and confidence pursue our own federal and republican principles, our attachment to our union and representative government. Kindly separated by nature and a wide ocean from the exterminating havoc of one quarter of the globe; too high-minded to endure the degradations of the others; possessing a chosen country, with room enough for our descendants to the hundredth and thousandth generation; entertaining a due sense of our equal right to the use of our own facilities, to the acquisitions of our industry, to honor and confidence from our fellow citizens, resulting not from birth but from our actions and their sense of them.
>
> (Jefferson 1939: 44)

Despite the number of years that he and other founders of the Republic had spent in Europe, Jefferson even went so far as to urge that the future leaders avoid traveling abroad for their education. An American student sent to Britain or France would have all the wrong experiences:

> He acquires a fondness for European luxury and dissipation, and a contempt for the simplicity of his own country; he is fascinated with the privileges of the European aristocrats, and sees, with abhorrence, the lovely equality which the poor enjoy with the rich, in his own country; he contracts a partiality for aristocracy or monarchy.
>
> (Jefferson 1939: 140)

The American distaste for European customs and ideas reflected in these statements by Jefferson, as well as paranoia about European motives after the Revolution, persisted into the nineteenth century. For economic thinkers, as well as for others, the implications of Jefferson's observations were clear: American intellectuals should turn inward and find through domestic rather than foreign experience the best ways to carry on their bold experiment in nation building. Foreign ideas and foreign experience were more likely to be misleading than to inform. Jacob Cardozo wrote from South Carolina in 1826:

> In this country we feel assured that the laws which regulate Profits, Wages and Rent can be more successfully investigated than in the old world. . . . It is reasonable to suppose . . . that a country whose institutions and laws have done less to derange the natural order of things than where a vicious social organization has resulted either from military violence or a selfish policy, will present the fairest field for analysis and speculation into the causes of wealth. The results of such analysis should constitute the principles for the guidance of the statesmen of the new world. . . . It follows that we ought not to be implicitly guided by the results of investigations pursued by European writers into the sources of wealth without an examination of the circumstances on which their systems have been framed.
>
> (Cardozo 1826: iii–iv)

American writers on political economy attended closely to controversies taking place in Britain over economic theory, but before the Civil War they made insignificant contributions to them. They continued to insist that the pure air of America was the ideal laboratory environment in which to settle disputes. For example, Daniel Raymond examined the question of whether government had a responsibility to maintain adequate "consumption" when faced with "the disease of accumulation," but he could find little guidance from the old world (Raymond 1820: 123). He observed that in modern economies "a state of comparative lethargy and torpor" tended to occur when the "supply of the manufacturing industry exceeds the demand" and it "became necessary to arouse its dormant energies, by administering stimulants" (1820: 294). In old countries, wars, "the expenditure of public money in public works," monopoly, domestic protection, and the colonial trade had all been tried as stimulants. Still, there was nothing to learn from looking abroad. Raymond was convinced that the "same causes" led to "embarrassment and distress" in America as in Europe, but Americans had a better opportunity to find an appealing solution:

> Americans certainly possess much greater advantages for studying the science of political economy, than Europeans, and, if we were not

> to make greater progress, it could only be attributed, either to intellectual inferiority, or want of application. . . . The advantages which we possess are altogether accidental, and arise out of the nature of our government and institutions. . . . Our country presents the fairest theatre on earth for the acquisition of knowledge in the science of government and political economy. Here experiments may be made with safety. Here we can see the operation of the principles of nature in the utmost purity, and here is to be kept alive, that spirit of liberty and equality which is yet to be diffused throughout the world, and is to warm and animate all the nations of the earth.
>
> (Raymond 1820: 464–469)

AWAKENING OF INTERNATIONAL INTERESTS

Over the course of the nineteenth century the turning inward was reversed—slowly at first, but with increasing momentum. American economic writers began to look overseas for at least five reasons. First, a few found it possible, even while condemning the old world in general, to find useful lessons there. Alexander Hamilton (1957) turned to the British case when seeking guidance on funding the public debt and on establishing public lotteries as revenue devices.

The second reason for American economists to look abroad was to reassure themselves of the uniqueness of their environment in key respects. In his *Principles of Political Economy*, Henry Carey (1837) surveyed economic development in a number of countries around the world and found that while all nations were governed by the same "laws of nature," the United States was characterized by steadily increasing economies of scale and "habits of kindness and good feeling" and was blessed with few of the "unproductive expenditures" that were commonly demanded by class-ridden and undemocratic social and political systems. (Other works with a similar message were by Ezra Seaman (1846) and E. Peshine Smith (1872).) Contempt for the experience of the old world could be expressed regardless of a writer's position on the major controversy of the time: for example, free trade, free banking, free land, or free labor. No matter which position a writer took, it could be argued that the American economy offered the best opportunity for the implementation of his particular recommendation.

The third reason why America's economic thinkers changed their perspective on the world relates to the changing behavior of economic agents. As the United States industrialized rapidly during the second half of the nineteenth century, foreign markets, and potential competition from foreign producers, took on new significance. Put another way, as the geographical frontier in the west arrived at the Pacific, the economic frontier of the wider world still yawned. As this change occurred, it became necessary to understand trading partners and the competition. After the Civil War, the great industrial tycoons of the late nineteenth century—Carnegie, Rockefeller, Duke, and others—all looked and adventured abroad in input and output markets with a new vigor and new questions. They asked what relationship they should have to these markets. Detachment? Active participation? Domination? What was the quality of their competition?

A fourth reason for decline in parochial economic thinking was that the Civil War had a profound impact on the American consciousness overall, and its horrors remained in the minds of American thinkers long after it ended. There was little fear that the internal struggle could break out again soon. But the consequences of relations with the rest of the world were less clear, and it seemed possible that the United States could become entangled in one of the destructive conflicts—colonial or not—that seemed to dog the European nations. With memories of their own recent carnage still vivid, this was a possibility to be carefully avoided. In his textbook of political economy published just after the Civil War, Amassa Walker warned that "the great systems of war" must exist "until the nations of the earth shall establish a code of international law, and institute a high court of appeal, to which their disputes shall be referred for adjudication" (1872: 421–427). He hoped that greater economic integration of the United States with other nations would demonstrate to the political leaders of the country the necessity of international arbitration of disputes and formation of a "congress of nations." "Common sense" would be the main stimulus for a move to some form of world government and rule of law, but other forces would be "a 'commerce' . . . its interests becoming more identified with the harmony of nations." Walker (1872: 426) reversed Jefferson's earlier argument for isolation:

> The rapidly increasing intercourse by travel between the different peoples is making them more acquainted with each other, and dissipating much of that ignorance and prejudice which, in times past, has been a prolific source of jealousy and distrust.

The fifth reason why American economists returned to the world was that so many of their young began to go abroad for postgraduate education, especially to German and Austrian universities, where they sat at the feet of the economic historians and the marginal revolutionaries. As Walker (and Jefferson) had predicted, this study abroad was a formative experience for intellectuals as much as for tourists more generally, and after their return home they and their students could not help but see the American economy differently—both in comparison to the older societies in which they had been immersed, and as part of global systems from which any serious thought of continuing isolation no longer seemed practical. By the 1880s it was simply implausible that the emerging discipline of economics could any longer remain parochial, with its new young leaders fresh from training abroad and imbued with a reformist zeal both for their discipline and for their economic system.

INTERNATIONALIZATION ON SEVERAL FRONTS

During the last two decades of the nineteenth century, the discipline of economics in the United States, like that in other countries, became professionalized in various ways: the American Economic Association was established, extended curricula were offered at colleges and universities, and serious scholarly journals began publication. Over the century since 1890, the number of economists and their activities in the United States have grown exponentially. From a few dozen serious journal articles in 1890, EconLit lists 13,546 for 1994. It was against this background of professional development that an evolving internationalization occurred. The purpose of the remainder of this chapter is to chart and understand the course of this internationalization in its various components.

A review of the literature of American economics over the past century suggests that there may be eleven fairly easily identified reasons (in contrast to the earlier five) why economists have been, in varying degrees since the late nineteenth century, interested in matters beyond their national boundaries. We set out to quantify international interests by constructing a database with this taxonomy, employing the eleven reasons as subcategories, within three broader categories, for classification of economics articles. We restricted our attention to articles in three of the main generalist core journals that published over most of this period: *American Economic Review* (*AER*), *Journal of Political Economy* (*JPE*), and *Quarterly Journal of Economics* (*QJE*). By opening all volumes and scanning their pages throughout, all of the articles in these three journals were examined. Those with significant non-American content—by our count, 3,051 out of a total of 9,893—were assigned to one of the three main categories and eleven subcategories. With these data in hand, we traced through time the level and composition of interest in international-oriented issues.

To provide a feel for the data set, an excerpt consisting of five years of data from *QJE* and an explanation of all the variables, including answers to several methodological questions, is presented in Appendix A. We now lay out our taxonomy—for present purposes, the most important variable in the data set—and illustrate its application with a few examples of classification; the taxonomy is presented for reference in condensed form in Table 17.1. Regarding notation: in addition to their category numbers, main categories of classification are denoted by their abbreviations in upper-case italic type; subcategories are denoted similarly in lower-case italics.

Table 17.1 Taxonomy

1-GLOBAL Articles exploring some aspect of America's place in global systems:
1a-trade International trade.
1b-macro Interrelated macroeconomics: including international monetary relations (exchange rates) and the international transmission of business cycles.
1c-defense Defense and international relations.
1d-empire "Empire": building and maintaining close military and economic spheres of influence.

2-SPECIFIC Articles containing context specificity, with specfic attention to:
2a-enemy "Enemies."
2b-friend "New friends," including developing economies.
2c-compare Comparative policies, industries, and institutions.
2d-test Model testing.

3-H&T Articles dealing with non-American history and thought:
3a-history Foreign economic history.
3b-h.e.t. History of economic thought: foreign economists of the past.
3c-current Current economic thought: foreign economists of the present.

TAXONOMY

1-GLOBAL (America in global systems)

Economists have been intrigued with the involvement of the United States in some kind of system in which the country might have freedom of action but in which membership was essentially compulsory:

- *1a-trade* (International trade). All the way back to colonial days American merchants were involved in importing and exporting goods and services. Moreover, economic writers from the middle of the eighteenth century appreciated that both parties benefited from trade. The principle of comparative advantage was well understood early in the nineteenth century, and the relationship between international trade and growth was a contentious subject for debate in America as elsewhere in the world. The articles in this category for the period after 1890 are concerned mainly with how, and under what terms, the United States can achieve the greatest benefit from international exchange. Example: Darity, "Determinants of Terms of Trade" (*AER*, 1990).
- *1b-macro* (Interrelated macroeconomics). This subcategory contains articles dealing with the transmission of aggregate economic disturbances across national borders through business cycles, price fluctuations, and shifts in aggregate demand. It includes descriptive accounts of booms and crises, attempts to explain macroeconomic events through rapidly

evolving theory, and proposals to alleviate problems through such devices as bimetallist conventions or cooperative bodies like the League of Nations, United Nations, and related institutions. There is often overlap in this subcategory with the preceding one on the international trading system, both in terms of objective (e.g., employment and growth) and policy options (e.g., alternative exchange rate regimes). The principal distinction between the two subcategories is that articles in *1a-trade* tend to be concerned with international economics in a narrow sense, with topics such as formation of tariff policy or the composition of trade flows, whereas articles in *1b-macro* are concerned more broadly with the impact of trade on employment, price levels, and related variables. Example: Smithies, "European Unification and the Dollar Problem" (*QJE*, 1950).

- *1c-defense* (Defense and international relations). American economists were highly sensitized by 1890 to the costs and dangers of war, and preparations for war, that could not be avoided entirely because of the mere existence of neighbors. Articles in this subcategory are of two kinds: first, those that deal with how to prepare for war, and, if necessary, prosecute it most efficiently; and second, those that deal with the question of how conflict may be minimized through unilateral, bilateral, or multilateral actions of some kind. Example: Anderson, "Fundamental Factors in War Finance" (*JPE*, 1917).
- *1d-empire* ("Empire"). The United States has seldom contemplated seriously the possibility of acquiring extensive territorial possessions. After the completion of the continental expansion in the nineteenth century there were challenges enough in digesting what was at hand. But the nation has from time to time thought a little about the opportunity. For example, after the Spanish American War the United States found itself almost by accident in possession of Cuba and the Philippine Islands, spawning a small literature on economic conditions in these areas. Example: Willis, "Economic Situation in the Philippines" (*JPE*, 1905).

2-SPECIFIC (Articles containing context specificity)

We can discern four reasons why American economists found it desirable over the time period examined to acquaint themselves with the *particularities* of various foreign countries, over and above their economic or political relationships with the United States:

- *2a-enemy* ("Enemies"). As soon as it became clear that even with a declared intention to remain remote from European internal conflicts, the United States still faced hostile, and potentially predatory, nations, it became important to understand these "enemies": their power, their weaknesses, and the determinants of their behavior. Spain was the first certified enemy worthy of study, followed by the Axis powers in the First World War and

Germany and Japan in the Second World War. The Cold War introduced real complexity in this category, with former enemies (Germany, Japan, Italy) becoming friends while potential enemies were identified more by adherence to an ideology (Marxian socialism) than from any hostile strategic interest or alliance. A whole subdiscipline, comparative economic systems, became involved with a study of communist enemies, seen collectively by some scholars almost as the anti-Christ and including the Soviet Union, the nations of Central and Eastern Europe, China, North Korea, North Vietnam, and Cuba. Example: Galenson and Fox, "Earnings and Employment in Eastern Europe" (*QJE*, 1967).

- *2b-friend* ("New friends"). The collapse of the empires of all the combatant nations in the Second World War (Britain, France, Belgium, Netherlands, Germany, Italy, and Japan) presented many of the people of the world in Asia, Africa, and Latin America with the choice of what kind of political, social, and economic systems to adopt in their stead: liberal-democratic and free market, authoritarian-collectivist, or something in between. In addition, these "new countries" had to sort out their relations with the rest of the world: to pick their own friends and enemies, to identify which alliances to accept and which to spurn. American political leaders concluded that the United States had a significant interest in these decisions, and that to the extent possible, they should attempt to encourage adherence by these new countries both to systems of market capitalism and to the "free" in contradistinction to the "communist" countries of the world. Influence, however, required understanding—so the economic subdiscipline of development studies, in the same way as that of comparative economic systems, received generous public and private support for what were essentially political reasons. Also behind the growth of this subcategory, of course, were the benevolent motive to assist the less fortunate of the earth, and the curiosity natural among economists stirred by the requirements of many new nations to, as it were, write upon an entirely clean slate. Economists writing these articles were presented often with the rare opportunity not only to comment upon but also to take part in the solution of complex problems. Many in the study of economic development became at the same time either advisers to developing countries or consultants to development assistance agencies, and they gave a distinctive practical flavor to this literature and momentum to this field. Example: Adelman and Morris, "Econometric Model for Underdeveloped Countries" (*AER*, 1968).
- *2c-compare* (Comparative policies, industries, and institutions). From the earliest days of the republic, American economists looked abroad for guidance on construction of domestic policies—taxation, bank regulation, collective bargaining, environmental protection, health, and social insurance, to name but a few. As these problems increased in number so did the evident opportunity to learn about them through the experience

of others. Also within this subcategory fall articles on the structure of foreign industries and institutions, whether or not comparisons are made explicitly to corresponding structures in the United States. Example: Hill, "State Railways in Australia" (*JPE*, 1894).

- *2d-test* (Model testing). As economists in the twentieth century turned more and more to the construction of formal models as explanatory devices, they have had to gain access to substantial bodies of empirical data by which to test their hypotheses. To the extent that economists presume economic actors behave essentially in the same way regardless of their location on Earth, they have been able to look overseas for data. Because development agencies have tended to be data-hungry, the data search and data bases have often (but not necessarily) been tied to the new nations. Example: Van Hoomissen, "Price Dispersion and Inflation: Israel" (*JPE*, 1988).

3-H&T (Non-American history and thought)

- *3a-history* (Foreign economic history). The subdiscipline of economic history has always seen the world as its subject area, although of course the comparative weight given to non-American material has varied over time. The contents of this subcategory reflect both this American versus non-American distinction and the relative emphasis given to economic history by the discipline at large (and more particularly by these three generalist journals). Example: Hamilton, "Wages on Spanish War Ships 1503–1660" (*JPE*, 1929).
- *3b-h.e.t.* (History of economic thought: foreign economists of the past). The same comments can be made for this subcategory as for the previous one. Again, three variables are reflected: the amount of attention paid to h.e.t. in the discipline, the amount paid to past foreign economists, and the willingness of these three core journals to publish research in this area. Example: S. Hollander, "Marx and Malthusianism" (*AER*, 1984).
- *3c-current* (Current economic thought: foreign economists of the present). This final subcategory contains commentaries on contemporary economists working outside the United States. Over time the amount of attention to this subcategory reflects interest in a "survey" approach to the literature of economics, and the extent to which competing schools of thought have been defined by geographical boundaries (particularly the Atlantic Ocean) as well as theoretical differences. Example: H. Moore, "Pantaleoni's Problem in Oscillation of Prices" (*QJE*, 1926).

WHAT THE DATA TELL US

Having assigned every "international" article to one of the eleven subcategories, we can plot the time series of internationalization of American economic thought at three levels of aggregation. Figure 17.1 plots international articles, aggregated over all categories and subcategories, as a percentage of total articles appearing in the three journals. Figure 17.2 plots the time series of each of the three main categories aggregated over their subcategories. Figures 17.3, 17.4, and 17.5 plot the subcategories themselves. To smooth out the volatility and facilitate simple scanning, we present most of the data as moving averages with weights adopted from the normal (0,2) distribution.[2] (Figure 17.1, however, superimposes the moving average on top of the annual data to illustrate the contrast.)

The following conclusions, at the highest level of aggregation, can be drawn from Figure 17.1. Since the end of the nineteenth century the overall

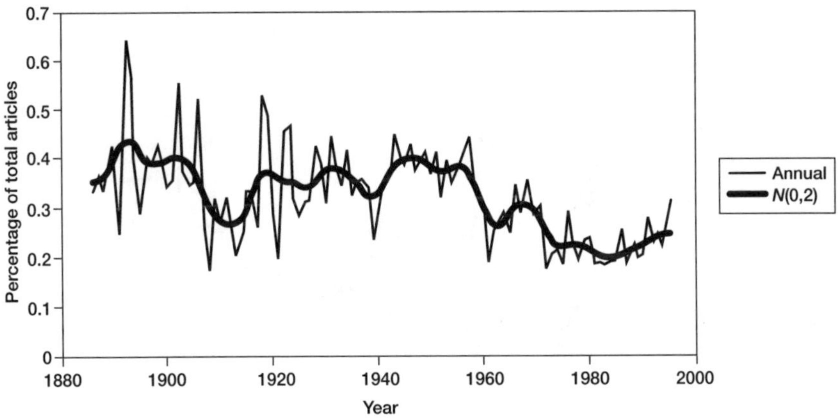

Figure 17.1 International articles, annual and N (0,2) moving averages

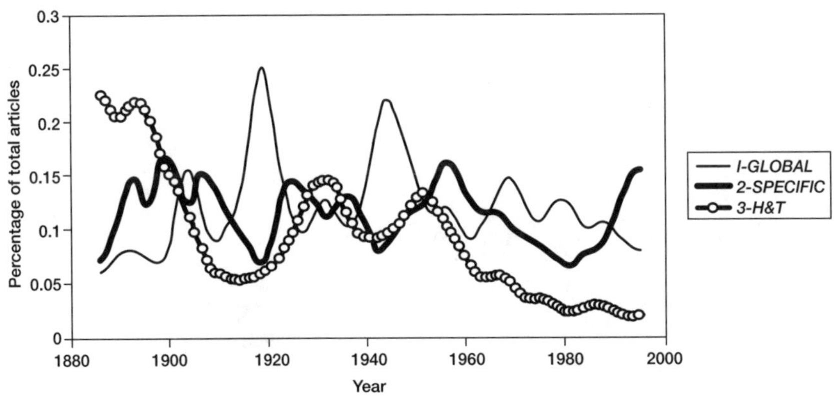

Figure 17.2 Categories of international articles, N (0,2) moving averages

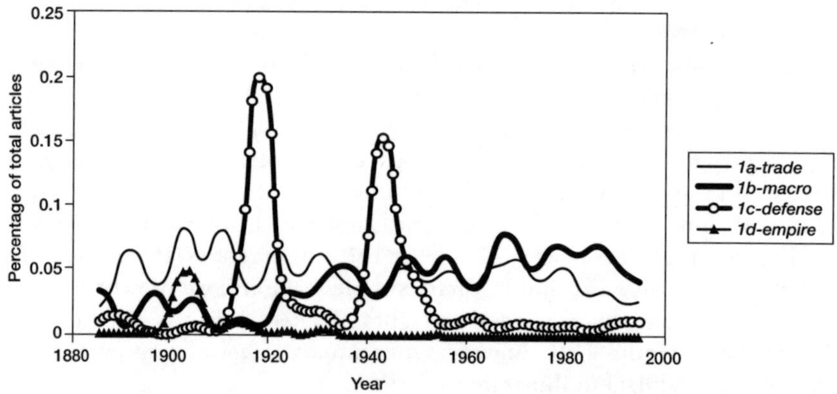

Figure 17.3 Subcategories of *1-GLOBAL*, *N* (0,2) moving averages

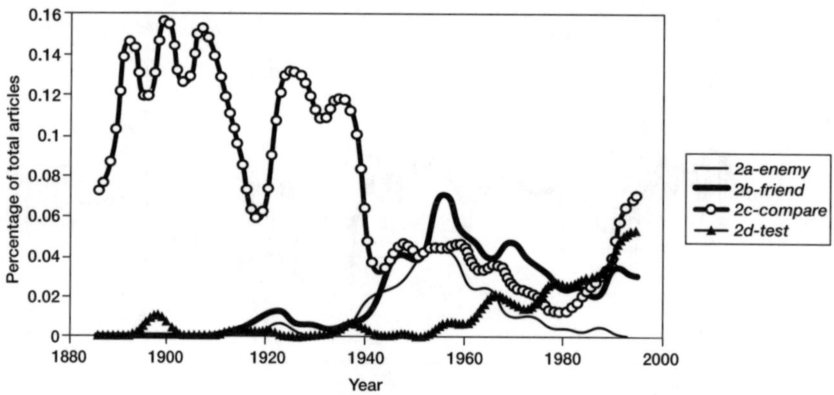

Figure 17.4 Subcategories of *2-SPECIFIC*, *N* (0,2) moving averages

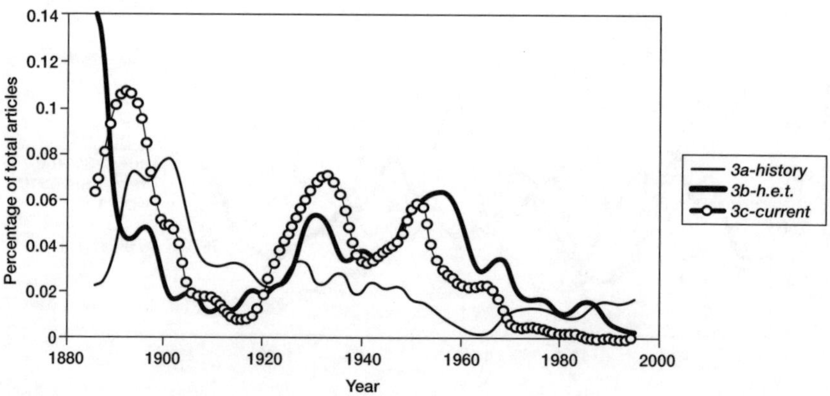

Figure 17.5 Subcategories of *3-H&T*, *N* (0,2) moving averages

international dimension of American economic thought has been in general decline, although with "humps." Looking simultaneously at the annual data and the moving average, four periods can be discerned within the general trend: 1886–1906, 1907–17, 1918–59, and 1960–95. Table 17.2 lists the average percentage of international articles over each of the periods. After beginning at an initially high level from the late nineteenth century until 1906, the international orientation of American economics articles then suffered a precipitous drop and remained at a low level until the end of the First World War. A dramatic rise in 1918 then marked the beginning of an extended plateau during which, were it not for two periods of sharp but brief decline in 1920–21 and 1938–40, the average percentage of internationally oriented articles would have been even greater than in the early years. The plateau reached its end in 1958–59. To the present day the international dimension has still not fully recovered from its subsequent plunge between 1958 and 1961, and the low average level of the period 1960–95 represents a turning inward even more than 1907–17. However, while the first twenty-five years of 1960–95 exhibited a marked decline in international orientation, the last decade has witnessed new growth.

The trends in thought underlying each of these periods may now be uncovered by turning our attention to the data at the lower levels of aggregation, and in its raw form—the articles themselves. Bear in mind in the following discussion that while we will refer often to the plots of moving averages for visual support, specific dates that are pinned down as turning points will be drawn from the annual data—which, except for the most aggregated data (shown in Figure 17.1), are not plotted.

1886–1906

Figure 17.2 reveals that the originally high level of international orientation is explained by *3-H&T*, which was quite high but declining over the period; and *2-SPECIFIC*, which was initially lower but growing. Within *3-H&T*, Figure 17.5 shows that *3b-h.e.t.* was initially dominant, but this should not be overemphasized, as from 1886 until late 1892 *QJE* was the only one of the three journals in existence, so the volume of data is small. Nevertheless, it is

Table 17.2 Mean proportion of international articles to total articles, by time period

Time period	*Percentage of total articles*	*Notes*
1886–1906:	.403	
1907–17:	.274	
1918–59:	.378	(without 1920–21 and 1938–40: 444)
1960–95:	.254	

worth noting that the first article published in *QJE*, "Reaction in Political Economy," was a history-of-thought piece with a focus on Great Britain written by the first editor of that journal, Charles Dunbar—and Dunbar maintained an emphasis on foreign history and thought (of all subcategories) during the ten years of his editorship that, as we shall find, would never be repeated. As the strength of *3b-h.e.t.* waned, the early prominence of *3-H&T* was maintained first by *3c-current* and later by *3a-history*. Articles in *3c-current* in this period focused in particular on Germans and Austrians, and were found particularly in *QJE*; Böhm-Bawerk's *Positive Theory of Capital* inspired extensive commentary beginning in 1889.

As *3-H&T* declined, *2-SPECIFIC* was rising, led by *2c-compare*—which, as can be seen in Figure 17.4, comprised nearly all *2-SPECIFIC* articles until the 1940s. As in *3-H&T*, the focus in *2-SPECIFIC* was on Britain and Europe. Subjects of greatest interest included rail systems and railway rates—for example, Frank Taussig's "Railway Management in Prussia" (*QJE*, 1894)—as well as foreign industrial legislation, social services, and forms of taxation. During this period, more than in any other, one gets the sense that the articles in *2c-compare* are really written to gain comparative perspective on *domestic* policy, rather than to study foreign institutions or policies as an end in itself.

1907–17

The dramatic drop in international orientation in 1907, which is quite evident in the annual data series plotted in Figure 17.1, was caused first by a decline in *3-H&T*, followed by *1-GLOBAL*, and sustained by a decline in *2-SPECIFIC* over the following decade even as *1-GLOBAL* recovered.

The decline in *3-H&T* articles began in the preceding period: *3b-h.e.t.* began falling already in 1887, *3c-current* in 1897, and *3a-history*—though most volatile—roughly in 1902. Between 1907 and 1917 *3-H&T* stabilized at a low average level. Combined with the low level of *3-H&T* was a sudden drop in *1-GLOBAL* in 1907; Figure 17.3 shows this came about primarily as *1d-empire*, which had risen suddenly in 1902 with discussion of the Philippines and the Panama Canal, and disappeared almost as suddenly in 1906–08.

At the beginning of this period *1-GLOBAL* began to recover, fed first by modest growth in *1a-trade*. Taussig wrote voluminously on U.S. tariff policy in *QJE*, the editorship of which he assumed in 1896. Tariff questions were also discussed at length in *JPE* beginning in 1907 and *AER* beginning with its first volume in 1911; "reciprocity" was the issue of the moment in these discussions, and Canada was the favored partner. (No comparable flood of literature appeared in the 1980s on the U.S.–Canada Free Trade Agreement.) An even more important catalyst for growth in *1-GLOBAL* was the beginning of the First World War and the consequent rise in *1c-defense*.

As *1-GLOBAL* rose, however, *2-SPECIFIC* fell, and this maintained the relatively low average level of interest in international problems from 1907 to 1917. As mentioned earlier *2c-compare* was the only important subcategory of *2-SPECIFIC* at this time, and it plummeted from .163 of total articles in 1909 to .036 in 1917 and continued to .014 in 1919—less than one-tenth of its 1909 level.

The crowding-out effect of the First World War and the growth in *1c-defense* are not sufficient to explain the drop in *2c-compare* from 1907 to 1917; this would describe a shift of relative importance between subcategories of the internationally oriented literature, but would still leave unexplained the low level of international literature in the aggregate relative to 1886–1906. *Something* must have encroached upon the aggregate international share of economics articles. Prominent candidates were a new interest in banking and currency reform (e.g., the "central reserve plan" versus the "Aldrich plan") and concern about trusts and industrial combinations. The former interest was reflected to a limited extent in internationally oriented literature such as Weaver's "Canadian Banking Legislation" (*JPE*, 1913), but by and large, and in contrast to the earlier period, economists writing in *QJE*, *JPE*, and *AER* in this period seem to have been more comfortable pursuing their interests without reference to experience abroad. This may be explained by the decline in graduate study abroad.

1918–59

When the average proportion of international articles rose once again it was due immediately to a peak in interest in *1c-defense* at the end of the First World War. But as interest in *1c-defense* abruptly ended in 1920 (causing a sharp but very brief drop in international articles from 1920 to 1921), international interest in general was maintained by a reversal in 1920 of the preceding decade's decline in *2-SPECIFIC*, and a renewal of interest in *3-H&T* in 1921.

Within *2-SPECIFIC* the reversal was led once again by *2c-compare*—and once again, the main regions of concern were Britain and continental Europe. Socialism, trade unions, and regulation of working conditions and wages captured the imagination of economists at the beginning of this period: R. H. Tawney's "British Coal Industry and Nationalization" (*QJE*, 1920) and John R. Commons's "Webbs' Constitution for a Socialist Commonwealth" (*AER*, 1921) were typical of this literature. The Soviet Union and communism also became topics of discussion; an early and prolific economist who published in all three journals, Amy Hewes of Mount Holyoke College, addressed the topics in articles such as "Russian Wage Systems Under Communism" (*JPE*, 1922).[3]

In *3-H&T* it was *3c-current* and *3b-h.e.t.* that led the ascent, while *3a-history* continued the decline that began in the preceding period. The subcategory *3c-current* peaked locally in 1933 at .091 of total articles; underlying this high proportion for the "current thought" subcategory were articles on various figures and ideas, such as "Frisch on Measurement of Utility" (*JPE*, 1933), "Mr. Keynes's Control Scheme" (*AER*, 1933), and "Sombart and the 'Natural Science Method'" (*JPE*, 1933). It is difficult to recognize a common theme binding together the articles written in this subcategory at this time. The revival of interest in *3b-h.e.t.* dealt with similarly dispersed subject matter, including Smith's battle against mercantilism and the monetary theories of John Law, among a number of topics.

In the midst of the 1918–59 plateau another crevasse took shape in 1938–40—not as deep as 1920–21, but a little wider and more mysterious. Figure 17.2 shows that although *2-SPECIFIC* declines around this time period, it actually does so two years too late for its influence to be felt in 1938–40. The crevasse is formed entirely by a decline in *3-H&T*; and within *3-H&T*, as shown by Figure 17.5, all subcategories fall simultaneously from 1938 to 1940. The mystery is that the decline in *3-H&T* cannot be viewed as a crowding-out caused by the onset of the Second World War and *1c-defense*, because that literature did not begin until 1941. So why the sudden lack of interest in foreign history and thought?

We find in 1938–40 the disembodiment of a subject of heightened concern (effective demand and business cycles) from the non-American personality who helped to bring it to the forefront of debate (J.M. Keynes) and lend it its originally international character (in our particular sense of the term). Keynes had recently written his *General Theory* and the book immediately sparked great interest in the United States, beginning with Alvin Hansen's "Keynes on Underemployment Equilibrium" in the October 1936 *JPE*. Notes on the *General Theory* by Viner, Dennis Robertson, Taussig, and Leontief followed shortly thereafter in a special symposium in the November 1936 *QJE*. All of this we regard as interest in Keynes and the *General Theory*—and as such, examples of interest in *3c-current*, "foreign economists of the present." But from out of this subject interest a quarrelsome discussion soon arose, regarding the definitions of savings and investment, which cannot be classified similarly. An exchange between Abba Lerner ("Saving Equals Investment" (*QJE*, 1938)) and Myra Curtis ("Saving and Savings" (*QJE*, 1939)) was a discussion with roots in Keynes's *General Theory* obvious to an amateur historian of economics, but in fact the articles contained little mention of either the man or his book. One gets the feeling that the authors perceived themselves to be sparring in the impersonal and geographically unbounded field of economic theory, rather than the confines of Keynes's backyard at Cambridge. The downturn of interest in international subject matter from 1938 to 1940 may thus be traced in large part, ironically, to the rapid spilling-over of the Keynesian strain of business-cycle research across international boundaries—including the Atlantic ocean.

The source of the renewal of interest in international problems after 1940 is much more straightforward. Figure 17.2 shows that the Second World War brought with it the predictable rise in *1c-defense*, with articles like R.

Rosa's "Multiplier Analysis of Armament Expenditure" (*AER*, 1941) and Richard Musgrave's "White Paper on British War Finance 1938–41" (*JPE*, 1942). And once again, when *1c-defense* declined at the end of the war, growth in *2-SPECIFIC* and *3-H&T* took up the slack. The difference, as evident in Figure 17.4, was that this time *2-SPECIFIC* was not led by *2c-compare*; instead, *2b-friend* and *2a-enemy* were the sources of growth. Economists' attention shifted away from Britain and Europe—toward Japan, India, Latin America, Africa, the Soviet Union, and China.[4] However, in many instances the articles in *2b-friend* did not focus on any particular developing region, presenting instead a more generally applicable development model: Hirschman's "Investment and Dualism in Underdeveloped Countries" (*AER*, 1957), for example.

In *3-H&T* the interest was again in *3b-h.e.t.* and *3c-current*. Articles in *3b-h.e.t.*, as usual, comprised a kaleidoscope, but some regularity can be found in *3c-current*. Reflecting in large part Hicks's contribution to the increased sophistication of dynamic modeling, a number of economists wanted to discuss his work: Arthur Burns in "Hicks and the Real Cycle" (*JPE*, 1952), Machlup in "Hicks' 'Revision of Demand Theory'" (*AER*, 1957), and Keunne in "Hicks's Concept of Stability in Exchange" (*QJE*, 1959), to name one article from each journal.

The high plateau of international orientation in American economic thought that had persisted for the greater part of the preceding thirty-one years ended in 1959. Referring to Table 17.2, the average proportion of international articles over this period, .378, rivaled the high proportion of the early years of *QJE* and *JPE*—and by far exceeded it, if 1920–21 and 1938–40 are excluded from the data. But by 1960 *1-GLOBAL* was nearly at a postwar nadir, and *2-SPECIFIC* and *3-H&T* were in rapid decline. In the following twenty-six years, the average level of international interest would hit a new low.

1960–95

From its low point in 1960 internationalism recovered somewhat through 1971, but nowhere near to the level of the preceding plateau. The recovery was fueled, as illustrated by Figure 17.3, by growth in *1-GLOBAL* and *1b-macro* in particular. International monetary theory was a matter of great interest in *1b-macro* as Bretton Woods began to fall apart. J. Makin's "Composition of International Reserve Holdings" (*AER*, 1971) represents this literature. But then *1b-macro* plunged suddenly in 1972 and the proportion of international articles fell further still—to .187 in that year. The average proportion of international articles then stabilized at a low level of between .20 and .25 for the following thirteen years.

In sum the period 1960–86 exhibits a downward trend for international orientation. Taking the place of the international literature were articles such as: Gary Becker's "Crime and Punishment: An Economic Approach" (*JPE*, 1968); Black and Scholes, "The Pricing of Options of Corporate Liabilities" (*JPE*, 1973); and Kydland and Prescott, "Rules Rather Than Discretion: The Inconsistency of Optimal Plans" (*JPE*, 1977). These articles focused on expanding the domain of microeconomics, financial economics, and the microeconomic (rational expectations) foundations of macro models. Surprisingly, in the *JPE* this shift in emphasis corresponds to Harry Johnson's tenure as editor from 1969 to 1977. His well-known (and widely published) international interests did not prevent the movement away from internationally oriented literature in *JPE*, let alone in the other journals.

In contrast to this downward trend in international interest from 1960 to 1986, the period 1986–95 has witnessed a new but noticeable upward trend. Since 1983, *2-SPECIFIC* has surged. Though *2a-enemy* has disappeared with the end of the Cold War, *2c-compare*, *2d-test*, and *2b-friend* have all grown. The growth in *2d-test* is a continuation of the trend that began modestly back in the 1950s, and the growth in *2b-friend* can be attributed both to the rise of the Asian tigers in the 1980s and 1990s and to the new development issues related to the demise of the Soviet Union in 1991 and the transformation of Soviet Russia and its satellites to market economies.

The rise in *2c-compare* has much to do with the renewal of interest in the determinants of economic growth in the mid-1980s, and while this interest may have been spurred simultaneously by work in the "new growth theory" instigated by Paul Romer in 1986 and the availability and improvement of the Summers and Heston *Penn World Table* data throughout the 1980s, it is primarily the latter influence that is represented in *2c-compare*. The Summers and Heston data facilitated the international comparison of growth rates and the testing of the "convergence" implication of the neoclassical growth model—and consequently launched a multitude of new regressions. Robert J. Barro's "Economic Growth in a Cross-Section of Countries" (*QJE*, 1991) is one of the better-known papers in this literature.

Finally, what has happened recently to *3-H&T*, the subject area of such importance at the launching of *QJE* one hundred and ten years ago? Figures 17.2 and 17.5 answer the question. First, *3-H&T* is at an all-time low, due to the virtual disappearance of *3c-current* and *3b-h.e.t.* from the three journals. Regarding *3b-h.e.t.*, it may be shocking even for historians of thought, who are well aware of the relative neglect of their subdiscipline by the mainstream of the economics profession, to review the recent publication track record of articles on foreign economists of the past in these three prestigious journals. *AER* has not published an article we could classify in *3b-h.e.t.* since A. Robson's "Stackelberg and Marshall" (1990). Were it not for a couple of pieces on George Stigler's foreign historical interests in a memorial minisymposium to him in the October 1993 issue of *JPE*, that journal would not have published a *3b-h.e.t.* article on an international subject since Gary Anderson's "Smith and the Preachers" (1988). In *QJE* the most recent *3b-*

h.e.t. article is R. Bishop's "Competitive Value when Labor is Scarce" (1985).

With regard to *3c-current*, it should be noted that the disappearance of this subcategory is contemporary with the increasing homogenization of the economics discipline worldwide. From the 1960s to the present, foreign and joint authorship has become commonplace in these journals, and foreign "schools of thought" have become more difficult to distinguish and associate with geographical locations. Reference to any body of literature is less likely to be classifiable as reference to "foreign" thought and thus counted in *3c-current*.

THE BIG PICTURE

Let us now leave the details of the data on which our account of the last century is based to suggest the story that we think can be told about this period. The century opened with a strikingly high level of internationalization based mainly on the sense of dependency felt by American economists on authorities overseas, and on the need they had to arrive at advice on a wide range of policies for a rapidly growing and industrializing nation. This intellectual openness was sustained especially by large numbers of young scholars who studied abroad and then returned home with reports on the doctrines they imbibed and the comparative perspective they had gained.

The rise of American graduate schools in the early decades of the twentieth century and the proportional decline in study abroad helps to explain some of the reduction in internationalization after 1907. More was happening in the intellectual landscape at home and less was known about what was happening elsewhere. Moreover, by 1907, after a brief period of indecision, the United States had set its face squarely against the idea of empire, and this international issue faded from view. The interest in international trade questions in the years before the First World War was not enough to counterbalance the other downward trends.

Understandably, the First World War revived the interest of American economists in the world and in economic aspects of conflict. An international orientation was sustained in the following years, first, by the hope that policy responses to the ensuing social and economic turmoil could be informed by the experiences of other countries, including the radical experiments in the Soviet Union, and then, by the confident sense that answers to the serious problem of recession could be found only in international cooperative action. The interwar years were also another era of limited self-confidence and relative humility for American economists, and this provided the necessary mood for openness to others. The substantial immigration to the United States of distinguished senior economists from other countries may also help explain this plateau of openness.

Economists were much more involved in the Second World War than the

First World War, and there were far more of them, in America as elsewhere. But the Second World War led to more than just an emphasis on defense economics. It also led to a new role for America in the world: as the political and military superpower, economic leader, and increasingly the educational and intellectual mecca. These developments led to counteracting developments within the economics profession: on the one hand, new specialties were created for the study of friends and enemies, including, ultimately, Cold War enemies. Old specialties like the study of trading and monetary systems were also given new life. But now, on the other hand, American economists came increasingly to believe that while the rest of the world was a place to study problems and gather data, it no longer was a place to go for ideas. Cambridge, Massachusetts, replaced Cambridge, England, as one center of the economists' universe; Chicago replaced Vienna as another.

We may speculate that the overall decline in attention to matters non-American that began in the 1960s is the result above all of three developments: First, a turning inward in American society generally that followed the debacle in Southeast Asia, the rise of the European Economic Community, and other responses to American policy that many Americans interpreted as bad taste or bad temper among foreigners. Why, many Americans thought, try to learn about and lead a world made up of such ingrates? Secondly, hubris among American economists rose to new heights, suggesting that their own research was now unquestionably supreme, that most foreign research was merely derivative, and that since many economic problems are generic there is little to be gained from non-American policy experience. Third, in macroeconomic theory in the 1970s, the innovation of rational expectations represented a microeconomic introspection on the part of theorists who temporarily left the world to focus on the structure of their models. All of these developments would certainly point toward a reduction in the international dimension of American economics, in both research and publications, and that is what in fact occurred.

The modest resurgence in the international dimension of American economics since the mid-1980s is explained by some weakening in the hubris of American economists about their understanding of certain developments both at home and abroad and by the discovery of a new role for the world—as a major data source to test theories. At home, various macroeconomic ailments such as low savings rates, spiraling fiscal and international deficits, and disappointing growth all made economists and policymakers wonder if other nations had some answers they did not. Secondly, the stark contrast in performance between some developing countries, such as those in Southeast Asia, and others such as those in Africa, gave a new challenge to development economics. Since the success stories in development seem related to the operations of a free-market system, the ideological support for this research has been strong. This latest international resurgence rests on a rather fragile base. Whether it will be sustained in the years ahead remains to be seen.

APPENDIX A: DATA SET AND METHODOLOGICAL OBSERVATIONS

Representing the international dimension of American economic thought as a time series of data points required a number of decisions regarding how and from where the data are to be gathered, how to define "international," and other issues. Our first decision was to gather the data directly from articles in the economics literature. By looking at every article published in the history of three U.S. economics journals we constructed a data base characterizing the extent to which, and the sense in which, the journal articles we looked at are "international." Our database has 3,214 observations in twelve variables. Table 17.A1 is an example: a clipping of five years of data from *QJE*. The variables and the methodology of data collection are now explained.

Variables

(a) Journal
(b) Year
(c) Issue
(d) Total articles
(e) International articles
(f) Article number
(g) Author(s)
(h) Affiliation of author(s)
(i) Nationality of author(s)
(j) Title of article
(k) "International" criterion number
(l) Region of interest

Observations of these variables were assigned values as follows.

(a) Journal

The three possible settings of this variable (suppressed in the following clipping from the *QJE* portion of the data set) are *Quarterly Journal of Economics*, *Journal of Political Economy*, and *American Economic Review*. Given our technique of data collection we were forced to limit our collection to articles from a small subset of the economics journals. We choose these journals because we believe they (better than any others) are representative of sophisticated professional American economic thought in general. All are general-interest journals, so any trends of interest in the professional economics literature should be detectable within their pages. They are also the longest

Table 17.A1 Data from the *Quarterly Journal of Economics*, 1920–24

Year (*b*)	*Iss* (*c*)	*TotArts* (*d*)	*IntArts* (*e*)	*Art#* (*f*)	*Author(s)* (*g*)	*Affiliation* (*h*)	*Am?* (*i*)	*Title* (*j*)	*Cr.* (*k*)	*Rg.* (*l*)
1920	feb	7	2	1	gras, n.	minnesota	y	present condition of economic history	3.3	gl
1920	feb			5	merchant, e.		y	govt. and news-print paper manufacturers	1.3	gl
1920	may	5	3	1	jones, g.	harvard	y	nitrogen: uses in peace and war	1.3	gl
1920	may			2	clark, v.		q	prices and currency in japan	2.2	as
1920	may			4	jastrow, j.		n	german capital levy tax	1.3	eu
1920	aug	6	3	2	pigou, a.	cambridge	n	report of royal comm. on british income tax	2.3	br
1920	aug			5	eldred, w.	virginia	y	grain corporation and guaranteed wheat price	1.3	gl
1920	aug			6	bernhardt, j.	johns hopkins	y	transition of sugar to competitive conditions	1.1	gl
1920	nov	5	2	3	tawney, r.		n	british coal industry and nationalization	2.3	br
1920	nov			4	einaudi, l.	u. turin	n	taxes on property in italy	2.3	eu
1921	feb	5	2	1	jeze, g.	u. paris	n	economic and financial position of france, 1920	2.3	eu
1921	feb			5	cunningham, w.	harvard	y	railroads under government operation, I	1.3	gl
1921	may	4	1	4	holcombe, a.	harvard	y	govt. of fabian socialist commonwealth	2.3	br
1921	aug	4	1	4	patton, h.	u. alberta	n	reciprocity with canada	1.1	ca
1921	nov	5	3	2	cunningham, w.	harvard	y	railroads under government operation, II	1.3	gl
1921	nov			3	hansen, a.	minnesota	y	technological interpretation of history	3.2	eu
1921	nov			5	cole, a.	harvard	y	domestic and foreign wool and tariff problem	1.1	br
1922	feb	5	2	1	durand, e.	u.s. dept. of comm.	y	agriculture in eastern europe	2.3	eu
1922	feb			3	graham, f.	princeton	y	intl. trade under depreciated paper	1.1	gl
1922	may	4	2	1	angell, j.	harvard	y	intl. trade under inconvertible paper	1.1	gl
1922	may			4	williams, j.	harvard	y	german foreign trade and reparations	1.3	eu
1922	aug	4	0							
1922	nov	5	4	1	taussig, f.	harvard	y	tariff act of 1922	1.1	gl
1922	nov			2	cole, a.	harvard	y	textiles schedules in tariff of 1922	1.1	gl
1922	nov			3	pigou, a.	cambridge	n	foreign exchanges	1.2	gl
1922	nov			4	joslyn, c.		y	british building guilds	2.3	br
1923	feb	6	2	1	graham, f.	princeton	y	aspects of protection further considered	1.1	gl

1923	feb			5	jastrow, j.	u. berlin	n	new tax system of germany	2.3	eu
1923	may	5	2	2	packard, l.		q	intl. rivalry and free trade origins, 1660–78	1.1	br
1923	may			5	warming, jens.	u. copenhagen	n	danish agriculture	2.3	eu
1923	aug	6	2	1	buchanan, d.	keio u., japan	q	rural economy of japan	2.2	as
1923	aug			4	douglas, p.	chicago	y	wages regulation in australia	2.3	pc
1923	nov	5	3	2	mcwilliams, r.		n	future of railway control	1.3	gl
1923	nov			3	graham, f.	princeton	y	theory of intl. values re-examined	1.1	gl
1923	nov			4	diehl, c.	u. freiburg	n	life and work of max weber	3.3	eu
1924	feb	5	2	2	silberling, n.	berkeley	y	monet. pol. of britain during napoleonic wars, I	3.1	br
1924	feb			4	douglas, p.	chicago	y	family allowance and clearing funds in france	2.3	eu
1924	may	5	2	3	silberling, n.	berkeley	y	monet. pol. of britain during napoleonic wars, II	3.1	br
1924	may			5	chandler, c.	corn exch. natl. bank	y	u.s. commerce with latin america	1.1	la
1924	aug	5	0							
1924	nov	3	3	1	taussig, f.	harvard	y	alfred marshall	3.3	br
1924	nov			4	copland, d.	u. tasmania	n	australian income tax	2.3	pc
1924	nov			5	taussig, f.	harvard	y	labor costs in u.s. compared with elsewhere	2.3	gl

published—since 1886, 1892, and 1911 respectively—U.S. economics journals, and throughout their histories have been among the most respected and widely cited by American academic economists.

(b) Year

To ease aggregation of the data across journals, the calendar year of each article's publication was entered and the volume number ignored. "Year" begins for each journal with the first year of publication and extends through 1995.

(c) Issue

This variable, expressed for visual convenience as a month rather than a numeral, is straightforward except in the case of *AER*. We did not count articles from the annual Papers and Proceedings issue of *AER*. Other than for that special case, "special issues" of journals were assigned for this variable the month in which they were published. If an issue was "Part II," it was assigned the same month as Part I.

(d) Total articles

This variable expresses the total number of articles appearing in the issue. To fill in values we were required to define "article," preferably in such a way that the editors of the journal would have agreed we were counting all the "articles" but nothing more. We allowed our definition to vary. For example, confronted with several very short pieces of work in the early years of *QJE*, we initially adopted a "five-page rule" to distinguish articles from nonarticles. The rule was shortly thereafter changed to three pages. We disposed of the rule altogether when the editors themselves distinguished on the title page between "articles," "shorter papers," and "comments"; we included only "articles." In most cases, when the editors provided a clue as to which of the works they considered "articles" (the primary works appearing in the issue) and which of them were less important—whether the clue was found in an explicit statement on the title page, in the page headers, or even in font size—we altered our definition of "article" accordingly.

This lack of stability in the definition of "article" should not in itself bias our general measure of the international dimension of American economics—"international articles" as a percentage of "total articles"—if the written work on international issues is evenly distributed between the categories of work included in the definition of "article" and those left out. One matter to consider, though, is that a definitional leniency in the case of *JPE* (including counting as "articles" works that for several years appeared in slightly smaller font on the title page, thereby helping to make the total volume of *JPE* data about 65 percent greater than *AER* and 55 percent greater than *QJE*) will give greater influence to *JPE* when the data for all three journals are aggregated, unless the data are reweighted by journal before aggregation. (In this study we have *not* reweighted the data.)

(e) International articles

This variable expresses the number of international articles appearing in the issue. This raises the question: Having defined "article," what is an "international article"? As suggested in the body of the paper, by an international article we mean an article whose subject matter involves heavy emphasis on at least one of the following:

1 A problem that is inherently international (e.g., in international trade, exchange rates, defense, or in building or maintaining an international sphere of influence).
2 A contemporary topic addressed in the context of another country (i.e., a country that may be a U.S. enemy, a developing country, or a peer). Addressing the topic may involve comparison of the country's economy or institutions with the United States', or it may involve using data from the country to test a more universally applicable model.
3 The history of another country, the thought of an historical figure from another country, or the thought of a contemporary figure from another country.

These three broad categories of international articles are precisely those already enumerated and explained as: *1-GLOBAL*, *2-SPECIFIC*, and *3-H&T*. Our definition of "international article" will be defined in greater detail when we come to discuss variable (k), the subcategory of classification.

(f) Article number

This variable, signifying the order in which the article is found in the issue, is included only to ease the task of checking and sorting our data.

(g) Author(s)

Here we list the last name and first initial of all authors of the article.

(h) Affiliation of author(s)

We list the institutional affiliation of the author(s), if that information was given. Where more than one institution is given for an author, we offer only the first-listed one. When more than one author has the same affiliation, we generally list it only once.

(i) Nationality of author(s)

This variable is intended to indicate whether or not the author is American—meaning affiliated with an American institution at the date of publication. The possible settings are "y" (yes, American), "n" (no), "j" (joint), and "q" (questionable). In the journals' early years the author's home city was often written after his name rather than his affiliation. In such cases, if the city is in the United States we filled in "y"; if the city is in a foreign country we usually filled in "n." In cases where neither affiliation nor city was listed (or in some cases where "nationality" in the sense we mean it could not be determined by the affiliation (e.g., the only listed affiliation was "World Bank" or "IMF")), we filled in "q."

The question of the author's nationality has become more tricky in recent years, when many articles are co-authored by economists in different countries, and when many authors are affiliated with several institutions in different countries. In *QJE* and *AER*, we filled in "y" if at least one of the affiliations of one of the authors was with an American institution, while in *JPE* we filled in "j" (for "joint") if the latter was true but at least one of the affiliations of one of the authors was with a foreign institution.

(j) Title of article

In most cases we paraphrased the title of the article for ease of entry into the data base.

(k) "International" criterion number

This variable returns us to the discussion of defining "international." We split the definition into the three broad categories listed in (e), and then further divided the categories into eleven subcategories. The complete taxonomy is presented above (see Table 17.1).

- *1a-trade* includes a large number of articles on tariff policy, and also models illustrating the causes of, and gains from, trade. Many articles might have found a home in either *1a-trade* or *1b-macro*. We tended to put an article in *1b-macro* if it emphasized the effects of international trade on some domestic variable or aggregate. Thus Taussig's "Tariff Act of 1897" (*JPE*, 1897) was put immediately in *1a-trade* and Flood and Marion's "Transmission of Disturbances under Exchange Rate Regimes" (*JPE*, 1892) was put immediately in *1b-macro*. A more difficult decision was required for Holzman and Zellner's "Foreign Trade and Balanced Budget Multipliers" (*AER*, 1958), which probably could have gone in either category; it landed ultimately in *1b-macro* because of its emphasis on the relationship of international trade to a domestic mechanism that is less commonly considered in relation to trade.

- *1c-defense* contains mostly articles relating to U.S. and foreign defense build-ups—including articles concerning domestic policy directly related to war, such as wartime market controls. Backman and Fishman's "British War Time Control of Aluminum" (*QJE*, 1941) is an example. International relations, including articles referring to treaties and international organizations such as the UN, is a less frequent subject in this subcategory.
- *1d-empire* is the smallest subcategory. It includes only a few articles, mainly (though not entirely) on U.S. possessions in the Pacific, Caribbean, and Central America: for example, Huebner's "Economic Aspects of the Panama Canal" (*AER*, 1915).
- *2a-enemy* includes articles that size up either wartime or Cold War enemies (or the economic systems, in the abstract, of such enemies). We classified implicitly and subjectively all countries as "friends" (including neutral countries) or "enemies," bearing in mind that a country designated an enemy at one point in time need not be so designated over the entire time series. We thus consider China an enemy from 1949 until the early 1970s, as we do the Soviet Union from 1946 through 1990, but both are friends before and thereafter. Hence Desai and Martin's "Efficiency Loss in Soviet Industry" (*QJE*, 1983) is included in the "enemy" subcategory, but Hewes's "Russian Wage Systems Under Communism" (*JPE*, 1922) is not, nor is Boyko's "When Higher Incomes Reduce Welfare: Socialist Economies" (*QJE*, 1992).
- *2b-friend* is most simply described as the subcategory of "context specific" in which the particular context is poor countries; we might also have named this subcategory "development." Not surprisingly, we find the American economics literature generally approaches poor countries with a different set of questions in mind than it does rich countries. Similar to the distinction between "friend" and "enemy," "poor" and "rich" are our subjective judgments and vary over time. We placed Hanson's "Growth and Inflation in Latin America" (*AER*, 1980) in this subcategory, as we did Laban and Wolf's "Privatization in Transition Economies" (*AER*, 1993).
- *2c-compare*—comparative policies, industries, and institutions—is a large subcategory in which we put most articles that dealt primarily with another country or group of countries, but not their interrelationships. The countries in question are generally wealthier than those providing the subject matter of articles in *2b-friend*; or development-related questions are not asked of their data, which are used only for comparison with other countries. A few examples are McLean's "Canadian Railways and Bonding Question" (*JPE*, 1899), Barro's "Economic Growth in a Cross-Section of Countries" (*QJE*, 1991), and Hayami and Ruttan's "Agricultural Productivity Differences Among Countries" (*AER*, 1970).
- *2d-test*, model testing, includes those articles which present an economic

theory or model which may have nothing to do with an "international" issue in the sense of our three broad categories, but use foreign or world data to test the model. Classifying an article in this subcategory sometimes required a tricky distinction from articles in *2c-compare*; after all, how does one decide whether foreign data are being used for "model testing" or "comparison"—or both?

On the other hand, there is a genuine difference between Halvorsen and Smith's "Measuring Natural Resource Scarcity" (*JPE*, 1984) and Prentice's "Canada and Hydro-Electric Power" (*JPE*, 1928)—and it is not just that "Canada" doesn't appear in the title of the former. Halvorsen and Smith's paper develops a measurement of resource scarcity and then applies it to Canadian data, while Prentice's examines the hydroelectric power industry in Canada. We might have said that both articles are "about" Canada, but not its interrelationships with other countries, and thus included them both in *2c-compare*. This would seem unsatisfactory, though. Halvorsen and Smith's emphasis is on their method of measurement, and the Canadian data are used only to provide an example—if Israeli data with the necessary characteristics were available, this might have been used to the same effect. (Yet it is still interesting to note that this article is "outward looking" and uses foreign data; so it is useful to classify it as "international" in some sense.) Prentice's paper, on the other hand, could not possibly have served its intended purpose if Israeli data were substituted for Canadian. For classification, then, the question we put to the article was this: Is the main point of the paper found in the model itself, or is it found in the application of the model to the particular data? By this criterion, Halvorsen and Smith's article was included in *2d-test*, while Prentice's was placed in *2c-compare*.

- *3a-history* is straightforward; the only major puzzle was how far back in time to draw the line between "history" and "present." We used a (flexible) thirty-year rule. Hoover's "Sea Loan in Genoa in the 12th Century" (*QJE*, 1926) was placed in *3a-history* without a second thought. We also included Lin's "China's Agricultural Crisis 1959–61" (*JPE*, 1990) in *3a-history* with just a little concern. On the other hand, although some portion of its period of study is on the appropriate side of the thirty-year line, we put Holzman's "Soviet Inflationary Pressures 1928–57" (*QJE*, 1960) in *2a-enemy* instead of *3a-history*. Cases like the latter provide our justification for keeping the rule flexible: Whether or not an article is "historical" is really a question of emphasis on the time line and relation to the present day, which should be considered case by case. If two-thirds of the content in Holzman's paper focused on 1928–30—or even 1932–33—we would probably have included it in *3a-history*.
- In *3b-h.e.t.*, history of economic thought (foreign economists of the past), we employed a similarly flexible thirty-year rule. The criterion became rather more complicated, though, due to the numerous articles eulogiz-

ing economists who had recently passed away. For this reason we adapted the thirty-year rule for application in *3b-h.e.t.* The question thus became: Has it been at least thirty years since this economist wrote the work that he is being remembered for (as opposed to thirty years since his death)? By this criterion, Schumpeter's "Marshall's Principles: Semi Centennial" (*AER*, 1941) was included in *3b-h.e.t.*, but his "J.M. Keynes, 1883–1946" (*AER*, 1946) was not.

- The latter article was placed instead in *3c-current*, current thought (foreign economists of the present), even though the economist examined was no longer living. More common in *3c-current*, though, are articles concerned with the ideas of living economists: Kuenne's "Hicks's Concept of Stability in Exchange" (*QJE*, 1959), for example. Inclusion in this subcategory requires the article to place heavy emphasis on the oeuvre of a foreign economist—not just to make a number of citations, for instance, to a paper jointly authored by an American and an Australian.

With *3c-current* we complete the list of possible settings of the variable "International criterion number." A final note: Even after following carefully the guidelines we have laid out here, a number of articles might well have fitted into two or more subcategories. In order to simplify the data collection and analysis, though, we thought it best to assign to each article one, and only one, international criterion number. We simply had to choose which one was best. In cases where there was some question about subcategory assignment, the decision was usually between two subcategories within the same broad category. Thus, while we find our subcategory classification scheme useful, aggregation of subcategory data into the broader categories is also useful. Some information is lost, but there should be less controversy about the information that remains.

(l) Region of interest

This variable is set to a two-letter abbreviation of the region of primary interest to the article. The regions are: af (Africa), as (Asia, also including Israel, the Middle East, and Japan), br (British isles), ca (Canada), eu (Europe, including Scandinavia, the former Yugoslavia, and Turkey), la (Latin America and the Caribbean), pc (Pacific, primarily Australia and New Zealand), su (the former Soviet Union and its satellites), and gl (general).

Many articles are concerned with some problem of the United States vis-à-vis nations from more than one region. There is no "U.S." region: such articles were assigned to the "gl" region, unless nations from one of the several regions dominated the discussion. In addition, articles that constructed a purely theoretical model—of international trade or exchange rates, for example—were usually assigned "gl." This caused "gl" to be by far the largest region in terms of number of articles assigned to it: Page's "Early

Commercial Policy of the U.S." (*JPE*, 1902), Bacha and Taylor's "Foreign Exchange Shadow Prices" (*QJE*, 1971), and hundreds of other articles on diverse topics were assigned to this region.

NOTES

1 We gratefully acknowledge assistance from the Josiah Trent Foundation and the Vice Provost for International Relations in the conduct of this research. We are grateful also to members of the Economic Thought workshop at Duke University and Jeff Biddle for helpful comments.

2 The $N(0,2)$ moving average calculated at year t places weights of approximately .20, .18, .12, .06, .03, and .01 on the data for years t plus or minus 0, 1, 2, 3, 4, and 5 respectively.

3 Since the U.S. relationship with the Soviet Union was not yet adversarial, we classified these articles in *2c-compare* rather than *2a-enemy*. See also note 4 and Appendix A.

4 Articles on Japan fell in *2b-friend* only in the first fifteen years or so after the end of the war; thereafter, we placed them in *2c-compare*. Articles on the Soviet Union were placed in *2a-enemy* for the entire postwar period up to 1991, and articles on China were placed in *2a-enemy* from 1949 to 1972; thereafter, both were placed in *2b-friend*. These shifts of subcategory reflect the changing extent to which the countries were generally considered to be industrial powers (*2c-compare*), military/political adversaries (*2a-enemy*), or likely aid recipients (*2b-friend*).

REFERENCES

Cardozo, J.N. (1826). *Notes on Political Economy*, Charleston: A.E. Miller.

Carey, H.C. (1837). *Principles of Political Economy*, Philadelphia: Carey, Lea & Blanchard.

Dorfman, J. (1966). *The Economic Mind in American Civilization, 1606–1865*, New York: Kelley.

Hamilton, A. (1957). *Papers on Public Credit, Commerce and Finance*, ed. S. McKee, Jr., New York: Liberal Arts Press.

Jefferson, T. (1939). *Democracy*, selected and arranged by S.K. Padover, New York: Appleton-Century.

Raymond, D. (1820). *Thoughts on Political Economy*, Baltimore.

Seaman, E.C. (1846). *Essays on the Progress of Nations*, New York: Baker & Scribner.

Smith, E.P. (1872). *A Manual of Political Economy*, Philadelphia: Henry Carey.

Walker, A. (1872). *The Science of Wealth*, Philadelphia: Lippincott.

INDEX